COURAGE *to* LEAD

COURAGE *to* LEAD

IN BUSINESS AND IN LIFE,
WITH GRACE AT THE HEART OF IT ALL

KWABENA DARKO

SAWMILL CREEK
PRESS

© Copyright 2023 by Kwabena Darko

All Rights Reserved. Without limiting the rights under the copyright reserved above, this book may not be reproduced, in whole or in part, stored in a retrieval system, or transmitted in any form or by any means (electronic, mechanical, photocopying, recording, or otherwise) except for brief quotations in critical reviews or publications without the prior permission of the publisher or author.

Library of Congress Cataloguing-in-Publication Data

Courage to lead, in business and in life, with grace at the heart of it all, by Kwabena Darko

ISBN:
978-1-7358852-0-9 Paperback
978-1-7358852-1-6 Hardback
978-1-7358852-2-3 Electronic

Includes bibliographical references and index
1. Leadership   2. Christian Living   3. Kwabena Darko   4. Agriculture, Poultry Farming
I. Title

Editor: E. Obeng-Amoako Edmonds

Rights for publishing this work or in non-English languages are administered by Sawmill Creek Press, United States of America.

www.KwabenaDarko.com

Praise for *Courage to Lead*

The style of leadership Kwabena Darko was comfortable with was servant leadership: leading by his own example. 'My leadership style is to walk beside people and facilitate their development. In many cases, I have the ideas, but it is only by placing good people around me, then empowering them to do a job, that an idea can be implemented'. He referred to it as growing fruit on other people's trees – the term borrowed from his friend Bob Buford. He [Kwabena Darko] was there to give, not to receive.

— *David Bussau*
Founder of Opportunity International
Excerpt from "Don't Look Back: The David Bussau Story"

Kwabena Darko, the real life inspiration for best-selling children's book "One Hen: How One Small Loan Made a Big Difference", has motivated school children around the globe to build businesses with small loans and invest their profits in community causes. As a youth who grew his backyard chicken flock into Ghana's first and largest poultry business, giving back to town and country throughout, Darko has shown kids that they can "rent" money to make money and help others. Now, in his memoir, Darko further inspires all who stand for social justice. He testifies not only to founding the fields of agribusiness and microfinance in Ghana, but also to engaging in the public square as a politician, pastor and educator who grew democratic institutions, financial inclusion and influenced social change across his country and continent.

— *Katie Smith Milway*
Award-winning children's book author and cofounder of OneHen.org

I am thankful for what God continues to do through my brother Kwabena Darko. . . great and mighty things beyond Full Gospel, not just in ministry, but also in business, in government, and in leadership in Africa, through Europe and America.

— *Jose V. Pascua*
The Joshua Generation International Network

I admired the simplicity of this great businessman, his smile, overflowing joy, and passion for involving Africa to the extension of God's kingdom. His remarkable zeal for the gospel proclamation and the inner flame that burned in him became contagious. I know that his work will not be in vain in the Lord.

— *Michael Kayembe wa Dikonda*
Former Secretary-General,
Full Gospel Business Men's Fellowship International (FGBMFI) – Africa

A good book can always wait! This is certainly true of Rev. Dr. Kwabena Darko's long-overdue memoir, *Courage to Lead*. A successful pioneer businessman, churchman, family man, and politician, what defines Kwabena Darko is the absolute integration of his Christian faith in all aspects of his life.

What makes *Courage to Lead* a must-have-must-read memoir, is the sheer scope of the experiences of Rev. Kwabena Darko, spanning the euphoric post-independence years of Ghana, to the cynicism of the current fourth republic. As a beneficiary of the bold and visionary policies of Ghana's first President Kwame Nkrumah; as a "witness" to the audacious nation-building spirit of Israel's founding leaders – Ben Gurion, Golda Meier, Moshe Dayan and others; as a beneficiary and victim of successive Ghanaian governments and their private sector policies; as an active participant in Ghanaian church politics, particularly the Assemblies of God, Ghana; as a Presidential Candidate, and thus an active participant in the rugged politics of the country; as the first African International Secretary of the Full Gospel Business Men's Fellowship International (FGBMFI); the life of Kwabena Darko has been eventful and extraordinary!

In sharing these experiences in a self-reflexive way, *Courage to Lead* becomes an invaluable contribution to Ghanaian political, business, and religious history – and its interplay with international political, business, and religious actors.

— *Dr. Paul Opoku-Mensah*
Executive Director, National Cathedral of Ghana

I have had the privilege to be impacted by the ministry of Reverend Kwabena Darko and the Full Gospel team since I was eight years old. Through his mentoring, I accomplished the major milestones of my life, and my entire life has been affected positively by him. I am so grateful to God to have been by his side. Generations have been blessed through him.

— *Reverend Obe Kumb Mbadinga*
Senior Pastor, The Messengers of Christ Church

Kwabena Darko, first and foremost, was and is a deeply committed Christian which underpins and drives him in everything he does. His company Darko Farms was a unique and almost mystic brand in Ghana in the 1970s through the 1990s. The company made a deliberate employment policy to recruit and maintain the best labour, and made a commitment to stay significantly above the average national wage market in all categories of employees. There were employment incentives and benefits like free daily lunch, free medical covering every employee and spouse plus up to four children. The company provided weekly free egg and chicken packages for all staff and free transport to and from work. This ensured that a highly motivated and committed workforce was in place at every area of the company, and work ethics which enhanced matchless productivity. There was a relentless commitment to training staff at all areas and sections, and the company lived up to one of its catchphrases, "pacesetters," in the literal sense of the word, by being the first in the use of modern technology in production and administration. Mr. Darko does not fear to dream, share his dream, and pursue his dream.

— *Reverend Barfuor Adu-Gyamfi*
Trinity Assembly (Kumasi), Baptist Church of Ghana

I am very thankful for God using people like Darko as an instrument to spread his Gospel. Kwabena Darko has always been a man who does so much for his country and for the world, and through Opportunity International, the Lord used a devoted man like him to do His will.

— *Richard O'Donnell*
Opportunity International

The memoirs of our "father", the Rev. Dr. Kwabena Darko comes at an opportune time when we stand at a crossroad as a nation, and need to be reminded of the 'ancient paths,' where the good way is, so as to 'walk in it'. From business, politics, church, marriage, and family life, Rev. Kwabena Darko has been a 'guardian' on the ancient path who imbues us with wisdom, hard work, discipline, passion, courage, and a solid faith in God. His memoir, *Courage to Lead* forces us to confront the trajectory and tragedy of our history and developmental experience as a nation. And as a society with a leadership vacuum that has immobilized and disempowered us, *Courage to Lead* is a timely reminder of our need for courageous leaders to both transform our country and strengthen the moral character of the nation.

— *Ken Ofori-Atta*
Minister for Finance, Republic of Ghana

Courage to Lead will inspire many thousands of people who read it, to trust God, as Kwabena Darko has done all these years, to take big steps of faith themselves. People of all ages can trust our big God, for divine courage to become leaders, and change the world!

— *Reverend Doris Hokett*
Hokett International Ministries

Working with Reverend Kwabena Darko with the International Leadership Foundation (ILF), African Union Prayer Breakfast events and AFREC has been a joy. His status and character in Africa provided much needed credibility for our team as we reached out to African government leaders.

— *Professor Delanyo Adadevoh*
President - International Leadership Foundation (ILF)

Dedicated to my Darling
Christiana Boatemaa Darko.

To my children,
Kwasi Edusei, Kofi Poku, Yaw Gyamfi,
Afia Serwaa, Abena Darkoa, and Afia Adoma
and both
my mother Yaa Serwaa Owusu
and my grandmother Nana Yaa Serwaa.

CONTENTS

Foreword xv
Introduction xvii
Acknowledgements xxi

Chapter 1: Hope Rushes In 1
Chapter 2: Chances And Destiny 7
Chapter 3: Feathers Closer To The Sky 19
Chapter 4: Grace Found Me 27
Chapter 5: Open Fields 35
Chapter 6: The Road Back Home 51
Chapter 7: A Life's Purpose 61
Chapter 8: Leap 71
Chapter 9: A Whisper Through The Rain 79
Chapter 10: Where The Heart Is 89
Chapter 11: Shifting Sands 95
Chapter 12: Like Vapor And Passing Shadows 105
Chapter 13: The Happiest People On Earth 115
Chapter 14: A Yearning For Change 125
Chapter 15: The Wisdom Of Lights 135
Chapter 16: Choices 151
Chapter 17: Mustard Seed 163
Chapter 18: Dreamers And Lifechangers 177
Chapter 19: A Promise Still Stands 189
Chapter 20: Worth Fighting For 231
Chapter 21: My Brother's Keeper 247

- Chapter 22: Outsiders 263
- Chapter 23: On The Brink Of Everything 275
- Chapter 24: Fourth Republic 293
- Chapter 25: Beyond Sunset 315
- Chapter 26: Turning Points 327
- Chapter 27: A Legacy Of Faith 343
- Chapter 28: Miracle Of Family 355
- Chapter 29: The Master Still Calls 369
- Chapter 30: What Leaders Hope For 387
- Chapter 31: The Promise Of Tomorrow 403
- Chapter 32: By His Grace 411
  - Afterword 425
  - Endnotes 429
  - Index 431

FOREWORD

Nearly 35 years ago, I had the privilege of going to CBN to preach for Dr. Pat Robertson and while I was there he introduced me to Rev. Dr. Kwabena Darko. Little did I know, that meeting and luncheon we shared, that our paths would cross again. I am grateful that they did. His stellar career and amazing journey have been a source of great inspiration not only in Ghana, but around the world. On every occasion that I have had to sit with him or when he would join us in service, I have been even more impressed the better I got to know him. As the proud pastor of his son, Jonathan and lovely wife, Grace; to be asked to write the foreword for his book is such a great honor. Rev. Darko is a true renaissance man endowed with a grace unprecedented for his time. His legendary career provides a template for international relationships that is exemplary and quite rare.

Kwabena Darko is one of the most influential business leaders in Africa and one whose work illustrates the impact each of us can make if we are indeed driven by a God-inspired passion and a commitment to excel. Courage to Lead captures his humble beginnings, challenges, and successes with an uncompromising reliance on God as his foundation. From his earliest days in Ghana, Kwabena Darko's steps were ordained to reach the world in which God had placed him, and he embraced that as a privilege to be an ambassador of his faith around the world. In this memoir, Darko weaves together gripping personal stories and his own evolution as a man. It is also about the private moments, with his wife Christina and children that he reflects on his most important role as a husband and father. What has always set Kwabena Darko apart was an unyielding character to pursue what he believed was the will of Almighty God, in business, in leadership, and certainly for his life.

Our paths crossed in an arena where we were both working to share God's message of hope and restoration to men from all walks of life. Even though he was a successful entrepreneur, the reputation that meant the most to Kwabena Darko was one of a Christian leader, and that he wore with exemplary humility and pride.

What makes this book an invaluable read is the experience-laden perspective he offers on entrepreneurship, politics, and belief in a way that is genuinely refreshing and instructive. He took a leap of faith as a poultry farmer to build a successful agricultural enterprise, and he has been grateful for more than 50 years of a remarkable journey. With stories and memories, he shares his views on leadership and governance, as well as a conviction that nations flourish when it is governed with God truly at the center.

Courage to Lead gives a detailed and revealing account of Darko's work with the Full Gospel Business Men's Fellowship, Opportunity International, and other visionary organizations as they embarked on a mission to influence societies and uplift nations. In the book's unflinching account of a life, a family, and a faith, Kwabena Darko writes from the heart, and for this reason, this memoir stands as a defining testament to the value of personal conviction and courage.

Bishop T. D. Jakes, Sr.
The Potter's House

INTRODUCTION

I was a young man when I heard the words "Unless the Lord builds, the builder labours in vain", and latched on to it. Some 50 years later, I have seen the truth of those words in many lives as well as my own. I prayed to live a life of dignity and audacity, one filled with conviction and gritty determination. When I had the chance to look back at my own life, I hoped it would be a story that is every bit as humbling and courageous as it is a powerful demonstration of God's grace in a life.

I set up the Darko Farms poultry business in 1967 and it grew to be one of the largest privately-owned agro-industrial companies in Africa. Had it not been for a missionary's random suggestion to my stepfather, a 16-year-old boy would never have stumbled into poultry farming, and ended up in the kibbutz and Moshavs in Israel. Now I know it was far from an accident; it was God's guiding hand.

The peaks and valleys of both my life and business were extraordinary blessings I had the privilege of walking through, and it was all by God's grace. Along the way, I was honoured to serve on the boards for both national and international organizations, including Full Gospel Business Men's Fellowship International, Opportunity International, Sinapi Aba Trust, Assemblies of God, and Edify. My prayer always was to become a facilitator of and for people, with a single commitment to live in God's will, and throughout my work around the world around the world. That remained my north star.

By 1978, I had been awarded the Grand Medal Order of the Volta, a national award for my contribution to agriculture in my native Ghana, and decades later, I served as a Chancellor of Regent University College of Science and Technology, in Ghana, I was ordained as a minister, and I served for many years as the International Secretary of the Full Gospel

Business Men's Fellowship International. It was all only by the grace of God.

From countries like Sierra Leone to Gabon and South Africa, to Brazil and the Far East in Philippines and Malaysia, sharing the message of Christ and leading people to Christ's salvation got the devil's attention, and he fought back. The devil attacked me and my family, my ministry and business, through everything from car accidents to bizarre premonitions and afflictions. Yet I stand today as a testimony to the living God whose promises are sure.

More than once, I was a casualty of unrelenting government policies that often stifled private enterprises, and it seemed the more I championed the amazing gifts that God had given to each of us to help build our economy, the louder my detractors became. What I believed about leadership and governance was what I had seen work, and there was no reason we couldn't uplift our nation with a bold vision.

I had no reason to be either complacent in my vocation or ministry, or lose faith in my God. I remember having to endure persistent persecution that disrupted budding international business relationships with Kentucky Fried Chicken (KFC) corporation, Tyson Foods and other major international brands. Yet, my hope was set on a God who was capable of finding beauty even in ashes, and I was confident that in His own time, only He made all things beautiful. There is not one accomplishment that I can claim to have earned on my own, and I am truly grateful that I lived through some of life's harshest emotional letdowns, and still found a resolve to keep fighting.

In 1992, I ran as a presidential candidate for the National Independence Party (NIP), with the same progressive political ideology and hope that guided my own journey. My stance on business, economy, governance and society was shaped by the simple human instinct that we will take care of what we own, and perhaps that may be what challenged us to work our hardest to contribute to our country. From Ghana to countries across the African continent, to Europe and the

United States, there were many countries where I was privileged to work with leaders and governments, and my only prayer was for governance that was guided by true Christian values. *If righteous governed, the people rejoiced.* If there was any way I could help men and women with integrity to lead with compassion and foresight, I was honoured to do so. And I did so, by God's grace.

Courage to Lead is hopefully a simple and unvarnished perspective of a businessman and poultry farmer who truly believed in building a house on God's sure foundation, a solid rock. In business, in politics, and in life, I am happy to have lived through every failure and success, and with unapologetic confidence in God's guiding hand in my life. I set out with a faith that was the size of a tiny mustard seed, and found the courage to live a life of integrity, of influence and with a passion for excellence.

What I learned about my God along the way, and what is probably most intriguing, is how God can order the steps of anyone who leans on Him, to someday see how so many of our life's biggest moments are made possible by some of the seemingly unimportant pursuits along the way. Every person is uniquely important irrespective of their talent or status because we are all created in the image of Almighty God. The labourer on my farm didn't earn any less respect than the Presidents and business leaders I met around the world. What mattered was treating everyone with godly kindness, and encouraging everyone to shine in their talents, the irreversible gifts given to each of us by God. I have found that the best teachers are those moments that nudge us to live in the awareness that everyone has a story. It is only by the grace of God that we are who we are.

In business and life, like the Apostle Paul, I hope we all see the present as a series of precious moments we will never get to relive, and to live our lives in honour of God. Only then will our lives leave the mark they were meant to leave. I thank God that I have been able to live through turning points and stumbling blocks, and still find a reason to hold on to hope, resilience and grace.

Hopefully, in a world with men and women seemingly desperate to amass fortunes and fame, and even trample on each other in pursuit of their aspirations, we will all learn that what matters most, long after our work is done, is to be able to look back at our own footsteps and know that we have treated our fellow men respectfully, lived honestly and fealesssly, and served our God honourably.

My courage is rooted in a God whose relentless love and faithfulness grounds those who truly lean on Him. His grace guides my every step, and His promise of a future and of hope is true indeed. In my life, a faith anchored in God's love is what gave a boundless optimism for living every day, for an extraordinary perspective of His amazing grace, and for the *Courage to Lead*.

ACKNOWLEDGEMENTS

My hectic schedule over the last ten years forced me to postpone finishing this book, until a pandemic across the world shut down everything from businesses and airlines, to international borders. Unable to travel, I was locked halfway around the world, with my manuscript and my editor, and no choice but to complete the book. And by God's grace, I did.

I wish to thank above all, my God whose matchless blessing has guided my every step for nearly 80 years. It has been very humbling to share the words sealed in my memory, but every one of them reminds me of a God who knows His children intimately, and cares about our every moment.

Writing this book has been exhilarating, because in a way, it has given me a chance to relive an amazing journey that God has seen me through. I have so many people to thank, for their friendship, collaboration, and support, and many more without whose talents my world would have been much different. I was bound to forget the names of many remarkable individuals with whom I worked, across Ghana, Africa, Europe, America, and other places, some as long as 50 years ago. I hope you know I appreciated every one of you.

Reverend C.B. Sercombe planted a vision in a 16-year-old boy and not a day goes by without my being grateful for a kindness that turned out to be the starting point for my future.

To Asantehene Nana Opoku Ware and Asantehene Nana Osei Tutu II, a very special thank you for their unwavering support to my work with both Darko Farms and Assemblies of God church since the 1960s. You have been instrumental in so much of my humble journey, and I thank God for his grace on your lives. I am truly honoured by Otumfuo's support for GILLBT's Bible translation work, and for a leadership that inspires and leaves a legacy for a people.

Full Gospel Business Men's Fellowship International will always be a special part of my life. I met terrific businessmen and Christian leaders who inspired me a great deal. People like Joseph Kwaku Kwao, D.W. Amoah, Modupe Tilapiers, Nana Kwasi Amoakohene, Gracien Desouza, Kofi Essaw, Kwakugan Apaloo, Michael Kayembe Wadikonda, Jose Pascua, Victor Jocktane, Simon Nyandwi, Reverend Alfred Nyamekye, George Prah, Tony Fosu, and Richard Shakarian; my heartfelt thanks to all of them. For Demos and Rose Shakarian, I will always be grateful for a wonderful friendship.

I extend my appreciation to President John Agyekum Kufuor, President Nana Akufo-Addo, Finance Minister Ken Ofori-Atta, Dr. Babacar Ndiaye, Senator Jim Inhofe, Pat Robertson, Richard O'Donnell, Chris Crane, David Simms, Professor Stephen Adei, Dr. Werede Vogel, and Astronaut Charlie Duke. I am deeply indebted to many of the kind teachers of the many lessons that served me so well. A few years ago, Katie Smith Milway shared my story with the world with the *One Hen* children's book, and I am very thankful for her support and for introducing both children and adults to the power of social entrepreneurship.

The world is a much better place because of remarkable leaders like Al Whittaker, Paris Reidhead, Jack Delaney, Jim Bergman, Mike Brazel, Peter King, Dr. Peter Boelens, David Bussau, David Freeman, Larry Reed, Lee Coleman, Reinhard Bonkke, Morris Cerullo, Reverend Lonnie Fox, and Reverend Gyan Fosu. All of them helped me paint fresh perspectives about life and faith, and I am especially grateful for their generously pouring their wisdom into my life.

I had the pleasure of knowing Reverend Nicholas Opuni, Reverend Arthur and Doris Hokett, Mark Powers, Warren Weinstein, Cary Summers, Professor Emmanuel Larbi, Ebo Hewton, Kwame Boateng, Dr. E. O. Gyenin, Lawyer Kwame Kodua, Isaac Antwi, Kofi Amponsah Effah, Dr. Oduro Boateng, Martin Asamoah–Manu, Reverend Baffuor

Adu Gyamfi, Dr. Paul Opoku-Mensah, Mrs. Pearl Saka, Obe Kumb Mbadinga, Ahmed Adjei, and Kevin Callwood. They all had incredible personal stories that served as a reminder of the places and people who shaped my journey along the way. Mr. Akwasi Peprah owned Akropong Farms and gave me a place to put my first chicks before I built my first pen. I am always very thankful to Madam Josephine Jenkins, Ambassador Dr. Barwuah Edusei, Mr. Yaw Owusu and Yaw Poku Mensah all of whom have been truly wonderful through the years.

In Darko Farms, honourable people like Gustav Acquaye, Dr. Michael Boadu, my brother Yaw Gyemfi, E.O. Quartey, Mr. Adade, Akwasi Kumah, Augustine Boateng, Fraincis Aidoo, Koo Ntim, and Joseph Cobinnah stayed with me through decades, all contributing immensely to make my enterprise successful, and I will forever be indedted to all the excellent men and women who poured their hearts into the work we did.

Reverend and Mrs. Professor Hans Adu Dapaah, Reverend and Mrs. Joseph Kwarteng, Reverend Kusi Boateng, Reverend and Mrs. Collin Agyei, Reverend Dr. Ahinkora, Reverend Selwyn Buckman and Reverend Mrs. Maxine Buckman, together with a team of leaders, pastors, and teachers stood side by side with me in this incredible walk of faith; I thank you all.

E. Obeng-Amoako Edmonds is a brilliant editor and researcher who took on this project with a mastery of eliciting stories from every conversation. I thank him very much for all the work to make this book possible.

A few people come into our lives and leave behind such incomparable generosity, thoughtfulness, and humility. George and Angelina Owusu became our family halfway around the world with such friendship, genuine kindness, and an untiring support. My family truly owes them a great deal of gratitude.

On a personal note, I have a profound gratitude to my children Sammy, Vernon, Joe, Maxine, Mercy, and Bernice. I am extremely fortunate to be their father. They each brought into my life an amazing inspiration, and for all that they continue to do for the next generation, I am eternally grateful. I will always look back and be thankful for Mr. F. K. Gyamfi for nurturing a young boy and challenging him to dream boldly. I have been blessed with wonderful men and women as part of our family, - *in-loves* Nana Yaa Darko, Vanessa Darko, Selwyn Buckman, Grace Darko and Frank Adu-Gyamfi, sincerely thank all of them for their immeasurable kindness and prayers. I pray for God's grace on all of their lives too.

My wife Christiana is everything to me - she has been my greatest teacher, and a remarkable confidante. It was her devotion and tireless prayers through the years that made it possible for me to juggle my leadership at Darko Farms with the tremendous demands on my time from the Assemblies of God church, the Full Gospel Business Men's Fellowship International, Opportunity International, Edify, GIILBT, Regent University, and a host of other organizations through which I had the chance to serve. For a million different reasons, I owe her much more than words can say.

Nothing I have earned or done in my lifetime deserves any credit, except unto my God, whose unfailing grace closed and opened doors, healed the broken places of my life and turned them into a testimony. It is His will for my life that will be done. The grace that guided my life was born from a faithfulness that comes only from Almighty God. I pray the same grace for anyone whose life has hopefully been touched by my own.

CHAPTER 1

HOPE RUSHES IN

Defining Moments. A Son.

"Kwabena!"

"Kwabena!"

My feet were stuck.

I was terrified, trapped in the raging waters heading downstream in River Birim. I was drenched in rushing dirt-stained waters, but it was even scarier looking up to see the violent currents and every silt and tree and stone they carried forcefully with them. I couldn't breathe.

In a moment, I was a 10-year-old boy fighting for my life in the rush of a river bearing down on me. It had been cloudy when we set out earlier in the day to a farm, when we walked through the shallow parts of the river. The farm belonged to my uncle's in-laws from the Kyebi area, and somehow all I was good for was digging cocoyam and potatoes, and carrying heavy baskets full of foodstuffs several miles home. There was no bridge on that part of the river, and like many people who farmed on the other side of the river, we crossed it every day without any thought of what could suddenly change our fate. That was before the torrential downpour.

"Kwabena, make sure you don't drop the basket of cocoyam!"

They yelled from the river's bank. Somehow, they had managed to cross safely and now all they cared about was for the basket on my head filled with cocoyam to make it across too. Not me.

I felt alone and afraid. Just then, I felt my feet slip from the small stone on which I was trying my hardest to guide my steps out of the river. It slipped too. The water dragged me with such force into the river, the basket of cocoyam flying through the skies.

I was drowning.

I yelled and tried to swim as fast I could but I was no match for the strength of the River Birim. I could see them running hysterically along the river's bank, screaming for help, but I was being carried away too quickly.

In a few moments, I felt my body smashed against a tree planted along the river, its branches grappling my shirt as if to snatch some debris from the furious water rushing downstream. I was stuck, the water beating across my face with relentless anger. Luckily, the branches were close to the edge, enough for my cousins to yank me from the water. A few minutes later, I felt pressure on my chest, with faint voices of panic, my eyes opening slowly only to fully fathom what had just happened. I had survived.

As a teenager, I had come face to face with death, and I couldn't hide my dread any longer. I had left Kumasi to live with my paternal uncle in Kyebi, a small town in Ghana's Eastern Region, only to find my young life turn into one of misery and gloom. I felt like a servant, when all I hoped for was to be treated like a son. My uncle didn't know much of what I endured every day in his home, and I knew he was doing his best to give me a life I didn't have, so I tried to manage. Now it was too difficult for my young life to suffer. I wept to go back home to Kumasi, back to my mother.

By the time I was 5, my parent's marriage had fallen apart and my mother was bent on raising 4 children the best she could. I had been born in Kumasi, in Apegya-fie. It was a place filled with so much of Asante culture and rich traditions, that we lived every moment engulfed in what it meant to be an Asante. We were supposed to be confident and proud of our heritage. We were supposed to celebrate our ancestry and royalty, even when our lives were rife with turmoil and the children felt the desolation of a broken home. Proud we were, still.

As the oldest boy among my siblings, I had been named after my grandfather, Opanin Darko, a man I never met. So much of my early life was cloaked in uncertainty and chaos. I could hardly remember much about my father, Opanin Kofi Poku. Most people called him Kofi Abebrese. The word "A-bebre-se" in the Twi language had often been said to mean a person who was destined to struggle in life. My father's name had been handed to him from his own mother, who had struggled through his birth, and wanted his son to bear the memory of her pain. Now, my father's struggle had become his children's pain.

I vaguely recall my grandmother hurriedly walking with my siblings and me to my father's drinking bar, *Patience Bar*, as it was called, on the busy Kofi Dagarti Main Road in Ashanti New Town. My grandmother was furious at his neglect of his children, and it seemed all of my father's every waking moment was to feed his single dream of becoming a chief in Asante Bekwai. I don't remember a moment we shared, or a word he said; all I saw was a man who wanted to be revered. That seemed to be what my father lived for, and even as a child, it was striking to see the incredible lengths my father would go to make his traditional sandals – *kyawkyaw* – look flawless, and meticulously arrange all his *kente* cloth as if to impress the gods.

On the days that he wore the *kaji kaji*—mascara under his eyes, it made his stature even more striking, and he exuded the confidence of having already achieved his life's purpose. Until his untimely death, every memory of my father was of the man whose entire life and hope were staked on chieftaincy, and perhaps in a strange way, the mirage had been worth it.

My family moved back to the Asawaase area near Manhyia Palace. I had become the focus of my mother's attention. I was the oldest boy, and she would always remind me that I was all she had, and along with that came a responsibility to help her provide for our household. I was barely 7 years old. I had been enrolled in Asawaase Methodist School after leaving Salvation Army Primary School in Ashanti New Town. My mother had inherited her own mother's grit and will to survive incredible odds. She would spend much of the night sewing clothes and wake up long before the break of dawn to get them ready to be sold in Kejetia Market.

On the days when she would make the long trip to the coastal town of Simpa, in the Central Region to buy smoked herring and other foodstuffs to sell at the Kumasi market, my sister Nana Yeguaa would go along with her. There was never a day when it seemed she found relief, and it was as though her life was overtaken by uncertainty and worry. Her days were long and she tried her hardest to hide her sadness.

My grandmother Obaapanin Yaa Serwaa couldn't help but be feisty. She was a devout Christian and unapologetically blunt. She saw her daughter's gloom, and tried to help her raise her four children with everything she knew. She knew God. She couldn't say for sure how God would change any of our fates, but she was convinced that if she kept her faith in the God she professed to believe in, God would hear her prayers soon. She would wake all of us up early, and after we had prayed, she wrapped cloths around our shoulders. We called these cloths "collars", and we would set out to sell.

Kuduo was a large round wooden tray on which my grandmother would put fresh plantain leaves, and then arrange the balls of corn dough neatly into rows. On the sides of the tray, she would put little bags of sugar. Before the break of dawn, we would roam the small dusty streets in Asawaase Estates, going from one door to another hoping to sell each of the balls of corn dough.

My grandmother was just as industrious and she was resolute. In the late 1940s, she had been one of the few traders who owned a passbook with the United African Company (UAC) that allowed her to buy from the international conglomerates established in Ghana, then the Gold Coast.

Chapter 1: Hope Rushes In

It had been difficult for my mother to provide for four young children, especially in the season when she sold only a handful of items, just enough to keep a roof over our head. That had to be the reason why when my uncle, who was a teacher at Abuakwa State College, suggested to my mother that I come live with his family in Kyebi, she readily agreed.

My two years in elementary school in Kyebi Government Boys School had been some of the fondest moments in my early years, until I fractured my right leg on a soccer field. I spent much of my free time playing the game with my friends, and in the school's team too. I enjoyed every moment of playing goalkeeper until one afternoon I dove to save a ball and landed awkwardly in the dirt field and fractured my leg.

My uncle hurried me to the native herbalist who carefully wrapped my leg with a few plantain leaves, shea butter, and other herbs. As was typical in the village, he also used short sticks on both sides of my leg to keep it in place, and tightly wound a long piece of cloth around my leg to keep the bone aligned. The awful pain lingered for several months before I could walk again. Kyebi bore a weight that was a little more than a teenager had bargained for, and the frustration took its toll.

After suffering the horror of nearly drowning in River Birim, and now the unbearable pain of a broken leg, I had to leave life in the small village behind.

CHAPTER 2

CHANCES AND DESTINY

Apostolic Church. Sercombe & Robin Hood.

The elders at the local Apostolic Church were livid. An Irish missionary, Reverend James McKeown who had arrived from England as part of a missions group to the Gold Coast in 1937, had begun unravelling their leadership and control. Once, it had felt like they had been appointed to lead for the rest of their lifetime without any concern of having another person take their seats. Now they couldn't be so sure.

As resident missionary of the Apostolic Church of Bradford, Reverend James McKeown had fallen in love with the Asante people, and was devoting much of his time witnessing to the locals in their homes and around the town. For Reverend McKeown, the church needed to inject new and young lifeblood into its flock and found an urgent need to invest in the young people in the communities. His hope was for his vision to help them find their place to serve.

In a few months, that desire to encourage young men and women had evolved into a youth training program. Reverend James McKeown turned his evangelism-focused program into a bible school, perhaps as a pathway to teach the theology of the Apostolic Church to a younger generation whom he envisioned would shape the future. The elders despised the idea.

In the Ashanti New Town area, many of the elders were illiterate, but had survived their positions in the church by virtue of their age and respect in the local community. It posed a huge challenge to be trained in theology to someday take over the pastoral work. As for the English missionaries, they hoped their leaders would be in a position to read the religious literature and disseminate the theology to more people to assist with the church's expansion. With literacy as a real stumbling block, Reverend McKeown had to look elsewhere, to the youth.

The clash of ideas caused the elders at the church to arrange for information to be sent to the mission head office in England. Their petition was for the office to withdraw Reverend McKeown. They couldn't watch the young men and women taking their places in the church, roles these older men had come to believe were their rightful places in the community. Soon after, Reverend McKeown was asked to return to England.

With Reverend McKeown removed, an irreparable crack surfaced in the church. The young men and women suddenly seemed to have found a new passion, but one that perhaps threatened the elders' grip on the leadership. Perhaps the young people were convinced that the leaders had managed to acquire a thin veneer of truth to mask their insecurities. They decided to leave, and start their own church, and the only hiccup would be the name they gave it, the Apostolic Church of Ghana.

It turned out the legal name of the Apostolic Church as it had been founded in Asamankese had been Apostolic Church of Gold Coast, without the word "Ghana", and the lively young men and women had found a key detail to buttress their case. The elders of the church were furious, and this turf war had deepened the rift between the two groups of the same church. The friction turned into legal wrangling between the church establishment who had every reason to keep fighting to protect their church, and a vibrant young group who also believed they were justified in their actions as kingdom builders on fire for God and who wanted to expand quickly.

President Nkrumah's administration had been dragged into this fissure, and the hope was for the two sides to find an amicable solution quickly. The name had been a technicality since the country's winning

Chapter 2: Chances And Destiny

independence in 1957, which had led to the country's name change from Gold Coast to Ghana. For his part, Nkrumah needed every institution in the country, especially the religious groups to continue playing their critical parts in nation building, particularly in regard to schools. After a lengthy stalemate, Dr. Kwame Nkrumah's government urged the new group to select a new name. Their name became Church of Pentecost. Soon after, Reverend McKeown would return to embark on his evangelism work with the new church, around Kumasi and other parts of the country.

In the early months of 1958, another missionary, Reverend Sercombe arrived from England to oversee the Apostolic Church of Ghana. Apparently, the church leaders had hoped to find a place at the Catering Guest House, the only hotel in the Kumasi area, but there was none. It turned out all the rooms had been booked, probably by the government officials visiting the Kumasi area. The Apostolic Church leaders needed an alternative.

The next Sunday was when I first saw the missionary. He was a tall man with streaks of grey hair, and a chubby physique. His deep voice was as striking as his charismatic personality. Reverend Sercombe seemed pleasant, with an inviting posture, seated calmly and dignified like a statesman. Then one of the elders made an announcement. They wanted any of the church members who had a room in their house to consider hosting the Reverend Sercombe, until they found permanent accommodation for him.

Just before the elder could finish his last few words pleading with the congregation, my grandmother leaped from her chair. Her hands lifted high into the heavens as she blurted out that she had the perfect solution. She said that would be something her son-in-law, Mr. F. K. Gyamfi, a lecturer at the Kumasi College of Technology would gladly agree to.

She continued, "You see, F. K. Gyamfi has a big house at the college compound with rooms for his wife, and Kwabena. He even has a nice big room prepared for a guest, so I don't see any reason why Gyamfi couldn't help". The church erupted with grateful applause and song for what was now an answered prayer. F. K. Gyamfi sat calmly toward the back of the room. There was little he could say.

* * * * *

My young life had taken a detour, because years after my father's death, my mother had remarried Mr. F. K. Gyamfi and moved to his house on the campus of the College of Technology, the only tertiary institution in the region. Mr. Gyamfi was a Physical Education lecturer at the college, a well-respected man in the town. My siblings and I stayed behind with my grandmother in Asawaase until Mr. Gyamfi asked my mother if I could join them in their home. Since I was my mother's eldest son, Mr. Gyamfi understood what responsibility society lay on my shoulders, and perhaps the least he could do was to give me a chance to grow in a new environment.

Reverend Sercombe, the missionary from England, came to live with us. He was to stay at least for the first few weeks of his six-month stay in Kumasi but it was not long before it became fairly obvious that both men had struck a genuine friendship. Having met my stepfather, Mr. Gyamfi, who was a well-read man with interests in a range of subjects, Reverend Sercombe found that the two had a lot to talk about. In Reverend Sercombe, my father found a curious missionary who seemed intrigued by everything he heard about our culture and our people. He seemed truly captivated by the world he had stepped into. My stepfather had been a Methodist, only having to join the Apostolic Church after he married my mother, so he too had many questions about the Apostolic doctrines for Reverend Sercombe. Occasionally I eavesdropped.

Curiosity and hospitality evolved into a genuine friendship between the two men from different worlds. I recall the evening I overheard Reverend Sercombe ask my stepfather what he would do when he retired. He enjoyed his time as a lecturer at the college, and looked forward to a retirement with nothing to do.

Chapter 2: Chances And Destiny

"Sure, you could do a lot on your compound here".

"Here?" my stepfather asked.

He could only hope that the missionary was not thinking about starting a church in his home. Their thoughts couldn't be much farther apart.

Reverend Sercombe spoke for hours about Newcastle, a city on the River Tyne in northeast England where the sprawling farmlands in the area had been home to many farmers, especially those who returned home after World War II. Then he patiently explained how many of the poultry farmers had begun on small parcels of land, raising chickens, and soon their work blossomed into successful enterprises. The compound reminded Reverend Sercombe of Newcastle.

The missionary urged my stepfather to consider poultry farming. The climate in Ghana seemed perfect for poultry farming, and all it was going to take was dedication and willingness to take a leap of faith. He reasoned it would be something worthwhile to do when my stepfather retired. My stepfather, having come from a Ghanaian society where most farmers were illiterates, didn't have any particular interest in the vocation. Reverend Sercombe handed my stepfather a small booklet that he claimed outlined every step he needed to raise chickens simply. My stepfather chuckled politely.

The missionary promised that upon his return to England, he could arrange to have 100 one-day old chicks, along with the necessary heating systems and basic feedstock we would need to raise them. Something that Reverend Sercombe said struck a chord in my heart. From the little that I overheard, I was hooked.

I picked up the small booklet *Poultry Keeping in Modern Days* a few days later and decided to read every single word. Some of the pages showed simple illustrations that even in my young mind seemed possible to carry out in Kumasi. This was definitely something I could do. I didn't know anything about poultry, but I was curious, unsure of what I would find. It was as if I had struggled to carve a purpose for my young life, and Reverend Sercombe's offer had suddenly opened a door in my mind. It would surely be something worth doing. At least so I thought.

It was in Bantama Local Authority (LA) school where I first met Teacher Nsiah. I was a student in Form 2. We had just begun a lesson in Nature Study, when I first learned about mixed farming. From what I heard, it was an agricultural method where both arable crops and animals are cultivated on the same farm, in such a manner that some of the crops end up becoming food for the animals, and the animal waste, in turn, is used as manure to fertilize the plants. It was intriguing to imagine a farmer rearing different animals on his farm, while also making the most use of his land by growing different crops on the same piece of land. Even as a young boy, my mind would travel to places I heard of, only to see the images the teacher spoke of in my mind's eye. I reasoned that I too could do it.

The teacher's words sowed a seed in my heart. My imagination would run wild, and for a boy who had spent much of my early mornings selling everything from corn dough and *tweapea*, I couldn't help but give myself something else to hope for. I wondered what it would mean to be a mixed farmer and to sell all the farm produce and animals that Teacher Nsiah spoke of.

A few weeks passed. An unexpected turning point for me was an old film shown at the school, in Bantama LA. It was about Robin Hood and Allan-a-Dale. From the original English folklore, the film's central theme highlighted a heroic outlaw who robbed the wealthy in the society, and handed the bounty to the poor. I was a teenager fascinated by the imagery and the culture of a world that was far from my own. I had no idea how a place like rural Nottingham could be, with its people and the tall grass on the sides of the winding pathways leading to the secluded cottages.

I was not particularly impressed by the clever tactics Robin Hood used to steal from the rich people. Instead, I was struck by something completely different in that film: a rather unexpected scene of a man eating roasted chicken.

Chapter 2: Chances And Destiny

I couldn't help but notice how, at one point in the film, a poor man was handed a sumptuous roasted chicken from one of Robin Hood's bounties. Watching the man devour the whole roasted chicken was an image I couldn't get out of my mind. It was hilarious, yet very striking.

I was a boy in a faraway town in Ghana, in a family where we often had little to eat every day and every night. In our part of the world, families would typically raise chickens in their backyards, together with a small garden where they planted crops like okra, tomatoes, and peppers. Eating chicken was for special occasions, and even then, it would only be a small piece, never a full chicken like I saw in the film.

In Ghana, the few entrepreneurs who engaged in commercial poultry farming brought chicken together with other foodstuffs from the northern part of the country, to the Kumasi area to sell.

On the long road trips, they would keep the birds in the big dry-straw-woven cages in the trucks. In the markets, the men would walk around in the scorching sun with chickens flapping their wings in baskets. For most people, buying chickens for a meal was a luxury only few could afford. If we were lucky, mothers would give children like me the small chicken legs or wings on the days those parts were available.

From Teacher Nsiah, I had learned about mixed farming, but it was the character in the Robin Hood film joyfully devouring the roasted chicken that ignited something powerful in my heart. Coincidence was now divine.

It was around the same time that I stumbled upon a construction project underway in the Bantama area of Kumasi. Crews were in the process of clearing the land for the construction of a new market. In a moment, a wide swathe of land was laid bare, and I couldn't help but imagine the land filled with different crops and animals, just like Teacher Nsiah had said. My young mind imagined it almost like a dream. I felt a rush of excitement quickly filling every corner of my heart. It was as if I didn't need to imagine much longer; I could almost touch it.

I stood on top of the small hill, with a faint smile. I imagined how fulfilling it would be if, by some miracle, everyone in my Kumasi town could eat a whole roasted chicken any time they wanted, just like the character I had seen in the Robin Hood film whose every bite into the chicken showed a joy only he could express. Maybe it was indeed possible for that to happen.

In a strange way, where reality would have strangled the dream in my heart, my childlike fascination and wonder nurtured every thought. I went back home into the small room and lay quietly on my bed to read the *Poultry Keeping in Modern Days* booklet, until I drifted to sleep.

It was about a month later, out of the clear blue, when my stepfather received a telegram from England. It was from Reverend Sercombe. He was arranging to send my stepfather 100 one-day-old chicks, brooding equipment, and feed, just as he had said. They would be arriving in Ghana on the British Caledonian Airways, and hopefully, my father had a place to keep them.

The next day, Reverend Sercombe sent a telex to confirm we had received his first message. He had done just as he promised, but my stepfather had taken their conversation with a grain of salt and never bothered to even open the book. Except now, he didn't want to disappoint his new friend Reverend Sercombe, but he hadn't cared to read even the first sentence in the little booklet.

"*Kwabena*", he yelled.

"*Eiii . . . Kwabena. . ., the missionary is sending the chickens, as he said*".

I couldn't believe it. I was ecstatic. My stepfather looked confused and perturbed, because he wouldn't know the first thing about keeping 100 day-old baby chicks alive. It seemed he was trying his hardest to recall everything Reverend Sercombe had mentioned about the chickens and poultry.

"He left a book, it was somewhere here," he added.

I nodded impatiently with a slight grin.

Chapter 2: Chances And Destiny

"*The missionary... Reverend Sercombe...*" my stepfather was trying to gather his thoughts on what he would do next.

"I know where the book is. I have it".

My stepfather looked uneasy.

As I hurried to the room to fetch the little booklet, I could see my stepfather pacing around the table, his mind wondering.

"Papa, here is the book". I couldn't contain my joy.

I had underlined almost every word, and the worn pages hinted to my stepfather that I had read through the book more than once. I knew every step it outlined and even though I had never seen much of the equipment it mentioned in real life, I had seen the pictures so many times that they had been imprinted on my mind. I had imagined every wood shaving, every lightbulb, and every cage, just like the illustrations in the booklet. I had replayed the scene over and again.

My stepfather was stunned.

"Kwabena, you mean to tell me you have read this book".

"Yes, Papa, I know exactly what we have to do".

I felt a confidence in my heart as my stepfather tried to understand why a young boy would latch on to a book about poultry, with information most children would find dull. As if I knew that was to be my destiny written on those pages, nothing in the little book seemed dull. It had given me something to spark a dream and I couldn't have imagined in my wildest dreams that I would someday be seeing that become reality.

By the time the chicks arrived in Ghana, my stepfather had arranged for a local carpenter to erect a small structure on his compound. There had been nothing more fulfilling in my life than the morning we set out to Accra in his black Opel car to get the baby chicks. I could almost hear every one of their little voices as they chuckled and paced back and forth in the two cardboard boxes perforated on all its sides. Back in Kumasi, I had prepared the wood shavings in the cage, and on the ground of a small garage in the house. Suddenly, this seemed to be something that was to give my young life its purpose, and I was delighted.

My stepfather quickly learned all he could about poultry and read through Reverend Sercombe's book too. Now we had 100 little chicks in our house in Kumasi, and never could we have imagined how this would become the turning point in both of our lives. It did.

Brooding chicks in the first few days were particularly delicate. From what I had read in Reverend Sercombe's book, we couldn't afford to leave the chicks unattended for a long period of time. I decided to not leave them at all. Occasionally the baby chicks would crowd on one side of the cage when they felt cold, as if to keep each other company, and warm. I wanted to be by their side and adjust the thermometer to the recommended settings at every hour. I couldn't wait to give them the right amount of food when they needed it. I would drift into sleep leaning against the concrete wall in the garage only to wake up in the middle of the night just to check the thermometer to make sure the cage was warm enough, and go back to sleep.

Over the next three weeks, I stayed with the baby chicks as much as I could and every minute of it brought me a great deal of joy. I just watched them. I never understood their chirpings, but I imagined they did. Often I would imagine what they also knew about my life and my world. I would sit for hours watching them pace back and forth in the wood shavings on the floor, wonder what made some use their hind legs to kick the dust as if to find a treasure on the floor. I was completely engulfed in the life of the chickens.

In a few weeks, we sent word to Reverend Sercombe. Apparently, it was common for about five percent or even as high as eight percent of chickens to die in the early days of breeding. Most farmers had come to accept that as their reality. I didn't know this, and naïveté has a way of drawing out the excellence in our hearts in a way we couldn't have possibly expected. With the chicks under my care, not even one had died.

My stepfather was excited, but Reverend Sercombe was beyond thrilled. He sent another telegram to confirm that indeed not even one of the birds had fallen ill or died. Something had worked. My stepfather was convinced that the information in the book was worth every word it had spelled out.

In Ghana, the small scale poultry farmers and individuals bred light breed chickens all of whom laid white eggs. That was all anyone saw in the local markets. Reverend Sercombe had sent us heavy breeds, the kind that laid brown eggs, and we never expected that this would be the first time most people in Ghana would be seeing brown eggs.

Word spread quickly across the campus residential area and Kumasi that F. K. Gyamfi had a poultry farm that produced rare brown eggs. It was not long before my stepfather had to consider buying a larger parcel of land and expanding the poultry farm.

It was 1958 in Anyimu suburb of Kumasi.

CHAPTER 3

FEATHERS CLOSER TO THE SKY

Career Turn

By the time I gained admission to Prempeh College, it was obvious that another challenge laid ahead. If I didn't qualify for a Cocoa Marketing Board scholarship like several of the young people whose parents had worked for the state-owned company, it would be impossible to attend the secondary school. Even though I secured a bursary to help defray the tuition costs, I had to watch that hope fizzle into thin air.

I enrolled in a correspondence course, in the Rapid Results College in England to prepare for the Ordinary Level certificate. I was determined to complete the course as quickly as I could. That was the only way to attend secondary school without having to dwell much on what opportunities life had taken from me. I had come to accept the fact that even though I would never have the chance to walk in the hallways of Prempeh College, I would survive on the satisfaction of staying home, closer to the farm.

Disappointment quickly turned into elation. I was to spend my time feeding baby chicks, watching them grow and someday to lay eggs, and watching their feathers flying into the skies. All this while, I was completing my studies as diligently as I could. I didn't know what would be ahead for my future, but all that brought me great joy was the present, a satisfaction of successfully raising a hundred chicks to grow into much more than we had started with.

Poultry farming had been an idea that had been handed to my stepfather by an English missionary Reverend Sercombe, and now it had become what defined our day. Suddenly a new sense of urgency had consumed my every moment, and as a 16-year-old, my life had set itself on a trajectory, and I was not too sure where it was heading.

* * * * *

Just like his contemporaries across the African continent, Dr. Kwame Nkrumah, Ghana's first president had become a revolutionary who was bent on championing ideas that impacted his people in a very real way. By 1957, he had become a household name for being one of the most influential statesmen in the United Gold Coast Convention (UGCC) and the Convention People's Party (CPP) to lead the country into independence. Sovereignty had given birth to self-reliance and the country would have to embark on a journey without any clear markers showing which way to turn.

Kwame Nkrumah's CPP had a red cockerel for the party's symbol. The bird was meant to signify a strong sense of leadership. Some Ghanaians ascribed their own interpretation to the symbol, even though no one had hinted that the government planned on giving everyone a cock or hen.

Coincidentally, the Nkrumah administration had created the Builders' Brigade, with one of its pressing mandates to be the feeding of school children, many of whom otherwise would be deprived of a balanced meal. Most families in the villages and towns across the country could not afford anything more than the basic necessities, and the government had an opportunity to step in. Nkrumah reasoned there ought to be a way for every child to eat an egg each day as a source of protein, but there was not even one commercial poultry infrastructure across the country to support his vision.

Chapter 3: Feathers Closer To The Sky

Nkrumah also established the Ghana Farmer's Council as part of a daring plan toward self-sufficiency through investment in agriculture. It was made up of mostly cocoa farmers, owing to cocoa having become the main agricultural export and revenue source for the country. A few months later, the Council added poultry farmers, and that would open the door for my stepfather Mr. F. K. Gyamfi to join.

Around the same time, my stepfather had been notified that his employment as a Physical Education lecturer at the college was to be moved to another tertiary institution in Ghana's Central Region, Winneba. Even though he loved the work, there was no way he would take on a job that demanded he travel more than 100 miles south. With this imminent change, my stepfather quickly decided to secure land in Anyinam, along the old Bekwai Road.

Mr. Gyamfi bought seven acres of land, and for a man who had been reluctant to be a poultry farmer, he had found a new lease on life. He now owned Central Egg Farm, which soon became the largest egg-laying poultry farm in Ghana. Prempeh College hired him as a P.E. instructor. The work was perfect for him, not only because he didn't have to travel away from his family, but also because he could quickly leave to check on the farm whenever he had a free moment. In the first year, my stepfather's chicks had increased to one thousand and he added another five hundred in the second year. Now a member of the Ghana Farmer's Council, Mr. F. K. Gyamfi had become a part of the core group whose enterprises would be instrumental in fulfilling Dr. Kwame Nkrumah's vision of feeding Ghanaians.

One influential person who immediately held up Dr. Kwame Nkrumah's well-intentioned yet lofty ambition was Golda Meir, an Israeli stateswoman, and Prime Minister. She had been an ardent supporter of self-sufficiency for any nation, having learned first-hand from her country's aggressive strategic planning that sparked an avalanche of successes in agriculture and industry. Where other countries had failed miserably, Israel had been an enviable success.

Golda Meir agreed to help Kwame Nkrumah. She suggested the country select young people in whom it could invest training resources and send them to Israel for training. With Ghana having established an embassy in Tel Aviv, Mr. Bediako Poku, who had been appointed ambassador to Israel, would coordinate this initiative. The partnership meant that the young men and women who were selected for this program would become the building blocks to one of the most ambitious agricultural projects undertaken by a young independent nation.

My stepfather had been in a meeting when this government initiative was announced and he encouraged me to submit my application for consideration. There was no telling what the selection criteria would be, but he reasoned that if I got the chance to share my love for the vocation, I would be the kind to embrace the opportunity wholeheartedly. I did. Apparently, there were more than 100 applications, all of us scheduled to be interviewed at the Famer's Council Hall in Accra March of 1959. All of us applicants were vying for six spots.

Mr. Avenin, an Israeli man who was leading the project's delegation, looked around the room full of hopeful young men and women. I imagined that some had come from as far as Brong Ahafo, Cape Coast, and Accra. The Israelis had come to help with the screening, and hopefully, identify people whom they thought genuinely had the potential to work in farming. It was not difficult for anyone to imagine that most people in the room had been exposed to some type of farming or even had real experience.

In that crowd, however, there was bound to be people who probably had no earthly idea of any farming routine, or even a desire to become a farmer, yet had gained the opening for an interview because of who they knew. There were many occasions when qualified people were left out and missed their opportunity because they didn't have any political or personal connections. Perhaps Mr. Avenin and his team could sift through all of us, and merit would win.

"Who knows anything about poultry?" he asked.

Chapter 3: Feathers Closer To The Sky

The room was silent.

"Poultry. . . who knows anything about poultry farming?"

I lifted my hand. The room was silent still. I was nervous, completely overwhelmed by the moment. No one said a word. No other person lifted their hands. I could see my world was changing fast and slowly, both at the same time.

Mr. Avenin sat up, and breathed a sigh of relief. I hoped so.

"What is your name?"

"Please sir, my name is Kwabena Darko".

"Kwabena Darko, what do you know about poultry farming?"

"Please, sir, I know about chickens".

"Chickens?"

"Yes sir, chickens". I was not too sure if that was the answer he expected, but that was all I knew.

Mr. Avenin smiled, looking straight at me. I imagined the rest of the people in the room were looking at me too.

"Kwabena Darko, tell me what you know about chickens".

My mind raced.

Everything I knew about chickens and poultry had come from Reverend Sercombe's little booklet he had given to my stepfather. I remembered every word. I could vividly describe every wooden structure and feeding process just as we had in my stepfather's compound. I told him everything I knew about heavy breeds and light breeds, his face beaming after my every word. I told him about my stepfather's farm being the first place to produce brown eggs in Ghana, and about my real experience of walking through the Kejetia local market selling eggs to strangers. Mr. Avenin looked surprised at the information that seemed to roam freely in my mind about chickens.

"Where did you learn all of this?"

I showed him the small booklet I had brought with me to the interview, *Poultry Keeping in Modern Days*. I was happy to share everything I had learned on my own, even the nights when I had to stay with the baby chicks to make sure they were well-fed and warm. I told him about how I had memorized every word in the small booklet and spent my days on my stepfather's farm taking care of the baby chicks. He flipped through the small booklet. I watched him smile at the sight of every word carefully underlined, and wrinkles along the worn edges that told a story of a poultry farmer who seemed to have fallen in love with his vocation. Mr. Avenin couldn't contain his joy.

"Kwabena Darko, you are going to Israel".

I returned to Ghana in 1961, having stayed in Israel for an additional year in order to complete my Advanced Level certificate which I had started with the same correspondence course at Rapid Results College in England. I had enrolled in Ruppin College in Natania, a city about 15 miles south of the capital Tel Aviv. I earned a Diploma in Poultry Science. Fortunately, life had shaped my character in such a manner that whenever I set my heart to accomplish something, I found the resolve to dedicate every second of my life to it. Studying at Ruppin College was no different.

Three years later, I was back in my country and I was honouring my bond to return to work in Nkrumah's farming initiative. The government had secured 35 acres of land in Dansoman, a suburb of the country's capital to construct a hatchery, animal feed mill, and a processing plant. The Israeli government had also kept their word and helped construct the entire facility.

Now, Kwame Nkrumah's administration counted on my training in Israel and I felt the weight of the responsibility. I had to complete my obligation for the government before I could go back to work with my stepfather in Kumasi.

Ghana Agricultural Poultry Farms comprised an agricultural development cooperation, and together with Mr. Avenin and Mr. Ofori, our work was to oversee the entire poultry project in Accra.

For the first time in Ghana, commercial poultry farming was set to undergo strict licensing and inspections to ensure that such enterprises were producing quality poultry. Ailments like Newcastle disease, fowl cholera and fowl typhoid had taken their turns devastating many farms around the world, but with my training in Israel I had come to understand the conditions that undergirded some of what once seemed mysterious.

Perhaps nothing shaped my earliest experience with the Ghana Agricultural Development Corporation Poultry Farms more than a marketing campaign that took on a life of its own. Mr. Avenin suggested we erect a signboard that would be large enough for any passer-by to see. The company was showcasing the government's effort, and it was important to use every avenue to highlight this. We settled on a huge white signboard with the image of a brown chicken at the center.

As it unexpectedly turned out, the picture of the chicken was what stuck in the minds of anyone who saw the signboard. The Dansoman neighborhood where the signboard was erected eventually earned a new name, *"Akoko Photo"*, the local translation for "a picture of a chicken". In a way, this was symptomatic of how Kwame Nkrumah's vision had begun to change the society's narrative on the success of the government to embark on bold ideas and to transform many lives, including my own. It had been a valiant dream to set the country on a path to solve one of its most basic, yet almost elusive promises: of feeding our own people. This project in Dansoman would be a start, and a chance for future generations to build on something even more impactful than signboards and chicken.

It had become one of the important crossroads for my life, and I only hoped that the next chapter of my life would bring the best years ahead.

CHAPTER 4

GRACE FOUND ME

Salvation

I was born in October 1942 into a home that was nothing more than ordinary. Yet, as far back as my memory takes me, my life seemed to be the target of strange, unearthly hands. This didn't feel like a premonition or a creation of my own imagination. It felt so real that I would be visibly shaken and panting feverishly for help anytime it happened. I would be suddenly gripped with anxiety and the ghastly image of two hands rushing towards me, as if to squeeze all the life out of me.

With this unsettling image lingering on my mind, I walked through each day dreading the night ahead. For me, it was especially difficult to explain to my family what I would see in my sleep. My mother desperately tried to make sense of what she assumed was a nightmare. But it also happened in the daytime, out of the clear blue. It felt lonely, as though no one could share in my horror no matter how hard they tried. But why me?

There would be days when I felt a slight sense of relief from this haunting experience, but just when I thought it was all behind me, another vision of the same fearsome hands would wake me up in the middle of another night.

More than once, my mother would have to rush into the room where I slept with my siblings to stop me from running into the nearby road. I would be fast asleep but running without any direction as if to flee the torment. I would wake up sweating profusely and screaming incoherent words as if to set myself free from a bad dream that just wouldn't go away. The haunting and eerie episodes continued through my teenage years and I only hoped my grandmother's prayers would be enough to put an end to the terrifying images.

With both my grandmother and mother being staunch members of the local Apostolic Church, I had been born into faith. It was not my own, but that of my mother and grandmother, both of whom had fervently sought God in their lifetime, and through the years, had their own personal encounters with Him. As for me, I had always attended church. I had sung and danced and seen congregations do the same. I had seen people's faces light up at charismatic preachers in the pulpit, but I had no way of knowing what personal encounters each person had with God, or even if they sought any.

I had memorized and uttered declarations of faith more times than I could remember, but I was yet to uncover what it truly meant to be a Christian. I had spent a lifetime in church, and on the nights when the strange hands kept me awake, I would pray quietly and hope God would somehow strip that fear away from me. My young life was in turmoil, something I couldn't explain, and I didn't know from where it had come.

I remember how by the time I arrived in Israel as part of the Ghanaian trainees for the agricultural program, one thing I knew for sure was that I wouldn't have my grandmother's comforting embrace when I was overwhelmed by dread. I could only hope my mother was praying for me. For the first time in my life, I had to find my own path through my faith. I tried my best to pray on my own, even fasting on several occasions in a desperate search for peace. By some weird coincidence, the terrifying episodes actually stopped. It was freeing, at least for a while, to put that unexplained dread behind me, and live my life like anyone else.

Memory was fragile for a young man in search of his own path. Life in Israel had slowly given me a poise I'd never seen in myself. Now

Chapter 4: Grace Found Me

that I was back in Kumasi, for the first time in my life I felt I had accomplished something meaningful and deserved every recognition that came my way. Interestingly, I thought I had to fight for everything in my life, and I couldn't help but notice the young women in the Kumasi area who seemed occasionally swept away in the little charm I exuded.

I had even managed to join a group of amateur singers who entertained in small venues around town. I loved to sing, and I had found a way to trade my Apostolic and Methodist hymns for pop music. I was starting to forget that what had carried me on its wings was grace.

It was a Saturday evening in 1962 when a friend, Kwame Amponsah, invited me to an evangelical crusade being held at Abbey's Park by the Assemblies of God Church. Until then, I had never cared much about anything outside either the Apostolic or the Methodist Church, but now both had taken a back row seat in the life of a young man whose life had arisen out of nowhere, but who now felt he'd found his life's purpose. Not long ago, I had been the boy with a cloth crisscrossed around my torso and tied into a knot at the back of my neck, walking through Kejetia Market, unsure of when my next meal would come. But now, open doors had begun to erase traces of that memory.

I hadn't stopped going to church; the only problem was that I was just attending services, nothing more. Perhaps I was no different from many people who went through the motions, with church being just a routine part of a person's day, and faith being something worth professing, at least occasionally. God had become a casual friend. Christianity was a journey I could speak of, and I had been fortunate to have a mother who made me learn Bible verses. She couldn't force me to have my personal encounter with God, and I never thought I needed one anyway.

And so, I reluctantly followed my friend Kwame Amponsah to an evangelical crusade at Abbey's Park. The crowd sang and prayed loudly. I had seen much of the same thing growing up. There was nothing special about the night. I found a big tree tucked away in one corner of the park and walked over to calmly lean on it. It was a Christian outreach event, nothing I hadn't seen before. In my mind, it was another opportunity for Christian missionaries to travel from town to town to amass church members and sell their doctrine. In some communities, it gave the people something to do.

I stood calmly in the back, and tried half-heartedly to listen.

Reverend Lonnie Fox was energetic and loud. His powerful voice pierced through the loudspeakers. His interpreter, the Reverend Gyan Fosu, was a local preacher at the Assemblies of God Church who was equally animated in his presentation. Out of nowhere, I heard, "Whoever dwells in the shelter of the Most High will rest in the shadow of the Almighty".

I straightened up slightly.

The word "shadow" rang again in my mind, somehow. *Shadow* connoted fright to me. I looked around slowly, to see if there were other people nearby who may have heard the same. I shrugged it off.

Then, in the next moment, I heard Reverend Lonnie Fox, "You will not fear the terror of the night". I was not sure if I heard him well. Then, "Nor the arrow that flies by day".

Neither of the two preachers looked in my direction, but I was suddenly convinced they were speaking to me. Somebody was. Now, I felt my whole body shaking. A strange feeling of warmth suffused my whole body and I was beginning to wipe the sweat off my face on what had been a calm evening. I was not sure what was happening to me and tried to lean on the tree to hold my posture. Deep in my heart, I felt a strong voice echoing the words of the scripture loudly but gently. All the times when I had dreaded going to sleep at night flashed into my mind. It felt as if a thick veil of distress had been stripped off my heart, allowing me to absorb the words clearly.

Abbey's Park was filled with congregants, yet it felt as though I was standing there all alone. I had stood as far back as I could, but I felt as though I had slowly drifted closer and closer. Every word in Psalm 91 pierced my soul. Tears began to run down my cheeks in a manner I never could explain, and I didn't care. It was a sudden calm, overwhelmingly bracing.

I had stood inside many churches all of my life and seen hundreds of people accept Jesus as their Lord and personal saviour, and I never truly could imagine what any one of them felt. I always thought that salvation's turning point was an intensely personal experience, but now I knew for sure. It had taken an encounter at Abbey's Park to hear the words anew. My hands were lifted up even before I could fathom what was happening to me.

Reverend Lonnie Fox asked the crowd if there was anyone who was willing to accept Jesus as their saviour. The preacher's every word carried such authority and sincerity, and I could no longer shrug off what I was hearing. It almost felt as if another force was pulling me towards the sound of his voice. The songs continued, the people clapping and shouting and praying. The preacher continued to challenge the crowd to take the first step of faith, saying that the moment was an appointed time for salvation, and that none of us had been in the park by coincidence.

The preacher's outstretched hands swept back and forth.

His words echoed in my mind, *"You will not fear the terror of the night"*... *"Nor the pestilence that stalks in the darkness"*.

That got my attention.

The missionary stretched out his hands again to the rows and invited the people who would want to take a bold step toward Jesus. He said that he was not talking about religion or finding a church, but rather, he was talking about a personal relationship with a Heavenly Father. No one moved.

"Who wants to come under the shadow?" I remember him looking through the crowd, as if he was expecting someone in particular.

"Who . . . who will come under the shadow of God".

The next thing I knew I was running as fast I could from one end of Abbey's Park to the front where the preachers stood. My heart was beating even faster. Suddenly, I turned slightly to see a sea of people rushing out of the aisles to the front. The preachers sang and kept praying. The last thing I remembered was one of the preachers touching me gently on my shoulder, and nothing else.

By the time I opened my eyes, I was sitting on the ground, covered in dirt and sweat. The crusade had ended and the people had gone home, except the preachers who had surrounded me. I must have fallen to the ground screaming and shaking repeatedly.

Interestingly, none of the preachers at the Assemblies of God Church knew me, or my story, yet it seemed I had been worth their time and their prayer. None of the men had met my mother or grandmother to know what church they belonged to, yet in an empty park in Kumasi, they were listening to me like I was the most important person in the world. Whatever the relationship my mother or grandmother had with Jesus was irrelevant; what mattered was my own. In that very moment, it had been a personal encounter for my own salvation in a way I never would have imagined would happen to me. What was true indeed, a new journey was set to begin for me, right in the middle of a dusty park in Kumasi.

The preachers listened to the deep fears that I carried with me every day and every night. I told of how scared I had been to fall asleep on most nights, never knowing if the eerie strange hands would ever leave me alone. They assured me that when a person accepts Jesus as their saviour, they are indeed a new creation, and all the promises in the Bible are true assurances upon which a person could stand. All I had to was to believe. The scriptures were not mere words, they were life. I had glanced and even read through the Bible over the years, but in that instant, there was nothing more liberating than the truth of God's grace for people like me.

I sang loudly through the night on my way home, walking through the streets of Kumasi to South Suntreso where my family lived. The same songs I had sung in church for many years had taken on a new meaning for me and every one of the same words was now amazingly reassuring.

The Assemblies of God preachers urged me to "put on the whole armour of God", and that meant a genuine decision to walk fully in the faith I had accepted. The metaphor sunk into my heart, that the spiritual warfare that lay ahead of me was against principalities, demonic rulers of the darkness, and spiritual wickedness, not the people or the things we could see with our own eyes.

The journey was to be my own.

I had to put on the whole armour of God,
In order to stand against the devil's schemes.
With the belt of truth buckled around my waist,
With the breastplate of righteousness in place,
With my feet fitted with the readiness that comes from the gospel of peace,
With the shield of faith to extinguish all the fiery darts of the devil.
With the helmet of salvation,
And the sword of the Spirit, which is the word of God.
I had to stand.

My life was never to be the same. I had no way of truly understanding what had caused me such horror all my life, but the freedom at that moment was one that was to be my testimony for the rest of my life. If there was one simple truth I had to take along my journey, it was that I could afford to take the word of God just as it is, and lean fully on every one of its provisions.

There was absolutely nothing in my life that was more powerful than the power of God's word, and I couldn't wait to read every single word of the Bible. I had found a freedom and a new start. Nothing was more important than carefully reading through the Bible from the first verse to the very last. It brought me newfound joy, and peace too. I truly believed in the salvation I had found.

The Bible became my life, and at 20 years old, amazing grace had found me.

CHAPTER 5

OPEN FIELDS

Ruppin College. Negev. Poultry Farming.

The Ghana Airways DC-10 flight landed in Rome, Italy and after a short layover, I boarded the flight for the second leg of the trip. We were headed for Tel Aviv, Israel. I was one of three Ghanaians on an intensive government-sponsored agricultural training program that was scheduled to last for two years. Ghana's partnership with Israel had been forged by a mutual sense of self-sufficiency that came from empowering its citizens to undertake every critical economic and industrial enterprise that would become a catalyst for lasting development.

Dr. Kwame Nkrumah's government was counting on this investment to be a model for us five young trainees. We would return home and impart any knowledge that we acquired to other young men and women in Ghana. Nkrumah had declared our independence in March 1957, and for true liberation to gain a foothold, there was the urgent need for an industrial framework to become the critical building blocks. If I was in any way successful, I would be one such block.

I couldn't contain my excitement. Every thought in my mind travelled back to every word I had seen in the Bible since I was a child about Israel. Even though I had read a lot about the country, I couldn't help but allow my mind to wander still. I had sung songs about Israel and dreamt of stepping foot in the land of God's own city. What was once a beautiful dream had now become a reality. Cities like Jerusalem,

Bethlehem, and Nazareth jumped to mind along with their incredible stories of significance, especially to my Christian background. I would soon be stepping foot on the land of King David.

My eagerness aside, it was interesting to find how people like my grandmother never imagined Israel being a real country in a modern world, and couldn't let a moment pass without expressing their disbelief at this rare opportunity over and over again. *"Jerusalem my happy home! Jerusalem my happy home!"* she would say anytime the thought crossed her mind. For such a devout Christian, just the thought of Kwabena Darko going to Israel was absolutely breath-taking, an answer to a prayer she couldn't have even imagined. It must have felt to my grandmother like I was actually going to Heaven.

Everyone seemed to stare from the plane's windows into the distance as we began our final descent into Tel Aviv. I clearly recall that what was most surprising for me were the long stretches of desert. In a way, I didn't fully know what to expect about the country and its people, the only images swirling around in my head being the ones I had seen in religious films, or imagined on my own. This would be the moment to step into reality.

We were met by Ghana's Ambassador to Israel, Mr. Bediako Poku. My eyes wandered ceaselessly over every wall and building as we headed into the city. Israel had just emerged from the 1948 Arab–Israeli War just 11 years earlier and the country seemed to be working day and night to shape their future. On May 14, 1948, Jewish Agency Chairman David Ben-Gurion had proclaimed the State of Israel which established the first Jewish state in 2,000 years. Israeli victory had given them the area that was the former British Mandate of Palestine, Sinai Peninsula, and southern Lebanon.

Life didn't seem hurried, yet it felt every bit as purposeful. I tried to pay close attention to everything I saw and heard, and did not want to lose sight of the dreamlike moments. In addition to what I was to learn in Israel, these were memories I would take with me for the rest of my life.

We spent the first two days in a hotel in Tel Aviv before the group headed in different directions. I was taken by an old bus to the settlement where I was to spend the next critical years of my career and life. This was all new to me, as there had been no way to find any information about Israeli towns and culture. I was ready to adapt. They lived in cooperative settlements they called *moshavim*, and collective settlements they called *kibbutzim*.

It was there that I found that the kibbutz was unique to Israel and they traced its history to the first agriculture-based kibbutz, the Deganya, located south of the Sea of Galilee. The Jews who had worked in draining swamp-land mostly for agriculture had built a settlement and a communal lifestyle that was to be woven into the fabric of the Israeli society.

In the settlements, there were Jews who had returned from European nations like Russia, Yugoslavia, Poland, and other parts of the world. Yet, what was most striking to me immediately was a sense of shared heritage that seemed to fuel an irrepressible patriotism. It was not long before any foreigner saw the grit in the eyes of a people who cherished the opportunity to return to their land. They seemed kind and welcoming, and even though I was well aware of their painful history, the people I met in the settlement seemed to have found a way to rise above it and take charge of their destiny. The kibbutz seemed to have been strategically constructed along the borders, some by the Jordanian border, and others near the Palestinian settlement, and some near Negev. I was in Negev.

The Negev area sat in a large desert region in southern Israel, and even though it was a very hot and dusty sparsely populated hilly area, the beautiful flowers and green shrubs that adorned the small pathways and long stretches of green fields were a reminder of the amazing things that have a potential to bloom in places where we least expect them to. This was in the middle of a desert. The Israeli seemed particularly confident in their demeanour, and I couldn't miss the extraordinary attention the leaders paid to every granular detail in every facet of life.

I was a student in a country that had been forced to be resourceful and industrious, living in a desert region without the abundant natural resources we had back home. Somehow, here I was, to learn from a people who seemed to have carved a world for themselves, and were committed to flourishing in whatever little they had. It seemed every waking moment in the Stibokir Settlement had become an enlightening opportunity.

Occasionally, I was envious of the other students who went to Givatos Settlement until I got the chance to live in those settlements also. I heard it was near the area archaeologists believe was the location of King Solomon's Mines just as it had been in ancient times. I was curious and I couldn't believe the amazing sights. Some of the students had come to Israel from other African countries, including Nigeria and Uganda.

The first three months living in Israel were immersed in required military training to ensure every adult in the settlement learned how to shoot anything from machine guns to artillery needed in war. It was as if the country couldn't afford to go a day without having to worry about its future and the constant presence of hostility along its borders.

Foreigners did not have any choice but to able to protect themselves in the event of any crisis, and that unnerving reality made a person appreciate every moment. What was striking was, everyone in the kibbutz constantly prepared for their daily lives with an understanding that at any moment they could be called upon to defend their nation.

Patriotism and a refreshing sense of identity seemed to have shaped the heart of every child and adult, of every man and woman. They were proud of who they were and who God made them be. For the Jews, it was evident that many of the horrors of their past had left indelible scars on their minds, that gave them every reason to rally around a nation, as one. The sense of attachment to the nation appeared to have translated into the attitudes and alliances with the other citizens, and they spoke

Chapter 5: Open Fields

of their country's achievements and failures with relentless devotion to their collective progress.

We were taken to the extensive underground bunkers constructed to house the people in a time of national emergency. It was rather fascinating to learn how a country had managed to prepare for moments other countries were not as concerned about. They had invested sweat and toil and wealth into shaping a nation into what they wanted it to become. Every one of the people knew exactly what was demanded of them when they heard the sirens. Despite the solace in knowing that my new neighbours were adequately prepared for any military crisis, it was nothing I wanted to live through.

In the kibbutz, everyone was part of the rotation program that included working in the nursery, farms, dining facility, and working in the hospitals. They had learned to depend on each other, and to work together. In the communal living, there were various professions like teachers and doctors and nurses carefully outlined to ensure that the people – every child and adult – had access to whatever they needed. Perhaps what made these arrangements possible was the fundamental connection they all shared and the sense of urgency with which they lived every day. It was impossible to live with the Israelis and not be impacted by their sense of duty and focus.

I was intrigued to see how the young women joined the army for a year and the men for three years before they all went to university. People in Israel must have come to terms with the reality that they would have to fight to defend their land, and had little choice but to live in constant preparation. Even when their huge tractors ploughed the fields, their machine guns strapped on the sides were ready to confront any attack.

In Israel, I had seen a world doing everything it could to adapt to circumstances that were often beyond their control and rally a people around a vision. The men and women in the kibbutz lived with a mindset that demanded great persistence and passion, and I often wondered what it would take for my brothers and sisters back home to adopt a similar focus in building our country too. Perhaps that was what Dr. Nkrumah had in mind when he sent five young Ghanaians for the initiative, and I could only hope that in the end, I would rise to the occasion.

Watching the Jews in the Stibokir Settlement relate to one another with a sense of brotherhood and common interest gave a window into the psyche of the people among whom I was to spend some of the formative years of my life.

* * * * *

After 3 months in Israel, I started the program at Ruppin College to study Poultry Science and Industry. The intensive curriculum required that all the students attend the practical sessions right after each lecture and that was probably designed to immediately translate every instruction into action. As an institution whose principal focus had been to train the next generation of farmers, they had gone to great lengths to ensure that there was never a wasted period, and that the students found value in every encounter once they stepped foot on the campus.

It was originally established in 1949 as Midreshet Ruppin, as a training center to provide agricultural management education for Israel's bourgeoning agricultural settlements. National leaders like David Ben-Gurion envisioned a hands-on training that was to serve Israel's immediate social and economic challenges, and students were required to engage in active learning, and take advantage of every resource to broaden their understanding. Those of us who had travelled long distances to enroll in the program were not treated any differently. The expectations were high, for everyone.

Occasionally, I would wonder if all my colleagues in Ghana I had left behind who attended other universities and trade schools were embroiled in such a vigorous training program. On the Ruppin campus, there was probably nothing more impressive than a system that did not limit learning only to the classroom session but found a way to create

Chapter 5: Open Fields

an immensely relevant curriculum. The lecturers seemed particularly focused on making sure that we actually understood everything they said, and be able to apply even the most insignificant of facts in the real world. Fortunately, the professors I came in contact with were some of the most experienced nutritionists, animal scientists, and also veteran professors in business and marketing.

In every lecture, they seemed to try their hardest to share every bit of knowledge they had gathered from a variety of research and field reports, all the while making the content just as applicable to each of the diverse regions from where we came. My life had been thrust into a rigorous academic and vocational environment surrounded by men and women who lived and learned with a curious sense of urgency.

It was at Ruppin College that I met Professor Kuperstein, a veterinary science lecturer. He was more than a person with a great deal of information and understanding of the subject. He had been an excellent communicator who dissected every word and listened carefully to every one of the students' questions to answer them precisely. It was striking to watch him pay close attention to a student's body language to try to decipher those questions we didn't even have the rights words to ask.

In education, just as it is in life, people like Professor Kuperstein were impressing on my young mind that if I truly learned to listen to the world around me, I would be able to reach people and teach them without having to fight through the self-inhibiting barriers people brought along with them. If someday, I was to share my experience in Israel with anyone back in Ghana, these attitudes and worldviews would be immensely crucial.

An extraordinary researcher I crossed paths with was Professor Bornstein. His focus was on nutrition and he spoke about it with a passion that made him endearing to every student. He taught with a smile. I recall every morning when Professor Borstein walked into the classroom with several food samples for every student to actually touch and see what we were reading about. His goal was to make learning an engaging process, rather than only a bland exercise to successfully remember facts to pass an exam.

By the time we were done with the nutrition course, Professor Bornstein had found a way to make every student appreciate the chicken as an intelligent animal whose true glow comes alive if it receives the right nutrients and lives in the best possible environment. In the minds of people like Professor Bornstein, nutrition was everything. I remember how he stressed that God in His own wisdom had given the chicken a clear sense of what they needed to survive. He would always say that it is for this purpose that a chicken can afford to spend a day walking through an open field and selectively pick what it needs to eat as it goes along. It knows what it needs, and our job as poultry farmers was to learn what the chicken knew, and to master it.

Science had to learn from that simple truth and feed the chickens exactly what they needed, nothing less. It was always remarkable to think of how just because of the way God made them, some of the food the chicken eats would inevitably be trapped in parts of their internal organs, and for poultry farmers, the best we could do for chickens on our farms would be to give them the right amounts of food to make it easier for them to digest.

Much of what lecturers like Professor Bornstein taught in the classroom was rooted in an understanding of the animals, and I saw the delight on the teachers' faces when it appeared as though their students were grasping the concepts. Our learning gave them a rare satisfaction.

One by one, the men and women in Ruppin College must have convinced themselves that they were raising a generation of students who would impact their worlds. In a short period of time, everything we were hearing and touching made perfect sense. There was a sense of camaraderie in learning from the people around us, because all of us had come with our own colourful backgrounds and there was a world of information from the places from where we came. The young Jews would be leaving the classroom to end up in the settlements where the community would depend on their work for their survival, and for them, everything they heard had an immediate and practical consequence.

I often thought about how we would leave a lecture about planting corn, and the next minute we'd be standing in the middle of a farm with corn in hand. It was not hard to imagine how the person planting corn with a hoe, and others using horses and mules with ploughs, or even tractors would be worlds apart. It was not difficult to understand why one farm would struggle all year and have little to show for the work, and another would engage in the same activity and have a plentiful harvest.

We were seeing pioneering technology finding its place with decades of research. On those large swathes of land, I found how technology was critical in every step, and there was nothing more fundamental than having the right equipment for the right work. Poor farmers back home in Ghana came to my mind more than once. They were doing all they could but the world seemed to have moved on a long time ago and left them behind. They worked for hours in the scorching sun, but it was easy to see how despite their efforts, they were still poor.

Professor Yudith Klein was another person who made quite an impression on me. She taught physiology, and carefully painted a beautiful picture of what gave the chickens life. Everything from how each cell functioned, even as detailed as to how the molecules interacted to give life gave a rather fascinating insight into the world of chickens. Nothing about their body or feather or beak had been an accident. Unless a farmer understood the underlying science in how a bird functions like a living creature, it would be difficult to appreciate why it responds and adapts to a range of things in the way it does.

There was certainly more to the chicken than the respiratory, reproductive, and digestive systems, and it took those years in Ruppin to truly appreciate the significance of its beak and skin and every feather that covered the body. As tough as Professor Yudith Klein had been to ensure that the knowledge we acquired became second nature to every one of us, her work created a sense of responsibility. A poultry farmer was a caretaker who ought to be excellent in all he did.

It was breathtaking to discover the care with which God had created the chicken. Just like all my fellow human students, I was spending every day learning more and more about a creature that God had carefully created, with every part of it designed for a purpose. All the feathers and scales seemed to cover the bird just perfectly. The comb on its head and wattle underneath its beak working to circulate the blood and regulate the temperature made it intriguing to think about just how unique God elects to make every creature in a way that may ordinarily never make sense to us. Why birds would have their nares tucked onto the beaks as nostrils, or have nine air sacs in their neck area, and a body cavity that functions to inflate their lungs were marks of a creator who chooses how He fashions anything and anyone.

Why a chicken will have gizzards to grind food particles, and how the colour of the egg will depend on the chicken's earlobes, is all in the hands of a maker who creates their world. These were truths that were not easy to miss, and on those farms, God's handiwork was an important reminder of His presence in every step along the way.

My colleagues who had been enrolled at Wiseman Institute, about 20 miles away, were studying Agricultural Administration and another focused on Forestry. It was interesting to occasionally sit together on the quiet weekends and to find that all of us had teachers who came to the program with a refreshing intensity and passion. It gradually rubbed off on each of us. We were falling in love with the knowledge of poultry and agriculture, and perhaps that was because of an interaction with people who had taken the time to design the programs in such a way that made every moment full of treasures of thought.

In the winter months, the cold winds swept in. This was my first time in such a climate and I had to adapt even on the days when it felt unbearable. We had to still go into the farm with jackets, my ears

Chapter 5: Open Fields

freezing on the cold hillsides. Most of the Israelis had returned from Scandinavian countries with much colder temperatures, and they were used to this kind of weather.

I went to Givatos, to a *moshav*, with a friend whose father owned a farm with grapes, apples, and oranges. She had invited me to visit the farm as it was harvest time for grapes. I ate a lot of grapes, never thinking for a moment that any would end up in my colon. In just a few days, the pain in my abdomen was unbearable. The doctors in the settlements diagnosed it to be appendicitis.

I was admitted to Tel HaShomer Hospital in Tel Aviv for four days. The doctors called the Ghana Embassy for an officer to sign the release for my surgery. Fortunately, Ambassador Bediako Poku in whose care all the trainees were in Israel, was able to rush to the hospital. The big relief was that the surgery was successful and I was able to recover quickly and be back to the farm.

Living in Israel felt as if we were cut off from the world we left behind. I missed my grandmother and mother back home in Kumasi, and I hoped they would be proud of the man I was to become. We didn't have any way to reach our families because it was very expensive to make international phone calls, even if we were lucky enough to find a phone. Fortunately, we were so engulfed in the training that it was as if that was all that mattered. The people with whom I was spending my days and nights worked hard, and it affected me too.

One picture that I would someday leave Israel with was the discipline with which the people went about their day. I saw leading personalities like Ben-Gurion, Golda Meir, and military leader and politician Moshe Dayan all doing the same work as everyone in the settlement, and it was almost surreal to see how unimportant they made themselves feel. I heard of how they held cabinet meetings at night, after they had spent the day with their community. They were the leading personalities in Israeli political society but in the settlements, their actions reiterated to their people that they were no different.

Everyone walked around in their brown khaki shorts and trousers, and work boots, with their shirts tucked in neatly. Their focus seemed stuck on pursuing excellence and resilience, with little regard for fleeting fame and notoriety. My outlook on life had been sharpened by the world around me. My added advantage had been that the Stibukir settlement where I was placed was also the seat of government so I had the occasional chance to interact with personalities I otherwise would never have met.

This is how I crossed paths with David Ben-Gurion, one of the most powerful men in the State of Israel and the country's first Prime Minister. He was a man whose charisma was as impressive as his leadership qualities. He, like most people I had the chance to work with, was incredibly hospitable and took every opportunity to share his experiences with a young aspiring farmer who had travelled for several thousands of miles. This was one encounter for which I would be forever grateful.

One afternoon, Ben-Gurion was urging me to ensure that when I returned home, I should buy any land I could afford. I remember even the occasional smile on his face. He tried to explain how God will not create any more land, but the millions of people who would be born in the future would need a place to live, and whatever land was mine would never lose its worth. Israel has learned that. His reasoning had come from of all the war and turmoil they had to endure just to get the piece of land they now occupied. I saw clearly the lenses through which they viewed life, and how determined they were to make the best of any opportunity.

I had come from Ghana, a place blessed with vast arable lands and plenty of rain. Israel was in a desert, and if they had found a way to harvest oranges in a desert, there was nothing else that should be beyond my grasp. I had no excuses. I had come from a place where I didn't have to wake up to the threats of military forces stomping onto my land or launching missiles to annihilate entire settlements, so I couldn't afford to live life callously and take peace for granted. I had to be even more resolute.

I was heading back home to Ghana unsure of what had become of the life that I left behind. For three years, I'd left behind friends some of whom had the chance to attend Ghanaian universities, both University of Science and Technology in Kumasi and the University of Ghana in Accra. All of them were to pursue courses in different fields from medicine to law and engineering. Others took on vocations to provide for their families. Life moved on. Our paths were different and I could only hope that their journeys would have been just as gratifying as the ones I had the chance to experience. A lot would be different, and some things were sure to stay the same.

I was curious to find anyone who had chosen a program in agriculture, and see if they'd fallen in love with the vocation as I had. I wasn't sure our country invested in facilities and instructors in the same way other countries seemed to have. I was aware of some of the challenges in the tertiary institutions at home, and now my experience had illuminated them even more. Throughout my early education, the emphasis seemed to have been on young students regurgitating information in textbooks with little worry about what the words meant. Most of us came to accept this as the way it was in our world, and it probably never changed.

What I remembered was that in many of the government schools, learning didn't challenge a student to think or even apply the knowledge acquired. It was a race to pass a test at the end of the school year, only to forget every word in the next minute. At Ruppin College, my world had been opened to question every thought and research, and to build on the knowledge I had acquired to suit my environment. Perhaps, the teachers back home had to confront the fact that there was so little investment in education that there was only very little they could do to give each student practical experience in any field.

I had spent three years in an agricultural program in Israel where the institution focused much of its learning on the student having a deep understanding of the work we did. Commercial poultry farming was much more than reading about concepts and systems. From the school's farms, we would be heading into the real world, and our learning would only be useful if we were able to translate the knowledge acquired into viable poultry enterprises. The young Israeli students were heading into the collective settlements to immediately use all the knowledge they'd acquired, and their sense of urgency spilled onto everyone in the program.

In Ghana, we had vast stretches of arable land, and a climate conducive to huge commercial agricultural projects, yet we were saddled with a host of economic challenges and social attitudes that stunted our growth. Our farmers worked through the sun and the rain but without the right tools, the right technology, and the desire to push themselves beyond their comfort zone. We had been blessed with enormous opportunities, yet we had defined our potential. Training in Israel had forced me to see beyond our limitations, and I dedicated long hours every day to nurture my passion for poultry farming.

In agriculture, I had learned how the technologies changed and new ideas enhanced every process. Institutions and organizations around the world worked hard on extensive research to develop countless vaccines, ideas for harvesting rainwater, and many breeding techniques for commercial poultry enterprises. From feeding systems, waterers, ventilation and climate control and lighting. There was a lot of information and science to consider, because in poultry farming, some of the seemingly insignificant steps had the potential to make a huge difference to any capital investment.

I had seen how there was extensive research undertaken by poultry scientists around the world to contribute new knowledge about hatcheries and types of poultry feed. Farmers seeking to establish successful enterprises that would provide eggs and meat to consumers who couldn't afford to ignore the nutritional means necessary to ensure the good health of the birds.

There was every reason to prevent diseases from viruses, mycoplasma, bacteria, protozoa, and other parasites. A lot of work went into finding vaccines to fight viruses that caused major diseases like Newcastle disease, Marek's disease, infectious bronchitis, laryngotracheitis, fowl pox, and fowl cholera. There was a host of technologies and new opportunities emerging every day, but unless a society like Ghana equipped training institutions to integrate the emerging ideas, it couldn't take any advantage of the innovative trends.

In Israel, it was remarkable to see how we carefully monitored the health of every bird, nutrition plans, temperature, humidity, and many other details that were to affect the farm and the profitability of the poultry business. In the real world, we would have to know a lot about how to control diseases, handle wastes, and implement sanitation of the poultry houses. Our success would be our own to manage. Whether we were raising a flock of broilers for meat production or layers to provide eggs rich in proteins and vitamins, our profitability would be tied to every one of the intricate details.

The Ghana in which I grew up embraced a fascinating misconception, that anyone who wanted to be a farmer could easily become one, and that it didn't take much more than common sense to do so. Men and women raised chickens in their own backyards and in small hencoops successfully for family consumption. Gradually it affirmed a delusion in our minds, and that attitude gave us reason to ignore any opportunity to gain new knowledge.

It was only when a person set out to operate commercial poultry farms that they quickly realized the complicated enterprise of poultry farming, and that raising five chickens in a person's backyard was vastly different from operating a facility with several tens of thousands of birds. While other societies desperately sought clever ways in farming to boost their agricultural sector, we didn't seem to bother. I hoped a lot had changed.

I had chosen the path of a farmer. There was nothing I would give to change that. I found an indescribable satisfaction from what I cared the most about and into which I could pour my heart. I was fortunate to have had lecturers in Israel who rigorously challenged passion with incisive research and pushed every one of their students to hone their skills. Becoming a poultry farmer was much more than owning chickens and a hazy desire to become an entrepreneur. Every bit of knowledge would have to be filtered and applied in the environment where I would be setting up an enterprise, and any success would be built on a full understanding of the vocation.

My education had stripped away my every ignorant belief about poultry farming and helped me to intimately understand the science of it. Just as any other professional would engage in lifelong learning to enhance their skill, I would be no different. If I wanted to succeed as a poultry farmer and contribute to the economic development in my country, I had to commit to a different approach, and one that required a relentless investment in myself and my trade.

God had given me every grace to thrive, but whether I succeeded or failed in the journey would be my own doing. A scripture in Genesis had become my mantra, that I was to "Till the land and eat out of it", and there was nothing else that I wanted for my life than to become a farmer. Just as I had once taken care of one hundred day-old chicks which Reverend Sercombe brought to Ghana in 1958, my commitment would be no different to care in that same way for ten thousand, fifty thousand, or a hundred thousand.

I had chosen to follow the path that God set ahead for me. Fortunately, before I stepped foot in Israel, I had the opportunity to begin my journey, making my mistakes and learning from every one of them. I prayed only to stay in God's will for my life, one that was capable of opening new doors of opportunities for my life and set me apart.

Someday I would have the chance to either take bold steps as an entrepreneur or learn only to copy the world around me. If I ever got that chance, I would choose to carve my own path. Going back home would come with a string of ups and downs to live through, but even then, I might get to look back someday and cherish every step that God had brought my way.

I had travelled to learn all I could about poultry science, and now I had learned much more. I know this, the favour of God had been with me every step along the way.

CHAPTER 6

THE ROAD BACK HOME

Ghana Poultry Farm, Apathy and Reality

Most of us smile at the thought of chickens being able to see and dream in full colour, but perhaps there is nothing as powerful as a perspective that is made even clearer through experience and time. In the case of chickens, because they are indeed tetrachromatic, they see many more colours and shades and things than humans do.

I had been deeply immersed in their world for three years in Israel, and had chosen to learn anything I could from it. I could only hope that I was returning to Ghana with a keener sense of awareness, and that I'd see the colourful world around me for all the opportunities it bore.

I returned home to Ghana in 1961, wide-eyed and excited to make a difference. It was then that I learned about a bond of service that I had agreed to before leaving for Israel. For a young man who couldn't wait to travel, it was not surprising that I couldn't remember any document I signed that stipulated my having to work for a state-owned company for two years before I would be allowed to pursue anything I wished. I had left Tel Aviv with my sights set on getting to Kumasi as soon as I could to work with my stepfather's company, Central Egg Farm. That had to wait.

I stayed in a bungalow in Accra, to work for the newly established Ghana Agricultural Development Cooperation, the poultry farm in Dansoman. It was with a group of men and women, most of whom had little experience. The effort was to get the crew up to speed quickly, and importantly, introduce every technique I had learned in the Ruppin College to the company. Mr. Avenin stayed on to help launch the project and was integral to every decision made for the agricultural development cooperation, Dansoman Poultry Project.

Our environment was much different from Israel, and unfortunately, so was our innate sense of urgency, and it didn't take a second to notice that. I hadn't returned home without any illusions, but my fellow countrymen's approach to the vocation was as striking as it was occasionally troubling. The challenge would be to carve a vision that the workers could appreciate and be eager to support because it uplifted the collective agenda, and wasn't meant merely to satisfy their individual motivations.

From my vantage point, Ghana had an inherent problem at the onset. It felt as though the mindset of the employees was that anything that belonged to the government belonged to everyone, and no one. When no one owned it, no one took care of it. This was an attitude that we had to push against and encourage them to shed if we were ever to reach the heights that Dr. Nkrumah and his administration expected of us. But it was much deeper than I could fathom. The country had made investments in training its people and had solicited help from international allies for the construction of a commercial poultry facility, yet our attitude towards the work had every potential to crush that hope.

Mr. Martin Appiah Danquah was the General Secretary of Ghana's Farmers' Council and the organization was instrumental to the direction of the cooperation. Mr. C.K. Annan worked for the Ministry of Agriculture and Animal Husbandry, and had been put in charge of the poultry project. His office organized a meeting to the State House to visit with Dr. Nkrumah and some of the members in his administration. This was my first encounter with the president, and even in routine exchanges with his colleagues, he exuded a confidence that was infectious. He seemed warm and focused. It was in that meeting that I

Chapter 6: The Road Back Home

saw what appeared to be a blueprint for the country's agricultural sector, painstakingly outlined.

Both Nkrumah's opponents and even members in his inner circle were publicly criticizing his ambitious obsession with African unity even when Ghana, as a new nation, had our own struggles to overcome. Through the Israeli partnership, both Ghana's Airforce and Black Star Line Shipping Company were on their way to becoming excellent corporations, and key cornerstones to the country's industrial agenda. Perhaps, the Ghana Agricultural Development Cooperation would also mark the government's priority to develop industries in Ghana. The construction in Dansoman included a hatchery, feed mill, and a processing plant.

The first few months were both exhilarating and challenging because the work was to help build an industry, and train people to shift the way they had always farmed into one that could effectively support the nation.

So much of what I had become had been shaped by the people with whom I spent time working and studying on Israeli farms. I came back from Israel with 12 white shirts and 12 pairs of khaki trousers. For the next two years, these were the same clothes I would wear to work every day. Sure, I could afford the *gabardine and rayon* clothes some of the workers wore to the facility, but a part of me couldn't stray from the simple and consistent approach I had seen work.

By 1964, investment in the cooperation had started to decline. Our achievements had been short-lived because cracks in the funding, investment in facility maintenance and accountability had started to emerge, and it was only a matter of time before the country would have to confront the consequences of our actions. Workers complained at the least opportunity, and most found excuses not to do one task or another. Indifference and bloated egos that were well entrenched in much of the society eventually came knocking at our door.

Then there was "Book it Dead" syndrome. It was as simple as managers and staff stealing chicken and eggs and making ridiculous excuses for it. "Book it Dead" meant whatever was taken from the farm or facility didn't need to be accounted for—for us to *consider it dead*. The chickens and eggs were ending up in lavish parties hosted by government officials and company managers, instead of finding their way to market. Sadly, our poultry farm was not alone; the looting had become a fixture at state-owned facilities. In the state-owned Animal Husbandry Farm in Nungua and another near Aburi, managers used a host of shameful excuses to steal from the companies. In the same way, the country's profits slowly eroded at the State Fisheries, and it was not hard to imagine why.

The half-baked patriotism started to rear its ugly head and it seemed people cared more about their personal gain than any honourable achievement for the country and our collective future. I had come from Israel with a hope, but it now seemed to be fading having to confront corruption and apathy every day.

The brazen and entrenched dishonesty squeezed the very farm the government was hoping would fuel its agenda. Feeding school children and making sure every child had an egg a day to eat had become an idea that would never see the light of day. Under the watchful eye of security officers, the staff stole from the poultry farm.

For President Nkrumah, even as his vision expanded, accountability did not keep up. I had learned from a system that worked, but standing in the middle of one that was exploited and strangled on all sides by politics and politicians, apathy and selfishness, painted a gloomy picture of where the company was heading. The problem went all the way to the top.

Around the same time, Nkrumah had formed the State Farms Cooperation to oversee the various agricultural projects in the country. There was the Builders' Brigade, young people who were supposed to provide manpower, dressed in beautiful light green khaki uniforms. The government secured large tracts of land and hoped the young people would take on the job with vigour, but the misplaced agenda stifled the once compelling vision. Unfortunately, most of the young people had

Chapter 6: The Road Back Home

come with a different outlook, that it was nothing but a "job for the boys". They had come for free money.

The Ghana Agricultural Development Cooperation designed to be a model for poultry farming in Ghana was soon doing all it could to push out the people who had been trained to lead the company. Whether it was because some of the staff were not well paid or they never cared to begin with, it was painful to admit that we, Ghanaians, had been the people responsible for undermining whatever benefit could have been achieved together. I saw warning signs, reported all I saw, but the system worked for some of the managers and they couldn't wait to take over.

In Ruppin College, I had come away with a conviction that leadership defines a company's culture, and unless the management embraces a culture of accountability, it will be a near-impossible task to charge the staff with the same.

In a state-owned company, accountability was surely the difference between success and failure. There were clear signals of things starting to go awry, as the people didn't feel a sense of ownership and drifted into spectator mode and watched as things failed.

I saw traces of corruption impeding agribusiness development, and ultimately it hindered the ability of the country to transform. It was a challenging position for a company to be in, and one that even if it became a footnote in history, would be etched in my mind for the rest of my career.

In places like Ghana, there seemed to have been an inherent sense of distrust in the agenda that the Nkrumah government pushed. In a way, it was their own, and the people hadn't bought into it. We were not prepared to sacrifice for a collective ambition. There was a prevailing idea: we said *"ewo me, ne ewo yen, enye pe"*, in that there was a big difference between what belongs to a person, and what belonged to an entire community. It was unfortunate but in Ghana, it was sad to admit that "when no one owns anything, no one takes care of it". It was a tiring reality working in a state-owned facility.

In just a few years, the Ghana Agricultural Development Cooperation had become a pale imitation of its former self, and it was time for me to head back home. I worked for two years and formally resigned at the end of the bond to return to Kumasi in 1962.

Central Egg Farm had 5,000 birds by the time I arrived. My stepfather had become the most prominent poultry farmer in Ghana, who stumbled into the poultry business, and worked his way up to become the chairman of the Poultry Farmers' Association. A year later, we grew to 50,000 birds and a 100,000 egg-laying flock the second year.

* * * * *

It was in my stepfather's house that I first appreciated how all of us make little choices every day, some of which end up having a big impact on our lives, and others that take us in unexpected directions. One single decision was to change my stepfather' perception of me, and for the rest of his life, it would change our relationship too.

In the months after I left the Ghana Agricultural Development Cooperation in Accra, and returned to Kumasi, I lived with my stepfather in Kwadaso Estates, a suburb in Kumasi. He had moved the farm to Anyinam in the Kokoben district, and poultry farming had become my life, spending every moment thinking about the business.

One evening, I was casually digging through a pile of junk that my stepfather had tucked away in his small garage when I saw an old electric stove. I wasn't sure it worked, and it looked as if he had no use for it. It appeared rusty on the sides and covered with dirt, but I hoped it would somehow work still. As a young bachelor, I was happy to have a small stove in my room to use to prepare tea.

A few months later, I moved to live with my mother's in her home in South Suntreso. I packed my belongings into a small suitcase, and the small stove too.

It was about a week later when I was reading a book by American evangelist D. L. Moody, *Repentance and Restitution*, when I came across an incredibly powerful idea of restitution. The author used several examples to carefully explain the importance of truth and the consequence of action. Even when no one knows our deepest secrets or even if we think our action is trivial, truth should guide our every thought and act. Restitution is restoring something lost or even stolen to its rightful owner. It was not enough to admit wrongdoing; restitution is a willingness to take action to salvage the moment, and to do the right thing.

In the mind of D. L. Moody, "If there is true repentance, it will bring forth fruit". The author wrote about what it meant to be sincere, and that if a person takes something that belongs to another, as long as the person was unaware of our act, it is theft. Confession and repentance is worthless unless we are willing to walk away from the action and sincerely give our best effort to try to be better, restoring the object or act. It was not enough to be upset or even regret; we had to act. If another person's belongings were in my possession, I had to take it back to them. In that afternoon, which reading through the pages of D. L. Moody's book, I felt the absolute conviction to return my stepfather's electric stove to him. I had it with me, I had not asked his permission to take it, and the Holy Spirit was sounding an alarm that it was theft.

I went back to my stepfather that afternoon. I began to tell him about *Repentance and Restitution*, and about how the author's words had pierced my heart in such a way that it was impossible for me to be blinded to the truth. The words were profoundly thought-provoking.

He wasn't sure what had weighed so heavily on me that I had come to confess. I had allowed the Holy Spirit to take residence in my heart, and now I had chosen to act on the conviction deep in my heart. I had no way of knowing if the electric stove was worth anything to him, but all I knew was that according to the Bible, I had stolen from him, and had come back to return it. It was not sufficient to regret the action. I had to live with my conscience and do the best I could.

I opened the portmanteau and took out the small electric stove. My Stepfather was stunned, in disbelief.

He had stood quietly listening to me explain repentance and restitution, but never could he have imagined that what had brought me to his house was an old electric stove that he had left in the pile of discarded appliances in the corner of his garage. For a moment, he wasn't sure he heard me right. He didn't find it humorous, he looked surprised.

Hearing me explain how theft was sin according to my Bible and I had come to seek his forgiveness was even more shocking to him.

"Forgive what? The stove?"

I nodded.

"Kwabena, this Bible has turned you into a madman!"

He tried to figure out if he had missed any part of my story. The whole time he had imagined I had probably done something terrible and that was why I sought his forgiveness. It didn't matter to him, but it did for me.

He was dumbfounded. He couldn't find the words to say what was in his mind. Then he continued, "So you do everything the Bible asks you to do?"

"Yes".

"Kwabena, you have gone beyond yourself".

I did not know what he meant, until he told my mother how he thought the Bible had turned me into an unhinged young man. He never imagined anyone would follow the word of God and every doctrine faithfully even when it involved something as trivial as a discarded electric stove. The Bible had become my mental compass, and I had chosen to live my life by its every word. For me, it was more than a discarded object, it was my heart's desire to please Almighty God that compelled me to act on the incredible conviction from reading *Repentance and Restitution*.

I didn't know how my decision would affect our relationship for the rest of his life, but just as quickly as this happened my stepfather turned over everything he owned into my care. Every asset and every aspect of the Central Egg Farm was now in my charge, because there was suddenly no one he trusted more. If my life was indeed guided strictly by the Word of God, there was no better custodian than a person whose heart's desire is to please God even with the seemingly insignificant objects. It wasn't until he took his final breath, years later, that I learned that he had entrusted me to become the executor of his will.

Choices have consequences, and every decision we make carries its own seed to bear fruits. There were choices in life I had no control over, but many that I determined which direction I would turn. I had chosen to acknowledge God in everything I did, and trusted Him to direct my path. My stepfather didn't have to understand my devotion to God's word, in a very small way, he saw the fruit of my faith and commitment in the most unexpected ways.

Following what I believed was the right thing to do with perhaps the most insignificant of items, had become the incredible act that allowed my stepfather to trust me with everything he owned. It was a decision that's probably determined the quality of life I was choosing to pursue, even if it was unpopular and unimportant. Perhaps it was the small rusty and dirty stove he left in the pile in the corner of his garage that led him to trust my judgment, and importantly, trust my God.

CHAPTER 7

A LIFE'S PURPOSE

Morris Cerullo

Providence gives us a window even when we least expect it, and God's guiding hands carry us through if we are humble enough to accept our own inability. Coming back to Kumasi had not only given me the chance to pursue my career as a poultry farmer, but more importantly, a life-altering encounter to embark on my Christian journey without any streak of doubt. God had found me, and I had chosen to walk with Him.

I had become the Youth Leader and Sunday school teacher at the local Assemblies of God Church in Kumasi. It was the largest charismatic church in the area, but had begun a few years earlier as a small church in Old Tafo. It was now grooming young men and women across the country to carry on with the church's vision. These open doors gave me a chance to share my faith. There was never a day that I lived without the awareness that it was grace that found me and set me on a new trajectory. Perhaps through my interactions, someone too would find the same encounter.

In most secondary schools in Ghana, non-denominational Scripture Unions and churches like the Assemblies of God had found an opportunity to connect with the students of the Protestant faith as part of an evangelical outreach. I was a Scripture Union leader, often visiting school campus events as their guest speaker and campus facilitator. It had been a real opportunity to serve young people in the Kumasi area and I learned to explain the faith I professed through my own lens.

There was nothing more fulfilling than having found a passion for teaching the word of God, and sharing the same gospel that had sunk into my heart a few years earlier. I had chosen to have a deeper relationship with Jesus and be sincere with my own walk. I had chosen to be a Christian, and I couldn't afford to be lukewarm. By the time I joined the Lighthouse Assemblies of God Church in Kumasi, near the old Jackson's Park, I had met other young men and women who were all on fire for the Lord, and in their own ways, each of them helped my faith find a firm footing as an ambassador of Christ.

We received word that American Pentecostal evangelist Morris Cerullo was coming to Ghana for a crusade. We learned that Cerullo's ministry needed several churches in the area to coordinate the event in order to reach people in the surrounding towns. The Assemblies of God, Christ Apostolic Church, The Apostolic Church of Ghana, and the Church of God all came together with our planning committees to host evangelist Cerullo.

In Ghana, we knew that he had founded his World Evangelism ministry in 1961 and spent decades preaching to millions across the world. Having been raised in a Jewish Orthodox orphanage in New Jersey, his empathy for people in pain drove him to some of the remotest parts of the globe to help people find faith and hope in Jesus Christ. This was the same commanding message he was bringing to the people in Kumasi.

We spent the next several weeks to raise money to print posters and t-shirts. Because both the Assemblies of God and the Church of God were denominations with American roots, the two churches took a leading role in the planning. Much of the work was to fall on the young people to use time and energy promoting the event, and gradually I had become one of the leading young men who spent every dreaming about the upcoming crusade's impact.

Chapter 7: A Life's Purpose

We marched from one area to another, excitedly with posters in hand, happy to tell anyone who would listen about *Kumasi for Jesus*.

Everywhere He went, He was doing good,
Almighty Healer, He cleansed the leapers,
When the cripples saw Him, they started walking
Everywhere He went, my Lord was doing good

I had been able to donate a new Volkswagen van to the church, what became the "Speed the Light" van, and it turned out to be the same vehicle that we had to drive around nearby towns, pasting huge posters on walls and signboards. I was beyond excited to see how our efforts were reaching people for Christ and this was giving me another taste of mission work, spreading the gospel to small villages.

Evangelist Cerullo sent his emissary, a young Hispanic preacher Ajamal Figueroa to Kumasi ahead of his visit. He arranged to meet with the youth from all four churches at an Easter convention in Akomadan Afrantwo in the Brong Ahafo region.

Then he spoke. It was a striking encounter hearing him teach the Word of God. Figueroa preached with such fervour and with powerful testimonies that his words shook everyone in the park. I was excited to see a man of God after whose preaching the whole city seemed to have accepted Jesus. His sermon was delivered with a genuine passion and conviction, and it was evident God was using such a man to proclaim His word. It ignited my own thirst to serve.

As we listened to Figueroa, the scriptures spoke boldly for themselves, and he took the time to expound on the biblical texts carefully. What struck all of us was how he was not seeking attention to himself, or using clever clichés and impressive exegesis to impress the crowd. By the end of the convention, he inspired even more evangelism in our hearts than we'd had before and we couldn't wait to be the hands and feet of Jesus in the towns and villages.

Figueroa announced the crusade date for Cerullo. If his emissary was this inspiring, we couldn't wait for the evangelist to arrive for a crusade that would affect the whole city and turn hearts to Jesus. Figueroa said we needed 500 youth as ushers. That was a lot of people. To print 200,000 posters, the ministry was to send money for printing at the Assemblies of God Press in Tamale who were to print them as quickly as they could.

The preparation started for the crusade in Kumasi. In no time, we had about 650 people signed up to be volunteer ushers for the weeklong event. It was unbelievable. Despite what little some of us knew about Cerullo, we were excited for an event that we imagined would be like the image we saw on the poster—a crowd of people with hands lifted up to Heaven, worshiping and praying. We couldn't wait for the weeks to turn into days.

Hundreds of young people took to the city streets, posting large paper posters on every wall we could find. The big bold letters of *"Kumasi for Jesus"* ran across the top of Cerullo's image with his hands outstretched to a people in a crusade held in Brazil. Every newspaper advertisement, and radio or television announcements during the days and nights invited people to an event to be held at the historic Prince of Wales Park at the city's centre, an area that was to someday become *Kejetia*. It was a venue often used for big events and coronations, and the expectation was for a crowd to fill every corner of the park.

It was on the day of Cerullo's arrival in Ghana that the organizers remembered a small detail they had overlooked. No one had arranged for a car to pick him up from City Hotel to the crusade grounds every evening. As the leader of Christ's Ambassadors youth group, I was chosen to pick up the evangelist in the same Volkswagen van that I drove around for the church's errands.

Out of sheer coincidence, I was to ride in a car with a man I had revered from a distance for the next four hours. It would be a chance to hear his every word without a cheering crowd of people waiting to have a

Chapter 7: A Life's Purpose

moment with him. This had to be a divine appointment. That was when I learned that Cerullo was a Jew, and after I picked him up, I found that my spending three years in Israel gave us much more to talk about, and instilled in me a greater appreciation of the person he was. I had become the chauffeur for the week and it was an incredible experience for which I could never have prepared. Men and women of all ages came from neighbouring towns and villages like Kanyaaase, Kwadaso, Ayigya, and Kantikrono. Some had travelled from as far as Bekwai, Ejisu, Obuasi, Konongo, and Dunkwaw and over the next seven days, hundreds and hundreds of people found a personal relationship with Jesus.

Morris Cerullo was an extraordinarily gifted spirit-filled orator and an anointed man of God. His every word was uttered with conviction and with such astonishing originality. I had been catapulted to the forefront of the organizers and developed a friendship with a man who ordinarily may have had only a few minutes to share with me. Now I was part of his every day in Ghana.

With thousands of people singing and praising God in the huge open park in Kumasi, Cerullo's captivating sermon and eloquence pointed all praise toward God. Night after night, he preached one fiery message after another. Hundreds of people came to the Lord every night, with amazing testimonies of God's healing power, and of marriages and broken lives restored.

I stood back, listening intently, and watching as Reverend Gyan Fosu interpreted perfectly to the crowd. It was evident Cerullo genuinely believed in every word he said, preached from his own strongly-held convictions and empowered by the Holy Spirit. He shared his personal story of how he had accepted Jesus as his Lord and Saviour when he was about 14 years old, and had lived the rest of his life seeking to understand every truth in the Bible for himself. It was refreshing to hear a spirit-filled man of God who connected the word of God to our own, not to win applause, but to explain the scripture and exude wisdom anchored in his faithfulness to God.

It was on the last day of the crusade that the evangelist turned his attention to broken homes. He prayed for God to restore families and for the Holy Spirit to bring home fathers, mothers, sons and daughters who had drifted away from home. He spoke boldly about drunkenness and addictions, all of which he stressed were not pleasing to God. It all came from God's word, not Cerullo's personal opinion, and for that, he could boldly declare that here was a chance for God to heal anyone who was willing to turn their lives over to the Lord.

Cerullo then began to direct an outward demonstration of surrender. He asked the people in the crowd who smoked cigarettes and tobacco pipes, but were ready to experience the redemptive power of Almighty God, to do as he instructed, on the count of three. They were to throw every cigarette or pipe in their pockets toward the platform, as if to reaffirm their own decision to throw away anything that was holding them back from becoming the men and women God had called them to be in their families and to their communities.

The next morning when we returned to clean up the crusade grounds, we collected about 7,000 tobacco pipes, and many trash bags filled with cigarette sticks and boxes. There was no way to know how many people came to the Lord that night, but the pipes and bags of cigarettes gave an idea of how many had heard the message of salvation and turned their hearts to Jesus.

Away from the nightly crusade at the park, Cerullo spent every morning teaching the missionaries, pastors, and leaders in charge of the program, most of whom were working in different remote parts of the country. Even though this was the evangelist's first visit to Ghana, he seemed to have a heart for people hurting in every corner of the world where he took the gospel. The morning meetings, Deeper Life sessions, were intensive training and prayer sessions to effectively reach people and bring hope to our communities and world.

For the first three days, I felt saturated with the word of God, so much that I was to immediately quit everything I had planned for my own life to become a preacher of the gospel. Nothing could be more important. My heart was full. Cerullo's every word had touched me greatly and had challenged my heart to diligently seek the face of God in all my endeavours. I was ready to leave my job on my stepfather's poultry farm and attend Bible school.

Nothing had shaken me to my core like the realization that there was a harvest of souls all around in our towns and villages, but the labourers were few. When an evangelist like Morris Cerullo was done with the crusade, there would be the need for committed local preachers to take the mantle and preach the good news to our own people. If anyone would heed the call to be a disciple, I wanted to be one. I was ready.

A few days into the program, Morris Cerullo asked why there hadn't been any local preachers on the huge stage during the services. Every night, there would be several foreign missionaries dressed immaculately who took their seats behind Cerullo, but the evangelist had a reason why he needed the local preachers to join him on the platform. In his mind, when his work in Ghana was done, it would be the local preachers who would work in the communities, spreading the gospel to the places and people that Cerullo would never be able to reach. They were the ones who should be seated on the stage for the crowd to see.

Then they showed up. There were about 20 local pastors from Kumasi and neighbouring towns and villages including Asante Bekwai, Akropong, Konongo, and Mampong. As honoured as that moment was, it was painful to watch the Ghanaian preachers climb on stage looking frail and uncomfortable. More than the awkward oversized outfits, their demeanour was a shattered image of lack and poverty. They wore loose-fitting and shapeless suits that were much bigger than their bodies and with the sleeves folded awkwardly into cuffs. The local preachers wore wrinkled white shirts with dark stains along the necks, and it was heart-breaking watching the men sit on the stage next to their foreign counterparts.

The sight of the men who I was sure were also faithful servants of God and perhaps even respectable preachers but looking frail and broken, was crushing. I was a young man with my own perception of God's kingdom as one where we confidently share His word. But in the faces of the local preachers that night, there was no confidence to share. Their countenance and appearance, as if there was no happiness in becoming a preacher of the Gospel stood out to me, painfully. The reality crushed my dream to become a preacher even before it took off.

Cerullo saw the dejection on my face the next morning at breakfast. It was hard to explain to him how I had been so convicted to go to Bible School until I saw the local preachers who couldn't make enough money to even buy decent clothes to wear. Some struggled to take care of their families, depended on charity, and I couldn't imagine quitting my job to become a preacher. No one was doing God's work for financial gain, but even in my young heart, I saw the men who seemed to be living their lives in such misery that I was not sure how they could offer hope to another person.

With tears running down the faces of the local preachers, Cerullo urged them not to weep. He said that God was raising businessmen and women across the country who would build His kingdom with their work and success. It seemed the preachers in the village could hardly support the work, but God saw their hearts and knew the weight of their devotion to the kingdom. There was nothing impossible for the Almighty God to do and I believed that indeed God was bigger than any earthly problems.

For every preacher who spent the days and nights caring for people, comforting broken lives and uplifting communities, maybe some of us who had been afforded the opportunity to thrive in the enterprise could become a backbone to their ministry. I shared with Cerullo how I felt caught between two thoughts, yet there was a burning desire in my heart that I couldn't shut off. I wanted to be a pastor, but their reality hindered me.

I remember the smile on his face. It was the affirmation I needed. The evangelist explained how he was able to do the work of God all over the world because he had brothers and sisters in faith whose generosity and commitment to the kingdom of God helped him to travel and be in every one of those places. He encouraged me not to feel dejected, but rather to heed God's call if He needed me as a businessman whose heart would be fixed on bringing Him the glory. What God needed was my heart set on serving him, from every area of life where I stood.

Evangelist Morris Cerullo shared a word of prayer with me, and challenged me to step out on faith to start a business so that I would be one that God could count on to support the kingdom with any success. He added that God would be faithful and make me prosper if I stayed humble and true to his calling. All I had to do was to be willing; God's hand of protection would cover my every decision and work.

Starting a company under a prophetic anointing and with a Godly declaration, that morning was what set the foundation on which I was to stand, and trust God to be faithful to keep every one of His promises. This was the vision for a new poultry farm, Darko Farms Company Limited.

CHAPTER 8

LEAP

Darko Farms

A week after Cerullo's crusade in Kumasi, I went to my stepfather to ask for his permission to travel to Saltpond for a three-day retreat. The Assemblies of God's Christ Ambassadors were hosting a Youth Retreat and I had planned to attend. I had done all I could to make sure my absence for those few days would not affect the work on the farm. My stepfather wanted all of his staff to be there, and had decided he would not extend any preferential treatment to me, even though I was in charge of the farm's operations.

My stepfather would not agree. For 4 years I had never requested leave because I knew how much the business depended on me. He had agreed for me to take leave for a week for Cerullo's crusade and he couldn't see why I needed another three days for a Christian convention.

I hoped he would understand. I tried to reason with my stepfather that I wouldn't do anything to jeopardize the company's operation, and that I could assure him that I had made every arrangement to make sure the staff was adequately prepared in my short absence.

I left and headed west, to Saltpond. It was in that retreat at the Southern Ghana Bible School campus that I had the chance to pray and reflect on God's calling on my life. I drank the Word of God like milk. I had become even more firm in my resolve to resign from my stepfather's farm. I started memorizing every word of scripture and decided to follow the dream that seemed to tug at my heart. Perhaps the evangelist Cerullo's visit to Ghana had been an urgent reminder and the reassuring truth that I needed to launch. He said God would raise faithful men and women in our land who would succeed in their enterprises and use their work to advance the kingdom of God.

I returned to work from the Saltpond retreat just as I had promised, but the tension clearly emanating from my stepfather demanded I share my heart so that he knew what I planned to do. I was confident.

"Papa, God has called me to open my own farm, so that I can do His work". He didn't seem interested.

For two years, my stepfather and I had a good working relationship and shared a sense of ownership. The family business had been successful largely because we treated it as our own, and my every waking moment was fixated on what I could do to improve operations and how to ensure our chickens were well taken care of. Chicken consumed my life, and Jesus too. And now, there was a strain in my relationship with my stepfather.

It was as if this time, our lives were now heading in very different pathways and there was little either of us could do to change that. If I didn't tell him the truth in my heart, it was only a matter of time before our partnership would fall apart. The days of reflecting on how the English missionary Reverend Sercombe had inspired both of us to start a poultry farm on my stepfather's compound was long gone. Even the days of my stepfather reluctantly stumbling into the life of a poultry farmer had given way to years of enormous success, and with that, he seemed to have forgotten about much of what sustained us through those years.

He suddenly was irate.

"Kwabena, just leave! Just leave! Just leave, and don't even come back!" His voice raised and the frown on his face said everything else he didn't have the words to say.

Chapter 8: Leap

This was the watershed moment and I had to take a leap of faith. I had thought about it but now I was convinced there couldn't be a much better time because the longer we spoke, the more my words aggravated him. It was sad that our relationship had come to this, but rifts and indiscretions had begun to create a wedge in our family. I had not told my stepfather I was quitting that very moment from his company, but he had snapped.

I could walk out of Central Egg Farm with my head held up high. For my stepfather, I had been everything to him: his labourer, supervisor, salesman, accountant, manager, and banker. He had trusted me with his company, never having to worry that I would take one *pesewa* from him.

He was fuming, and we had come to an unfortunate crossroads. In anger, he took away the Volkswagen van he had given to me to use for the company's errands. In my heart, I was at peace because I had never dishonoured him in any manner, or even once stolen from him—not money, not even an egg. I didn't bear any grudge because I had been honest with him and diligent in my work every single day on the farm.

What was different, God was asking me to start a business and I heard His voice deeply echoing in my heart. There was a boldness that seemed to stop any doubt that occasionally surfaced in my mind. I believed that God had put a hunger in my heart and I had to trust that He would bring the right people across my path when I needed them. All I had to do was to hold on to what I already knew about the faithfulness of my God. A Bible verse leaped into my heart again, *Jeremiah 29:11* that God had a plan for my life and it was one that was to bring me to a fulfilling future and a hope.

Stepping out on faith to start my own company brought along a stream of uncertainties and questions. There was so much that I was not sure of, and how it would work out. *Was it indeed God's plan for me to leave a successful company and start over? Where would I buy land or property for a farm? What if the business doesn't survive? Did I even hear God right?* My mind raced often, and I tried to pray even more.

The small booklet, *Poultry Keeping in Modern Days* had been my foundation when I sat in the small room in my stepfather's house many years ago. The truth about foundations was that they never changed, and so I could go back to whatever first sparked the love for poultry farming in my heart, and start over. My advantage this time was that I had spent years training in Israel, working with companies, and had life experiences that I didn't have at 16 years of age. Now they were guideposts. A barrage of questions still remained, just as it would for any young man setting out to start a business, but for me, I had a God on my side who had made provision for me. That was my true advantage.

From Saltpond, I picked up my friend Kojo Akowuah. I shared with him what I intended on doing and that I needed his company to ride to Akropong-Asante, about ten miles on the outskirts of Kumasi, on the main Sunyani road.

I purchased ten acres of land to start my farm. Mr. Kwasi Peprah owned Akropong Farms in Akropong-Asante, and just a few months earlier I had trained several of his employees, and struck a friendship with him. Now he was the same man who was willing to help me start my own company. He agreed for me to rent a space on his facility, a small room where I would put my baby chicks while I constructed a structure on the new land.

It was January 1966, I was setting out with 900 chicks, and all of my life's savings from Barclays Bank, one thousand cedis. In those years ninety seven Ghanaian pesewas were the equivalent of one American dollar, hence I was using almost one thousand dollars for this venture. Sure, I had taken a risky plunge as an entrepreneur and started a company that I was convinced God had impressed upon my heart to do, yet I was taking off on a much rockier ledge than I imagined I ever would. There was genuine vigour and imminent purpose every morning to hurry to the farm, but the voices of doubt and defeat were loud still.

I had to fight through. I had rested on a firm foundation that what my God had said, He would do.

It took a few weeks before my stepfather tried to persuade me to change my mind. He was desperate, and he'd had time to change his stance. He said he didn't mean for me to quit Central Egg Farm and that I could stay if I wanted to. He was willing to double my salary and give me any allowances I needed. I heard the sincerity in his voice and I remembered how he had been instrumental in my life, but it was too late.

The biggest problem that had brought tension and heartache was his betrayal of my mother's trust. One thing I was sure about was that nothing stained a person's integrity more than indiscretions that broke sacred covenants and showed a character flaw that I couldn't condone. It was hard to confront my stepfather, but I had to. I couldn't afford to break my mother's heart and tell her all that I saw at the farm's office, but I had no interest in grieving the Holy Spirit. I hoped my life had been a testament of integrity to my stepfather, but in the end, it was his choice to live his life as he wanted.

I had to move on, with confidence that *if God was with me, no other person would be able to stand against me*. Sure, if he needed my help, I was willing to serve him at any time, but God had called him in different directions and I was not turning back.

My mother tried to plead with me to return. Apparently, in a short space of time, my stepfather's company had begun to fall apart. Unfortunately, the people he had hoped they would replace me, were young men who had shown up on the farm to make money. I remember how I had tried to explain to my stepfather a long time ago, that not everyone was born to be a farmer, and for people who didn't have the love for the vocation, they would leave at the first chance they got. Some of those truths had found their way into reality. Central Egg Farm was dealing with its own troubles.

It was when my stepfather reached out to American missionary Reverend Vernon Driggers, a man whom he knew I had so much respect for, to help him sway me. That desperate gesture was what convinced me even more that I had made the right decision. There was no way I could return; my vision was much larger than raising chickens and displaying riches. I wanted to impact lives and support the work of God.

Reverend Driggers was in charge of the local Assemblies of God Church, and called me to hear what he also thought. He wouldn't discourage me from my calling, but urged that I find a way to work a few hours in each day on my stepfather's farm, to help him adjust to the inevitable change. If I could work with him for at least another year, that would give him ample time to gradually groom a successor. My stepfather agreed to the new arrangement, and offered to also help where he could, for me to support my new venture.

Even though we had not gone our separate ways on good terms, I didn't bear any grudge. I was convinced that God was calling me to do His work and the God who had sent me would provide whatever I needed. The arrangement helped me to slowly take flight while I was doing my best to leave my stepfather's company to other men and women who would take over permanently. In the months when grains were in short supply, I could buy the same grain I had stored at a cheaper rate in the large silos on my stepfather's property to feed chicken on my own farm.

By the end of January 1966, President Kwame Nkrumah was on television asking Ghanaians to tighten our belts because the country had found itself in an economic rough patch, the Cedi currency devalued, and state-owned industries were heading in a downward spiral.

The Reverend Driggers was right; God had humbled my stepfather's heart to reach me, and had given me the grace to be humble also. In a season where Ghana's economy was tumbling and everything we needed on the farms was in short supply, and that could have shut down operations at Darko Farms. Instead, God had taken me back to the same place where I had worked hard to store grains and feed in large silos, and to buy them even cheaper.

I was benefitting from the same work I had done in the years on my stepfather's farm, as if God knew that in a few years, I would need every one of those grains. I needed animal feed for my birds at a reasonable price. God had made provision for me, several years before I even had the problem. Really, I got to trust that *the steps of the righteous were ordered by God*. On February 24, 1966, President Nkrumah was overthrown in a military coup, and plunged much of the country and many enterprises into uncertainty.

If living in Israel had taught me one thing, it was that a person could start a thriving venture in the middle of nowhere, under any circumstance, even in a desert. My training had given me reassurance that I had all the knowledge and skill I needed for the moment, and I couldn't let what I couldn't clutch in my own hands make me forget that God had not abandoned His word.

I was serving a God who was always faithful and had promised to reward those who diligently seek him and acknowledge Him in all of their ways. The scripture in Hebrews 11:6 was unequivocally assuring, *"But without faith it is impossible to please Him. For he that cometh to God must believe that He is, and that He is a rewarder of those who diligently seek Him."* That I had decided to do. It was 1967.

I had started Darko Farms Company Limited with little money for investment capital, but I had a bigger God with whom all things were indeed possible.

CHAPTER 9

A WHISPER THROUGH THE RAIN

Surviving Storms in New Business

An older gentleman I knew, Dr. Opoku Ampofo worked for the Agricultural Development Bank (ADB) in Accra. The company offered a host of banking and short term loan services for commercial and investment purposes. Since I was a farmer, my friend suggested that I submit an application to the branch in Kumasi to secure a loan. I needed 5,000 cedis and I had heard that if I had a business plan that reasonably outlined the purpose of the loan and how I intended to pay it back, it should not be a problem.

Unfortunately, it was.

The manager at the Kumasi branch of ADB was kind enough to meet with me, but asked that I return the next day to meet with a project officer. The bank required evidence of the property lease, and I showed them the documentation for the three acres of land for which I had all the legal documentation, as well as the indenture documents for the remaining acres.

I had started a new venture and I needed the money to buy feed. I explained that I needed the bank's help to get my birds to a point of lay, after which I was confident I would pay back any loan and accrued interest in no time.

"Do you have a house?"

They asked for documentation for any property I owned that could be used as security and collateral for the loan.

"No sir, I don't own a house".

Then he continued, "A car?"

"Yes, I do. I own a Volkswagen van, a microbus".

Mr. Atsmah, the bank manager flipped through the documents I had submitted.

"You're asking for a loan for what?"

"For my poultry farm, sir," I replied quickly.

I carefully outlined my plan for 5,000 birds in the first year of operation and how I would be able to pay back the loan in two years.

The manager laughed.

"Two years?"

"Do you know anything about chicken?" His eyes were staring into mine, as if to force me to admit that I did not even know why I had come to his bank. He looked uninterested, and the smirk on his face was one that quietly mocked my application as he occasionally mumbled a few words under his breath. I told him of how I had been one of five people President Nkrumah had sent to Israel to train, and that I had spent three years in Ruppin College studying Poultry Science.

I also hoped that my work over the last several years at Central Egg Farm would give them some assurance that I indeed had a good idea of the business, but it didn't.

"Israel," he chuckled snobbishly, "Is there even a real Israel somewhere".

It was as if the bank manager was finding every conceivable reason to discredit my application. Then he lifted his head, clearing his throat, and said I wouldn't get a loan from ADB because I didn't have any credit, neither did I have any collateral.

"Sir, please what about the buildings that I have constructed on the farm?"

Chapter 9: A Whisper Through The Rain

Mr. Atsmah didn't mince his words. "My friend, a chicken coop is not a house".

Agricultural Development Bank, the one financial institution that I reasoned would understand the nuances of farming and perhaps evaluate my business plan with a real sense of the industry, had shut the door in my face. Nothing I would say would make a difference to a manager whose mind was made up. They could not give me a loan for 5,000 cedis.

I left the ADB office in Kumasi unsure of where I would get such a loan. I couldn't afford to give up that easily. Over and again in my life, whenever I had felt like giving up on myself, the only thing I knew to do was to hold on to what I knew to rely upon, the word of God. I had not set out with some rosy idea that I would live my life without any obstacles, but I had assured myself that despite the constant struggle that was bound to come my way, there would always be a God who would run in my direction, even when all hope seemed lost. At that moment, with rejection staring into my face, I saw the closed door as a test of my faith.

Sure, I had no credit, and I did not own a house to use as collateral. What I had was a God who was much bigger than anything I needed, and I had decided to take him at His word, literally. I didn't have any other options. Often when our backs are against a wall in life, what we are made of is what rises to the top and forms our immediate reaction. This was no time to cede ground to fear and unbelief.

I went home to pray, and to do so persistently. In my mind, I reinforced my hope with a decision to stand firm and push through what I believed despite the difficulty that would otherwise force me to give in.

I had to keep trying.

I prayed through the night, with every hope I had staked on the fact that God had assured his children that if we are bold enough to ask, what we request shall be given; what we seek, we will find; and if we can find tireless courage to knock long enough, the doors that had been shut would open. My life was immersed in God's word and I meant every word I said. My heart was heavy, but I had the confidence to keep my eyes fixed on Jesus. I couldn't give myself permission to focus on the rain or the storms of life.

I headed to the ADB head office in the capital city Accra the next morning to meet with the Managing Director E.N. Afful. I had never met the director before, and had no idea where he would be, all I knew to do was to go to Accra. The first person I met at the bank's office was an old security guard.

"Good morning sir, I am here to see the Managing Director".

"The M.D.?"

Something about my self-assurance didn't match my appearance, at least so it seemed in the eyes of the security guard.

"Do you have an appointment?"

"No sir. But I came from Kumasi and I have to. . . ".

The man didn't even care to hear my last few words.

"No, no, no. No appointment, you can't see M.D. like that".

I didn't have any reason to challenge him. In fact, I was not sure what I expected when I left Kumasi, but I had prayed through the night on a proposal that I had done all I could.

A small door led to a small office downstairs. I went in. Fortunately, I saw a book with the company directory and found the phone number to the Managing Director's Secretary. I still didn't have an appointment, but at least, now I knew his name and knew I was in the right building. I had probably found my way to the part of the office downstairs where I shouldn't have been, but I found a phone nearby and called the Secretary's line.

It rang.

"Good afternoon, Madam".

She seemed polite, not hurried.

"Good afternoon, how can I help you?"

I told the lady my story as quickly as I could. She didn't interrupt or hang up the phone so I assumed she was listening.

"Please do you have an appointment?" she asked.

"No please, but . .". I suddenly didn't know what else to say.

She politely explained the processes to review business plans like mine, and that I would need to schedule an appointment with a project officer to first evaluate the document, who would, in turn, forward it to their manager, and ultimately to the M.D. It was a process, and it was impossible for all that to happen in the same day. I understood.

"But, please do you have his number? The M.D.?"

Surprisingly, she didn't hesitate and gave me the number to his direct phone line. I called the line immediately. A man picked up.

By then I had repeated my business plan several times and I thought I had to make my case quickly before he asked about why I had called his office directly. Then I told the man about how I had prayed the night before and God charged me to persist. That is why I was in Accra, and that is why I didn't walk away when the security officer asked me to leave.

Then there was a pause on the other end of the telephone.

"My secretary will come downstairs and wait for you. Come up".

I was not sure I heard him well. I didn't have enough words to express my gratitude.

The Managing Director E.N. Afful sat behind a large office desk with a pile of papers on each end, others left in a stack by the window. I couldn't help but wonder if my business plan would have sat in one of those piles if I had sent it to him.

He listened to my every word and asked one question after another. As grace would have it, everything about my educational background and training was precisely what he hoped most of his clients had. We spoke about my training in Israel and about Central Egg Farm. He knew about my stepfather's success through the years and seemed thrilled to know that I had been the man who had worked behind the scenes all of those years. I told him about how Mr. Atsmah and his team in Kumasi had made fun of the very idea and application I had submitted to ADB.

Then he carefully went through the business plan.

"You did all this yourself?"

I nodded.

"And you need only 5,000 cedis?"

I explained how all I needed was enough money to buy the feed to get my birds to a point of lay. I had raised enough chickens through the years to know just what I needed.

"Also, sir, I plan to pay back quickly, in two years so that I can build my credit with ADB".

The M.D. was stunned.

"Credit?"

I understood how a person's creditworthiness was critical to establishing and maintaining a successful business. It was one thing promising to pay for a loan from a financial institution, it was another having a good appreciation of the relationship it creates with the institution. Most of the local farmers did not have this basic understanding and banks like ADB often struggled with finding entrepreneurs whose businesses they could support without having to plead with them to honour their promise to pay.

ADB approved a loan for twice the amount I had originally sought. There was a one-year moratorium on the loan and that inspired me to work even harder to pay the loan off quickly. For the first year, Darko Farms had 5,000 birds, and by the second year, I had 10,000 birds at the farm. I made my way to ADB to pay the loan amount in full, just as I had promised. I remember vividly the loan officer pleading with me to use the money in the business, take my time and pay it over a five-year-period as most people. I was not most people.

My life and enterprise were guided by God's word, and it was not a casual fondness for scripture. It was my life. I had learned of Romans 13, where a God asks to *"owe no man anything, except to love one another"*. I didn't want to owe anyone, not even the Agricultural Development Bank. I was afraid that if I was to die suddenly and stand in front of

God, I wouldn't be able to defend why I had left the earth with debt in my name. I didn't want to offend God.

The ADB Project Officer seemed perplexed. "My friend, do you use the Bible for everything?"

"Yes sir, everything".

In a few days, the Managing Director of ADB drove from Accra, picked up Mr. Atsmah who was still the manager at the Kumasi branch, to Darko Farms. The operation was much more than he imagined. I had learned that "those who know their God will do exploits," and if I was able to succeed in this venture, every credit was to God, who had given me the grace to do so. Nothing had been on my own.

"Kwabena, what else do you want from ADB?" Mr. Afful asked.

He couldn't believe how the operation had followed the plan I had meticulously laid out, just as he read it in his office. I had paid the bank every pesewa I owed.

He smiled broadly. "Kwabena Darko, the bank is yours . . . whatever you need".

* * * * *

In the early years, I spent all of the time on the farm with one labourer, an older northerner gentleman who had come to Kumasi seeking odd jobs. He became the watchman, the labourer, and everything else we needed on the farm. We mixed the chicken feed in the middle of the night with shovels and placed them in large buckets for the next day's feeding. My goal was for the chickens to get every nutrient they needed from the different ingredients even though I didn't have enough money to buy expensive feed. What I knew was the science behind the nutrition, having spent years studying the effects of every nutritional value of the chicken.

I would drive around Kumasi in my Volkswagen van picking up the corn bran that people typically threw away when they grind the corn. I had found an intriguing fact, that many people didn't know the nutritional value, hence they threw away the parts of the corn that they should have kept. I was there to collect them for free. That was a source of energy for the chickens.

I would buy anchovies from Senya Breku, common saltwater forage fish we called *Keta School Boys* in Ghana. It had a ninety percent of protein value, and this knowledge gave me a reason to look elsewhere for chicken feed when other poultry farms were spending huge amounts of money to feed their chickens. Darko Farms' feed costs were about seventy percent less than most companies in the same business.

At the heart of everything I did was an overreliance on God's word, the only thing I believed was a sure foundation for my success. I remember around 1972 when a contagious infection swept across the country and killed many thousands of birds. Poultry farms suffered such a demoralizing setback that some were not able to survive afterward.

Decades earlier, President Nkrumah had set up the Ghana Veterinary Services in Pong-Tamale, to oversee disease control and vaccine development for indigenous livestock breeds, mostly to support the large cattle farms in the Northern regions. Over time, their work extended to the health of other animals, including poultry. The facility produced vaccines for Fowl Pox, Newcastle disease, and a host of other common illnesses, and most commercial farmers routinely vaccinated all their chickens. At Darko Farms, we did too.

Yet, out of nowhere the virulent Newcastle infections took over the country. Diseases that typically occurred mostly in the dry season must have appeared in Ghana because of birds migrating south from the Sahara Desert.

In no time, Akropong Farms had lost more than 6,000 birds, and other farms in the area were losing several hundred and even thousands of their birds to the sudden onslaught. It was devastating, and there was little that anyone could do to help.

On my commercial farm, we had more than 50,000 birds, and even though I had vaccinated the entire flock, it was gut-wrenching to even

Chapter 9: A Whisper Through The Rain

imagine what would happen if one of them was infected. I chose not to imagine that, instead to keep my focus on Jesus. I had learned that even when it was most difficult to lift my eyes, I had to stay at rest in the faith that God would fight my battles for me, where I could not on my own.

I asked my church to help me in prayer for farms and farmers across the nation. All it took was one infected chicken, and they could wipe out an entire farm. I refused to accept that as my reality. I fasted and prayed fervently through the night. Once, in a dream, I saw one chicken on my farm infected with Newcastle disease. It felt almost real, and I woke up suddenly at dawn and rushed to the farm. In one pen, just like I had seen in the dream, one chicken stood in the corner alone. It looked sick. I was not dreaming.

The same morning after the veterinarian killed and dissected it, that chicken had a pure Newcastle disease. Even though I had records of all the vaccinations, the disease had found its way to my farm. Dr. E.O. Gyenin, who was deputy Managing Director for the Ghana Veterinary Services brought a team to the Kumasi area to see how best they could help the large poultry farms concentrated in the region. The veterinarians suggested I slaughter all the chickens before the infection spread through the farm. Slaughter all 50,000 of them. They were sure all of the chicken, at least most of them would be dead in a week. I decided not to kill any of the chickens.

There was nothing that was impossible for God to do, and if that was a test of my faith, I was willing to take God at His word. I had seen His hand on my life over and again, and I was certain the same power would protect Darko Farms. A week later, four chickens had died. Another four died two weeks later, and just as if the wind that blew the virulent infection to Ghana had found its way out, none of the birds on the farm died of any infection.

I always believed that for those who lean on God completely, He would *rebuke the devourer for their sake*, and now I had seen this to be true in my life. It was Malachi 3:11. There was nothing more calming than living a life not defined by wreckage left behind or the fear of what was ahead. Indeed, the best thing I had done for myself and my company was never taking my eye off Jesus, who had promised to stand with me. In a period when it felt dark and hopeless, and disease threatened to bring me to my knees, God had covered me.

I had to leave the rains and the storms of life to Jesus, so that I could ride on the waves. So that my testimony would bring glory to Him.

CHAPTER 10

WHERE THE HEART IS

Darling

Scripture Union has always been an interdenominational and evangelical Christian group whose work in Ghana primarily centred on secondary schools, ministering to young people in their most vulnerable, yet equally receptive and formative years. There were young people from diverse backgrounds who ended up on the same campus, and our work was to continually encourage them in their walk with God. I served in the Scripture Union chaplaincy program in charge of Prempeh College, Opoku Ware Secondary school, and Yaa Asantewaa secondary school, all in the Kumasi area. Scripture Union had become a central part of my life, with an opportunity to fellowship with young people and to lead them to Christ.

A void remained in the young people who left secondary school and universities, but without the network of brothers and sisters with whom to fellowship, their faith gradually unravelled. The idea for a Scripture Union Town Fellowship was to create an evangelism avenue in the community, mostly attracting young men and women, some of whom had even started their careers. Soon after the Town Fellowship started, lecturers and young professionals joined. Members of the Scripture Union were often invited, and that was how my cousin Paul Aidoo asked me to come along to a fellowship meeting.

A printer, Mr. Wobil lived in an estate in the South Suntreso neighborhood, and he volunteered his house to be the meeting place for the fellowship. Eventually, the KNUST campus had a location where the people could meet, until another teacher at Prempeh College, Mr. Goodfellow Thiesens also agreed to host the bible study fellowship on late Sunday afternoons in their bungalows.

For several weeks, I had arranged to drive the young ladies in the Nurses Christian Fellowship who often came as a group to the Town Fellowship, to the nurses' residential facilities near the Okomfo Anokye hospital. My dark blue Volkswagen van was the same vehicle that I used on the farm, with every seat covered in feathers, chicken feed, and stains. By Sunday, it was new, without any hint of having been on any farm. I dropped off the young ladies, and occasionally watch them walk away.

I felt in my heart that I was ready to marry. The Assemblies of God Church had several young ladies in the choir who smiled charmingly, but I hadn't felt any connection to any of them. Occasionally, a friend passed a comment about the girl in the church supposedly fighting over me, and we laughed and never cared to pay any attention to it. I was convinced it was best to pray about my desire, and let God order my steps.

I found a confidante in another young cousin, Kwame Amponsah, who was working as a pharmacist in North Suntreso Clinic. I told her about a young staff nurse who I needed his help to meet. Kwame knew her because they both worked in the same hospital. I was taking Kwame to work for the morning shift, and he said he could ask the nurse to come out for a few moments if I was not shy.

"Her name is Christiana".

I knew that.

It was impossible to forget the first day I saw her at the Town Fellowship meeting. Everything about her, from her perfect smile to the lovely earrings tucked in her neatly combed bushy hair make my heart skip a beat. She seemed calm and confident. Over time, I heard her speak, and I listened to every word she said, and even the beautiful way her lips moved. I had seen her for several months, and I was sure she was the answer to my prayer.

All Christie knew about me was probably from what she saw at the Town Fellowships, but I was sure the nurses spoke about me whenever I dropped them off after the Sunday meetings. Perhaps someone had told her that I was a youth leader in the Assemblies of God Church and a leader in the Scripture Union also.

"What will you tell her?" Kwame asked with a slight chuckle.

"I am ready to propose". That I was sure about.

"Propose!" He ran through the entrance doors.

I waited in the car. Kwame was going to find Christiana and let her know that I was waiting in the car to speak to her. I was nervous and calm at the same time. Confidence washed the doubts quickly from my mind, but then they appeared again.

Then Christiana walked out.

I had seen the young lady several times, but never had I paid attention to every step she took, with a smile brightening the cloudy morning. She wore her dark green uniform with the white strips along the sleeves and around its neck, and her spotless white shoes. She had no idea what I had in mind, but something about my edgy demeanour made her nervous too. She was shaking slightly.

"Good morning Brother Darko. Please do you need something?"

Everything else was a blur in a split second.

"Yes".

I suddenly couldn't find my words. "Yes, good morning".

She had been kind enough to walk out of the clinic for something Kwame must have told her was important, and now she stood next to me, even more beautiful than I had seen her on Sunday afternoons.

"What time do you close?" I asked Christiana.

"12".

"Please, I will be back at 12 PM to pick you up. There is something I want to ask you, and hopefully you will consider it prayerfully".

I was back at South Suntreso Clinic at 12 PM, my white shirt tucked in neatly, and every crease in my khaki trousers in its place. Christiana walked up and I jumped out of my seat to open her door. She didn't mind going to lunch with me at the YWCA restaurant in Adum, opposite the Ashanti Pioneer newspaper building.

"I will not waste your time Christiana. It is you that I want to marry and spend the rest of my life with".

She was lost for words, yet her perky smile said it all.

I had spent nights praying quietly to God for a woman who would be more than a fairy tale in my mind, but one who would come alongside me and experience life to its fullest potential, together. I had been praying for someone who would brave the messiness and uncertainty of the world by my side, but most importantly would be a partner in faith. Christiana seemed grounded in God's word, and judging from everything I had heard her speak about in the Town Fellowship, her confidence was even more elegant, and with a sincerity rooted in Christ.

I had found the woman who wore her authenticity just as beautifully as she did her imperfections. She radiated a kindness that was genuine, and her personality I knew to be one that inspired everything in my heart. There was nothing more delightful than knowing her whole life's ambition was to please God in everything she did.

We learned all we could about each other that afternoon.

I asked her to come with me to see Reverend Vernon Driggers at the Mission house on Old Bekwai Road. He was happy to see me, and to hear about Christiana.

"Kwabena, have you two courted?"

We hadn't. I told him we were both ready to be married and courting was not necessary. We had met a while ago at the Town Fellowship, and we had no idea that we were both praying for the same thing and admiring each other from a distance. I had guarded my adolescent and adult years with a warning in the scriptures–1 Corinthians 6–to flee fornication. If indeed I had heard from God, I was ready to marry.

Chapter 10: Where The Heart Is

Christiana did not expect any of this so soon, but she was thrilled. Reverend Driggers had a lot of questions, still. He wanted to know if Christiana loved the Lord, and was not just a young lady who attended church and Town Fellowships. Coincidentally, there was a scheduled meeting for the Assemblies of God Church board, and these would be the same people I would like Christiana to meet, so I asked Reverend Driggers if he would be kind to give me a few minutes at the board meeting. I was the youth leader in the church and it was important to me that my elders knew of my decision, and of such a significant moment in my life.

My mind was made up, and Christiana's too.

She came along to meet my mother. Then my grandmother the same day.

"Is she Asante?"

For my grandmother, what mattered to her was the shared heritage and tribal identity.

"No, from Koforidua".

Christiana's father was an Akyem from the Eastern Region, and her mother, a Ga, from the Greater Accra Region to the south. Neither were Asantes, and women like my grandmother, whose appreciation of value systems had always been rooted in tradition, wished I would marry someone whose family were also Asantes. What had attracted me to Christiana was her heart and her trust in the Lord, and I was sure that was a foundation upon which we could build a future.

I assured my grandmother, "The God in whom you have raised me in His ways, has selected this woman for me".

I asked Christiana to meet my stepfather the next day. She agreed. Mr. F. K. Gyamfi seemed happy for us, but wondered if we weren't moving too quickly. Christiana and I had decided we could have a wedding in a few months. All she needed to do was to tell her parents and the rest of her family, and set a date for a customary marriage ceremony in Koforidua.

We were married at the Lighthouse Assemblies of God Church in Kumasi, on 7th September, 1967. People spend a lifetime in search of true love, seeking someone whose love will not just be an emotion, but a devotion. Most people pray for what we found, and I was eternally grateful God chose Christiana for me.

We decided, that very day, to call each other "Darling".

CHAPTER 11

SHIFTING SANDS

Acheampong, Busia, Limman and Rawlings.

Ever since I first watched 100 baby chicks find a home in 1958, my life as a poultry farmer had its share of ups and downs. Spending every waking moment as a poultry farmer and participating in the industry had a way of dragging a person's life into the political arena.

I returned from Israel in 1961 at the height of President Kwame Nkrumah's agenda to uplift Ghanaians with economic and social programs that would be funded and operated by parastatal agencies. By their very nature, the state-owned institutions were to have all the political backing, such that even though they were separate from the government itself, their work benefited the government.

The fundamental idea, I thought, was not too different from what other countries had embarked upon through the years, albeit with varying degrees of success. In Israel, I recall watching the men and women in the collective settlements go about their day with such an enviable sense of collective purpose. In those places, there was a shared hope that brought the best in all of them, and it seemed most people carried their weight. I saw first-hand how the Ghana Agricultural Development Corporation, despite the government's financial investments and international support, fell apart block by block. I saw how government officials looted the company and staff, and walked around each day in search of loopholes to undermine the company.

I was a poultry farmer, who saw the outcrop of any government's decision in a way that most Ghanaians never could. Feeding the people in the country where uncertainty reigned made the work much harder than it should have been, and the people often didn't have a voice loud enough for the decision-makers to acknowledge.

As for Ghana, we had inherited the systems that the British colonial masters had left behind. In some companies, they could afford to have Ghanaians as directors even though they didn't have any power to make any meaningful decisions for the company. For organisations like UTC, UAC, and CFAO, the instructions came from England, and the directors only executed them.

President Nkrumah's establishment of the Ghana Cocoa Marketing Board was one such arrangement that didn't benefit many cocoa farmers. Most were incredibly hardworking but illiterate, and they spent their days and nights in small farms, without much of a choice but to trust the government infrastructure to treat them fairly.

Cocoa farmers took all the risks, but the revolving doors or management and staff at state-owned corporations made it impossible to develop any meaningful relationships with the bureaucrats who determined their fate. They kept the industry afloat with sweat and hard work, but their profits ended up in the coffers of the Cocoa Marketing Board.

Would it have been much different if a government policy had created an infrastructure, and stepped aside to let the citizens to build the businesses? That was a question that remained for most people, especially farmers, who questioned the value of the government taking over the marketing of cocoa. What became the reality for the farmers I knew, when any decision was made from the government, they had no input. Those who became rich were men and women who never stepped foot on a farm; instead, they weighed the products at the depots and supervised the fate of the farmers.

Even President Nkrumah's idea of a scholarship scheme to support the children of the cocoa farmers to pursue education, ended up being a vehicle to supported bureaucrats for whom the program was not intended. The poor cocoa farmers in the village never benefited from the programs as they should have, and they remained poor.

Poultry farming faced the same challenge, because the ideology that had given birth to the parastatal organizations that oversaw cocoa, was the same that was to oversee poultry. Unfortunately, the policy of state farming did not survive in poultry. Dealing with live animals and perishable products demanded a sense of urgency that was inherently absent in state-owned companies. Unless a person had a genuine sense of ownership in a business, it was impossible to cultivate that.

Pomadze Poultry Enterprise was a Ghanaian state-owned company that didn't survive, even with 2 million dollars' worth of capital investment from the Canadian government. Agricultural Development Corporation in Accra, Kumasi, Takoradi, and in other regions eventually fell apart. Farming was a business that required constant energy from tireless labour, and it was no surprise that companies owned by individuals survived when the state-owned corporations with enormous financial and regulatory backing struggled to remain profitable.

I remember my years working in the Ghana Agricultural Development Corporations until 1963. I thought our work was to be a pilot project, and a model for the private enterprises to emulate. President Nkrumah's socialist agenda turned the government into active players in a proverbial field of play, when they would have been better suited to be referees.

As for farmers, we always hoped the government would institute concessions and provide reasonable tax breaks as was necessary to regulate the industry, and support the economy with forward-thinking interventionist policies. The fundamental flaw in the Nkrumah years had become state-owned corporations edging their way into the business, but without the collective vision to support it.

Perhaps, one of our biggest challenges as a country was the fact that every collective patriotic spirit we shared in 1957 was slowly eroding as the different factions of society prioritized their own selfish interests and used the state-owned corporations as the conduit to achieve their goals.

After Nkrumah's overthrow, both J.A. Ankrah and Akwasi Afrifa's National Liberation Council struggled to enact policies that would restore confidence for the country. Kofi Abrefa Busia's Progress Party took over the helm of Ghana's government, for the Second Republic from October 1969. Busia had previously Chairman of the Centre for Civic Education, with much of his work focused on educating the public on voting and other civic duties, and also served as the Chairman of the National Advisory Committee for the National Liberation Council, led by General Joseph Ankrah, the military head of state.

By the time he was Prime Minister, Busia's focus was to create the building blocks upon which the country's social, economic, and political future would rest. Edward Akufo-Addo who had been Chief Justice served briefly as President in the 1969 election, and sought to entrench the rule of law and push a pro-business agenda that would be a departure from the veranda boys who felt marginalized in society and saw the government as an opportunity to change their fortunes in the Kwame Nkrumah years. Cocoa prices slumped and the devaluing currency set in motion a period of anxiety. Farmers didn't see any investment or incentive from the short-lived administration. We could only hope the administration would find a way to assist the men and women who rose at sunrise and worked in the searing heat, tending to crops and animals to feed our nation.

It was the same with Hilla Liman whose People's National Party during Ghana's Third Republic didn't get the opportunity to deliver on any commitment to farmers. Limann had come to power in September 1979 in the country's return to party politics, after a coup earlier that year. The People's National Party's symbol was corn.

I was in Kumasi when I received a call that President Hilla Limann and his team were heading to Darko Farms. They had chosen to announce their agricultural policies for the country from my farm. As

Chapter 11: Shifting Sands

surprising as it was for a moment, it was not unusual. What was perhaps unusual was the fact that I had no dealings with any political party, and the only explanation I was given was that the President needed a neutral but thriving farming business to inspire his agenda.

But despite Limann's government's well-intentioned policies and plans to embark on an extensive irrigation project, none of them saw the light of day.

Rather, it was Lieutenant Colonel Ignatius Kutu Acheampong, the military officer who overthrew the Busia government in a coup d'état, whose agricultural agenda left a mark on the nation. The new National Redemption Council (NRC) military government introduced programs and commissioned projects he reckoned would uplift the country. In 1972, "Operation Feed Yourself" was the government's agricultural response to food shortages, and it was directed at increasing production for domestic consumption. It was an ideological agenda aimed towards self-sufficiency, and the government counted on farmers to be an integral part of this vision.

The program's first "Five Year Plan" set an ambitious goal for agricultural output, based on the reasoning that it would positively impact employment around the country. In the first year, it gave incentives to farmers, and encouraged every citizen to take up a form of farming so that the country wouldn't have to rely on anyone for food. Every television and radio program championed this government agenda, and sought to create systems for collecting, transporting, and trading foodstuffs. Government agencies like the Meat Marketing Board, Food Distribution Corporation, and State Fishing Corporation had become integral parts of the operation.

The government also asked poultry farmers to plant our own corn to use as feed on our farms. This forced me to buy 1,000 acres of land in Ejura, near Asante Mampong for this purpose. For all the administration's shortcomings, the first few years saw surplus food supply in the country. For many, *Operation Feed Yourself* subsidized the prices of fertilizers and seeds. Tax exemptions were instituted and the government planned to abandon any import duties and taxes on agricultural machinery. Even though a lack of infrastructure remained the Achilles heel of the policy, corruption and bureaucratic red tapes strangled the life out of it.

Yet, until his government was removed in a palace coup, following his unpopular Union Government—Unigov—agenda, the directors of the state corporations profited immensely, perhaps because many of the military leaders did not have any idea about the farming business.

Under the military regime, Ghana's gross domestic product, export earnings, and living standards saw a free fall. As multifaceted as governance is, farming is perhaps even more complex, yet every leader and citizen erroneously assumed that farming as a vocation, whether for crops or livestock, required little skill and would lead to inevitable success.

But before the national agricultural initiative, was a brazen stance by the Acheampong administration heralded by the *"Yentua"* policy. It simply stated *"we will not pay"*, which meant the government blatantly refused to pay any national debt it had supposedly accrued in bad faith by the civilian government it had just ousted. The International Finance Corporation (IFC) and Word Bank were not exempt. Many Ghanaians cheered in the streets, when in fact private investors and international governments seeking to invest in the country had to immediately divert their assistance elsewhere.

By the time Ghana realized its part in the global economic system, the damage had already been done. For farmers and private entrepreneurs whose work was intertwined with foreign manufacturers and suppliers, the government's declaration froze any such relationship. In the United States, I had developed business relationships from Washington D.C. and Kentucky, to Florida and Iowa, but now all were burned to the ground. International partners I had secured for my business' supply chain understandably walked away because there was no way to do business amidst such uncertainty and risk. It was devastating.

Chapter 11: Shifting Sands

Through the changing of government and politicians with different nation-building ideas, one truth that remained was the endless tussle between investment in parastatal organizations and private enterprise. The years since independence were fraught with instability, all at a steep price for the country to bear. It was unfortunate to see how Ghana's first President Kwame Nkrumah's futile socialist ideologies showed up over and again, and the same idiosyncrasies that stifled their success remained too.

Lieutenant Colonel Ignatius Kutu Acheampong who overthrew Abrefa Busia and Akufo-Addo Progress Party a little over a year into their governance in 1972, would be deposed in a palace coup in 1978 by a military group led by Fred Akuffo. Jerry Rawlings and the Provisional National Defense Council (PNDC) stripped power from Lieutenant General F.W.K. Akufo Supreme Military Council government in 1981. The PNDC's central agenda was to take power away from the wealthy in society whom they blamed for Ghana's difficulties, and hand over the country to the "people". For their agenda to work, the military government said they were embarking on a cleansing mission, one that would rid the nation of corruption and mismanagement.

From the start, there was no real policy for agriculture, but the distrust of private enterprises was bound to bleed into individuals and companies that were into farming.

The private sector bore the brunt of PNDC's anger, and economic policies like dropping subsidies and price controls to reduce inflation, and devaluing the currency in order to stimulate exports gradually took their toll. People were terrified of the kangaroo courts, and there was no telling who would be the next target.

Most Ghanaian entrepreneurs were engaged in trading, and many who were illiterates did not keep any records. The same was the case for the cocoa farmers who had spent their entire lives in small village farms, having to give up much of their profits to the Cocoa Marketing Board, and barely keeping any records of their company's activities. For these people, it would be impossible to declare any assets over a seven-year period, and their lives and businesses quickly disintegrated into chaos.

At the time, I sold eggs to soldiers in the military barracks, and to hospitals and other corporations, but I had been careful to not align my business with any political party or military regime. My focus had been the same since I started the company in 1966, a complete reliance on God's provision for my life and my work.

The military approached me to set the control price for eggs. For whatever reason, they had decided my prices ought to be the standard, and anyone who sold above that price would be subjected to public floggings or even jailed for price gouging. I tried to explain to the men that there was no way I could do so because I was a wholesaler. The men and women who bought from my farms understandably had added costs which I could not account for, and it would be unfair to force them to sell at the same price that they had bought from me.

The PNDC soldiers were setting prices without having any idea of the individual costs that the entrepreneurs bore to bring their produce to market. My refusal had made me a target. They asked me to show up for vetting, a process whereby the military government could confiscate any private assets they assumed had been acquired through corrupt means.

Citizen vetting was conducted in every region, and business owners were required to declare seven years of assets. I was given a form to complete, and I had to declare every asset, from cars, to houses, to businesses, and everything else I owned, even my wedding ring. In Kumasi, the PNDC had gone to the Internal Revenue Service to review all the files to find loopholes to make their case. Darko Farms, in 1981, had 201 million cedis in assets, the equivalent of 100 million U.S. dollars.

I packed all my accounting and financial records the boxes in the back of a pickup truck and headed to the Ashanti Regional Office. Fortunately, I had all the documents they required. It was only after the terrifying interrogation that I learned why I had become a target and how much more the soldiers would harass my company.

Chapter 11: Shifting Sands

On one occasion, ten soldiers arrived at my farm, toting guns and walking around hurriedly as if there were something to find. They demanded to know why I had stored grains in my silos. I explained that I had typically purchased grains during the major harvest season and stored them in my 1,000-ton silos, and using them in the lean years. They accused me of hoarding.

And the harassing began. Sadly, I was not alone.

Darko Farms made preparations by saving all the grains it would need as part of raw materials needed to feed the chickens. We prepared for growth, and for emergencies, and we were better at managing the changes life brought our way. To run a successful enterprise, Darko Farms took a long-term perspective. With soldiers forcing their way into businesses whose operations they hardly understood, I had to fight back and let them know that I stored in the harvest around July and August, and also around December and January, all in preparation for the lean season.

It was not long before another group of solders showed up at my farms, this time to demand that I elect some of the low level employees to my company's board. The PNDC military government had commanded every company to establish a People's Defense Council (PDC) to include the workers in the decision making process. A majority of the farmers and staff at Darko Farms stressed that they didn't need to, and they were witnesses of how transparent and supportive the company had been to their personal growth and success. The company had given free accommodations and real incentives to ensure that their standard of living exceeded that of employees in similar companies. I had treated every man and woman just as I would my own son or daughter.

One employee, somehow, saw the military government's demand as an opportunity to disrupt the company's activities. He organized some of the people to march into the offices, making the same wild demands that the military had made on national television. The angry mob went as far as bringing syringes and enemas, filled with disinfectants from the entrance vehicle baths, and they swore they would inject the poison into every senior manager. Somehow the management of the company had become the bane of their existence. They made their threats and assured the company that they had the backing of the government to take the law into their own hands. "We no go sit down make them cheat us", they chanted.

How did I cheat them?

Their aggression failed, but it was crushing to see how a leadership that demonized private enterprises, or one that pushed a socialist agenda found a way to push all the blame on the people who had suffered to build companies.

Then an unprecedented string of bushfires in 1983 plunged Ghana into a famine, one that made an already hobbled economy even worse. Farmers suffered mightily as the parched earth hurt production. Farmers felt the pain of the uncertainties of Ghana's different political regimes, and it was now only worse with the bushfires. It seemed the battle for government disruptive involvement in the economy came at the expense of allowing private enterprises to build the nation. Men and women who poured their hearts and souls into their vocations under the scorching sun and pouring rain had to learn to thrive.

It was entirely possible that the challenges that we the farmers endured were an indicator of a much larger problem in Ghana's economy.

CHAPTER 12

LIKE VAPOR AND PASSING SHADOWS

Accident & Testimony.

I did not see the petrol tanker parked awkwardly in the middle of the road. The last image I could remember was my Volkswagen van driving at full speed into a head-on collision, and a huge bang. In one moment, I was a young man full of life, fueled by my ambitions of what life held in store, but in the next, I would have no way of knowing who would rush my comatose body to Okomfo Anokye Hospital.

I had been admitted to the emergency ward at the hospital for seven days, and even when I started to regain my consciousness, I couldn't fully grasp what had happened to me.

* * * * *

My cousin Paul Aidoo was visiting from Berekum, where he was working as a pastor in the Brong Ahafo region, to the north of Kumasi. He had completed his studies at the Assemblies of God Bible School and this was the first time I was getting a chance to hear about the exciting things he was doing in his church, and for the Lord.

I had been invited as the guest speaker at an event organized by the Scripture Union at the nearby Kwame Nkrumah University of Science and Technology (KNUST) campus. The group had asked that I speak on the topic *"Man's life is like Vapor"*. I was thrilled to be speaking on a subject that stressed the urgency of the moment, with a humbling awareness that nothing in the present belonged to us.

The Bible, as I had come to discover, was full of many illustrations about the fleeting nature of time and our lives, but if we are to embrace the fact that our fragile lives are indeed short, we will appreciate every precious minute and second we have, and this will give us a renewed understanding of committing our lives to Almighty God. The topic touched my heart, and I couldn't wait to share what I believed would stir the hearts of the students at the KNUST campus, and urge them to be faithful stewards of every breath we are blessed to have. Paul was happy to come along.

In 1969, KNUST had added a new residential building for students who had just completed the O-Level Certificate but not yet Sixth Form to take the Advanced Level Certificates, a requirement to apply to any university. KNUST used this program to attract and nurture young students who were interested in the sciences, by giving them the opportunity to be affiliated with the university as a stepping stone. The University Hall residence was nicknamed Katanga Hall, taking its moniker from the breakaway state that proclaimed its independence from Congo in 1960. Yet, during Scripture Unions, some university students joined the sixth form students in fellowship.

"Man's life is like Vapor". The theme came back into my mind over and again. I couldn't wait to share a powerful truth about the brevity of life to young people who often imagined we have a lifetime of eternity, and hence never paused to comprehend how our mortal lives are only in this world for a brief moment in time, and the next second is not ours to control.

One of the organizers had been a young Kwesi Andam, who exemplified the gusto of the young men and women in the Scripture Union. He was Muslim, having grown up in the Ahmmadiya enclave in the country's Western Region, where many of the residents had migrated south from the predominantly Muslim communities. I couldn't hide

Chapter 12: Like Vapor And Passing Shadows

my excitement at the idea of winning souls for Christ, and on a campus that seemed to bring many young people from all over the country. It was Monday evening.

I dropped off my wife Christiana at the local church for the usual choir rehearsals. Paul hopped to the front seat. We got back on the main road, on our way from the Kwadaso Estates to the Akwatia line neighbourhood. What I hadn't taken time to observe was how most of the cars in those years all used 6-volt batteries, which affected the brightness of their headlights. The Japanese cars that had found their way onto Ghana's roads had noticeably brighter headlights because of the 12-volt batteries. I was driving at full speed, my mind distracted with the topic I couldn't wait to preach about. Paul and I laughed and talked about our lives and what filled our days.

It happened quickly and suddenly. An oncoming car beamed its bright lights, and completely blinded me for a split second. The Volkswagen van drove straight into the large petrol tanker that had parked closer to the lane where I drove. The impact was so strong that it mangled the Volkswagen van, the driver's side flung open and I came flying out of the car onto the tar road. I had no recollection of any noise or screams, any panic or lament. Life had truly become like a passing shadow, with two young men lying on the side of a Kumasi road covered in blood.

When I opened my eyes, I was lying in bed in Okomfo Anokye Hospital in excruciating pain. That was when I learned I had been in a coma for about a week and that my wife had been sitting by my bedside every night nursing me back to health. She was praying that God would keep me alive to finish the work I had set in my heart to do with my life.

For weeks, I couldn't open my mouth, and the nurses had to force a small tube into my mouth to help me take a sip of water. It was when I could fully fathom the magnitude of what I had endured, that I heard there had been a surgeon, Dr. Akiwumi and his Egyptian orthopaedic surgeon colleague, Dr. Tsodagah who had been carefully trying their best to save every limb on my body.

A nurse told me about how my mother had fainted by my bedside when she first walked in to see my condition. She was broken. Paul had been like a son to her, and in one hospital and in one night, both of her sons laid in the intensive care unit fighting for their young lives.

My mother admitted that her family hadn't been fond of my wife ever since I first told them she was partly Ga, a different tribe. It had taken the gruesome accident and my family watching Christina spend every minute of her life caring for me, watching her gingerly clean the gashing wounds above my right eye, for them to see her worth as a woman and my wife. They had harboured their own distrust for a woman they hardly knew, but now couldn't find enough words to thank her.

Indeed, the stone which the builders scornfully rejected had become my cornerstone. It took a few weeks before I could take my first steps, slowly. My chin had dislocated and my fractured jaw was healing, also slowly. My head was swollen still, half of my face covered with scars. I tried to find Paul.

His legs were still hoisted up, and much of his face was still covered with bandage. It was even more painful to watch my cousin lying there with no words to say. In our human eyes, our lives had come to a grinding halt, and I could only hope that God into whose hands we had both committed our lives, would turn our adversity into a testimony for His glory. I was hospitalized for six months.

Paul was transferred to the 37 Military Hospital in Accra. He still had a long road to recovery ahead. He was still fighting for his life, with broken bones, shattered legs, a jaw fractured beyond repair, and cuts all over his body. Apparently, Paul had survived another miracle because of Reverend Driggers rushing to Okomfo Anokye Hospital when he heard of the accident. As a para-medical doctor, he observed signals of internal bleeding and inserted his whole arm in Paul's mouth to make him gag and vomit. Blood that had been trapped in his chest and lungs flew around the room, covering Reverend Driggers' clothes and all over the bed. The doctors quickly worked to resuscitate Paul.

Reverend Vernon Driggers came to the hospital every single day to visit with Paul and me and encourage us to keep our focus on God, who would be our healer. Paul's legs were supposed to be amputated in Accra, but the doctors elected to put metal braces on both of his legs and hope for the bones to slowly straighten and heal. God healed him.

God was truly faithful and kept His word even in what seemed like our darkest hour. The young nurse, Cecilia Agamavi, who sat beside Paul the whole time when he felt so broken, turned out to be the woman with whom he would spend the rest of his life. Paul went on to become the first radio minister for the Assemblies of God Church in Ghana, and later in life, a lecturer at the University of California in Los Angeles.

Surviving this grisly accident had become the greatest miracle of my life, and a year later I would be invited back to KNUST Katanga Hall to preach *"Man's life is like Vapor"* again. Once I was going to preach about my interpretation of God's word. Now I had a testimony. I can never forget preaching to a room full of young people, about 300 of them, all making a decision to turn their lives over to Jesus and accept Him as their saviour.

The accident had not only revived my faith, but had given me a deeper understanding of the Scriptures, *"For to me, to live is Christ, and to die is gain"*. Every moment alive meant I would live for Christ, and dying would be even better because I would be in the arms my Heavenly Father. With that assurance, nothing could sway me to leave the grasp of Almighty God.

* * * * *

I shared a story a few years ago at the Saint Cyprian's Anglican Church in Kumasi. I had been invited as the guest preacher for their morning prayer meeting. It was in 1981, when I was travelling to England that I sat next to B.M. Kuffuor, a wealthy businessman and a timber contractor who owned a huge sawmill in the Kumasi area. I knew him, and most of the people in the region saw his success and sway across the country, just like many of the prominent local businessmen at the time.

I had been exhausted from a busy week and I bought a first-class airline ticket on the Ghana Airways flight so that I could get some rest on the journey. I reasoned that the first-class seat would give some added comfort, and I might be able to sleep for a while. I sat near the window quietly, in Seat number 1A. B.M. Kuffuor sat in 1B. He exuded such confidence that came from having enormous wealth and influence in his world.

Just as the plane took off, the flight attendant walked up. She would be serving any beverage of our choice, expensive wines, exotic champagnes, or any alcohol of our preference.

I heard B.M. Kuffuor say, "Give me gin, on the rocks". His voice was deep with poise, like a man who was used to others serving his every need.

"No problem, sir".

The lady politely handed him a glass of gin, hard liquor. And rocks too.

That was the first time I knew what the rocks were—ice cubes. Mr. Kuffuor had said it with such sophistication that I was shocked to see that was all they were, ice cubes.

The flight attendant turned to me, "Please what would you like to drink?"

I asked for orange juice. And I didn't even need rocks.

A few moments passed.

Mr. Kuffuor couldn't hold his thoughts in much longer. Something about my request for orange juice tickled him. He gulped the glass of gin. Then he tilted his head towards me.

"Young man, what is your name?"

"Please, Kwabena Darko"

"And what do you do, if you don't mind me asking?"

"I am a chicken farmer, sir".

Chapter 12: Like Vapor And Passing Shadows

He seemed either intrigued or confused. I had boarded the flight hoping to drift quickly to sleep but now I was engaged in curious and unexpected chitchat. Something about my asking for orange juice in the first-class section of the aircraft instead of expensive wine or alcohol had sparked a conversation.

"Do you know me?" He asked.

"Yes sir, you are Nana Kuffuor, nice to meet you". In addition to his business, he was chief of Nkawie, a town in the Atwima Nwabiagya area, in Ghana's Ashanti Region.

Then he asked the question that seemed to have been lurking in his mind for a while.

"Why did you get a first-class ticket?"

"Oh sir . . . I had a long day and I have meetings scheduled when we arrive in England, so I wanted a seat where I could sleep a little comfortably on the flight".

B.M. Kuffuor was even more surprised.

"My friend . . . so you bought the expensive first-class ticket so that you could sleep?"

I nodded.

"You could have bought a cheaper ticket somewhere in the back and slept if that is all you needed. Aren't you wasting your money?"

I smiled.

All I remembered for the rest of the flight was Mr. Kuffour pacing back and forth occasionally, as if he were restless on the long flight. Then he took another sip of his gin on the rocks.

It was two weeks later, returning on the Ghana Airways flight, that I sat in the same seat as I had before, seat number 1A. Maybe if Mr. Kuffour was returning, I would see him again, and maybe he would drink another glass of gin on the rocks. But he never did; his seat stayed empty.

I sat by the window, looking out while the men unloaded the bags one after the other on a long conveyor belt into the luggage and cargo compartments underneath the plane. Just then, the pilot, the first officer Captain Ampomah whom I knew back in Accra, stepped out of the cockpit, and we spoke for a few minutes as we had about half an hour before all the passengers were aboard.

There was one curious piece of luggage, a long narrow box, moving slowly on the conveyor belt. The pilot looked out also and shook his head.

"What is that?" I was curious.

"Kwabena, you travelled two weeks ago with a man named B.M. Kuffuor, do you remember?"

I nodded.

"He died in England, and his corpse is in that casket, on that conveyor belt." It felt somewhat surreal because I could almost remember every word he spoke and the elegance he exuded just two weeks earlier. He was confident in what he had achieved and seemed even more buoyant because of the piece of the world his fortune had carved for him. "He traveled alive as a man, and now he will return home as luggage," the pilot added calmly.

It was a few weeks later that I was invited to speak at the cathedral at Saint Cyprian's Anglican Church in Kumasi. I spoke about God's grace and how much of the live we live is outside of our control. Every moment is surely in the hands of Almighty God, and in a blink of an eye, it could be our last breath. Then I shared a testimony of a prominent man with whom I had sat on a plane just two weeks earlier. On one flight he drank the most expensive drink, gin-on-the-rocks, and walked confidently back and forth. Nothing could have suggested that was the last time I would see the man alive, but it was. It was a sad truth.

It was after the service that a woman introduced herself to me. Our worlds had been much closer than apart. The testimony struck her deeply because it was a part of hers too. She knew of me, because her husband had told him of a chicken farmer who was drinking orange juice in the first class section, and she couldn't forget that story. She had been the reason why the man occasionally walked back and forth because she was seated towards the back of the airplane. It was then that I learned the couple was travelling to England for a medical check-up.

Dressed in black, the lady was mourning her husband's death. The man had once carried himself assuredly, as a wealthy man whose life was brimming with confidence. But now it was even more baffling how a person with any critical medical condition would spend most of an evening pacing back and forth in an airplane, and gulping gin-on-the-rocks, one glass after another. In one moment, he was drinking gin-on-the-rocks in an expensive first-class seat seemingly without a care in the world, and now was tucked in a wooden box in the airplane's cargo section, lifeless.

Our life, and every moment in it, is like vapor. We are here in one moment, and we do not have any idea what will happen tomorrow. Like mist, our every next moment is dependent only on God's grace, and His will. My life's journey had been littered with too many markers to miss the fact that life is ever so brief, like the early morning fog that vanishes with the rising sun. It is by God's grace and blessing that we are alive to serve Him and others, and it is He who gives the gift of life. All we can do is capture the fragile moments and treasure them. My purpose had become to live for eternal things, rather than for fleeting ovations and temporal things of the earth.

It is by God's grace and blessing that we are alive to serve Him and others, and it is He who gives the gift of life. All we can do is capture the fragile moments and treasure them. My purpose had become to live for eternal things, rather than for fleeting ovations and temporal things of the earth.

For I am persuaded, that neither death, nor life, nor angels, nor principalities, nor powers, nor things present, nor things to come, nor height, nor depth, nor any other creature, shall be able to separate us from the love of God, which is in Christ Jesus our Lord. — Romans 8:38, 39.

CHAPTER 13

THE HAPPIEST PEOPLE ON EARTH

Campus Crusade. FGBMFI. Ghana Outreach.

In 1977, I was invited to Swaziland to join a group of Christian men and women who supported American Evangelist Bill Bright's Campus Crusade for Christ. He had begun his ministry on the campus of the University of California, Los Angeles, in the early 1950s to evangelize to university students. His work flourished from the California coast to many cities across America, and countries around the world. It was for this same vision that Bill Bright sent another American missionary, John Austin, to Ghana to explore the possibility of establishing Campus Crusade for Christ in the country.

John started on the campus of the Kwame Nkrumah University of Science and Technology (KNUST) in Kumasi, and with Scripture Union's outreach already in all secondary schools and universities in Ghana, much of our work coincided and we supported each other's vision. I had met Bill a few years earlier in the United States, and I accepted the invitation to the conference in Swaziland. I was traveling with my wife Christiana, and another Christian couple, Mrs. Regina and Enoch Agbozo.

Before we set out on the Ethiopian Airlines flight from Accra to Addis Ababa, Ethiopia, and later to Nairobi, Kenya, we had been warned of the odd apartheid system in South Africa. I had heard deplorable news stories about the regime for many years, but I had to be in the country to truly feel the weight of the oppression. After four days in Nairobi, we travelled to Johannesburg, South Africa where the organizers had arranged for all of us to spend the night at the Holiday Inn hotel near the airport.

I stepped out of the aircraft into a beautiful airport, lined with more than 10 Boeing 747 aircraft on the tarmacs, and for a moment I imagined how South Africa managed such economic success despite the pressures from the international community. Just before I had the chance to be impressed, all the black passengers were directed to a different arrival hall. The white people were taken in another direction. It was incredibly shocking, and that taste of white supremacy and overt racial segregation was nothing I could have imagined.

Throughout the airport, the black people did the cleaning and every menial job, and although they didn't say a word, it wasn't hard to see the pain in their hearts bursting through their strained smiles. It was awkward for the white missionaries who had travelled with us from Nairobi to be escorted into an air-conditioned bus, while the rest of us were instructed to climb a wooden truck, rattling and shaking all the way to the Holiday Inn. South Africa was a reality that intrigued and dismayed in equal measure, but it was inevitably infuriating to see what people were subjected to in their own country because of the colour of their skin.

The entire group headed out to Mbabane, Swaziland, in three buses the next day. Riding along the steep hills was nerve-wracking. For a moment, the warnings we had been given ahead of the trip not to look outside the windows while the bus was descending, seemed more ominous than comforting. The bus felt as though it was just moments away from tilting over into the grass-covered valley on either side of the road. We made it to the conference venue and spent the next week in Swaziland.

A moment that stayed with me for the rest of my life was during one of the seminars when Henry Brandt, a Christian psychologist, tried

Chapter 13: The Happiest People On Earth

to explain parts of the Christian doctrine in a way that I didn't believe was consistent with the Scriptures. In a place where we had all come to seek the face of God with prayer and direction for outreach, I saw no manifestation of the Holy Spirit, as I knew it to be the speaking of tongues. I had to ask the question.

"Do we believe in the baptism of the Holy Spirit? What about speaking in tongues?"

There was a pause.

Henry tried to sift my question through his own training and Christian teachings. Bill wasn't surprised I had raised the question, and I was happy to explain my reasoning.

In many of the Christian teachings, most of the churches that considered themselves evangelicals believed that when a person accepts Jesus as their saviour and is born again, they are also born of the Spirit. For men like Henry, since the Word of God is Spirit and life, and lives in the heart of a believer upon accepting Jesus Christ as the Son of God whose death on the cross gave them eternal life, there was no need for a separate baptism of the Holy Spirit.

Pentecostal teaching shared the same Christian understanding, but encouraged the believer to know the difference between water baptism unto repentance, what the Bible describes as the remission of sins, and the baptism of the Holy Spirit, the gift that was manifested by the speaking in tongues as the Holy Spirit gave utterance. It is an essential part of the Christian journey. It is this power that fills the believer to become an ambassador of Christ's salvation to our world.

The Pentecostal teachings lean on one of the most significant encounters in the Scripture, the Day of Pentecost, where Jesus, after His resurrection, tells his disciples to wait in the Upper Room for ten days, praying until the Holy Spirit descended upon them. "But ye shall receive power, after that the Holy Ghost is come upon you: and ye shall be witnesses unto me both in Jerusalem, and in all Judaea, and in Samaria, and unto the uttermost part of the earth" Acts 1:1-26.

Our Christian backgrounds may have been different, but we were serving the same God, and our great commission was to evangelize for the same kingdom. The discussion that ensued that afternoon formed a new relationship, and we would soon be heading to our respective countries, as committed witnesses of the Gospel of Christ. We were to go into our world to preach the good news, and this conference in Swaziland revived my own zeal to become a vessel and a committed ambassador of Christ. It was in 1977.

It was a year later, in October 1978, when a young student, Dela Adadevor, who had been discipled by John Austin, took over the ministry work on the KNUST campus and across Ghana. John was heading to New York as part of the ministry's outreach at the United Nations, with a focus on world leaders, ambassadors, diplomats, and government delegations. With Dela committing himself to the ministry's local outreach across the country's universities, I was honoured to support the organization's vision, witnessing sincerely and boldly to the nations, building the kingdom with young men and women in the universities, many of whom were soon to be influential people in their societies.

By the 1990s, Dela had transitioned to the Campus Crusade head office in San Bernardino, California, and the work had grown into the International Leadership Foundation (ILF) evangelizing to leaders across the African continent with a plain message of Christ's gospel. From university campuses to presidential hallways, the message remained the same, and the urgency of bringing people to the knowledge of Jesus Christ reigned.

* * * * *

I was in England, at a Stonely Poultry Show, when I received a letter from D.W. Amoah from Ghana. He was a member of a new organization in Ghana, they called themselves the Full Gospel Business Men's Fellowship International. They had heard about my commitment to the

Chapter 13: The Happiest People On Earth

work of Assemblies of God and Scripture Union, and were extending an invitation to me to share my personal testimony at their upcoming meeting.

It was later that I learned about how a young Ghanaian evangelist, Alfred Nyamekye, who had been in Nigeria as part of his evangelism work, met a Nigerian Christian businessman Chief Uwadie. Alfred had struck a friendship with Uwadie, and both men gradually nurtured a trust in each other as they remained in the network of Charismatic Pentecostal preacher Archbishop Benson Idahosa.

Uwadie had imported goods into Ghana, only for his cargo to be stuck in a clumsy documentation process at the Tema Port. Alfred, who was also in Nigeria, sought to help his Nigerian friend, and needed someone who knew the local business landscape and could assist in preparing the documentation that was needed. He called his cousin Joseph Kwaku Kwaw.

Joseph's help forged a business relationship between the two men. It was a few weeks later that Alfred called his friend again, this time to share a thought that had crossed his mind. He mentioned how Uwadie was part of a Christian network for business people and it seemed it could be something Joseph would be interested in. Alfred suggested that Joseph take the time to speak with Uwadie, who was the International Director of the organization in Nigeria.

Joseph was thrilled to learn about the organization, and agreed to start a chapter in Ghana. With what he knew, he quickly formed two chapters with three of his friends in Accra and Tema, a few friends and businessmen meeting at a restaurant or the home of anyone who volunteered. It was 1976.

It was later that year when Archbishop Benson Idahosa held a crusade in Accra, "Ghana for Christ", and crowds of people flocked to the Continental Hotel. It became an eye-opener for Joseph and his friends. They realized that they too could use the hotels for their meeting venue. Full Gospel Business Men's Fellowship International was launched.

By then, Kofi "Simms" Mensah, a prominent electrical contractor, had embraced the vision of the fellowship and agreed to serve as an advisor to the chapter president. Together with Papa Amoakohene, who readily supported the organization with a hefty 10,000 cedis, men like Simms would turn out to be immensely helpful to the new organization. Another young businessman, Kwasi Amoakohene, owned a chain of A-Mart Stores around the country, and he volunteered to finance some of the chapter activities. The men hoped to open chapters in the large metropolitan areas around the country, like Kumasi and Takoradi, and invite Christian businessmen in those communities to join and help. They held a convention at the Ambassador Hotel in 1981, and that was when I was invited to be the main speaker.

Full Gospel Business Men's Fellowship International had been founded in 1953, with a vision to connect business people with opportunities to reach out and ultimately build communities, with God's grace at the centre of their work. The founder was American businessman Demos Shakarian, who often reasoned that there were indeed more businessmen than preachers, and the kingdom's message in all its fullness would reach the ends of the world if the businessmen chose to spread the gospel.

The Shakarian family had escaped the Holocaust in Armenia, and settled in California. The family's farm with three cows ended up with more than three thousand in 1943, and soon gained prominence as the largest private dairy company in America. Ten years later, Demos Shakarian started a network of businessmen who would meet every week in Clifton's Cafeteria in Los Angeles, to share their faith and testimony of God's provision for their lives.

Joseph Kwao, Kwasi Amoakohere, and D.W. Amoah shared this same vision, committed Christian businessmen daring to make a difference in their world. By standing together, businessmen in Ghana would found a network that continually equipped men to fulfil the Great Commission, reaching the nations for Jesus Christ.

Chapter 13: The Happiest People On Earth

I had arranged for my driver to pick me from the Kotoka International Airport upon my arrival from England. I planned to change quickly and head to the Full Gospel Business Men's Fellowship International convention at the Ambassador Hotel. Instead, G. A. Acquaye, who was the office manager at my company in Accra was at the airport to pick me up. Something had to be wrong.

It was moments later when I spoke to my wife that I learned that the driver, heading from Kumasi to Accra that evening, had been involved in an accident. A tipper truck had rammed into the back of the Mercedes Benz and the driver had been fortunate to swerve just in time to have avoided any major injury. Thank God his life had been spared.

"Devil you're a liar! God will move today".

Nothing was going to stop me from sharing my testimony at the convention. My faith was charged even more. I had a wrecked car in my garage to prove that whatever the devil meant for harm, God always had a way to turn it for our good. There were more than 400 men in the conference room, and I was not sure if they knew anything about me. What mattered most was that they left that evening knowing about Jesus.

It was interesting to sit in a Christian meeting where the people shared their testimonies rather than listening to a preacher or evangelist. Full Gospel Business Men's Fellowship International was not a church, but an assembly of men, and women also, whose commitment would be to fearlessly expand God's kingdom in their towns and cities. I shared my story of the eerie hands that had pursued me through my childhood. I shared my testimony of God's provision when I had been struck by illness, and when my mother found me sleeping on a mat in the middle of the street, haunted by nightmares and strange visions. I shared my story of how God had found me on a Saturday night in 1962. It was one thing to speak generally about the saving grace of Almighty God, but nothing could carry the power of relating such experiences.

The men in that room had come with their own expectations, and perhaps belonged to their own local churches. They may even have accepted Jesus as their saviour, but I was sure they knew that until a person has walked through life's trials of fire and faced the enemy, and felt the pain of brokenness and dejection, "talk is cheap". I knew what God had done in my life. God was looking for people who would take a stand in their homes and in their communities.

As for me, I had found a family of believers whose vision had been the same as what had set me on my journey. These were the born again businessmen and businesswomen I had sought to reach; together we would build the kingdom. One Saturday after another we met and prayed and encouraged each other. We reminded each other of the four things that guided our lives: that God is our Father in Heaven, the significance of water baptism, the need to be baptized in the Holy Spirit, and testifying to the world.

We set out to open several chapters in Accra. We had not been saved because of some good work we had done on our own, but because of Jesus, in whom we believed. The Fellowship was a Charismatic movement that stressed living a life that brought glory to Jesus.

We opened a Full Gospel Business Men's Fellowship International to Kumasi in 1982. Dr. Nii Adjere Wellington joined as Vice President, Mac Obiri-Mainoo was the Treasurer, Henry Boakye Ababio as the New Convert Administrator, and a young Kofi Amponsah Effah as the Fellowship's secretary.

We opened five new chapters in Kumasi. At our opening in Kumasi, we invited a young charismatic pastor, Nicholas Duncan-Williams as the keynote speaker. I set up an office for Full Gospel Business Men's Fellowship International at the centre of Kumasi city, and hired a young man as the administrator. I was soon to become the Field Representative, and my burning desire was to open new chapters in all the major cities across the country. I headed north.

We opened a chapter in Sunyani, in Brong Ahafo. About a month later, I opened a new chapter in Tamale in the Northern Region, and then another chapter in Bolgatanga, in the Upper East region near

Chapter 13: The Happiest People On Earth

Burkina Faso. At the same time, Joseph and the team in Accra were opening new chapters in different parts of the Greater Accra region. By 1983, we had opened several chapters across the country, and decided to organize a national convention. We invited the International Coordinator Jose Pascua to Ghana.

This was the first time Full Gospel Business Men's Fellowship International office in America was stepping foot in Ghana. We had been fortunate to open several chapters in a short time, and with a very active membership. Jose Pascua and a team arrived from America, and joined us in an energetic teaching seminar at the Ambassador Hotel. The place was crowded with men and women hungry for God's word. Their job was to explain the vision of the organization and how the international office supported the local work and the hierarchy, as well as to share the literature that uplifted the work of God in many nations.

Over one week, the chapters in Ghana formed the national leadership board and helped us to develop the chapter manuals. Our first national office was along the busy Ring Road in Accra. I was selected as the National Treasurer; Joseph became National President; Kwasi was National Coordinator; D.W. Amoah, the same man who had first contacted me three years earlier, remained as the National Secretary. By 1984 we had successfully opened 40 chapters in Ghana.

One group of people we supported were men and women who were part of the Fellowship, and we had become a resource to one another. The lawyers and accountants and others with varied skillsets took turns sharing their knowledge and experiences, and teaching godly values to the people in our network.

Jose Pascua and his team took a report back to the founder Demos Shakarian and the international fellowship, and that opened the door for what were to become some of the most humbling and awesome years of my life.

CHAPTER 14

A YEARNING FOR CHANGE

Outreach Africa. AFB and Mandela.

My hands were lifted high in praise to my God. I was standing on stage at the Full Gospel Business Men's Fellowship International's world convention, held in Anaheim, California in June 1984. Thousands of men and women from all parts of the world lifted their voices in song and joined in prayer. God had taken me from a humble start, a teenager who fell in love with poultry farming in 1958, and never looked back. Now, all I had was my testimony. I spoke for a few minutes but I could feel the presence of the Holy Spirit in the auditorium. Demos Shakarian hugged me as I walked down the stage, "Darko, you have lifted Africa today".

The next morning, my picture was on the front page of the Fellowship's newsletter, along with my testimony that was to go to corners of the world where I had never been. I returned home with my faith invigorated, ready to find men and women who would join hands to build the church and the nations. I was persuaded that the Lord had laid it on my heart to go to the countries in West Africa.

My first trip to a Fellowship chapter was to Monrovia, Liberia. It was an American colony with many professionals who had spent years in American universities and other colleges overseas. The country also had many English speaking communities and we were able to organize a breakfast meeting where we introduced the Full Gospel Business Men's Fellowship International and opened a chapter.

With both Joseph and D.W., I headed to Sierra Leone afterward with plans to open the first chapter in Freetown. I had elected to pay 200 pound sterling for the breakfast, as I had always done, hoping to have at least 100 people in the venue. An older Sierra Leonean gentleman who often worked in Ghana, Modupe Tilapiers would be our contact. He was willing to connect us with people in the country who he was sure could be of help.

We landed in Freetown, and travelled by ferry across to Lungi, a small coastal town in the Northern Province. We had spent our days praying and fasting ahead of the trip, and was happy to see Tilapiers. Our conversation gradually turned into an exhortation and prayer. We all felt the Holy Spirit descend.

The most amazing thing was to see Reverend Modupe Tilapiers' daughter cleaning dishes in the adjacent room suddenly start praying in tongues and interpreting. She was consumed as she prayed in the spirit. Tilapiers was an Anglican priest and a man who had never encountered the baptism of the Holy Spirit, something that was not as significant to him before. Now, he stood utterly perplexed, shaking, knowing in his heart that God had brought us to Sierra Leone.

Reverend Modupe Tilapiers suggested we meet Dr. Thomas Hope, a Christian businessman who was with the Assemblies of God Church. He was a respected Water Engineer and had previously served as the first board chairman of Ecobank in Africa. I had no idea Dr. Hope was now the Board Chairman of Standard Chartered Bank in Sierra Leone. Modupe believed that if his schedule would allow, Dr. Hope might be a great influence to help us connect with business men and women around Freetown.

We waited outside of his office. What I never could have known was how my name and picture ended up on Dr. Hope's desk. And it did. Even stranger, it was exactly that very morning when I was arriving in Lungi.

Chapter 14: A Yearning For Change

A few months earlier, my local branch of Standard Chartered bank had rewarded my business with the company, by paying for my expenses to the Stoneleigh Agricultural Show partially sponsored by the bank. They also arranged for me to meet with the Chairman of Standard Chartered in England. As a gesture, I took with me a small wooden carving from Ghana, one that depicted three people interlocked as one. Back home, the local name was *Eti baako nko agyina*, and it meant it was ideal for more than one person to carry the weight of any moment. But, a thought crossed my mind to give it my own meaning.

Handing over the carving to the Chairman of Standard Chartered Bank, I told him what it meant to me, the trinity. I explained simply the theological doctrine of God as three distinct, independent persons— Father, Son, and Holy Spirit— yet simultaneously existing as a single, unified being. Just as coincidence would have it, there were cameras in the room while I handed over the small gift to Chairman who was thrilled at receiving a present with such deep meaning.

A few weeks later, a photograph with the Chairman of Standard Chartered ended up in the company's monthly bulletin, sent from England to managers in all of the bank's branches worldwide. It turned out the morning we were in Lungi, sitting right outside of his office, Dr. Hope was opening his mail, which included the bulletin. My picture with the Chairman of Standard Chartered Bank was on the front cover.

When we walked into his office, he listened to why we had come to Sierra Leone, and why Tilapiers had suggested we meet with him. I introduced the two men with me.

"This is Joseph and D.W".

He smiled.

Then I told him my name again; he was lost for words. He spoke excitedly.

"This is God. God has done this". The bulletin sat on his table and he couldn't believe the coincidence.

"So, you are Kwabena Darko, the poultry farmer".

Dr. Hope was surprised and excited to see me, and to hear more about my plans for Full Gospel Business Men's Fellowship International.

Dr. Hope introduced us to his friend from the prestigious Fourah Bay College, Dr. Marcus Jones, and his wife Philippa, who said she would be glad to assist. Apparently, they had a network of business leaders and businessmen and women who we could invite. Philippa's brother, Welben Short, was eager to join the breakfast meeting and he mentioned several other people he would invite as well.

In every country where we set out to plant chapters, it was particularly important to engage the local church leaders to embrace our work. Full Gospel Business Men's Fellowship International was not a church, and we had no intention to compete with the local churches. That was a message we had to make sure was clearly shared with the church leaders. For this reason, we invited them to a meeting to share our vision.

Just as we had done in Liberia, we were in Sierra Leone to reach out to our kind—businessmen and businesswomen with whom we shared common challenges in our vocations, and whom we knew would be great ambassadors to the kingdom of God. Full Gospel Business Men's Fellowship International was only interested in training the men to help their local churches and we wholeheartedly believed we were building leaders who would make a difference in their nations. If there was anything we wanted to be known for, we were in the country to catch the men, equip them with the Holy Spirit and give them back to the local churches to support.

Dr. Hope agreed to assist with setting up the breakfast meeting as well as inviting many of the nation's leaders he knew who lived in the nearby cities. Full Gospel Business Men's Fellowship International was more than a Christian network for prominent leaders and doctors and court judges. It was an invitation for men and women of different social and vocational backgrounds to revive the urgency of the great commission, to go into our world and spread the gospel. The full gospel. I had

Chapter 14: A Yearning For Change

come to believe wholeheartedly, just as the Scriptures had taught me, that "When the righteous are in authority, the people will rejoice".

Across West Africa, Full Gospel Business Men's Fellowship International had an immense opportunity to affect change by strengthening committed Christians in leadership positions in every sphere, those who would hold high the banner of Christ and become the light in their world through their example.

We left Sierra Leone after opening a new chapter. Dr. Hope became the President, Wilben Short was Secretary, Dr. Marcus Jones was Treasurer, and Modupe Tilapiers was Coordinator. I had the honour of setting the stage, but it was God who moved mightily in Freetown.

Back in Ghana, the men and women now in charge of Darko Farms were incredibly diligent in every area of business. The more I stepped out on faith to work for the Lord, the more God multiplied my influence and built a hedge of protection around everything that concerned me. With my business in good hands, my wife Christiana was able to come along as I headed to Conakry, Guinea to open a new chapter. Then we went to Abidjan in Cote D'Ivoire, and Banjul in Gambia for a successful opening of the first chapter in that West African country.

Travelling north to Senegal meant I needed the help of the Assemblies of God Church whose local congregation also had committed Christians ready to serve, and it was a huge blessing to have them on board. A few of the Ghanaian flight attendants who worked with Ghana Airways, and also the Regional Director of the airline based in Dakar, agreed to assist. There was an incredible group of men and women, all of whom were willing to be building blocks to opening a new chapter in Dakar.

Senegal was also where I reconnected with my friend Anta Babacar Ngom, who was also a chicken farmer. He was a Muslim. We had met in one international poultry conference hosted by the USAID and the Corporate Council for Africa, and struck up a friendship. He had often brought several of his employees to train with my farms in Ghana, and through the years, he had been a remarkable business leader in his country.

I called to let him know I was heading to his country. I was humbled by Brother Ngom's acceptance of the invitation to join us at the breakfast meeting, and in that morning, my friend gave his life to Jesus and spent the rest of his life preaching His good news. He became the largest chicken farmer in Dakar, but nothing warmed his heart more than reaching men and women for the kingdom.

Then I turned east. I spend the next several months opening Full Gospel Business Men's Fellowship International chapters in Lomé, Togo, and Cotonou, in Benin. Nigeria had established several chapters across the country, and I was happy to support every effort to make their work impactful. I introduced Advanced Learning Training Seminar (ALTS) to equip the Fellowship's leaders in Nigeria. The vision of the Fellowship had become my life. I prayed that all the people I had the chance to meet and share the faithfulness with would have their encounters with Almighty God and give them their own stories.

Kenya had opened a chapter of Full Gospel Business Men's Fellowship International several years prior, with many of the American tourists who travelled to the region for safaris and expeditions also finding an opportunity to network with Christian businessmen and women. Jerry Kibarabara was the National President, and was also Africa's representative to the International Board for the fellowship.

I travelled to Libreville in Gabon, to open a new chapter and a few months later, to Yaoundé, Cameroon. Together with the team from Gabon and Cameroon, we opened a chapter in Kinshasa, Congo. A young man, Michael Kayembe Wadikonda was selected to be National President and his passion for Christ's work was refreshingly contagious. Some of the leaders in the region disliked Christian missionaries and what they perceived to be the influence of foreign philosophy in their society. Carefully and boldly, Wadikonda started opening chapters in Central Africa. With him, I travelled to Malabo in Equatorial Guinea,

Chapter 14: A Yearning For Change

and a few months later, to Brazzaville, Congo, opening and supporting chapters in both countries.

Beyond the Fellowship, however, whatever influence God had given me I was careful to represent the same God I served in every other area of my life. For every world leader and politician I met along the way, I prayed that God's grace would guide their hearts to be of service to their people. From Étienne Tshisekedi and fellow countrymen Mobutu Sese Seko, Omar Bongo and Thabo Mbeki, to Americans Ronald Reagan and George Bush, my truth never wavered.

As for every businessman whose love for wealth and fame trumped their thirst for integrity, I prayed for and trusted the Holy Spirit to turn their hearts to Christ.

In 1990, I was elected Vice President of the African Business Roundtable, a committee of business, political and social leaders, independent, non-partisan, non-profit private sector-funded organization committed to promoting African private sector-led economic growth and social development in Africa. It was funded by the African Development Bank, and headed by Senegalese Dr. Babacar Ndiaye who was also serving as the chairman of the bank. In that year, the horror of apartheid had pushed South Africa to a brink, a sobering reality of racism and oppression.

F.W. de Klerk had been elected leader of the National Party and soon after, President. He took a significant step toward peace by meeting with the imprisoned South African leader of the African National Congress (ANC), Nelson Mandela. African nations were particularly enraged over apartheid's grip on the black Africans, and despite his earlier missteps, F.W. de Klerk began a process of ending apartheid. Removing the ban on liberation movements like the African National Congress (ANC), Pan-Africanist Congress (PAC) and South African Communist Party (SACP), was a start.

The Full Gospel Business Men's Fellowship International in South Africa had only white members, and leaders like de Klerk saw an opportunity to solicit their help to reach Africans in the fellowships from other African countries to rally support. The men and women in our group were some of the instrumental decision-makers at the African Business Roundtable. It was through this effort to meet with influential African leaders like Nigeria's General Ibrahim Babangida, that F.W. de Klerk sought the help of the African Business Roundtable and the Corporate Council for Africa.

A series of meetings with the African groups piled pressure on F.W. de Klerk to make significant inroads to releasing Mandela quickly. I remember a chill in my heart as I stood with a group of African leaders on Robben Island, miles from Cape Town, a place of exile where the white South African leaders sent opponents of apartheid, to isolate them from their people and crush their morale. The peaceful end to an evil regime came, as South Africa transitioned to democratic rule. Nelson Mandela was released from prison after 27 years.

I remember how Cyril Ramaphosa was a trade union leader who worked hard to uplift the people in the Soweto area. Full Gospel Business Men's Fellowship International had little choice but to integrate, and the leaders reached out to me to help open new chapters in places like Pretoria, Johannesburg, and Victoria. They also needed my help with setting up farms for aspiring entrepreneurs who were now in search of their future without the boundaries of apartheid.

The Fellowship had taken me to almost every nation across the African continent, prayed with leaders, and helped men and women take a stand for Christ in their professions and in the privacy of their homes. In 1991, I remember travelling out of Ghana 53 times, at a cost of more than $50,000 on tickets, to places that I was convinced needed to hear the truth about Jesus. My guiding light has always been God's word, that He will bless me, so that I will be a blessing to my people.

Back in 1984, with thousands of people in the Anaheim Convention Centre hearing my testimony, I didn't have a glimpse of where God would take me, or of the power of prayer to touch the hearts of men.

The gospel had taken me around the world, with the honour to speak to nations. Every quiet triumph and gallant effort had been to bring all the glory to Almighty God.

In 1991, I was the International Secretary of Full Gospel Business Men's Fellowship International, operating out of Costa Mesa, California. It had been incredible to see how through the years, the vision remained unchanged. I had no interest in politics; my only yearning was to see Christian leaders lead the land, in every country—steadfast Christians whose hearts were completely set on Jesus.

All that I had been, the places my feet had walked to share the good news, had been because of an undeserved grace in my life. I always prayed, just as my friend Demos Shakarian had declared over my life many years ago, that I would *lift Africa every day of my life*.

Most importantly, I would lift the name of Jesus Christ.

CHAPTER 15

THE WISDOM OF LIGHTS

Parastatals. Private Enterprise. Paris Reidhead.

It was in Israel that I saw a *moshav* cooperative agricultural settlement which the farmers in the early part of the 20th century had organized. They had been given several acres of land each on which they worked long hours in the day, their horses ploughing the land. The underlying principle in the moshav began with private ownership of land, and an avoidance of hired labour which meant that the farmers were intimately connected with every activity on the farms. The success or failure fell on their shoulders.

Even more important were the communal marketing and mutual assistance which gave them a real understanding of market factors and opportunities.

At central locations, they marketed the produce in such a way that no one person carried the burden of selling. There were men and women whose every attention was on the sale, that being their contribution to the cooperative.

It was 1960, and I was particularly intrigued to see workers producing crops on separate properties, yet with pooled labour where needed, and ultimately with all the profits being shared among themselves. They appreciated the infrastructure which was made possible by their taxes, and ultimately it became a society where everyone was willing to play their part. Hardly a perfect system, yet one thing was unmistakably true, that the farmers took all the risks and poured their hearts into their work simply because they had a stake in every success.

Even though the world from which I came always had a clash of ideas with different business models, it was easy to see traces of cooperative systems, people working for themselves, and taking an entrepreneurial risk in the hope of making a profit. I remember when I first knew of the Ghana Cooperative Society, which had been set up by farmers, but with the necessary regulatory assistance they needed coming from the government. It worked well in Ghana, mostly for the cocoa farmers. That was until the arrangement was overtaken by government-run institutions.

Gradually, parastatals took centre stage. They were the state-owned companies that had been set up to compete with private enterprises in any industry, were managed by government appointees and had all the backing they needed from the government. The state-owned companies immediately gained the upper hand in the market. Their rise, without much surprise, dwarfed the cooperatives and the farmers had little choice but to struggle to survive. It was unfortunate, because nothing would have been more ideal than a government whose every focus remained on creating an infrastructure that allowed private individuals to build businesses and take care of them to flourish, eventually becoming the bedrock of nation-building. With changing governments, Ghana toggled back and forth between different ideas for a functioning economy.

In farming, one farmer's story was strikingly similar to another's, and I saw how unless a man or woman wiped their sweat in the scorching sun tending to their crops and livestock, they hardly took care of it. It was difficult for any policymaker sitting in an office far away from the farming towns and villages to truly walk in a farmer's shoes even for a mile, and know what drove them. For instance, I vividly remember the years when Ghana's Cocoa Marketing Board took over as the only buyer in the country. They set up produce-buying centres and assured the cocoa farmers that they would in fact be the only entity responsible for marketing.

Chapter 15: The Wisdom Of Lights

Farmers did not have any chance to weigh in, especially in a sector where the state-owned marketing boards replaced the cooperatives. The opportunities that the local farmers in the villages once had to pool resources and establish mutually beneficial storage facilities to be able to sell directly to large multinationals quickly eroded when the government took over.

In Tema Harbor, Ghana's first President Kwame Nkrumah had partnered with companies to build huge silos and depots to store cocoa, buying them cheaply from the local farmers. From the village farms, the farmers complained about policies that crumpled their enterprises, but the country often chose to head in a different direction where state-controlled companies became an integral part of the political apparatus, as a job creation vehicle.

The one problem in those years was that even though cocoa was the country's major export crop, there were bureaucrats negotiating prices with both the buyers and the farmers, often to satisfy a political agenda, but the men and women who tilled the land and tended to the cocoa didn't have a chance to affect their own future. Despite the huge investment in the state-owned companies that had once been touted as the engine of economic progress, the parastatals quickly became the architect of their own demise.

Whether it was in cocoa farming, or in poultry farming, the underlying issue was still true: when no one owned anything, no one took care of it. It was human nature and instinct to take care of ourselves and our own, and convincing people to give the same commitment to something in which they didn't have any stake became a tall task.

Farming has always been a difficult job, something farmers knew all too well, and it seemed others didn't have a reason to imagine that was the case. Regardless of the capital investment, there was the dependence on the climate, the constant threat of diseases and pests, and a host of challenges beyond our control. To thrive, we had to learn to adapt, and we hoped that government interference would not become an added strain.

In the same vein, economies survived on men and women working their hardest to overcome business challenges, compete and innovate. Private enterprises ended up having to take a hands-on approach to be willing to take on all the risks just as much as they would any gains.

What worked, whether in a developing or developed country, was a government that embraced a rather basic logic that crushing private enterprises meant crushing a nation. Over and again, I had seen economies flourish when the government created a framework within which a society ought to function and spent all its energy in making sure it worked. I shared the opinion that where it can, the government offers incentives for individuals and enterprises to produce. No one thrived in a society without the Rule of Law and the necessary safeguards that prevented society from drifting into chaos. The government's involvement in any economy was vital, but only as a broker and watchdog of an economic engine.

Much of what I saw as efficient models in other countries was when a government that took on the role of a regulator. In Ghana, only the government could set the rules and make sure individuals and companies competed within them. In agriculture, the government could afford to create systems like the Pong-Tamale Veterinary Service, and the Food and Administration Authority whose work undergirds the economic activities in the sector.

In Ghana, another such system was the establishment of the West African Cocoa Research Institute (WACRI) in 1944. It had first been set up in Tafo in 1938 by the Gold Coast Department of Agriculture as the Central Cocoa Research Station to investigate diseases and pests which had considerably reduced cocoa production. Decades later, it continued to function and support the industry even when all other state-owned companies crashed. Perhaps, because research institutes like WACRI exist to support an industry, they thrive instead of state-owned companies that seek to play in the same field where they are best suited to be the referees and set the rules.

In Ghana, perhaps we have struggled to rid ourselves of a system that didn't push us into ownership. The British colonial government handed over power after independence and mostly left Ghana's shores. The large trading companies stayed behind. In hindsight, it is easy to understand their mindset in setting up companies in countries and hiring locals to serve as managers. Even though they trained the local managers, it was to serve their business' goals. All decisions emanated from England, from the men and women whose money was invested in those companies. The British government brought along multinationals like United Africa Company (UAC), Cadbury's and Cadbury Schweppes, and the Lonrho conglomerate, who were interested in investing in Ghana, and their government's only job was to ensure the business climate was conducive to reaping profits.

They made the private sector companies do the work. For any profit they earned, the British government stood to gain in taxes, which in turn created a chain of benefits for every one of the companies. Often, we pointed to some of the world's thriving companies and marvelled at their success, yet the building blocks were the same. It was evident that state-owned companies are best served when they exist to support a private sector.

One thing that was difficult to ignore was the fact that the British had arrived to seek their own interest, not Ghana's. They were happy to buy everything we produced as cheap raw materials and turn them into valuable finished products, and sell them back to us. Sad to admit, but there were cocoa farmers who had never tasted chocolate, and had no idea where their cocoa pods ended up. The foreign companies that came along with the British government to Ghana did not find the need to build factories in Ghana, and they must have reasoned that any such investment would not be a prudent use of their capital. They were entrepreneurs in search of greener pastures.

As for all the locals the British trained to be caretakers of their companies, they did not take their eyes off them. Companies had invested huge sums in a faraway country and they had to put every mechanism in place to ensure they earned their returns for their investment.

Then the British left. Many of the Ghanaians who ended up in charge of these companies, since the companies were now state-owned, saw a golden opportunity to take all they could. Corruption and theft gained a foothold in a company that Ghanaians didn't own, and whose failure they could easily walk away from. The state-owned companies became an avenue for free money.

A government is inherently ill-suited to run an enterprise. The unfortunate outgrowth of government takeover of factories, farms, and private investment projects was that the individual citizens hardly saw themselves as owners of the state-owned company, so it was easy for them to see any profits as *"government's money"*. As disheartening as that was, it was a prevailing mindset, one whose genesis was difficult to pin down.

In poultry farms, *"book it dead"* ruined companies. Everyone from the managers and staff to the security guards could afford to collude and siphon products and profits year after year. The worst that could happen was the business crumbling, by which time they would have found every avenue to pillage.

I remember Ghana's *Daily Graphic* newspaper on August 9, 1977, reporting the government's new directive for poultry farmers with more than 5,000 birds to buy their feed solely from the Ministry of Agriculture. Pomadze Poultry Enterprise was at the heart of this forceful initiative. Other farms were required to get their feed supplies from government agencies like the Muus Agency, Brenhya Distributive Agency.

For its part, the state-owned enterprise promised a bright future, one in which the government agencies guaranteed feed supplies to farmers across the country. The irony was in how Pomadze Poultry Enterprise eventually crumbled,¬ even with millions of dollars of capital investment, while private farms like mine were able to thrive with a paltry 1,000 cedis to start an enterprise.

Chapter 15: The Wisdom Of Lights

Years ago, I met a woman whose life revolved around traveling to remote parts of Ghana to buy tomatoes to sell in the local market. Her story touched my heart, but it was incredibly instructive too. She travelled north for several days on a treacherous route to large tomato farms tucked in the bushes in Ghana's northern regions near the Burkina Faso border. The woman slept along pathways and under trees in the middle of nowhere waiting for her turn to carry her load.

As she was perched on the side of the main road with her carts of tomatoes packed, a driver heading south to Kumasi and Accra, knowing the woman was desperate to get her tomatoes to market, demanded sex in addition to a fare. With her heart pounding, the woman fought to keep her dignity, refused him, and decided to wait through the night if that was what it would take to get her load on top of a small bus or truck heading south.

By the time she got to market, some of her tomatoes had rotted under the sun's heat, and she could only hope to sell enough of it to afford to make the trip again. The woman had chosen to take every risk as an entrepreneur, and all she hoped for was security and infrastructure to ensure half of her produce would not spoil by the time it ended up in the local market. As a private entrepreneur, she guarded what little she had.

After such an ordeal, just like many of the farmers around the country who shared her fears, her prayer was that someday our country, our leaders and most importantly our people would understand a powerful truth that seemed to so easily elude many of us: the rise of any nation will always rest on the shoulders of a vibrant private enterprise willing to sacrifice and thrive at all costs.

* * * * *

On 5th March, 1971, I received a telex out of the blue from the United States. The man on the other end said his name was Paris Reidhead. He said he was a missionary who had travelled and worked in Southern Sudan, and had been given my contact information by the Ghana Embassy in Washington D.C. He was interested in learning about my work in Ghana, and wanted to find out more about me. I agreed, but I didn't give it any more thought. Perhaps he wanted to visit Ghana for his next mission work. He arrived in Ghana two weeks later and made his way to Kumasi.

He seemed curious about what drove me to pursue poultry farming in Ghana, and politely asked one question after another. By now, I was curious too. He asked if he could come along to visit my farms and see how we cultivated our crops and raised our animals in Ghana. Then he told me in great detail of a series of events that had sparked questions in his mind, and that now he was on a quest to create solutions in parts of the world where he had been fortunate to travel.

It was in that evening that I learned that Paris had indeed been in the Southern Sudan for several years, working with a group called the Sudan Interior Mission. Apparently, he arrived in the small town when the drought and lean harvest had caused a famine in the region. The incidence of hunger was not unusual in the towns when they had little corn, sorghum, and healthy cattle for food during the dry seasons. For years, the people had resigned themselves to starvation, and waited on corn from the northern parts of the country.

But in the area were wide stretches of arable land covered with tall grass as far as the eye could see. Paris' mind travelled back to his hometown outside Chicago, Illinois, where he had seen large farms of corn, wheat, and sorghum. What was so different in the soil in Illinois that the farmers were able to grow many acres of food to feed millions of people? In his mind, the tall grass fields he saw everywhere he turned were sufficient proof that something else could thrive in the area.

He returned to South Sudan from his break in Chicago, this time taking seeds with him. He grew corn and sorghum in his backyard. It was the rainy season and it seemed in just a few weeks, he had rows of corn and sorghum soon to be harvested. Paris asked the leaders for three

Chapter 15: The Wisdom Of Lights

acres of land and did the same with those. The sorghum survived the heat even better, but both crops had thrived with the rain. He reached out to the people in the area, most of whom were nomads, and shared an idea.

Within a few years the people had grown enough food to feed the families and much more to store for the dry seasons. There would also be plenty for their cattle. This revelation led Paris to wonder why there weren't huge farms littered across Africa, especially in the regions where the continent was blessed with abundant rainfall to support a long planting season. Paris was a missionary who reasoned that if the people to whom he had travelled thousands of miles to minister were starving, there was nothing he could say that would touch their hearts. In Southern Sudan, he had seen the power of an idea, and the willingness of the locals to embrace it.

He went back to the United States. He was part of a prayer group in the Washington D.C. area where returning missionaries and other professionals who lived or worked in the neighbouring cities often held Christian fellowship meetings. The man behind the Fellowship at the time was Douglas Coe, and they called it *The Fellowship*. It was in that prayer group where Paris shared his idea with another businessman, Al Whittaker.

Paris reasoned it would be best to have an organization that would seek African students who had completed agricultural programs in the United States and were willing to return to their home countries to apply what they had learned. As part of the organization's vision, he would reach out to people in a variety of agricultural businesses and other corporate executives to assist with their experiences. One such person would be Al Whittaker, and Paris hoped he would be able to impart business knowledge to farmers and help them turn their farming into businesses.

If what Paris learned in South Sudan was any indication of what was possible in parts of Africa, it was possible for young men and women from the continent to return home with technologies and farming techniques to support the local economies. If it could work in Iowa and Illinois, it should be able to work in Africa.

Paris occasionally visited student groups on university campuses. On one occasion, he spoke to a group of students from different parts of Africa. He asked if anyone knew of a farmer or any person who had studied any aspect of agriculture and applied that knowledge somewhere in their countries. Paris said he needed that practical example to explain to other young men and women that it was indeed possible to develop commercial farms in African countries, and to do so successfully.

A young man from Ghana said he had heard of one such person in his country but didn't know the person's name or in what part of the country their farm was located. All that he knew was a *"Darko"* name and that the person was a poultry farmer. Paris ended up at the Ghana Embassy in Washington D.C. to find any information he could.

There at the consulate, he met with a commercial attaché but who said he didn't know anyone by the name Darko either, but was willing to inquire when he travelled back home in about a week. If what Paris had heard was true, it wouldn't be hard to find the Ghanaian he was looking for. That was how Paris received my contact information and decided to reach me in Mach of 1971. This is why he sent the Telex.

By the time Paris Reidhead arrived in Ghana, I had just purchased one thousand acres of land in Ejura, about 60 miles on the outskirts of the main Kumasi city. He came along to my farms in Akropong – Asante, and then agreed we would drive along the narrow main road to Ejura. Paris' neck turned every minute to see every large tree and truck and bush and person we drove past. It was as if he was determined to not miss any sight on his trip in Ghana. He spoke about his excitement at seeing vast stretches of beautiful land. It reminded him of home.

After a week in Kumasi, Paris headed back to the United States. He wrote to say that another friend of his, who was a businessman, would be coming to Ghana to visit with me. They had agreed that if he found a person in whose business they could invest their time and resources, Al Whittaker would travel to train the person. While in Ghana, he would also visit with another person who had started a publishing company in Accra.

Al Whittaker arrived in Ghana in January 1972. By the time he was leaving, they were making arrangements for me to visit their network of Christian businessmen in Washington D.C. Apparently, there Fellowship included not only Christian politicians, but also businessmen, bankers, factory owners, and farmers, all of whom would be happy to share their experiences for my venture in Ghana in any way they could. Al and Paris both believed that it would be encouraging and perhaps even instructive for me to see the kinds of work other farmers were doing in their parts of the world. It turned out it was on this flight back home when Al Whittaker became convinced that they would to set up the Institute for International Development Incorporated (IIDI).

I arrived in Washington D.C. about two weeks later. They arranged for me to live in a beautiful residential unit of The Fellowship. I had no idea how many senators, congressmen and prominent American business executives would show up the next morning for fellowship. Many of them supported the work of missionaries around the world. It was remarkable. They listened to my testimony, and some shared theirs.

One gentleman, Jack Delaney, owned a private jet, and had volunteered to take me to a few agricultural facilities across the United States that very day. Jack was tall and confident. He owned a large future company, and even with his imposing figure, he shared genuinely about how he had found Christ, and why they relished the opportunity to put their faith into action.

He said the same thing Al had said, that it was best to see what was possible, if only I kept my focus on God to lift me higher. Every experience outside my comfort zone caused a paradigm shift and introduced me to a world bigger than I knew existed. I was curious and open-minded, but most importantly, willing to walk in the path God had set for my life. "We want you to see it," Jack said.

I was travelling with Jack in his private jet, next to him in the cockpit, leaving Washington D.C. for Chicago.

"Darko, you know you can fly this plane, right?"

I chimed in quickly, "No, no, no. . ."

"Why not?"

I was sure Jack could hear the shudder in my voice. Just sitting in the cockpit was scary enough.

"Thank you Jack, please let me enjoy the flight this way," as I tried to smile, I was still in awe.

Jack understood my apprehension, but didn't give up. He tried to explain every altitude indicator, radar display, and navigation control. In a few minutes, we had ascended to a safe altitude, and he asked me to take over the control. Every nerve in my body froze.

"Darko, this is why Paris told me to take you to places you didn't imagine you would be, and doing things you didn't see yourself doing".

It was a powerful illustration, but nerve-wracking nonetheless. We landed in Midway Airport in Chicago and drove to a large supermarket that sold only poultry products to wholesalers and distributors. Maury Cable owned the facility, with the name in bold black letters, Chicken Unlimited. We walked around, as if to inspect the operations, paying attention to every detail in the facility. I had never seen a poultry processing facility this sophisticated and impressive. I quickly realized that Jack was talking me on a tour that would be eye-opening and equally life changing.

From Chicago, we travelled to huge corn fields outside Des Moines, Iowa. There were miles and miles of cornfields, and it was evident the commercial farmers in these regions had invested a lifetime into such grand operations. From above, a string of combine harvesters and many trucks went through the fields harvesting corn, and other farmers were working near the huge silos on one end of the farms.

Chapter 15: The Wisdom Of Lights

We spent time with the owners and some of the workers who had just finished their work in the large air-conditioned combined harvesters, blaring loud music, and eating large hamburgers. There was so much to learn in a short space of time, and my eyes captured everything they could.

We left Iowa later in the day and headed south to Gainesville Florida. My time there was spent in one of the largest poultry farms in the area. As of 1972, the company had large hatcheries and even larger industrial poultry hatching machines that were capable of processing 100,000 baby chicks at a time. With ten of such impressive Jamesway incubators working in the facility, it was easy to imagine the reach of such a business. I had time to ask every question running through my mind. I had seen impressive facilities in Israel, but in Gainesville where they didn't have any constraint on land, every facility was much bigger.

Occasionally, I would think aloud, *"Can I do this in Ghana?"*

Jack Delaney would gently remind me, "Darko, sure you can. You can do all things because of Christ who strengthens you".

I remember travelling north to Kentucky. Jack pointed to a field ahead, to my right. It was the large horse tracks that hosted the popular Kentucky Derby event.

He quickly added, "That's where the gamblers go, I won't take you there".

From the airport in Kentucky we drove to the large Pepsi Cola office complex. There was a man Jack wanted me to meet, Colonel Sanders. Even after he sold his company in 1964, the Colonel's office displayed all of his work through the years, from selling chicken in his roadside restaurant to his patented cooking method. He spoke of his faith, and with a sense of humour, talked about some of the challenges he had live through as a businessman in America.

He joked, "Darko, I hear you are a poultry farmer too. Well, people grow chicken, I just fry them".

Colonel Sanders spoke about the Kentucky Fried Chicken (KFC) company for which he was now a brand ambassador, and assisting with franchising.

"You should get a franchise".

This was my first time a thought about franchise had crossed my mind, and now it was Colonel Sanders who was extending an invitation to me.

"When you're ready, you let me know, it is easy".

Jack Delaney tapped my shoulder, "We will talk about that".

A rush of thoughts swirled in my head. We returned to Washington D.C. on 8th February. Paris and Al were to take me to the World Bank to meet executives of Bank of America the same day. They explained their organization's work in developing countries and guaranteed financing for any project I wanted to pursue in agriculture, up to $10 million. Typical funds for African countries seeking to invest in the private sector incurred a 2% interest rate with a ten-year repayment period. For this loan, I had two years for a moratorium. Fortunately, Al Whittaker had spent the time to review my business plan in great detail. The IFC executives were very supportive and securing a loan for such an amount had been much easier than I could have ever imagined.

The next morning was the annual National Prayer Breakfast that was being held at the International Ballroom of the Washington Hilton Hotel. More than 3,000 leaders who had come from around the world were in attendance, including executives in government, the diplomatic corps, and industry. I sat near the stage with Paris and Al, listening intently to every speech and taking every moment to reflect on how far God had brought me.

United States President Richard Nixon spoke that morning, and told a story of President Abraham Lincoln and his men at war, when one asked, "Is God on our side?" Lincoln is famously quoted as telling the man, "I am more concerned not whether God is on our side, but whether we are on God's side".

Chapter 15: The Wisdom Of Lights

His words couldn't be truer. There had never been a moment I didn't pray I was on God's side, because I rested in the confidence that only He could raise me into the future He had set for me.

We spent much of the next day on Capitol Hill to meet with several of the executives' friends who were Senators and members of Congress. Paris wanted to share some of my observations on the large American factories with some of his friends, whom he explained had a heart for any businessman who sought to uplift his community through his work. Over the next four days we had several meetings with different business and faith leaders, as well as many missionaries who were doing great work in some of the remote parts of the world.

I was heading back to Ghana with a new passion for Darko Farms Company Limited. There had been so many things I had seen that I couldn't help but allow them to rekindle my commitment to business and faith all over again. I had set out to build a business to support God's kingdom, and I had been fortunate to spend two life-changing weeks with men and women who devoted their time and hearts to doing the same. I had learned a great deal and had been fortunate to align myself with people who had come into my life, as if only to carry me to the next height that I couldn't reach on my own. I had a band of Christian brothers supporting my every step, and above all, a God who was capable of doing the impossible on my side.

By the time I received the pro-forma invoices from manufacturers and equipment suppliers for the long list of machines I needed, I was ready to expand Darko Farms and develop other business lines, just as I had outlined in my business plan. Ten million dollars had been earmarked to ensure I was successful every step along the way.

Then Ghana's military government under Colonel Kutu Acheampong declared Ghana had decided it would not pay any foreign debts. His policy was *"Yentua"*, which boldly stated "we will not pay", because indebtedness didn't mean a person should starve—*"kafo didi"*. Unfortunately a man who didn't seem to have a good grasp of international business was declaring Ghana would voluntarily kick itself out of international commerce. This stance destroyed the country's economy, and overnight, crushed every plan I was ready to embark on.

All of my hopes, and those of Paris and Al, shattered into a million little pieces. Every funding from the World Bank and investment from the men with whom I had met in the Fellowship at Washington D.C. came to a screeching halt. But for every fire that burned my vision, God was still capable of redemption, and an assurance that our story was far from over, because God reigns over our lives. As disappointing and infuriating as this had become, God surely had a plan of His own. In His own time, God knew how to make beauty from our life's ashes.

* * * * *

In Ghana, military governments crushed private enterprises in ways they couldn't even imagine, and in turn crippled the fragile economies. For every decision made by a country's policy makers, there was always a ripple effect across industries that I wished they'd had the honesty to put at the forefront of their bold declarations. Private investors had been able to take on business risks and make guarantees with their hard work, but unless the governance truly supported a vibrant economy, there was little that an individual could do to make a change.

There was wisdom in learning from the world around us. Economies don't thrive by chance and I had seen that over and again. The triumphs and shortcomings were like lampposts and lights to anyone and any country whose curiosity for truth guided their appetite for building enduring foundations for an economy.

CHAPTER 16

CHOICES

Darko Farms. Business Lessons. Liberia.

The success of Darko Farms Company Limited was never one to be left to chance. That I knew. Ever since I brought 900 baby chicks to a farm to start my company, I decided to employ everything I knew to create an environment that fostered hard work and appreciation. Every moment another person spent on my property was a moment they could be elsewhere, and if I wanted everyone to give their very best to my enterprise, I couldn't ignore reciprocity.

In my business, I followed every legal guideline, from paying taxes to guaranteeing workers' welfare, because I understood that I was part of an economic engine. The overriding principle for me was that if I was not able to hold up my end of the bargain with uncompromised honesty, I wouldn't have grounds for complaining when an employee was dishonest. I paid taxes to the government faithfully, just as the regulations required. I had to make sure every employee who set foot in my company understood this. I paid myself a salary for my work and paid every tax accordingly.

I often thought back to the needless provocation of private enterprise by the PNDC military government in 1981 when the leaders demanded seven years' worth of my company's records. I had every piece of information that supported every business transaction, every cedi, and every pesewa. I worked with men and women to whom my character and leadership was an example, and it was important I set a stage for how integrity ought to lead, even when no one watched.

To succeed as a private business, I had learned that it would take a culture that attracted great people, and retained them. In addition to hundreds of farmers and scientists, I hired accountants and compliance officers, not only to conform to rules but to take every step to ensure our records were accurate. I was helping myself to know where the company stood at every turn.

The poultry business required unwavering dedication. My work was to set a direction, and challenge strangers to believe in it. Decades ago, I had spent nights in my stepfather's garage making sure the chickens were warm and safe, and that passion didn't fade. I had to hire men and women who would be willing to do the same. I understood clearly that it was my responsibility to make sure they had enough for their own survival in order for them to make my vision a priority. The staff's well-being was important to me, because if they succeeded and were willing to work hard, I succeeded.

Back in the early 1960s, I remember working in the state-owned poultry company in Dansoman in Accra, where the workers who had been charged with maintaining the incubators often showed up late or didn't come to work at all. Their role was crucial to our business and for every missed workday, the company suffered. Darko Farms in Akropong-Asante was 12 miles away from the city, and I bought two 40-seater buses to make provision for the people to be at work on time. It was my company, and I had to do whatever it took to make it successful.

It is easy to forget the difference an attitude of excellence can make in a company with a motivated workforce. The small and seemingly insignificant acts added up to become our company's competitive advantage. Success always hinged on paying attention to the details that others might overlook—the little things. My plan was to develop people for their next step, whatever that might be, and in whatever venture they wanted to pursue, even if that was not with my company.

Chapter 16: Choices

For years, I purposely cultivated a culture that rewarded resourcefulness in our employees, and challenged everyone to follow the footsteps of those who worked hard and were invested in our collective success. I had come to believe that if I treated them well, and we worked together, the men and women in the company would be willing to stay and build our business.

As an entrepreneur, I had learned from the moment I embarked on this journey to raise chickens that this was not a business I could do alone. I needed a dedicated workforce, and it was my job to build just what I imagined. I knew what it took to find high-performing talent and give them the tools to excel, and that was driven by a determination to build a company where people felt valued.

In business, I reasoned that training my workforce instantly added to their value, and in turn, added to their worth to the company, and I had to pay them salaries commensurate with the work they did. I couldn't afford to lose the people on whom I had spent money to train, only to have them end up working somewhere else. In farming, as it is with most businesses, continuity works to a company's advantage. As it turned out, people appreciated the genuine recognition and the shared sense of ownership. Even with more than 400 people working in the company at any time, many became a steady and essential part of the business, some for as long as 40 years.

For the senior management staff at Darko Farms, I built apartments in the area so they could live with their families at no cost. It was a cost of doing business. People like the hatchery managers, farm managers, feed mill managers, and processing plant managers were critical to the operations of any poultry business, and it was imperative that they feel a sense of ownership and had a stake in the success of the work they did. It paid huge dividends, because some of the men who lived near the farms were happy to check on the chickens even when they were not on their shifts.

I strategically constructed the Feed Mill, the Hatchery, and the Processing Plant close to the farms. Also, I built twelve three-bedroom flats in the Kumasi town for the management staff that needed accommodation, also at no cost to them. We paid them to afford what they needed to take care of their families. It was an enormous investment in the staff's welfare, but in a real sense, motivation had become the beating heart of a successful enterprise.

I arranged for many of the employees to attend training programs in universities in Israel, Holland, England and Germany. My hope was that every one of my employees would see Darko Farms through my eyes. There was probably nothing more rewarding than investing in men and women to stand on their own. It was my private enterprise, and one where I prayed and worked day and night to see the vision I set out for myself come to life.

One thing I didn't walk away from was an investment in myself. Besides being diligent, I had to be intentional about my own growth. I travelled to institutions like Cornell University in Ithaca, New York for poultry programs, and spent time on several large breeding farms in England. The market changed quickly, and technology, even quicker. As a company evolved, especially one that enjoyed any level of success, what was important was avoiding complacency, and that started with me. I couldn't stop learning, and I couldn't get comfortable.

Ever since I left Ruppin College in 1961, I had ample opportunity to gain practical knowledge from many people with whom I worked. Everyone came with their own expertise and background, and there was something to learn from every one of them. Even the unfortunate relationships from dishonest business partners and insatiable employees taught a lesson worth keeping.

I joined the World Poultry Science Association and attended the yearly International Production and Processing Expo held in Atlanta, Georgia, in the United States. It was in Atlanta that I learned about some of the most impressive scientific advances in the poultry industry. Leading drug manufacturers like Pfizer, Novartis, and GlaxoSmithKline displayed innovative drugs, and medical device companies like Siemens and Abbott Laboratories brought pioneering technologies into commercial agriculture.

Prominent research universities across the world shared their own insights on animal science including tracing and preventing common diseases. I took technical literature back home, and most importantly, took the time to review all of it with my staff. If I wanted to build a successful company and give myself a fighting chance through the turbulent economic and political regimes, I had to invest in myself, just as much as I did in the people who worked on my farms.

Early on, I was in Springdale, Arkansas, in the United States to visit the Tyson Foods facility. As a food processing company, it had become one of the world's largest processors and marketers of chicken, beef, and pork to retail grocers, foodservice distributors, and restaurant chains. It was impressive to see the hundreds of scientists working on a large compound to develop different poultry products, spices, and even machines they needed for their operations. There was much to learn from their operations, and for every company I visited, I looked for what unique traits we could learn.

In a few years, my wife Christiana resigned from the hospital and set up a clinic at the company's head office. She hired nurses to rotate weekly schedules and a doctor from Okomfo Anokoye Hospital in Kumasi town to assist. There was no clinic in the area where the farm was located, so it was a blessing to the community having a facility where the farmers and their families could receive medical care.

Investing in our people and our community was incredibly important to me. I had learned that first-hand and I had been blessed to be able to implement the same in my company. Now, I was pleasantly surrounded by men and women of different backgrounds and skill sets working together to build a company. It was particularly humbling to see how even at the height of the famine that swept through Ghana in 1983, the staff still had plenty to eat at the farm's canteen, and they were happy to be at work. On the farm, it felt like a world away from the anxiety and gloom. It was true indeed that when you treated people well, they did their best, even in the face of incredible odds.

It took a shock event one afternoon in January 1983 to drive home the value of planning ahead in any business venture. Often, life's harshest winds blow unannounced, and for people who fail to plan, occasionally all it takes was one disaster and to wipe away everything they've built through the years.

In one afternoon, all we saw at first was thick smoke blowing towards the farms. A bushfire had started in the dense forests from the neighbouring acreage, and it was travelling quickly. It was the dry Harmattan season and the sudden sight of a wide swath of burning bushes marching towards my farms struck unimaginable fear in all of us. Everyone hurried to the fire stations we had constructed at the perimeters of the farm.

We had trained our staff to respond to such emergencies, having planned for it with fire drills over and again, but praying we never had to go through it. It was the same forethought to prepare for the worst that had made us erect huge disinfectant baths at the company's entrance to ensure that all vehicles entering the property were properly inspected and sanitized. There were more than 50,000 chickens to protect. Safety was an attitude I had embedded in my operations, and on that afternoon, with raging fires bearing down at my property, I was thankful for the wisdom to have installed commercial firefighting equipment. But fires burned, quickly.

What saved Darko Farms were the hydrants that had been installed years before any such incident occurred. The fire hydrants on the farms had been carefully constructed at vantage points to combat fires, and I had seen how effective they had been years ago in several farms around the world. In Ghana, no one required me to install hydrants on my farm, but I knew it was the right thing to do, and that was an investment I was willing to make.

Sadly, even the large cities in Ghana didn't have any fire hydrants in cases of emergency, and the ones that had been erected decades ago had been abandoned. In many places, there was not even a steady supply of water in the event of an emergency like raging fires. I couldn't afford to overlook such vital installations, and risk lives and livestock on my property.

The men rushed to the water stations connected to large water hoses and jumped to fence lines. By the time the Ghana Fire Service crew arrived, the staff had combatted a fire that would have easily overpowered them, simply because they didn't even have the right equipment to fight that vast stretch of burning bush. I remember how after only a few minutes of trying to help, the fire service crew run out of water. Their plan was to rush to the nearest water source, ten miles away, and be back as quickly as they could. Counting only on their help would have left behind clouds of dust and loss.

In every step I took as a businessman, I had made huge investments to protect my farm because it meant everything to me. Thankfully, I had developed the muscle of veracity, instead of seeking outside validation to do what I knew in my heart was right.

* * * * *

It was in 1990 that my life got caught in the crossfire of what became the brutal civil war in Liberia. I lived my life in complete trust that God's grace always protects His children in moments where only He can carry us through.

William Tolbert owned the Mezzarado Group of Companies, which had a lot of investments in large poultry farms. It had large feed mills and hatchery. The company also invested in large fisheries along the Liberian coast and several other companies that brought Tolbert enormous wealth.

After a coup d'état that brought military leader Samuel Doe to power, businessmen like Tolbert whose private enterprises were mingled with politics lost many of their assets to the military. Even though they had confiscated many companies that belonged to former government officials, the military officers had no idea how to maintain the properties.

Tolbert's wife Kamina came to meet me in Ghana. She had heard of my company from one of the companies whose employees I had trained on my farms. Her husband's assets were in decline and the army had by now constructed living quarters on the property. She had seen her husband build the business for many years, and now, none of the soldiers they had put in charge had any real experience to manage such a huge farm.

Kamina needed my help. She promised she would reach Samuel Doe, who was Head of State and plead with his military government to allow my company to help save the farm. I was a poultry farmer in Ghana with facilities in Akropong-Asante, and several offices in different parts of the country. I had formed business relationships with commercial farms and entrepreneurs in different parts of Africa, and it was one such contact that led me to Monrovia, Liberia.

Doe invited me to Liberia shortly after. The farm was huge, yet some of the very modern and expensive machines sat in the same place they'd been for several months. A poultry farm with such huge economic potential was struggling to keep its flock alive. The chickens looked frail and sick. Some had died and it looked as though the rest of the birds were infected.

I walked around the facility and observed some of the simple maintenance they had ignored, which had quickly turned what must have once been an impressive poultry farm into a facility that was falling apart. Most of the chicken had Coccidiosis, a parasitic disease that affected chicken and poultry through ingestion. Their ruffled feathers and the blood in the droppings told the story of how unkempt they had been. It was easy for parasites to enter a chicken's system through food or drink water contaminated with infected soil or faeces from other infected birds. That was certainly the case on this farm. I recommended we quickly get the birds the drugs that had been sitting on the shelf the

Chapter 16: Choices

entire time. Amprollium and Clopidol helped to block the parasites from multiplying and worsening the infection in the intestinal tracts of the chickens. The drugs had sat on the shelf while the chickens were dying, but the soldiers had no idea what they were.

I was in Liberia for three days, and by the time I was ready to leave, the birds were full of life again. The military supervisors told Samuel Doe.

Kamina Tolbert was excited that Doe agreed for me to officially become a consultant, as someone who actually knew how to run a poultry farm. Even though the tension and rumours of another civil war swirled, Samuel Doe had no reason to believe that his government would be short-lived.

I went back to Accra and had two of my staff begin a thorough review of the contract terms and begin the appraisals. I returned to Monrovia a few days later to begin the final negotiations and commence work on the farms.

I was at the executive mansion with Samuel Doe and his military soldiers getting ready to sign the contract when Doe received word that Charles Taylor and his the National Patriotic Front of Liberia (NPFL) and with Prince Yormie Johnson's rebel group, the Independent National Patriotic Front of Liberia (INPFL), were advancing toward Monrovia in what was bound to be an all-out bloody confrontation.

Samuel Doe asked me to leave immediately. He sensed a bloodbath, and assured me that his people would contact me to return once the dust settled. The soldiers whisked me away to the Roberts International Airport. We reached the airport just in time for me to board the Ghana Airways flight that had just arrived from Dakar, en route to Ghana. I was in the air by the time the violence took over Monrovia and plunged the country into one of the bloodiest civil wars in Africa's history. Every day I heard the news of the atrocities and gruesome murders in the Liberia civil war, I couldn't help but remember that afternoon when I arrived at the airport just in time to fly out of the country. It was surreal, as if the plane had landed in Monrovia just for me. God had made a way of escape and spared my life.

With Samuel Doe dead in the civil war, and Kamina Tolbert leaving for the United States, the Monrovia farm project never took off. Yet, I had nothing to be disappointed over. Even though the poultry project in Liberia would have opened new doors for my business in western Africa, nothing compared to the agony that the men and women endured having to flee the civil war in the country. They had to leave everything they knew, and sometimes even painfully, family members, to make it out on a boat heading to Sierra Leone, Côte D'Ivoire, or Ghana. They had no idea of who or what awaited them on the other side, but it was an ordeal they embraced, with rebel forces hunting down anyone they could find, and gunfire filling the Monrovia skies.

Some were heading to Ghana on the Black Star Line. Fortunately, many of the people with whom I had worked setting up the Fellowship in Monrovia were safely aboard the ship heading to Tema, Ghana. I was in Kumasi when I received a phone call from an operator on the Black Star Line. Provision had been made for the refugees who were able to make arrangements with someone they knew in Ghana to assist upon their arrival. I arranged immediately for a young Asamoah Manu to rush to Tema to meet Richard Morris.

He had been fortunate to have survived the dread of war, and landed in Ghana with his wife and family. They were now refugees, all hungry, angry, broken, yet grateful. The road ahead was bound to be challenging, and all that some of us could do was to support them in any way we could, and give them hope.

I had arranged for about 35 of my Christian brothers and sisters from Liberia and their families to live in a residential compound I owned in the Tema area. Another 30 came to live in several of my properties in Kumasi. I couldn't fathom what went through their minds every day, but there was a shared sense of gratitude even though their lives were now in disarray, never knowing how much they could ever salvage. I was fortunate to be able to help the few people with whom I shared many of their days in Ghana. Many of them stayed with my family for about a year after which they either obtained a visa to the United States, or travelled to Côte D'Ivoire.

Over the next few months, Ghana's government organized soldiers to join the ECOWAS Ceasefire Monitoring Group (ECOMOG) peacekeeping force. The ECOMOG was a West African multilateral armed force established by the Economic Community of West African States (ECOWAS) to help end the civil war in Liberia. Over the next several years, they would be part of the difficult work of halting the bloodshed. Hundreds of thousands of Liberians died in the country's ruthless civil war, and more than one million people were forced to flee their homes.

Darko Farms had supplied chicken and eggs to the Ghana military, as one of our customers in Ghana. It became another great opportunity to donate eggs and chickens to the ECOMOG peacekeeping forces. As the crisis continued, Ghanaian government set up a camp for Liberian refugees in Buduburam, a town that was a few miles west of Accra. Darko Farms was blessed to donate to the families in the refugee camp, and with every tray of eggs that I hoped would bring a little smile to someone's heart, I remembered how I had been blessed not to have been caught in the same bloody conflict.

The only time I went back to Liberia was to supply day-old chicks to Baker's Farms, in Monrovia. It was after the war, this time to a farmer I had met while studying in Cornell University in Ithaca, New York. Nothing brought more reassurance to my life than knowing very well that God's hand had indeed guided my feet, and pulled me away from harm.

Over and again, I had seen His provision in my life and my business. I chose to honour God with everything I had. God opened doors I never dreamed of, and gave me the resources to open some more for others. God had also shut those doors that weren't in His will for my life. He had been my very present help in a time of need.

CHAPTER 17

MUSTARD SEED

Sinapi Aba. Opportunity International. Hope.

"I tell you the truth, if you had faith even as small as a mustard seed, you could say to this mountain, 'Move from here to there,' and it would move. Nothing would be impossible".
~ Matthew 17:20

In 1993, I was at my company's head office in Kumasi, making final preparations to travel to Hong Kong and China, when four gentlemen walked in: Jonathan Wilson, a minister with the Christian Life Center (CLC) in Australia, David Freeman, a Ghanaian preacher who had been living in Australia, Larry Reed, a businessman and missionary working in small towns in Zimbabwe and Kwame Opoku, who was assisting Freeman in his work in Ghana.

They had come to discuss a business partnership, a micro-lending institution. They were forthright in why they had come to me. Their venture was one that required the backing of a businessman, and importantly, a person who would have the heart to uplift people who might otherwise never get a helping hand. Inasmuch as I wanted to hear the details of their proposal, my mind was occupied with another potential business venture with Chinese partners who were waiting on my arrival in Hong Kong in a few days. All I remember the men saying over and again was that their vision was to *help the poorest of the poor*. The timing didn't help.

The men agreed to schedule another meeting upon my return. The best they could do was to give me every piece of information they had on the proposal, and I would have more than ample time to review it once I was on my flight to China. As with the evaluation of any business opportunity, even one that was not meant for profit, I still had to do my own through review rather than taking another person's word for it. I had a good sense of what key information I needed to make sure the proposition was worth my time and investment. I promised to give them my response upon my return. At least, I would let them know of my thoughts about their proposal.

Davis Freeman had returned to Ghana from Australia to set up a local CLC church, and was working with his fellow CLC preacher Jonathan Wilson, who had travelled along to Ghana to help find new opportunities to expand the CLC's footprint in Africa. To them, missionary work was much more than a spiritual outreach and inviting people to join church fellowships. They wanted a tangible and practical way to uplift local communities in small towns and villages, especially men and women who were stuck in an endless cycle of poverty and dejection.

Larry Reed was a missionary in Zimbabwe in southern Africa, committed to reaching people in remote communities, not only in large cities like Harare and Bulawayo. He had set up Zamboku Micro Lending Institution, a program established by the international non-profit group, Opportunity International. The organization was non-denominational but had an urgent goal of helping to eradicate extreme poverty around the world. Their task was daunting, but the men who set out to embark on this journey believed that there was nothing impossible for their God to do in the lives of men and women who commited themselves to work their hardest, and turn their hearts to God. The founders of Opportunity International, Al Whittaker and David Bussau, had decided back in 1971 to take a bold step into developing countries, and that was what took Larry to Zimbabwe. Now they wanted to start the same program in Ghana.

Chapter 17: Mustard Seed

The four men had reached out to me because if they were to set up a non-profit organization in Ghana, they needed a businessman in the country to serve on its board. On the flight to Hong Kong, I read everything—brochures, flyers, and newsletters. Aboard the British Airways flight, I smiled broadly to myself. Every word in their proposal felt like a *déjà vu*.

Two years earlier, I had planned to set up Kwabena Darko Foundation with the intent of reaching people across Ghana with programs that would empower them to support themselves and their families, while ministering to their spiritual needs. I had discussed setting up a foundation with my friend Richard Morris, who was in Ghana when the Liberian Civil War had ravaged much of his home country. He had served as the President of the Fellowship there.

Back in Liberia, brother Morris had been in charge of a small savings and loans company and had been an excellent resource. In one evening, I remember him sitting behind a desk and outlining an entire business plan in great detail, but with a simplicity that came from experience. He understood every nuance in setting up such a company, and was especially diligent in working with international organizations. I completed all the legal documentation and marketing material to start Kwabena Darko Foundation, but I had to wait until an opportune time to implement the non-profit idea.

It was a rather remarkable coincidence that the vision of Opportunity International was the same as what I had intended to do a few years earlier. It was more than a coincidence; it had to be God's hand. Around the world, and particularly so in developing countries, there was an opportunity to give hope to millions of people who were determined to invest in their future through some vocational or entrepreneurial endeavour. It was not difficult to see the facts on the ground in Ghana, most didn't have any meaningful resource to step out. That was a reality I was well aware of, and one that had been a pressing need to my heart.

I had no reservations in joining the vision of Opportunity International, in fact, this was a chance to merge the vision of Kwabena Darko Foundation into another, to serve the same purpose. I did not know anything about Opportunity International at the time, but everything I read about the organization sparked joy in my heart to step up and help.

In a few days, I sent word to Larry Reed that the work they planned to embark on in Ghana was exactly what I had always wanted to do. We arranged to take the next step. At the heart of the vision was one thing that I knew very well, that Ghanaians were not lazy. Often so many are stuck in cycles of poverty that irrespective of their hard work, they never are able to break free.

Shrewd individuals, who also recognized this, took advantage of their work ethic, often making the men and women work for every minute of the day, and still have almost nothing to take care of their own families. It felt disheartening watching the people in the country's busy streets plying trades as hawkers who sold anything they could find. The men pushed handcarts in every corner and through crowds to find someone to buy their goods. Pregnant women and mothers with infant babies tightly strapped on to their backs ran through cars and motorcycles chasing a smile from a driver or passenger who might buy something they carried. Their lives were crushed when all the items they had carried to the roadsides ended up on the ground, or even worse, their lives were cut short in the middle of a street at the hands of an innocent driver who didn't see them running. There had never been a moment whelm their plight didn't strike me to my core.

I felt their pain, because I had walked in their shoes before. I had woken up early in the mornings and with a large wooden tray on my head, walked through lorry parks and local markets hoping to sell everything my mother and grandmother could find. As a young boy, with a cloth wrapped around my neck into a "collar", another tightly wound into a cushion on my head—we called it kashire—I walked the dusty

Chapter 17: Mustard Seed

streets every day just to earn just enough for my mother to provide food for her children. No one saw my mother's pain. I did. I remembered still.

It had taken God's providence and grace for me to stand when I was now, and I knew there were many hardworking women just like my mother who struggled every day and night but seemed to get nowhere. My poor mother was desperate but she was determined to do whatever it took to take care of four young children. She couldn't let her children see the agony of poverty, but now I knew enough to realize what the men and women in those situations must go through every morning. My desire was to find a way to change their destiny and hopefully that of their children by given them an opportunity like the one I'd had. The solution had come to me with involvement with Opportunity International.

We agreed to send Kwame Opoku to Zimbabwe to learn how Zamboku had successfully reached the towns and villages with a sustainable micro-lending initiative. Our world was not too different, and if it worked in Zimbabwe, there was much of its application we could easily implement in Ghana. And we did. We decided to set up the non-profit organization in Kumasi and start with the people in the surrounding areas, like Kwadaso, Tanoso, Bantama, and AshTown. Across the country, there were millions of micro-enterprises all with the same basic problem. If any program were to fulfil their ambition, they desperately needed financial support, financial literacy, and a realistic pathway to changing the course of their family's future.

Together with Jonathan Wilson, Davis Freeman, and Larry Reed, I set up the board with other local business leaders and preachers who shared the vision, and understood the heart of the work we wanted to do. There was no intent on turning this into a profit-making enterprise; instead, it was a single vision to empower the poorest of the poor, stuck in a perpetual cycle of poverty and misery. The most powerful thing we could do as Christians was to find a way to uplift our brothers and sisters.

For the people whose livelihoods depended on what they sold in a day, what drove them every morning to the busy roadsides was a desire for dignity in their own lives, an industrious work ethic, and hope. They set out every day without a trace of what they would find, but in their hearts, the God who takes care of even the birds in the sky, would take care of them. They were people who didn't ask for charity; they wanted an opportunity.

Opportunity International had worked in developing regions in Indonesia, Philippines, India, and many parts of Asia, and had incredible experience and resources. They agreed to help train the group in Ghana. In every meeting, the training team emphasized the underlying vision, seeking to emulate the Good Samaritan whose compassion transcended culture, religion, and status. The work was to transform lives. As a non-profit organization, we would be able to solicit funds from donor agencies and individuals who saw our hearts' genuine intent to help, and saw the need.

We agreed to use my home in Kumasi as a start, while we worked through every detail in setting up the organization and the outreach strategy. Soon after, we moved to occupy some of the offices I had in Adum, Kumasi. Fortunately, all the equipment and furniture I had used for the political campaign and election in 1992 were still arranged neatly in the offices, as if God knew I will need all of them for an entirely new purpose.

The opportunity we had to share our faith in a real way meant people would see the Jesus we confess to, and hear the message of freedom and hope, without even having to lift a Bible. If we truly cared about our neighbours as ourselves, our hearts would bleed for the pain they endured. Now, we had a chance to do something bold, something new. It was more than stepping out to be generous. Our guidance was to run a sustainable program driven by the accountability of anyone in our network, and also the compassion to see everyone as extensions of ourselves.

Chapter 17: Mustard Seed

We needed a name for the organization. We prayed. Jesus' parable of the mustard seed was a powerful illustration of what we were believing and what we hoped to do in Ghana. In the scriptures, Jesus had told his disciple about how "The kingdom of heaven is like a mustard seed, which a man took and planted in his field. Though it is the smallest of all seeds, yet when it grows, it is the largest of garden plants and becomes a tree, so that the birds come and perch in its branches". That was our vision. A seed does nothing until it is planted in fertile soil, and that was what we had an opportunity to do. "Mustard seed" translated in the Twi language as *sinapi aba*. The organization was named Sinapi Aba Trust.

In the popular parable, Jesus referenced a seed so small it is almost impossible to see why He would imagine that faith that size could move anything. It was a powerful illustration of potential. It was the same small mustard seed having the ability to grow into a huge tree and capable of ripping through structures that once seemed insurmountable. The imagery was one of how our faith in what God can do for each of us doesn't have to be outwardly large to make an impact in our world.

We were setting out on a simple mission but one that was incredibly powerful. We were asking men and women in places where banks and financial institutions wouldn't go, to have the faith to change themselves and their families. We were inviting men and women to take a first bold step out on faith, for God's grace to meet them where they could not walk on their own. We were setting out to empower people to invest in themselves, irrespective of their stations in life.

In our organization, the men and women we hoped to reach were the ones with a dedication to work hard every day and every night, and all they needed was an opportunity. Every one of the people who devoted his or her time and energy to this mission truly believed we could make a difference in all the lives we touched. Sure, we were imperfect people, yet we believed that a person didn't have to be a prominent evangelist, a charismatic politician, or wealthy entrepreneur to make a difference in their world. A seemingly small act of kindness by anyone can be the mountain-moving influence in someone else's life. I was selected as Board Chairman of Sinapi Aba Trust in June 1994.

In no time, the fruits of our hard work were evident in some of the women who walked through our doors. We had become the family they never had, and the friends they'd prayed to find. It was sobering to hear the stories of young women who travelled long distances from villages around the country in search of greener pastures in the urban areas. They didn't have any permanent residential addresses and no collateral to secure any financial assistance.

Many slept in storefronts in the heat and the cold, holding tightly to their little children; some of their nights even saw the horror of rape and crime. Many of them didn't have even a person who could be their guarantor. Their poverty was bound to be perpetuated, and there were also people in society who were happy to take advantage of their predicament. Those were the poor in our society struggling to change their lives, and were the ones Sinapi Aba sought to uplift. We were choosing to take a risk, and to do so in the faith that anyone with whom we shared our purpose would honour the trust we had placed in them.

The eye-opening misconception in micro-lending was the belief that these men and women who needed our help might not pay, and the organization would not have any way to find them. Surprisingly, they were faithful, and that gave us the confidence to open our organization to more and more people. It was as if our own mustard seed had blossomed in front of our very own eyes.

We were able to provide financial assistance and entrepreneurial training to individuals and groups from tailors and seamstresses, shoemakers and bag makers to furniture makers and hairdressers. We helped the food sellers and chop bars, ice cream makers, bakers, and confectionery owners. We aided men and women in poultry, vegetable farming, and small scale retailers of foodstuffs like beans, rice, maize, and groundnuts. The impact was immediate.

Chapter 17: Mustard Seed

Years ago, I told the story of a young woman who would show up at Darko Farms only to buy four trays of eggs. Each tray contained 30 eggs, and that was all she could afford. There would be a stretch of days when she didn't show up, but she would suddenly reappear after a while. She left the farms every time with a spark in her eyes, a sharp contrast to the broken demeanour with which she had walked in. She told how if she was lucky enough to have an individual lend her money to pursue any trade, the lenders wanted 60%, 100%, or sometimes even more in return. She remained indebted to lenders, but still hoped she would be able to have a few cedis left over to buy food for her family.

I was willing to help, if she was willing to keep her end of the bargain. As a micro-lending organization, we demanded accountability and a willingness to learn from people who were able to assist in financial literacy programs. She agreed and started the program with the same four trays. With a lending rate that was almost negligent, she could afford to sell four times what she had sold in a few days, because she didn't have to charge exorbitant prices just to make a payment to a lender. After a while, she could afford to buy more eggs and have enough money to pay for everything she bought immediately. The young lady excelled, and her hard work paid an immediate dividend in her finances, and also her life.

Her story was no different from the women who owned small bakeries, but used dilapidated ovens that burned their faces and eyes every time they reached for the loaves of bread. They had borrowed money from lenders at high-interest rates to buy flour and now they had little choice but to sell all the bread they could quickly, so they'd be able to return the money. They spent every night unsure of what the next day held in store.

Then there were female head porters—*kayayei*—most of whom had migrated from other parts of the country to find work in the cities. If they were fortunate, all they owned would be the large pans they carried on their heads, in which they piled heavy loads from the markets throughout the day. Occasionally some found their way into jobs as domestic help. Many wanted more for their lives and their future, and wanted an opportunity to learn a new trade in which they could earn a decent wage and take care of their families.

The work we had taken upon ourselves to do demanded Christ-centred values to see the worth of a person, just as Christ saw them. Ours was an organization built on the teaching that the strong in society can indeed help the weak. Our programs charged interest, but only minimally, just to ensure that everyone in the program learned the value of money and how to successfully manage their own finances.

Perhaps the best part of Sinapi Aba Trust was widening our reach in such a way that the women brought in people in their network who needed the same help they had secured. By now, the participants had people to guarantee for them and an added responsibility to honour their pledges, not only to pay, but to strive to reach higher. Our community needed everyone doing their best, and if we could help pull many out of the clutches of poverty, we would have given them the hope to dream much bigger than the confines of their current station in life. It was amazing to discover how even a little financial assistance could have a powerful ripple effect on the lives of the men and women we met.

Sinapi Aba Trust had access to Opportunity International's training materials, rooted in Christian values and in different areas of business and finance. We used these as a resource to offer business advice and support, and most importantly give the workers a platform to share their own testimonies with each other. The most effective witnesses were the ones who had truly experienced the freedom that only came from God's grace, and their own persistence. We were privileged to pray with them and lead them to the knowledge of Jesus Christ.

Opportunity International helped to raise funds to assist with the local programs and to enable us to reach even more people. We were blessed with a one and half million dollars funding from United States Agency for International Development (USAID), the independent

United States federal government agency that administers civilian foreign aid and development assistance around the world. There were also generous sponsors like Opportunity Network, Official Development Assistance (ODA) in the UK, Hilden Charitable Fund, Archbishop of Australia Fund, and the Christian Life Center (CLC). Their generosity reaffirmed our faith to keep pressing ahead and bringing hope to rural communities and towns. I have been blessed beyond my own expectations with a privilege to tell our story and also to raise millions of dollars for the outreach projects.

From its start in 1994, Sinapi Aba Trust had grown into a micro-lending organization that built more than vocations for young men and women in Ghana's rural areas. We built hope. Their joy and opportunity to step out of the shadows of life was our priceless reward. Devoted men and women like Joseph Ebo Hewton, David Asante-Adjei, Thomas F. Asare, J.K. Kodua, Dr. Dorothy Danso, Ken Appenteng-Mensah, Dr. John Oduro-Boateng, and J.E. Acquaye, joined the board and continued to work pro bono with our focus remaining on guiding the organization.

Another part of our work that brought me so much fulfilment in Opportunity International was a leadership training with Haggai International, an American-based Christian organization that seeks to equip leaders to increase their knowledge and influence in any area where God had placed them. All around the world, they taught the leaders about how transformation in communities happens when people with compassionate and Christ-centred values lead.

Haggai International operated from the United States Island of Hawaii, and that was one place where I witnessed an incredibly powerful program aimed at tackling broader social issues and transforming communities and nations with Christ's provision at the centre of its vision. My years in the Haggai International were some of the most critical ones in my Christian leadership training. The organization had set out to train leaders to redeem nations and transform every aspect of life through the Gospel of Jesus Christ.

For two weeks, men and women who were seasoned business professionals and leaders and established entrepreneurs sharpened their faith and knowledge as part of the organization's Senior Servants' Ministry. Founded by John Haggai, the purpose was to encourage all of us to use the talents and opportunities that God had given us to reach other leaders, and encourage them to grow in the Lord. We were servants for Christ and the organization hoped to strategically position men and women to demonstrate the Gospel of Christ in their nations and to their people. Even though I had committed to doing the same as part of the Full Gospel Business Men's Fellowship International, it was incredibly rewarding to have the chance to inspire others. We were seeking to build leaders in different fields.

In the years after I had first attended the meeting in Hawaii, I had the privilege of sharing my testimony to others who had travelled from different parts of the world. For Haggai International, I was honoured with the role of selecting individuals for sponsorship to the immersive three-month program in Singapore, Southeast Asia, where the focus would be on preparing their hearts to serve the needy. As tasking as it was, it was rewarding as a servant of Christ to meet with high-ranking policymakers in the United States and around the world who shared the same passion for outreach. My work started to open many doors to other international organizations and prominent businessmen who heard the testimonies of the men and women from the villages and towns in Ghana, and saw how every credit was to God who had given us the grace to reach our world.

In all the years, the organizations' focus remained the same as it had been from the start. In Opportunity International, there were still the Support Partners around the world; organizations, government agencies, and individuals, and Implementing Partners who were local organizations who did the work at the grassroots, and interfaced with the local communities. No individual owned Sinapi Aba Trust, rather, it was an implementing partner of the program, and every fund raised was to address a specific purpose in the Opportunity International vision.

Chapter 17: Mustard Seed

The biggest surprise for me as part of Opportunity International was crossing paths with Al Whittaker again. This was too much of a twist of fate for me to believe it was an accident. Again, it had to be God. It was the same Al Whittaker I had met in 1972 through missionary Paris Reidhead, and who together with a group of Christian businessmen in America did everything they could to encourage me in my business.

It was through Al and his friends at the Fellowship that I first walked through the doors at the World Bank and secured a $10 million investment, a seat at the National Prayer Breakfast in Washington D.C. with business and faith leaders from all over the world, and an offer to own a Kentucky Fried Chicken (KFC) franchise in Ghana, all in 1972. Sadly, the doors were shut on one huge investment opportunity after another in Ghana, because of the country's military government at the time. It had taken 22 years for our lives to come back full circle.

It was unbelievable, and the joy in both of our eyes during a reunion in Al's home in Chicago paled in comparison only to our embrace, like long lost brothers who never imagined how God would bring us together again. I was reading a book Al had written, *Opportunity Knocks*, where he recalled having travelled to Ghana in the early 1970s to help two young businesspeople, one being a poultry farmer in Kumasi. It was on his way back to America that he felt the urge to devote his life to the Institute for International Development Incorporated (IIDI), which eventually became Opportunity International. Until then, I never had any idea that he was involved in any such project.

By 2004, after serving for 10 years as the Board Chairman of Sinapi Aba Trust, I was appointed the Board Chairman of Opportunity International Worldwide, and was also elected to the U.S. Board, working from my office in Chicago, Illinois in the United States.

Opportunity International Savings and Loans (OISL) was founded also in 2005 to offer deposit services and increase outreach to marginalized rural families and communities. Separately, Sinapi Aba Savings and Loans Company was set up as an independent non-banking financial institution that specialized in accepting savings deposits and extending financial services to micro and small enterprises.

Across Ghana, the message of hope and opportunity for a *mustard seed* to bloom into its full potential travelled as far west as Axim and Dormaa Ahenkro, Aflao and Hohoe to the east, and north through Techiman and Salaga to Bolgatanga. It was this same servant's heart that opened a new opportunity for me to serve on the Bank of Ghana Board. God had given me the grace to serve and to reach people in Ghana and across the world to a much higher degree than I had hoped for. There was much more to be done, and I could only pray that many people in our communities who were able would find it in their hearts to reach others who needed their help, and invest in their future.

Indeed, God has been faithful to His word, His plans were much bigger and bolder than my own. I have been blessed beyond all measure.

CHAPTER 18

DREAMERS AND LIFECHANGERS

Luke Society. Edify.

I remember meeting Oduro-Boateng when he was a teenager at Opoku Ware Secondary School, in Kumasi. It was one of the schools under my care as part of the chaplaincy committee to evangelize in Catholic schools in Ghana. We were on the school's campus on Sunday afternoons and occasionally during the week to meet with the students and encourage them in faith. It was in one of such meetings that I met a young John Oduro-Boateng.

I had not seen him again, until he showed up at my residence some thirty years later. He came with a request for me to serve as Board Chairman for a medical mission organization in Ghana. Apparently, after his secondary school in Kumasi, he had continued to the University of Ghana medical school and was later awarded a scholarship to continue his medical education at the University of Copenhagen hospital network. In Denmark, he practiced medicine in both the Glostrup Hospital and Rigs Hospital in the Copenhagen area.

I never knew that John had secured a job with Uniroyal Company to work as a resident medical doctor in the company's rubber plantations in Buchanan City, Liberia. The burden on his heart was for him to return home, to Ghana.

John remembers joining a Christian fellowship on the massive rubber plantations with several missionaries who lived in the small bungalows in the area. They were part of the Christian Reform Church, and when they heard about John's craving to serve in his country, to do medical missions and evangelism in his village, they encouraged him to write a letter to Dr. Peter Boelens.

Halfway around the world, Dr. Boelens, an American medical missionary working to reach developing countries around the world, was working in Latin America and Asia, having opened medical facilities in Iloilo Island and Negros Island, in the Philippines; Tuni, India, and later Olancho, in Honduras.

The organization was the Luke Society, an interdenominational Christian ministry whose focus was finding indigenous medical professionals who were willing to serve in their local communities, to bring hope and physical healing found only in Jesus Christ. The ministry's work was a striking departure from the traditional mission because it understood the fundamental relationships that existed in communities, one that would take decades to establish, but a person could reach his or her own people overnight because of the bond they already shared.

At the very core of the mission was a requirement of the medical professional to be a person with a heart to serve, and to lead men and women to the knowledge of Christ's salvation. This was the reason why the Luke Society required the medical professional to also be a committed Christian who saw this as a rare opportunity to minister, not one to suit a personal career ambition.

Dr. Peter Boelens reached out to John Oduro-Boateng and expressed interest in working with him in Ghana. John was thrilled at the opportunity, one that would help him establish a clinic in his hometown, Kasei, in Ghana's Ashanti region. There would be no greater fulfilment for him.

For the program to work, however, John needed to find a born again Christian entrepreneur who would be willing to come alongside him,

Chapter 18: Dreamers And Lifechangers

to serve as the chairman of the local organization's non-profit board. A young John Oduro-Boateng spent days thinking about anyone he could reach, anyone who would satisfy the two requirements by the Luke Society.

Out of nowhere, John said my name popped into his mind. The last time he had seen me was in 1967 while he was in secondary school. The moment came back to him as if it had just happened. What he couldn't forget was that I had been the Scripture Union leader who had helped him anchor his faith in Christ.

I was scheduled to travel to Manilla, Philippines, by the time he reached me. It had been nearly 30 years. He spoke about the Luke Society with such a joy that it was evident he had found something that gave him the rare chance to serve the Lord and his community with his skill. I asked him to give me some time to think about his request, and said I would discuss it further when I was back in Ghana after a few weeks.

Apparently, Dr. Boelens had called John to find out if he had made any progress finding a Christian businessman or businesswoman who would be interested in supporting the vision in Ghana. John explained that he had mentioned the idea to me but I was busy making preparations to travel to a Christian conference in the Philippines and had promised to contact him when I returned. He gave my name to Dr. Boelens.

Dr. Peter Boelens knew all about the conference in Manilla, Philippines. His ministry had supported American evangelist Billy Graham through the years and he knew all about the Lausanne Conference. They had no plans to attend, but if the one person John Oduro-Boateng needed was heading to the Philippines, Dr. Boelens decided he would too.

The Lausanne conference in 1989, Lausanne II, expected more than 7,000 Christians from all corners of the world, and somehow Dr. Boelens and his wife hoped that they would find me. He tried to find information from Billy Graham's office in Charlotte, North Carolina but the only way to ensure our path would cross would be to travel nearly 10,000 miles to the Philippines. He prayed that God would somehow lead him to a Ghanaian businessman named Kwabena Darko.

That was when I arrived in Manilla. I had no way of knowing Peter Boelens and his wife had flown from North Carolina to the Philippines to find me. The only problem is that they had no idea what I looked like, so they hoped they would bump into a delegation from Ghana, and that one of them might know me. Elders from the Assemblies of God church like Reverend B. Asore, and other charismatic leaders like Baptist preacher Reverend Steve Asante, had been invited. I had received an invitation, together with my wife as Christian leaders from Ghana.

We were in a long line together with hundreds of people to get our registration bags and conference tags. There were about five lines on either side of ours. Occasionally our eyes met those of the people either standing behind us or in front of us to exchange a polite smile, or say hello. No one started any conversation.

My wife Christiana and I reached the registration table and received our tags. I pinned hers on her shirt. She in turn pinned my tag on my pocket. We had to walk over to the next line for another set of information, but just as I turned, the couple who had stood behind us the entire time stepped towards the registration table. Their eyes glanced at our tag and the name "Darko" leaped at Dr. Boelens.

He exclaimed, *"Darko! Are you from Ghana?"*

I nodded slowly but was a little unsure about the sudden excitement from a man who had stood behind me for about 20 minutes and never said a word.

"Are you Darko, the poultry farmer in Ghana?"

"Yes, I am Kwabena Darko".

My wife assumed he must have been a person I crossed paths with at a Full Gospel Businessmen's meeting, or perhaps he had heard my name

Chapter 18: Dreamers And Lifechangers

from someone, and now coincidentally we had met. This was far from a coincidence. This was much bigger.

Dr. Boelens had flown from America to the Philippines to look for me in a crowd of more than 7,000 people at the conference, only to have stood behind me in a registration line. What were the odds?

"Thank you Jesus! Thank you Jesus!" He could hardly contain his excitement.

"You know John, from Ghana." I tried to remember which John he would be referring to.

"John. . ."

Then he blurted out, "John Oduro-Boateng".

"Yes, yes, I know John".

That was when, still lost for words, he explained how much they had prayed every minute on their way to the Philippines that our paths would cross so that he would get the chance to share the vision that John Oduro-Boateng had brought to me. He said they had prayed that morning while they left their hotel that God would lead them to me.

It was in Manila that I learned about the Luke Society and its incredible mission to work alongside local medical professions to minister to people in local communities, transforming lives and hearts to the glory of God. This is when Dr. Peter Boelens spoke at length about a vision in 1964 of a group of physicians and dentists from the Christian Reformed Church who stepped out to save the Rehoboth Mission Hospital in Gallup, New Mexico. They set out to help construct a new hospital and used the opportunity for community outreach.

I accepted to serve on the board for Luke Society in Ghana and was honoured to work with men and women whose dedication to serving was both remarkable and truly inspiring. This was proof that God is always looking for people who are willing to heed His call. He is not just looking for people who are equipped. We may think we do not have all that we need to make a difference in the world around us, but the God who has called us to serve His purpose knows exactly whom to put in our path to lift us up, and where to find them, even in a crowd of more than 7,000 people. Indeed, God can orchestrate a man's path to be only a footstep away from wherever he needs to be, in His own time.

John Oduro-Boateng remained incredibly faithful and committed to the vision of the organization. He had been a young man whom I had the privilege of leading into Christ's salvation, and I never would have imagined working with him nearly some 30 years after the last Scripture Union meeting, and for many more decades healing the needy and bringing them hope.

From Kasei, Luke Society reached out to N'Dali, Benin; Bamenda, Cameroon; Moundou, Chad; Kinshasa, Democratic Republic of Congo; Northern Egypt; Nairobi, Kenya; Monrovia, Liberia; Kaniaka, Mali; Kayes, Mali; Segou, Mali; Madaoua, Niger; Dahra, Senegal; and Kampala, in Uganda. I reached out to doctors in the Full Gospel Business Men's Fellowship International like Dr. Ntem from Cameroon, who were willing to serve in their communities. John became the coordinator of all the African outreaches for the Luke Society, working diligently in his hometown as a medical missionary.

I remember the afternoon at our home in Kumasi, when my wife and I were paid a visit by Mrs. Ruth Billman. Together with her husband Dr. Hebert Billman, they had founded and operated Emmanuel Eye Clinic for several years in the East Legon suburb of Accra. They had decided to retire and return to America, and wanted us to help them find the ideal person who could take over their business. They didn't need the money, but what was dear to their hearts was that whoever was interested in operating the facility would promise to keep the same passion to serve the community just as they had done for many years. What had brought them to Ghana was an opportunity to share Jesus Christ with men and women, even in a time when the pain and discomfort of illness had clouded their hearts.

The Luke Society team in Ghana would be the perfect organization in whose care they could be sure the Emmanuel Eye Clinic would

Chapter 18: Dreamers And Lifechangers

continue the work they had done in Ghana. John agreed to oversee operations in Accra, with the facility in his hometown having now improved and become a district hospital to serve many more people in the surrounding towns and villages.

Many years ago, what took me to secondary school campuses was a servant's heart, and a privilege to impart the Gospel of Jesus Christ to young men and women. Nothing hinted at what God had in store for my life. I had nothing, except a heart fully committed to the service, just as Christ had invited all of us. I had always believed God had called me to be a facilitator, and my work with the Luke Society through the years caused a joyful impact on my community. God didn't ask for what we owned or who could vouch for us. Jesus does not ask for our ability; all He asks for is our willingness to serve.

* * * * *

Just as with the Luke Society, I had the rare privilege of working with Edify, an organization with a remarkable influence and commitment to building communities through education. What drove the founders Chris Crane and Tiger Dawson to find a pragmatic solution for proprietors who were willing to establish schools and learning centres in some of the remote parts of the world was no different from what drove me to help the people I was fortunate to meet along the way.

It was through Opportunity International that I met Chris Crane. I was serving on the organization's board, and in every discussion, it seemed my presence brought to light a much different understanding of the plight of poor Africans who lived in the remote villages and towns. African countries were as diverse as they were complex. Africa is characterized by a bizarre coexistence of wealth and poverty, side by side.

There were board members whose worldview of Africa was through the lens of African-Americans they saw in American cities, and it was challenging to explain how our universe was a bit different. Then there were others who understood Africa through the distorted images they saw on television, and to whom it was even more challenging to paint reality. Not everyone in Africa lived in rural villages, and in poverty. The few board members who had travelled to the continent had a much better appreciation of our world in all of its diversity, and understood the intricacies of the programs we were overseeing to achieve their intended aim.

Without knowing the impact of my strong opinions, I was slowly helping several of the people alter their skewed worldviews. Opportunity International's focus was micro-lending, and in almost every country in Africa, that meant supporting poor women stuck in a seemingly endless cycle of poverty. While the mission was incredibly honourable, there were several people on the organization's board who pushed for widening our scope to ensure we were creating lasting solutions in the developing countries we were serving.

That was Chris Crane's standpoint. He encouraged the Opportunity International board to raise money for *edufinance*—financing of educational initiatives in the developing countries. He tried to impress upon the rest to consider the challenge that small organizations and individuals faced while seeking to build schools in areas where the government had not invested any resources. Such organizations were struggling to do their work, and it was only a matter of time before the burden forced them to leave. Schools were expensive to construct and even more difficult to maintain. With the influence of Opportunity International, Chris was sure the organization could zero in on education, in addition to micro-lending, and assist the private sector on this initiative.

In one board meeting after another, the issue arose, and surprisingly was often met with the same lack of support because the focus was to remain on micro lending, not large capital investments, even if the intent was noble. At several of the board meetings, I had to speak forcefully. I knew all too well the plight of the children that Chris was advocating for, because I had been one of them many years ago. I urged them to objectively consider how any assistance we gave to a mother in

Chapter 18: Dreamers And Lifechangers

a rural area in any African country would make an even greater impact if their sons and daughters were in school, because eventually they too would add to the change we sought to make. Educating the children in rural poverty-stricken towns and villages was an incredibly powerful avenue to break the cycle of deprivation.

It was probably in sharing my own story that I developed a friendship with Chris Crane. In one board meeting after another, the people disagreed still.

Chris agreed to visit Ghana, and came along with me to places like Nkawie, Brofuodo, Asuo Yeboah, Nwiah Nkwanta, and many small towns where we had a great opportunity to change lives of young men and women. If we had taken the first step through Opportunity International to reach the women, investing in education for the children would be another courageous effort to make an even significant impact. He left Ghana with a renewed passion to press ahead.

The board eventually agreed to the *edufinance* proposal Chris had advocated. The plan would be to support the individual proprietors to build and maintain the schools. This new step led Opportunity International to open Opportunity International Savings and Loan in 2005, as one of the vehicles through which the organization could channel loans and ensure that they got to the right people doing the right work. I served on the organization's board. Fortunately the arrangement meant that Opportunity International could solicit funds, specifically for the Opportunity International Savings and Loans, separate from the micro-lending initiative. Benji Montemayor brought his banking experience to serve as the Chief Executive, working alongside a great team of Ghanaians whose focus remained the support of proprietors seeking to operate educational facilities around the country. I remained the Chairman of the board for another ten years.

By then Chris had resigned from Opportunity International and launched a new program, Edify. It was the same awareness of how millions of children in different parts of the world might never have the opportunity for an education, and how that perpetuated the cycle of poverty and limited opportunity to affect their own futures that inspired him to hope Edify would address these problems. He invited me to serve on the Board.

In Ghana, the work was to support school proprietors to build facilities and hire teachers to educate young children, especially in places where such schools were desperately needed. Loans were disbursed through lending institutions, mostly savings and loans, who would in turn guarantee that any funding was for educational purposes. Edify worked with organizations like Sinapi Aba Savings and Loans, which remained connected with Opportunity International, to finance educational initiatives with low-interest rates to relieve financial burdens on the proprietors.

I had learned that God will use any one of us to affect communities and nations if we are willing. It is true also, that if we don't step up, He will use the next willing person whose heart seeks to do the one powerful thing that God is asking of all of us—to love our neighbour.

Edify didn't set out to be a hero or seek any applause for the selfless work in difficult situations. What we knew, if any challenge was difficult for us helpers, we could only imagine what a young child in such a situation went through. I hoped we could be problem-solvers in every community in every part of the world, but at least, we got to begin with the corners where we were planted.

Through the years that I was able to serve with Edify, it was humbling to support communities with Christ-centred solutions, the only solutions that we were confident would make a lasting impact in the lives of all young children and their families. The opportunity was to transform millions of lives with quality Christ-centred education in disadvantaged areas.

Every mother or child we were able to reach surprisingly reminded me of my own childhood and my own family in Asawaase Block E11. I couldn't help but remember seeing my mother sitting quietly in the middle of the night in the corner of a room, arranging corn dough on a tray. She would need me to carry the tray around the Asawaase area early in the morning to sell what I could before I went to school. Now, my story was theirs. I hoped to do all I could to share the same opportunities I'd had. There had been men and women, just like in Chris' case, with whom I had been privileged to serve, and who showed uncommon compassion to use every resource they had to help other people who were less fortunate than they were.

God worked in so many incredible ways to impact people around the world with Luke Society and Edify. I am always humbled to find what God does in the rifts and difficult environments when our human logic only sees roadblocks. He opened windows of opportunities much wider than we could have on our own. What is true is that there will never be a more perfect time to reach back, to make a difference in another person's life than *right now*.

CHAPTER 19

A PROMISE STILL STANDS

Setbacks. A Faithful God.

I met with a Chinese company that was interested in a $20 million investment project in Ghana in 1989, in Takoradi. The company, together with its international stakeholders based in Seattle, Oregon in the United States, was interested in establishing a sawmill and lumber factory in Africa. After careful due diligence, they had settled on Ghana. They had come to Ghana to meet me because of a recommendation from an American investor, and they needed a local partner to make the project possible.

After a month, I headed to Hong Kong and China afterward to discuss the proposition further. They arranged for me to visit large wood processing facilities in Beijing and another in Tianjin, where the company was producing a range of products. Ghana had fallen on their radar because of the timber industry that had produced some of the largest timber with the quality they needed.

As a large multinational company, they previously completed huge projects in different parts of the world with major investors and international donors, so they were confident they could assist me to raise my share of the project value. The project was estimated at $20 million, and the Chinese company had agreed to invest $14 million.

I had to raise the remainder, and because of my work in Ghana as an established businessman with a credit standing with several financial institutions, they would introduce me to their banking colleagues at the International Finance Corporation (IFC). The institution does much of its work as part of the World Bank Group, the largest global development institution whose primary focus is on private sector development in developing countries. The IFC team was excited to support me, having completed their own due diligence with independent parties in the United States.

I spent a week in Tianjin and went through every detail with a company whose value proposition was rather simple: produce and process hardwood in Ghana and ship to China. Rather than ship the raw materials to China, the business plan and agreement was to build a wood processing company dedicated to this project and to be able to meet the veneer demand.

For Ghana, this was to be an incredible investment in the southwestern area of the country, one in which a private investment would fuel employment, create a significant source of export revenue for the country, and ultimately, widen the tax base for the government. The location in Takoradi had additional strategic benefits, because additional timber was to be imported from Gabon and Cameroon to be processed in Ghana.

The project offered an exciting opportunity for many of the saw mills companies in the Takoradi area, because any success was bound to open a new world of opportunity for their businesses too. We signed all the contracts and I proceeded to buy ten acres of land in Takoradi. That's was when the most improbable thing happened.

I received a letter from my Chinese partners clearly outlining their regret that they had been forced to abandon the project. They had been notified that the ruling PNDC government will not approve the project, only because I, Kwabena Darko, was their local partner. They had been advised to cut their ties with me, if they wanted to proceed with the project.

Fortunately, their letter disclosed the identity of the official who had been bold enough to openly undermine my business venture, and

Chapter 19: A Promise Still Stands

who didn't hide behind his clout in the government. He suggested the Chinese company work with his son instead, and that he would ensure the project took off. He was a high-ranking official in the PNDC government, but this was disgraceful and heartless. Worse, this was a man I knew personally because he had sought my assistance over and again for his family's private business. The betrayal had been by a man who had once counted on my help, but was now guided by greed. It was much more painful than the lost business opportunity with the Chinese partners. He was the last person I would have ever thought would perform such a callous act, but this had become routine for several of the government officials who were happy to sabotage anyone and use their position to unravel any venture.

Unfortunately, the Takoradi timber project was not the kind where that the Chinese company could easily replace a local partner because the IFC's funding was dependent on my reputation and business as collateral. The project crashed. Sadly, the conniving ways of doing business in Ghana were too rampant for anyone to curb, and the military government's officers didn't care about whom they trampled upon.

With every investment in this venture now a wasted effort, I had little choice but to move on. Truth is, I hadn't been alone. The irony of men and women who touted socialist ideals in public, only to try every means to secure private business deals, was baffling. On one hand, they were bent on implementing economic programs that were doomed from the start, knowing very well that the very private-run system they sought to destroy had been the lifeblood of every thriving economy we saw around the world. It was not difficult the see the consequence of the government's economic policies that undermined and demonized every private investor and entrepreneur, and spiralled the nation into an economic freefall.

Once there had been companies like Appiah Menka Complex Limited in Kumasi that manufactured Apino Soap and who at its height employed hundreds of Ghanaians and supported other private investment around the country. The military government called for a boycott of the company's products because of its apparent support for opposition groups. Industrialists like J.K. Siaw established Tata Brewery Limited in 1969, but it was brutally seized by the Armed Forces Revolutionary Council (AFRC) regime, just as Siaw's assets were taken overnight. B.A. Mensah's International Tobacco Ghana Limited (ITG) manufacturing company was also confiscated by the military government. The long list of private companies that became the target of the military's rage against entrepreneurship crippled any infrastructure intended to build a nation. It also emboldened the crooked politicians and scheming officials who were now confident they had the backing of the government to crush anyone they considered a political opponent.

Because of such efforts to thrash private investment, the country had decided to abandon any hope for ingenuity and individual pursuit of excellence. Over and again there had been countless examples of governments doing all they could to nationalize major industries and create a system that left economic decisions in the hands of government, supposedly seeking the welfare of its people. What it turned out to be, was erecting huge roadblocks in our own paths and believing that someday a government would fix all of our problems. Sadly, what we had masterfully sabotaged had become our country's future, and one only to regret in hindsight.

It was in the mid-1980s that Darko Farms qualified for an ECGD loan that was being administered through British financial institutions like Standard Chartered Bank and Barclays Bank. It was during some of Ghana's tumultuous economic years with a struggling economy, and there was no way for private businesses to secure Letters of Credit to fund its operations. I had applied through the British Council and the last step that was required was for Ghana's Secretary for Agriculture John Ndebugri to append his signature, verifying that indeed Darko Farms was a reputable business supported by every audited financial document and business investment plan.

Chapter 19: A Promise Still Stands

The Secretary visited my farms in Akropong-Asante, together with his team of government officials. By the time they left the facility, we had addressed every requirement and outlined the need for the capital to import vaccines and other raw materials critical to our operations. Unfortunately, the more Secretary Ndebugri learned about Darko Farms, the more he hated the thought of appending his signature to any document that would make the company survive for even one more day. Apparently, he did not care to hide his disgust, venting to his officers, *"One man owns all of this?"* Why couldn't one man own Darko Farms?

He ripped the loan documents and cancelled my company's application for the ECGD loan. He was the government official in charge, and if he had his own way, his government would have the power to determine who succeeded and who failed.

In 1992, Jerry Rawlings had just won the presidential elections in which I had also competed as flagbearer for the National Independence Party (NIP). I had campaigned on my genuine belief in the ability of private enterprises to uplift a nation, and to create competition and excellence through entrepreneurship. In my heart, I believed in the Ghanaian's dignity and ethic to work hard, rather than waiting on handouts and windfalls. I had seen petty traders work through days and nights and rain and beating sun to earn an honest living. I had seen farmers, old and young, till the land and find their worth in their harvest, and I had met entrepreneurs who had faith in their knowledge and their God-given abilities.

I had absolutely no faith in centralized plans to build state-run companies. I believed in the ones that could survive market changes, and ones whose employees would care for them, as if the companies were their own. In the absence of any incentive to compete, all that such policies were good for was stifling economic growth, rising unemployment levels, and devaluing of our currency. I was confident that all any government was well-suited to do was to create an underlying framework upon which private individuals and corporations would be the chassis of economic activity. That was the basis for my disagreement with Jerry Rawlings and his National Democratic Congress (NDC). Nothing his military officers had done to my business over the previous ten years was reason to bear a grudge against him. Now he was president, and everyone had to wish him well to succeed, so that the nation succeeded too.

After the election, Jerry Rawlings declared, *"Ghanaians should not buy Darko chicken"*. My enterprise had become an enemy of the state, and my political difference had become a reason to crush my business. It was not a coincidence that for many years, the officers in the country's Internal Revenue Service (IRS) in Kumasi also felt bolstered to find every avenue to choke my business with bogus allegations and threats. It was unfortunate that Ghana had missed the much larger point, that a thriving private enterprise, regardless of its size, becomes the catalyst and fuel for any sustainable economic progress. In Ghana, we have had ample reasons to know that government is not a business, and *"if no one owned it, no one took care of it"*.

* * * * *

It was in Atlanta, Georgia, at the annual International Production and Processing Expo that I first discovered Tyson Foods. As a member of the World Poultry Science Association, I had attended the event held every January which attracted some of the largest poultry companies around the world to display technology, equipment, and a host of services in the industry's supply chain. There were also innovative ideas in processing plants, feed milling, veterinary drugs, poultry housing systems, and even drinking fountains purposely designed for chickens. Every scientific seminar and elaborately designed booth was an educational experience, and one that I returned every year to implement in Darko Farms in Ghana.

For ten years I had visited Tyson Foods' display at the convention. I was particularly fascinated with the company's work and their carefully orchestrated marketing displays to tell their story plainly and effectively.

Chapter 19: A Promise Still Stands

I introduced myself year after year, and it was as if the Tyson Foods Company had become a model for my own, as I watched their operation from a distance. At their booth, the company had interactive displays that often gave a sense of what it felt like to walk through their farms.

After ten years of building a professional relationship with some of the marketing and business team at the Atlanta conventions, I decided it would be best to visit the company's location and see some of the leading manufacturing equipment and impressive technology first hand. I handed over to John Tyson a marketing video of Darko Farms that highlighted our work and our vision for West Africa. By then, I had learned about how the company had become the largest chicken company in the world, having expanded its processing plants to countries like Mexico, and as far east as Japan.

Tyson Foods invited me to visit their headquarters in Springdale, Arkansas. I took my sons Sammy, Vernon, and Joe along, and from the little I knew of the company, I thought it was an experience I didn't want them to miss. John Tyson had followed in the footsteps of his father Don and his grandfather John. W. Tyson, who set out during America's Great Depression in the 1930s to build a company that had thrived with decades of innovation and resourcefulness.

Tyson executives were particularly excited, and I remember John sharing his own love for the work and how he had seen the same in the Darko Farms video. He spoke of how both of our companies were doing the same thing, except that Tyson had managed to scale its business through the years. Nothing was more moving to me than seeing his grandfather's office, in the same state in which he had last left it, and a large portrait of John W. Tyson on the wall. Even the pencils and small sheets of paper were neatly arranged, just as his grandfather would have them every day, and perhaps for John the grandson, this was a potent reminder of his humble beginnings and what it took to build such a company.

For two days in Springdale, I had seen their operation, and seen their remarkable use of science and technology to develop different chicken products. There was also a vast network of private outgrowers throughout the area, from Springdale all the way to Little Rock, Arkansas. The company supported the relatively small scale farmers to whom it sold the baby chicks and feed, and also made sure they had access to the capital and resources that were made possible by the Tyson relationship. The outgrowers had installed well-designed cooling systems, drinking and feeding structures, and benefitted immensely as part of a network of transportation systems that took the chickens from their farms to the Tyson processing facilities.

With the integration of poultry systems, Tyson Foods slaughtered several millions of birds each day to end up in large grocery outlets and restaurants across the United States and the world. The company's success had been built on decades of meticulous planning, and strategic partnerships. Every image that hung in their office walls, every logo and design on the company's trucks, and product labels, was purposeful. The company had invested millions of dollars into its marketing with an insatiable thirst for innovation.

John Tyson asked a lot of questions about Ghana. Regardless of what he knew from his own due diligence, he wanted the reality from my vantage point. I had set out in 1958 to Israel to learn about poultry science, returned to Ghana to work for a state-owned company, and eventually for my stepfather's farm. Venturing out on my own in 1967 to start Darko Farms demanded an undying commitment to hard work and finding opportunities to survive. I had chosen to thrive at all costs, and trusted my God to see me through.

Doing business in Ghana, just as in most African countries, demanded a level of faith and fortitude to stand through the changing governments, each with their own understanding of private enterprises, some hailing them as a source of tax revenue, while others blamed them for every one of society's ills. Yet, there was no greater satisfaction for me than working in my country and being able to add value to my people and my home. There was no challenge or political pestering that would force me to give up.

Ghana had a hope to shift to democratic ideals, away from the coup d'états and military interventions that instilled fear in private entrepreneurs that didn't support the chaos. Fortunately, as a country emerging from a peaceful transition to democracy, there was optimism for a renewed outlook, and a need for private enterprises to help resuscitate our country.

John Tyson wanted to talk further. We agreed that I would send an employee from Ghana to train at Tyson Foods' Springdale facility. The visit had been eye-opening and I had struck a friendship with another poultry farmer whose love for the work seeped through his every word. That was the beginning of the discussion to extend Tyson's footprint to Ghana and Africa.

I returned to Tyson Foods several months later in 1999, this time with my son Vernon, and Kwasi Poku, an economist and agriculturalist whom I had just hired to work for my company. I met with William Kuckuck, Senior Vice President of Tyson Foods International, Roger Parette, Director of Sales for the Atlantic Region, and several other executives, and we went through a series of detailed presentations about the venture in Africa.

Tyson Foods agreed to invest more than $50 million in Ghana's poultry market, as a gateway to serve the West African region. The partnership with Darko Farms would instantly inject new life into an entire sector whose resources were too scanty for them to be able to compete on an international level. The tide was bound to turn in Ghana's favour and the timing couldn't be more perfect. The agreement was announced on national television together with the Minister for Agriculture Owusu Akyeampong, and USAID executives.

Tyson Foods gave Darko Farms $100,000 to immediately begin work on a strategic framework and marketing plan to supply chicken products from Senegal, Sierra Leone, Liberia, Cote D'Ivoire and across the West African coast to Nigeria. For Tyson Foods, Ghana had become the anchor to supplying new customers across a continent that relied on importing chicken and meat products from overseas. The Tyson strategy was to develop Ghana with every technological capacity as they had in Springdale, Arkansas, and create a market even for smaller farmers who would see an immediate uplift in their own investment. Other American companies, to whom Tyson had supplied products through the years, were to follow to Ghana.

The United States Department of Agriculture (USDA), USAID, and the U.S. Embassy in Ghana had been supportive of the American company investing in Africa, as a new market opportunity. The company shipped several chicken products in a 40-foot container, 1,000 tons of chicken leg quarters as samples to demonstrate the magnitude of the work to be undertaken. We invited both large and small grocery retail outlets in Ghana to an unveiling of this business in Accra.

The Minister of Trade and Industry for the NDC government, Dan Abodakpi had a different agenda. He went on national television soon after, to voice the government's opposition to the Tyson Foods' partnership. The sham complaints included everything from Americans supposedly displacing Ghanaian poultry farmers, a Ghanaian pathologist alleging that the Tyson chicken contained dangerous fats that would kill Ghanaians, and even worse, that the venture was designed to bring dead chickens from America to dump into Ghana stores.

For a country that was still importing chicken from Brazil and several European countries, a venture with Tyson Foods that intended to construct facilities in Ghana, and add significant value to the industry, the "sabotage" was devastating. The deal that had been transparent from the start, and gained every legal business and scientific approval, was now to be abandoned because the government suddenly didn't approve.

For the first time, Ghana had a true investor to support a poultry industry to international standards, to make the country self-sufficient

Chapter 19: A Promise Still Stands

and to provide a direct market for agricultural products like soybean, sorghum, and other grains. The immense benefit for small poultry farmers and the opportunity to create jobs in the country, vanished.

There had been the chance for export revenue to Ghana with a huge market from Dakar, all the way to Port Harcourt, and to the southern African region, but the deal was now cancelled. Even in a democratic society that supposedly embraced a free market, the haunting of the military government's brazen declarations and assault on private entrepreneurs had resurfaced. Just seven years earlier, President Jerry Rawlings had urged Ghanaians *not to buy Darko chicken*, and now Dan Adodapki, a political appointee, was echoing the same sentiment.

For international companies like Tyson, it was not worth being embroiled in political machinations in Ghana. They walked out. Tyson Foods had come to Ghana because of our shared business ideals, and what they had seen me do in the country since 1967. They were not interested in striking a business deal with any government, and Ghana's would be no exception.

Not surprisingly, investors refrain from doing business with governments because a government in its true sense, is not an enterprise. Governments are successful at enacting laws and ensuring that the regulatory framework in any society thrives, acting as a referee to an economic engine, not a player on its proverbial turf.

As short-sighted as many of the assaults against the private investment in Ghana had been, there was no successful state-owned entity in the country to support the reliance on utopian ideas that had no place in reality. Darko Farms was destined to outlast every one of these bizarre sabotage and baseless attacks, that I was sure of. Unfortunately, it is our country that suffers. Economic policies that gave bleak signals to the Ghanaian entrepreneur and the world ultimately crushed our nation's spirit to build and innovate, and at best, produced erratic progress. History suggests clearly that any nation that stands against private investments and entrepreneurship is one that sets itself to fail.

What I knew also, was that God's way of opening doors and closing others was hardly like my own. In the middle of storms, I wore a garment of praise, with a determination to trust fully in God and not lean on my own understanding. My confidence and security rested in Almighty God. I had seen God's footprints in my life enough to know He would turn things around. I trusted Him with everything and lived in a place of peace because, in spite of the setbacks and needless humiliation, there was nothing that anyone could do to derail God's plan for my life.

There had been delays, betrayals, oppositions, and frustration that I could not understand. I chose to remind myself that God was in control of the universe and every situation, and he had surrounded me with His favour. Even in uncertainty, I knew my every step was ordered into a God-ordained destiny. Despite what looked like a dead end and another obstruction, God knew exactly what He was doing. Surely, everything *was working together for my good.*

Kwabena Darko and Christiana Boatemaa Darko

Kwabena Darko, Christiana and children

Mercy, Vernon, Bernice, Sammy, Maxine, and Johnathan

Kwaba Darko and family

CHAPTER 19: A PROMISE STILL STANDS 205

With Vernon and Pat Robertson at the inauguration of George W. Bush, Washington D.C.

With United States Senator Jim Inhofe in Accra, Ghana

With Sammy and Vernon at Darko Farms facility in Akropong-Asante, Ghana

With Ken Ofori-Atta (Ghana Minister of Finance) and Robert Ilakov at the Jerusalem Prayer Breakfast in Jerusalem, Israel

Chapter 19: A Promise Still Stands

With Senator Jim Inhofe in Washington D.C.

Kwabena Darko presents award at Regent University College of Science and Technology graduation ceremony in Accra, Ghana

Kwabena Darko speaks to students at Babson College in Wellesley Massachusetts

With Katie Smith Millway at the launch of *One Hen: How a Small Loan Made a Difference*

Chapter 19: A Promise Still Stands

With John Tyson of Tyson Foods Inc. in Springdale, Arkansas

With Douglas Coe, founder of The Fellowship and host of the United States' annual National Prayer Breakfast

With Citibank executives in New York City, New York (2001)

With Full Gospel Business Mens' Fellowship executives in Libreville, Gabon (1991)

With President John Agyekum Kuffuor in Accra, Ghana

Kwabena Darko with business leaders in Arizona, United States

With Amway founder Richard DeVoss

Inspection of first equipment delivery for Darko Farms Abattoir, Ghana

Chapter 19: A Promise Still Stands

Rev. Christiana Darko with Bishop Irvina Miller of Oasis of Love Ministry, Shippensburg, Pennsylvania

Kwabena Darko with Alhaji Asoma Banda at the Kwame Nkrumah University of Science and Technology in Kumasi, Ghana

Wedding ceremony, Kwabena Darko and Christiana Boatemaa Darko (1967)

Wedding celebration of Kwabena Darko and Christiana Boatemaa Darko at Kumasi Assembly of God Church, Ghana (1967)

With Christiana Darko, Mr. Hanson Asiedu and my sons Samuel, Vernon, and Jonathan in Koforidua, Ghana

Rev. Mrs. Christiana Darko with leaders of Women's Aglow in Monrovia, Liberia

With Astronaut Charlie Duke, President Agyekum Kuffuor and staffers at Ghana's first National Prayer Breakfast

CHAPTER 19: A PROMISE STILL STANDS 217

With Mr. Odoi-Syke, Pat Robertson, Dr. Apraku (Minister of Trade), and Paul Crouch at the inauguration of President George W. Bush (2001)

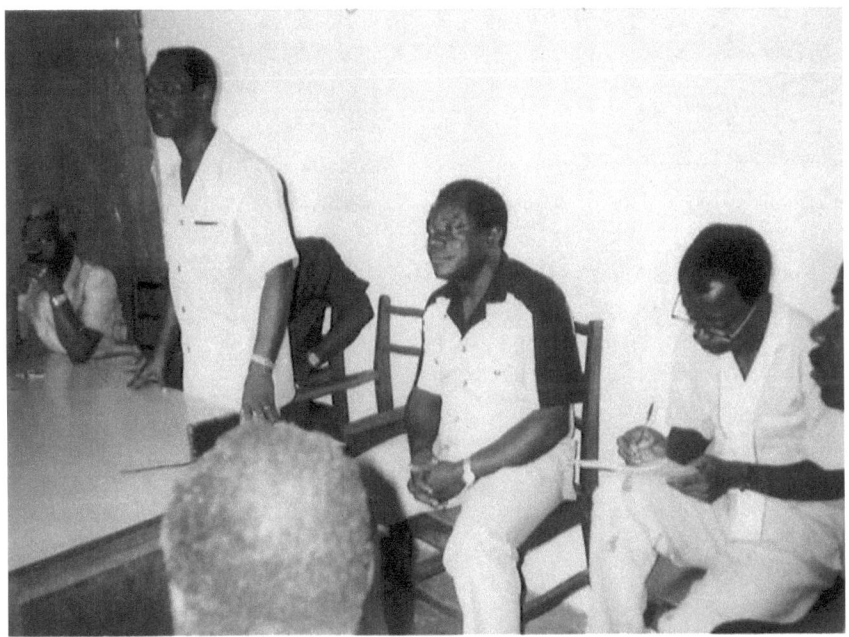

With Col. Bamfo and Isaac Antwi during the 1992 presidential election campaign

With Mr. Addo Kuffuor, Defence Minister (left) and Hon S.K. Boafo, Ashanti Regional Minister and United States' Congressman J.C. Watts (middle) in Kumasi, Ghana

Meeting with President Laurent Gbagbo of Cote D'Ivoire at the Kumasi Airport, Ghana

Board of Governors, Bank of Ghana (2001 – 2008)

With Edify founder Chris Crane and wife at the Oasis of Love International Church in Kumasi, Ghana

Opportunity Network Board's visit to Krakow, Poland

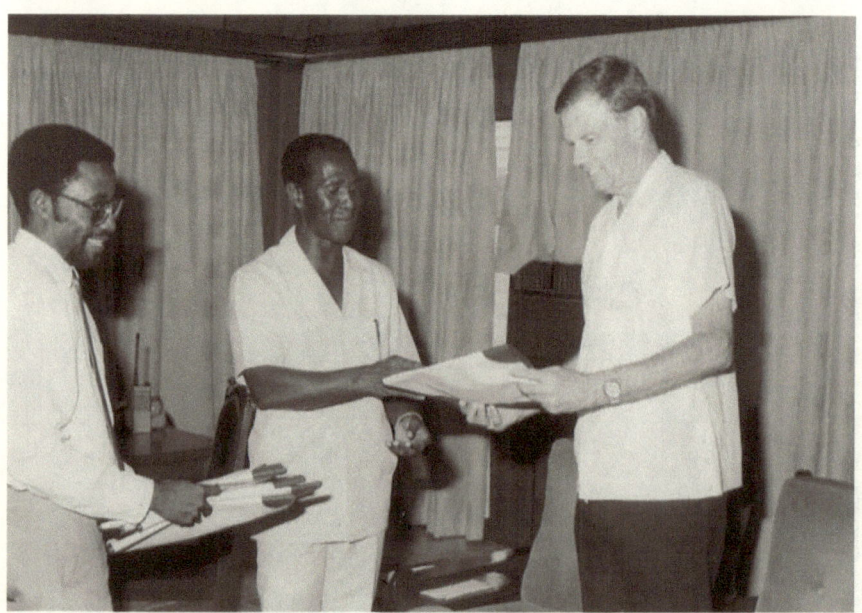
With Baffuor Adu Gyamfi and Australian Ambassador to Ghana at Darko Farms Co. Ltd, Akropong-Asante, Ghana

Chapter 19: A Promise Still Stands

Kwabena Darko presenting Tyson Foods' joint venture poultry project at Manhyia Palace, Kumasi, Ghana

With Women's Aglow leaders in Monrovia, Liberia

With entrepreneur Richard O'Donnell in Houston, Texas

In Krakow, Poland

Full Gospel Business Men's Fellowship members in Anaheim, California

With Bank of Ghana executives in Ghana, Accra

With Richard Shikarian at the Full Gospel Business Men's Fellowship in Lagos, Nigeria

With Paul Crouch of Trinity Broadcasting Network in Washington D.C.

Chapter 19: A Promise Still Stands 225

First Network Board Design Council of Opportunity International Worldwide

United States Congressman J.C. Watts and Ghanaian delegation visits Asantehene Otumfuo Osei Tutu II, Kumasi

Asantehene Nana Opoku Ware II visits Assemblies of God Church (Lighthouse Assembly) for its 50 years anniversary in Akwatia Lane, Kumasi (1981)

With my wife Christiana Darko and the leadership of Tyson Foods, Inc.

With Princess Anne and Ghanaian delegation at the IDiF meeting in London, England

With Demos Shakarian and Full Gospel Business Men's Fellowship African executives in Toronto, Canada

With Ken Bamfo, Don and Marlene Ostrom in San Diego, California

With Full Gospel Business Men's Fellowship executives in Anaheim, California

With Evangelist John Avanzini at the Full Gospel Business Men's Fellowship conference in Anaheim-California, United States

With Demos Shakarian, founder and President of Full Gospel Business Men's Fellowship International.

With Cary Summers, President Nana Akufo-Addo, Bishop T.D. Jakes, Rev. Kusi-Boateng, and Dr. Paul Opoku Mensah (2022)

CHAPTER 20

WORTH FIGHTING FOR

Mission Work. Assemblies of God. Fences Within.

What I believed God said about my life had taken root deep in my heart, and I had chosen to see my world through the eyes of faith. This powerful realization is what gave me the courage to live freely as a child of the Most High God and my life's mission became one that supported the gospel reaching as many hearts as it could.

In 1966, I remember sharing my heart with American Evangelist Morris Cerullo when I was torn between a life as a preacher and that of an entrepreneur. If I had been blessed in my career, it had been to, in turn, become a beacon of light and hope to the world around me. It all began a few years earlier.

It was a Saturday evening in 1962 that my paths crossed with Reverend Lonnie Fox and his ministry interpreter Reverend Gyan Fosu in Abbey's Park, in Ashanti New Town, Kumasi. A chance moment in the humid and dusty park turned out to be what would change my life forever. I had a choice to leave behind the lifestyle and the thoughts that occupied my day, and step into a new world of salvation, completely.

Until then, I had always been in the church even as a little boy, but that was all I had done. My mother and grandmother had been devout members of the Apostolic Church and committed their lives to prayer and allowing their every path to radiate with righteousness. They had been the ones who hoped I would also follow in their faith's footsteps, but all I did was to follow them to church and to hear about Jesus. I knew about the salvation story, perhaps, like anyone who attended church services, but Jesus was not in my heart, and I didn't even know what it meant to truly have a personal relationship with Him.

I was no different from many of the young men and women who showed up in a church with broad smiles on Sunday mornings, and went back to living any way we pleased until it was another Sunday morning. Most of us were casual churchgoers. On Friday nights, with a group of friends, I would be standing on stage as part of the High Class Diamonds band, gyrating wildly to charm any girl who had come to see us perform. My cousin Kwame Amponsah had introduced me to the band, and because I loved to sing, I became a vocalist, entertaining crowds at drinking bars.

Often we would take sips of alcohol and other concoctions with marijuana to distort our presence of mind. Feeling high and in a world made blurry with drugs gave permission for us to misbehave and perform wildly to entertain a crowd. I remember how we would show up at the Kumasi Asafo Jamboree and dance through the night. With my friends, our evenings ended up in drinking bars, and spending the night looking for girls to impress, and rounds of whiskey and gin to give us the feeling of ecstasy. Unfortunately, after an evening of drinking and what I thought was fun, my nights would be troubled with the same eerie premonitions that had haunted me all through my life.

My cousin Kwame knew of my trepidation, and occasionally he would suggest I gulp enough shots of alcohol to numb my fear so I could drift into sleep peacefully. It didn't work. I had told him that anytime I tried to fall asleep, after a long day, it was only a matter of time before the nightmares began. The scary and eerie creatures that seemed like large hands rushing to squeeze every life out of me would appear over and again. Fear shook me. All alone, I would wake up, sweating and screaming.

Chapter 20: Worth Fighting For

With the wild nights behind me, I still made it to church on Sunday mornings, like most people. The church was something to do, something nice. I assumed Jesus was understanding of our human imperfections, but I was young and I thought I had a life ahead of me to enjoy. I was making a mockery of God and myself. I had convinced myself that I was not ready to turn away from the freedom and happy-go-lucky lifestyle. Only when the haunting continued, did I wake up in the middle of the night troubled and unsure of why such horror seemed to have followed me all these years. I was mortified, and it always felt as though something was pulling me to my death.

Coincidentally, it was Kwame, the same person who had invited me to join the pop music band, who suggested I come along to a crusade he heard about. It had been organized by the local Assemblies of God church. He told of how he had heard of some of the preachers who were powerful and might even be able to perform miracles; perhaps one of them could help me. There was not much left to lose, but I was not too sure I was ready to share my problems with perfect strangers at a crusade.

That is how I ended up in Abbey's Park on that Saturday evening in 1962. Standing under a tree tucked away in the far corner of the park, a part of me was desperate still. Yet, I was not sure I was ready to walk away from my carefree life as I knew it. I was a young man, who had found some success working on my stepfather's poultry farm, earned a scholarship to study abroad, and returned to a familiar life in Kumasi. I was one of the few young men in my community with gainful employment, brimming with confidence and conceit. But I was empty.

When I heard Reverend Lonnie Fox quote Psalm 91, what jumped at me was the phrase *"dwells in the secret place"*. For a moment I thought my cousin Kwame had told the preachers about my problem, and that they knew I was standing as far back as I could, hiding near a large tree. Then he continued, *"Will never be afraid in the night, nor the pestilence that haunts in the day . . ."*

The words pierced my heart inexplicably and it felt as though every word he spoke was to me. Reverend Gyan Fosu, the local translator, reiterated every message, and spoke with such eloquence and force. I remember how they ended with an assurance from the Lord that swept me into the arms of grace, that for anyone who was courageous enough to surrender, God said, *"I will rescue him; I will protect him . . . He will call on me, and I will answer him; I will be with him in trouble . . . With long life, I will satisfy him and show him my salvation".*

The message couldn't have struck harder. I needed a way out of my silent misery and the horrors of ghastly images, and even though I had spent all my life following my mother and grandmother into church services, this was my encounter, and it was not just about religious routines and dogma. This night was about finding salvation.

I never will forget the moment Reverend Lonnie Fox extended an invitation to the crowd for anyone who wanted to accept Jesus as their Lord and saviour. I was standing by the tree, shivering and sweating, and I felt something gently pulling me away from where I stood. No one in the crowd moved, but suddenly I didn't care if anyone moved. It was my moment of grace and it was not passing me by. I was tired of living as though my life were perfect, when in fact I desperately needed a rescue. I took off running towards the stage. Suddenly, I turned to see men and women from all across the park running too, to where the Reverend Lonnie Fox stood. We were running to Jesus.

That night turned my heart and my life completely around. God was no longer a casual reference. He was my Heavenly Father. I didn't know what happened to me once I reached the stage and fell to the ground. When my eyes opened, with my dirt-stained clothes and face covered in sweat, something amazing had happened to me. The preachers told of how I had been covered in dirt, shaking and screaming on the ground and at one point praying in the spirit, in tongues. They could only invite me to accept Jesus Christ, but it took the Holy Spirit to turn my life around and set my feet to walk on higher ground.

Chapter 20: Worth Fighting For

The men who had prayed with me and encouraged me that night in 1962 assured me that accepting Jesus as my saviour meant the end of my old life, and I was starting anew. I believed it wholeheartedly. I didn't have to walk in fear of any nightmares and eerie hands haunting me at night. I had the word of God to stand on, if only I could believe every word as the perfect truth, with absolute power to break every chain. The two preachers invited me to Assemblies of God church.

A reliance on God's word gave me a completely new purpose. I joined the church's choir, the Youth group, and seized every opportunity to immerse every fibre of my being into the church activities. The same diligence spilled into my work at Central Egg Farm, and it was as though I was working for God, not my stepfather. Evangelism and outreach became what stirred my every waking moment, and through the years, the vanity that had once given me some semblance of happiness was the farthest thing from my mind. I had committed my life to Jesus, and I was no longer the same *Kwabena Darko* who showed up in church casually because it was something to do. I was a man whose heart was turned to Jesus and whose mind was consumed with His every word.

Years later, Assemblies of God had become my church, a fellowship to nurture my faith, and I had been fortunate to have opportunities to serve in any place I was needed. I was now an elder, and I had seen God's hand on my life, on my work, and on my family. I had decided to follow Jesus, and there was absolutely no turning back.

Reverend Nicholas Opuni was transferred from a small village, a few miles on the outskirts of Kumasi, to serve as resident pastor at Lighthouse Assemblies of God. He was to work with Reverend Vernon Driggers for a while, and to take over the church leadership when the missionary returned home to the United States. From the start, Reverend Opuni's vision was to establish churches in surrounding towns and villages to ensure that people didn't have to travel long distances to come to the main church in Kumasi. He was remarkable in his dedication to the

Lord's work and challenged the young men and women to work with him to reach our local communities.

Within the first year, we had opened a church in Bantama, South Suntreso, Santaaase, and soon, Atonsu, Kwadaso, and several others. We set up churches as far north as Mampong. Reverend Opuni's presence stirred my faith, and it was refreshing to follow his lead as a fiery believer whose only joy came from evangelism and reaching people with the message of Christ's salvation.

Growing in faith in the Assemblies of God church, I had found my joy, and if there was anything I was to spend the rest of my life doing, it would be creating places of worship, and supporting the church with everything I had.

Our work was the Lord's, and everything He had given to me was meant to serve Him. I didn't need any recognition to buy a Volkswagen van for the church to support the "Speed the Light" program, or buy clothes and food for church leaders who were in need. It would be much later in my life that I could afford to buy lands and houses and properties for churches, and to give away possessions to help preachers do the work of God. At every turn, whenever I met someone in need, I couldn't help but remember where I was when God found me. God had been merciful and watched over me throughout my young life even when the devil haunted my days and nights with premonitions and dread. Now, I knew for sure, that my life had been in a battle, and grace had won.

Two friends, Kwame Ofori Amankwa and R.K. Mensah, both of whom worked for me at Darko Farms, came along to oversee some of the new churches. None of us had attended Bible school, but we knew we had a calling to minister to people in our community. God was choosing ordinary young men without any qualifications, but given us a testimony to share. We worked with Reverend Opuni, helping with the church leadership at the new churches until resident pastors were assigned to the locations.

Chapter 20: Worth Fighting For

There was no act of generosity to my fellow man that I thought matched God's faithfulness towards me. I was quickly learning a powerful truth, that there was no way I could give more than God gave me in return. My greatest desire had been to succeed in business, and to use every profit to build God's kingdom. It was amazing to find how He opened doors for me to help preachers and churches, being able to minister to specific needs. I determined long ago to follow where God led, and not do what would give me applause. I was not donating my money or time to any church to earn a front seat, or to stand in their pulpit. I prayed for a generous heart, one whose only reward would come from Almighty God, as having done exactly what I had been called to do.

Beyond Kumasi and the Ashanti region, I was able to support the Assemblies of God General Council and other churches across the country. It was the same humble knowledge of Christ's provision that led me to purchase land for the church in places like Atonsu, Kwadaso and New Tafo, or to buy 1,000 shirts for all the pastors in the villages who needed new clothing, or Tomos motorcycles for ministers in the villages so they could drive through the narrow pathways to minister to their communities. If all I had was the suit or shoes in my closet to make sure a preacher in a small town felt his best, I was grateful to have become an answered prayer. That is what I was determined to do, and I only prayed for the grace to do so.

In 1981, the Assemblies of God church in Ghana was to celebrate its 50-year anniversary. The church that had started in Ghana's northern regions by missionaries traveling south from Burkina Faso, which was then Upper Volta, had now made large footprints across the large cities and towns in Ghana. The anniversary was to be held in Kumasi, and since I was a youth leader, God laid it upon my heart to renovate the large church building that the missionaries had built that needed new flooring.

It would be expensive, but my faith had taught me that there was nothing my God couldn't provide. All I needed was a willing heart and faith the size of a mustard seed. It was humbling to galvanize men and women, old and young, to stand together for one vision. It was amazing watching one person after another volunteering to buy cement and stones, and others eager to work as masons and carpenters to do whatever was needed.

For six months, we sang and built. We tore apart the old dirt and cement floors and rebuilt every piece with terrazzo. Seeing the heart of the people in fellowship affirmed my faith in a community of believers who could stand together to bring glory to God. I remembered the biblical story of Nehemiah, a Jewish leader and his people choosing to rebuild the wall of Jerusalem. I could only imagine the overwhelming joy he must have felt, brick by brick, doing all he could for the glory of God.

I had been blessed to have God take over my life completely, and now I wanted to live my life, and be the hands and feet of Jesus in my world. I was grateful for opportunities to assist missionaries who had travelled long distances to help our churches, and to do outreach. I met many devoted men and women of God who were incredible bible teachers, doctors, and others with skills that they were happy to share with us. Often, I told the foreign missionaries about my own life, how an Englishman, Reverend Sercombe had come to Ghana to serve with the Apostolic Church, lived in my stepfather's home, and introduced me to poultry farming.

But the ministry had its gloomy moments too. Self-centeredness and bruised egos took over for many in leadership, both foreign missionaries and local preachers. There was no worse feeling than watching how the infighting and petty misunderstandings tore apart the unity to serve. Occasionally it was frustrating and humiliating to see how far people went to advance their personal agendas in the church, when our focus had to be on a collective vision to share the good news.

I remember in 1983, when I was invited to the Assemblies of God church's head office in Springfield, Missouri, to meet with the

Chapter 20: Worth Fighting For

international leadership. I was leaving Ghana at the height of a famine that had ravaged communities and set panic in many parts of the country. The church's worldwide mission's overseer was Reverend Phillip Hogan, and together with the General Superintendent, Reverend Zimmerman, they wanted a chance to introduce me to some of the leaders in the United States who were instrumental to the work in Ghana and across the West African region. I travelled to Springfield, Missouri with my wife, who was also serving as the National Women's Coordinator for the Assemblies of God churches in Ghana.

The church's office in America did not know much about the severity of the famine in Ghana, and I was able to express the urgent need to help in any way we could. Various churches and missionaries were sending essential food to their congregation across the country, and I suggested to them that if the Assemblies of God church were in a position to assist the local churches, food supply would be immensely appreciated. I spent time with several of the board members, including J.C. Penney, who also shared their hearts and willingness to help.

The church arranged for five 40-foot containers packed with food items to be donated to church members in the hard-hit areas. They also brought various seeds that would be needed in the planting season as soon as the drought was over, and farming tools like hoes and cutlasses used by many of the local farmers.

It was also on this trip to meet with the leadership that I learned about the frightening allegations some of the American missionaries were levelling against their fellow missionary serving in Ghana, Reverend Arthur Hokett. The accusation that reached the church's office was that Reverend Hokett was a CIA operative disguised as a missionary, collecting sensitive information for the American government.

A group of missionaries and elders banded to make the scathing allegation. The Reverend Arthur Hokett I had known was incredibly devoted to the mission work and was one whose heart was wrapped around outreach and serving the rural communities where he was stationed. He also worked across the northern border, into Burkina Faso, and his genuinely friendly demeanour and compassion for the people he preached to, endeared him to the locals.

Coincidentally, some of the local preachers wanted the position which Reverend Hokett occupied in the church, and other American missionaries had allowed jealousy to take root in their hearts against him. Apparently, despite the allegations, the leaders who were peddling the story did not have any proof to substantiate their claims, but pressure mounted on the missions' office to remove him from Ghana.

It was unfortunate to see a man with such enviable devotion to the work of God, especially in rural areas where most people would not care to spend a moment, treated this way. The Arthur Reverend and his wife Doris and young son Jeff lived in the Wale-Wale area, and they did more than just learn the language; they became a part of the local community. I had heard of how he travelled the long dirt roads across the northern borders to buy petrol just to have enough to drive for mission work. Now he would have to leave his post because other missionaries bore a personal grudge.

In Ghana, local churches sincerely appreciated the work of missionaries who had travelled long distances and sacrificed a great deal to preach the good news to some of the remote parts of our world. Reverend Hokett had made enemies from the last group of people he imagined he would. He had been accused of undermining the work in Ghana, working as an informant for the spy network Central Intelligence Agency (CIA). They had said the Ghanaians didn't like him, and here I sat in front of the church leaders in the Missouri office, trying to convince them that I could not think of one reason why anyone would dislike Reverend Hokett's work.

He was a man of faith who had done all he could to empower the local preachers. He was the same missionary who arranged for a delegation of Ghanaian Assemblies of God leaders to visit the head office in Missouri to build relationships with the leadership. Coincidentally, it was some of these same men, whom he supported for several years, that ended up championing the allegations to remove him. Eventually, they succeeded, sending him back to Houston, Texas. It was amazing to find how he and Doris went on to launch a new ministry, and constructed more than one hundred new churches in the northern parts of Ghana.

Even worse, the church was not immune to bigotry. There were other American missionary leaders who openly derided African preachers, launching one attack after another. It was as though some of the men had determined to sow discord in the body of Christ, and worked hard to see it take root. There were some who did their best to make sure the Ghanaian preachers were not elected to the Executive Council, and others who undermined every work of other local preachers as though their service was to a different God.

One incident that I witnessed in Washington D.C. was as troubling as it was sad. I was visiting the United States, and found a local Assemblies of God church to attend for Sunday fellowship. I sat at the back of the church. Coincidentally, the church had allowed missionaries who had returned from Africa and other parts of the world to speak for a few minutes to share their testimony and some of the highlights of their work. It was an opportunity for the missionaries to raise funds for their next trip.

For most missionaries, this fundraising opportunity was to appeal to the generosity of the congregation and even the local church, and that meant showing images of the unimaginable conditions in those countries to demonstrate their sacrifice. Pictures of abject poverty tugged at the heartstrings of the congregation, and to some, created a sense of urgency for the missionary to head back into those remote villages to help. This missionary was a man I knew, and he was describing Ghana. I sat quietly in the back, watching the video presentation and the heartbreaking pictures.

Supposedly, he was telling a story about a small village where he had lived and worked, but he had done his best to exaggerate the community's plight. It was nothing like he described, but there was no way for the congregation in America to know. He showed a video of himself walking across a stream with a fallen tree as a bridge, and told of the dangers he had to endure every day. The missionary was standing in a church, shamelessly claiming that he lived in the thatch-roofed tiny building in the bushes near a small church, but that too, sadly, was all a lie.

It was while he spoke that his eyes panned through the crowd and met with mine. I was the last person the missionary thought he would see in that Washington D.C. church, and he looked as if he had seen a ghost. Sadly, I was sure he was not the first to perpetuate the lies he was telling. There were many men and women like him who stained the message of hope with their own selfish interests and clamoured for recognition. Their work in faraway remote towns and villages had been for the benefit of their careers, not the kingdom of God. There were always men like him who exploited the generosity of the Christians who supported work in parts of the world they knew little about.

Others showed up in Africa, but without a heart to serve. It was a heart-breaking truth, but there were many such missionaries around the world who were not there to do the work of the Lord, and thankfully, whose selfish ploys were only short-lived. They brought shame to the missions, but God was raising men and women with pure hearts of love and service, and upon whose shoulders the message of Jesus would reach the farthest corners of the world, people like Reverend Arthur and Doris Hokett.

*****

Meanwhile, at the Assemblies of God's head office in Missouri, the most contentious issue had become the Assemblies of God printing press that the missionaries insisted should be relocated to Togo because of their fear of Ghana's new military government. It was the facility where we printed all church materials that were distributed across Ghana, and to other parts of the West African region. The missionaries didn't hide their fear.

What had caused the rift was the 1981 coup d'état by the PNDC military officers led by Jerry Rawlings. With the overthrow of democratically elected President Hilla Limann, the months which followed were marred by uncertainty and fear. The missionaries feared that it was only a matter of time before the PNDC seized the Assemblies of God printing press, just as had happened in Nigeria during the country's civil war. Togo, to them, was a safe bet.

The local church leaders disagreed. I vehemently opposed the idea, and I was determined to take a stance against the foreign missionaries. For years, the press' role of printing Sunday school materials for the various ministries had become critical, and despite our repeated assurance that the PNDC military government would not do any harm to the facility, the missionaries didn't find any comfort in our words. They stressed that a military government was unpredictable and wanted to make the decisions that their colleagues had overlooked in Nigeria.

Back in Nigeria in 1967, a civil war broke out when millions of Igbos to the south-east wanted to part ways from the Northern-dominated federal government. The Republic of Biafra launched a secessionist campaign with military officer Emeka Ojukwu as the leader. It would take another 30 months of fighting before Biafra surrendered, but not before Nigeria plunged into one of the country's darkest years, with millions of lives lost.

At one point, Ojukwu seized the Assemblies of God press, which was used to print the Biafran currency and other propaganda. General Yakubu Gowon and his northern Nigerian forces, as part of their attempt to crush the Biafran stance, bombed the press. Thus with Jerry Rawlings' military's rise to power in Ghana, the missionaries couldn't help but imagine a repeat of what had happened to the church's printing press in Nigeria. We understood their concern, but we tried to impress upon them that our circumstances were much different.

The missionaries threatened to leave Ghana. It was at the meeting at the church's head office in Springfield, Missouri that I reiterated Ghana's position to the missions' overseer, Reverend Phillip Hogan. If the missionaries wanted to leave Ghana, we could not force them to stay; however, we had capable professionals who could run the press successfully. Our productive work in the country and around the region was immensely critical and there was no reason to be alarmed that the PNDC military officers would seize the church's asset.

Eventually, I spearheaded a business plan to operate the press in Ghana, continuing to print ministry resources and Sunday school materials for Assembles of God churches across West Africa. I was invited to a leadership conference in Abidjan, Côte D'Ivoire where the church's international leaders agreed that we should operate the facility in Ghana. The General Superintendent from Nigeria, Reverend Ezibo, who was well aware of the current reality, also backed the Ghana proposal. Unfortunately, an irreparable crack had emerged with the competing ideas, and gradually the foreign missionaries left Ghana.

Competing ideologies in church had caused several people to takes sides on the issue. I was leading a charge that I believed was the right thing to do, and I was confident that despite the political crisis in Ghana, we had no reason to believe that what happened in Nigeria would repeat in Ghana. The national office of the Assemblies of God church in Ghana went ahead and set up a management team. I had the privilege of serving as Chairman of the Board for the next ten years. It was bound to be a challenging road ahead, but like any business, we had a firm understanding of the marketplace, and how to sustain the venture. We were now successfully printing for churches and other organizations across West Africa, as a commercial entity, known as the Assemblies of God Literature Centre, A.G.L.C.

Christians weren't perfect people, but there were also people whose character tainted the message we worked to share. Disagreements happened in churches, and even between people of faith. Some were even heart-breaking, and I am sure it grieved the Lord also. Once, it had been unfortunate to see a Christian brother mismanage $20,000 of funding from an international donor organization and blame an entire ministry for it. It had been strange to see men and women openly sabotage another missionary's work, even when the allegations were blatant lies.

In another instance, I arrived in Nairobi Airport, Kenya, with my Christian brother Joseph Kwaw to assist a ministry, only to learn I had been reported to the authorities as being a *Gaddaffi agent*, a spy. The allegation was intended to land me in prison as an adversary to the Kenyan government. I have never been a spy for any agency, and worse, it was the same ministry leaders whom I was travelling to assist, who found me as a threat, and concocted a plan to ruin my life. My saving grace were other business leaders and Christian brothers who were on hand to vouch for my identity and credibility.

What was most unfortunate was when people we believed shared our faith, damaged every relationship, and soiled the reputation of the church. But in the end, only the truth of Jesus Christ prevails. One thing I was sure of: God will raise pure hearts willing to serve Him honestly and reach the world with His good news, and upon such people's shoulders He will build his kingdom.

Years ago, I had set out a young man determined to chase after righteousness and commit to missions and ministry. My only prayer has been to remain faithful in every work, and for God to grant me the courage to guard the opportunities and people He entrusts into my care. My life's single purpose is to live with a clean heart and to share the good news of the gospel everywhere I set my feet. All of us will still need to push through darkness and let the light in our hearts lead our way; in the end, my hope and my faith will forever be worth fighting for.

CHAPTER 21

MY BROTHER'S KEEPER

Apaloo. Bonnke. Full Gospel Leadership.

In 1986, the Full Gospel Business Men's Fellowship International hosted its world convention in Grenoble, a town in the Auvergne-Rhône-Alpes region of south eastern France. With my wife Christiana, I arrived in Paris' Charles de Gaulle Airport, and boarded speed train heading to Grenoble. Apparently, the Fellowship had made arrangements for a chauffeur to meet me upon arrival, but I hadn't received the message before leaving Ghana.

Grenoble was cold by the time we walked out of the train station, yet the clear skies made the town feel inviting, especially for people who were excited to be at such a conference. We needed a taxi, and tried a few times to get the attention of some of the porters at the station, and ask them for directions to our hotel. Fortunately, my eyes met those of a tall black man standing across the street. I imagined he was French, probably waiting on someone. He smiled courteously. I nodded gently, as if to say hello but without being a bother. The man saw us trying to ask for directions, in English, and walked over to help.

He introduced himself as Kwakugan Apaloo, and said he was from Togo. It was unbelievable. I knew many Africans from Francophone countries lived or visited France frequently, but it was as if he had waited for us at the train station.

"I am Kwabena Darko, from Ghana. My wife is Christiana".

"Welcome. I just arrived here, from Canada".

"Canada?" I was curious.

"Yes, I came here for a Full Gospel Business Men's Fellowship International conference, not too far from here," he added.

We had travelled from Ghana to attend the same conference, so it was a welcome coincidence to bump into Apaloo, who was fluent in French, and would help us get to the hotel easily.

We hopped into the taxi. It was during our conversation that we found that Apaloo was the Togolese Ambassador to Canada and had been incredibly excited about the opportunity to join other men and women from around the world at the convention. He couldn't contain his joy when he also learned that I was Africa's representative on the board of Full Gospel Business Men's Fellowship International.

We spoke briefly about the Fellowship's impact and about some of the featured speakers who were scheduled to attend the Grenoble convention. I remember when the taxi arrived at the hotel and I reached into my pocket to pay the taxi fare, he insisted he would be delighted to pay.

I stepped out of the taxi, only to find that the Fellowship had arranged for someone to meet us at the airport, but had missed us. I introduced Kwakugan Apaloo to them as a diplomat from Togo and said they should assist him in any way to make his stay comfortable. They made arrangements for him to stay in the same hotel that had been reserved for my wife and me, and he agreed to have dinner later to talk more about his work and life. That was when Apaloo told of how he had first seen Demos Shakarian, the founder of Full Gospel Business Men's Fellowship International, on television in Canada. He was in a hotel lobby, watching Christian television, and hearing Shakarian speak challenged his heart. On that same program, Apaloo listened to American evangelist Oral Roberts preaching to a crowd and that was what made him give his life to Jesus, right in front of the television screen. The program later mentioned the convention in Grenoble and that is why he decided to attend.

Chapter 21: My Brother's Keeper

In the seminars, while I sat on stage, I arranged for Apaloo to also be given a seat near me, among the government dignitaries. Throughout the convention, I had the chance to share my passion and faith with him and also encourage him in his walk with the Lord.

I urged him to consider the fact that God had placed him in a position of authority, in a leadership role for his country, and it was important to not waste any moment but rather to become a shining example for his people and bring glory to God. I shared a lot about the Great Commission that was at the heart of the Fellowship's vision, to empower men to become active in their churches and impact their local communities. Meeting Kwakugan Apaloo had been a coincidence, but little did I know that God would use this encounter to redeem millions of people thousands of miles away.

On the last evening of the convention, thousands of people were scheduled to gather in a large arena for a dinner meeting. On the table were bottles of wine. For a Christian Fellowship, it was bizarre to find what looked like a sea of wine bottles on every table. Apparently, we were in an area of France where the natives ate their meals with glasses of wine, and someone had assumed it was acceptable for the fellowship's meeting.

The organizers had gone to great lengths to even put a picture of Demos Shakarian on the wine bottles as part of the detailed decoration. At the first chance he got, Shakarian spoke unequivocally about the wine, that *"The Bible clearly tells us to be filled with the spirit, not wine"*. He was polite, but didn't mince words telling the crowd that it was unacceptable and that was not what the Fellowship stood for.

The German-American Pentecostal evangelist, Reinhard Bonnke, was the featured speaker. He too, could not help but see the duplicity and used the opportunity to speak directly against drunkenness. If we were hoping to be ambassadors of the Great Commission, our every act and every attitude ought to represent the Jesus who had saved us and called us to be heirs of the kingdom. We were not of this world, and our desire ought to be to please Almighty God, not to conform to culture and social norms. Having bottles of wine on the convention's tables, with some of the people happily indulging without pausing to wonder if that was something a Christian ought to do, flew in the face of what we had gathered in Grenoble for.

The theme of the event and the scripture in Ephesians could not have been any more succinct, *"Do not get drunk on wine, which leads to debauchery. Instead, be filled with the Spirit"*. Bonnke preached about the baptism of the Holy Spirit. He called for men and women to rise up to please God in everything we did, and to be truthful ministers of His word. At a point, I remember him leading the crowd in prayer, where just as he stretched his hands, he struck one bottle, setting off a domino effect where the sea of bottles instantly fell down on the tables and floors with the force of a rushing wind blowing through the whole arena.

Many of the guests, some of whom had only assumed it was a networking event, had found salvation and turned their hearts to Jesus. That was my first meeting with Bonnke, an evangelist who preached the truth of God's word fearlessly, and led millions into finding their healing and restoration in the power of Christ.

After a week in Grenoble, I was leaving the town revived. I had also made a new friend in a Christian brother, Kwakugan Apaloo. It was through him that we were to launch a new chapter of the Full Gospel Business Men's Fellowship International in Togo, in August of the same year. In 1991, I organized the West African convention for the Fellowship in the capital city Lome, Togo. By then, I had launched chapters from Senegal, Gambia, and Sierra Leone, to Guinea, Liberia, and Côte D'Ivoire. For the convention, many travelled from across West Africa to the capital city of Togo, more than 5,000 people having arrived in buses from Nigeria alone.

As we had done in every country, the first meeting was with many of the Christian pastors across Togo to share the Fellowship's vision, and to emphasize especially how we were not a church. It was important to

Chapter 21: My Brother's Keeper

reiterate our focus on raising Christian businessmen to support local churches and outreach. Young men like Martin Asamoah-Manu and George Prah, both of whom served in the Fellowship in Ghana, assisted with a tremendous amount of work in preparation to ensure that the program proceeded without a hitch. We printed every brochure in both English and French at the Assemblies of God press in Ghana, and took them all to Togo.

Gracien Desouza and Kofi Essaw, who was the Togolese Ambassador to Ethiopia, were some of the men in Togo who dedicated their time to reach as many people as they could. I was immensely grateful for their commitment, especially in a country like Togo where it felt as if other religions competed for the hearts of the people. After several days of hosting smaller Fellowship meetings, our big challenge had become hosting the last day's rally together. In Togo, there was no indoor venue that could host more than the 15,000 people who were in the country for the West African convention, and the only venue would have to be one that was suitable for an open-air rally, like a stadium.

Togolese President Gnassingbé Eyadema, since ascending to power in 1967, had banned every open-air meeting for political rallies, and extended the ban to religious crusades, conventions, and any other type of social gathering. But the most improbable thing happened. God had made provision to change the hearts of rulers for His glory. Through the ministry, a young man who had been one of President Eyadema's trusted inner circle officers, accepted Jesus as his saviour and decided to turn away from every cult into which he had immersed his life. He was grateful to have stepped into freedom from bondage and begin a walk with Christ. He took it upon himself to speak to President Eyadema.

The theme for the Full Gospel weeklong rally, scheduled to start on February 3, was "Discerning the Time", and the event was announced on national television and on every radio station in the country. With President Eyadema's approval, the Full Gospel Business Men's Fellowship International held its convention at the national sports stadium, attracting more than 20,000 people. It became a night of tremendous teaching service and a Holy Spirit-filled encounter where many people gave their lives to Jesus.

John Darku, the Ghanaian emissary to evangelist Bonnke, called about two weeks later. He had heard of Full Gospel's outreach in Togo, and spoke of how Reinhard Bonnke had hoped to minister to the people in the country but with the decade-old ban in place, they hadn't been able to do so. But now the roadblock in Togo was no more. I arranged for a Fellowship leader in Togo to work with the country's leadership and President Eyadema to get an invitation.

Eyadema agreed for the evangelist to host a three-day event in a stadium near his hometown in the Kara Region, and another three-day event in Lomé, the capital city. This was beyond anything we could have asked for. From the first Fellowship meeting in Hôtel du 2 Février in Lome, Togo, we could never have imagined the powerful testimonies that were to arise out of the West African nation. I had been privileged to have become a vessel to preach the good news, but it had taken a chance meeting with Kwakugan Apaloo at a train station in Grenoble in 1986, to open an incredibly unexpected door in Togo.

Two years later, Reinhard Bonnke was set to arrive in Ghana in 1993 for a crusade. His Christ for All Nations ministry drew millions of people to Jesus across the African continent and it was a privilege to help in any way I could. A network of churches collaborated to form a planning committee, working with Bonnke's team to arrange the event. Often, the Assemblies of God church took a leading role in some of the advance planning with the foreign emissaries, as did John Darku, the evangelist's local representative in Ghana.

I volunteered to pick up Bonnke from the airport in Accra for the 4-hour drive to Kumasi. This turned out to be a rare opportunity to hear him speak from the heart, and we traded stories about where we had both been, and some of the amazing things we had seen God do. From being a guest in my home, to coming along to visit Asantehene

Osei Tutu in Manhyia Palace, his visit to Kumasi had been incredibly refreshing for him also.

Over the next five days, I witnessed a series of powerful nights of worship overflowing with testimonies of amazing miracles and praise. He spoke to men and women who had accepted the call to salvation to join a local church, and had decided to walk fully in Christ's redemption. The evangelist was grateful for every gesture of kindness that I had willingly extended to him, and everything I had been fortunate to do to help with his outreach work.

It was a few months later, in June 1993, at a convention in Boston, Massachusetts that I learned that Bonnke had been so incredibly moved by a sense of generosity and devotion that he couldn't wait to share his gratitude in a letter to Demos Shakarian, the founder of the Full Gospel Business Men's Fellowship International.

For many years, Demos had learned about my work in Ghana and across Africa, but perhaps the pictures from Bonnke spoke in a manner that words couldn't describe. Bonnke's letter to Demos was humbling, and as a farmer who had heeded God's call to rally Christian businessmen to support ministry work, he saw his vision coming to reality around the world with Full Gospel leaders creating avenues for men and women from different nations to worship the one true God. It touched his heart greatly.

On the stage in Boston, large prints of scenes from Reinhard Bonnke's Kumasi crusade were displayed next to each other. It meant the world to him that our paths crossed, working together in the Full Gospel leadership to be instrumental in such a powerful outreach. I had served in the Strategic Planning Team for the Fellowship for several years, and on that evening in Boston, Demos appointed me the International Secretary. For a man who had been invited just to speak at an event in 1981, I didn't know how far God would take me some twelve years later to speak His truth to many leaders and businessmen, from Indonesia and Japan to Brazil and the United States, Kenya and Malawi and all the way to Australia.

I was still serving as the representative of Africa on the Pan African Council (PAC), and also as international director of the Fellowship, but what was more moving was when Demos smiled and asked that someday when his life on earth was done, and his son Richard was to continue the work of the Fellowship, that I watch over him. It was a father's trust in a Christian brother whose world had been much different from his own, but our lives had come together to serve the same Great Commission. It was a fellowship that had connected me to my kind—business people who stood for Christ, and who chose to make a real impact in the marketplace and their communities.

I began my work by travelling across African nations and working with local leaders to revive the hearts of businessmen to serve in God's kingdom.

I remember how, soon after the Togo convention, Victor Jocktane and people in Gabon urged that we head to their country for a similar event. The hope was to build on the success of the work in one Francophone country into another. With my wife, I headed to the Gabon consulate in Lome, Togo, to apply for a visa. Despite the purpose of our visit, entry into Gabon had become difficult because of the country's oil wealth that encouraged the government to restrict the entry of foreigners. Hence, we needed an official invitation.

We received the invitation a week later, and had to travel to Abidjan, Côte D'Ivoire, to board a plane into Gabon. Full Gospel Business Men's Fellowship International planned to host an All Africa Convention in the capital, Libreville. We also received word that Prime Minister Simon Essimengane would arrange for us to meet with himself and President Omar Bongo. As a Fellowship, our outreach had always been to businesspeople and leaders, and when we had the opportunity to share our message with a country's President, that was always an answered prayer.

We arrived in Gabon, and were taken to the President's residence. Together with Christiana, Rose Kogombe, Prime Minister Simon Essimengane, along with Richard Shakarian, International Treasurer

Ronny Svenhard, we fellowshipped with the President in his home. He listened to every word. For a man who was Muslim, there was no greater demonstration of obedience to God's will than watching the President ask his wife and children to join us in prayer, as they knelt on the floor in submission to the one true God.

In Gabon, we had seen the manifestation of God's powerful presence even before we set foot in the convention auditorium. President Bongo wanted to support the work that was to impact his own country, and he offered $20,000 to help defray much of the cost of accommodation and facilities for the thousands of people who would be in attendance for the Pan African Council's meeting of the Full Gospel Business Men's Fellowship International. For every man and woman who surrendered their lives to Jesus in Gabon, I deemed it a privilege to have stood with a group of committed Christian brothers and sisters to share His hope and His redemption.

I ended up in Lusaka, Zambia, encouraging Christian businessmen to appreciate the opportunity each of us had to become missionaries even as we did our work, because most of us had a rare opportunity to travel and lead in our communities in ways most preachers and religious leaders might never be able to do. In all my years of serving with the Fellowship, what had touched my heart the most had been the fact that no one received payment to serve, but it had given businessmen and women a chance to use every wealth and influence to do the single most important work on earth, sharing the truth of Christ's salvation.

Several people had been part of the Fellowship that had been started years earlier by the American tourists, but it was time to rejuvenate the chapter and boldly open our doors to men and women to stand in their faith, and lead in their work. In Zambia, President Frederick Chiluba joined the Fellowship's Presidential Breakfast held in Lusaka, and it was in this meeting that he declared Zambia a Christian nation. Without forcing the faith on anyone, Chiluba prayed that his country would be one whose leadership and people would commit to working with each other, helping each other, with values and sincere actions that will bring God all the glory.

In countries like South Africa, Malawi, the Democratic Republic of Congo, and Uganda, we had a chance to revive many of the Fellowship chapters, and I was humbled to lead work whose impact was to last long after I was gone. John Njaw worked tirelessly to revive the chapter in Dares Salaam, Tanzania. It was in Kayembe Wadikonda, a brother from Kinshasa, Congo, that I saw the incredible heart of a man with a conviction to lead and compassion to serve.

From the moment we established the Pan African Council, Wadikonda accepted the appointment to serve as secretary, and even though he had a family to care for and a business to tend to, he found the energy to travel across the Central African region to open chapters in many countries and encourage other leaders.

I was with Wadikonda when the Fellowship was invited to help negotiate peace between Congolese President Mobutu Sese Seko and Prime Minister Étienne Tshisekedi. Unlike the former, whose leadership and repressive regime struggled to win public opinion and the support of the international community, Tshisekedi's work as Prime Minister put him in the middle of the day-to-day governance of the country. Apparently, President Mobutu was threatened by Tshisekedi supposedly amassing power to overthrow him.

In a country that had struggled through the years of instability and torture, many of the leaders hoped the rift between the two men wouldn't plunge the country into further chaos. Several of the political leaders and business community who were part of the Fellowship pushed for a meeting to diffuse the impasse, and resolve the differences.

I travelled with Richard Shakarian, John Carrett, Bruno Burton, Kayembe Wadikonda, and an interpreter, Kolongi. From Kinshasa, a private aircraft took us to a huge palace where President Mobutu lived, in the mountainous and woody parts of the country. We held a successful meeting, prayed with him, and later travelled back to Kinshasa to meet with Tshisekedi to do the same. The Fellowship did not have any political affiliations, and the tangible faith we professed had become one that gave us the courage to share a peace that can only come through Jesus Christ, irrespective of the situation and the personalities.

For the Congolese men and women whose lives and families were often torn apart in the horrors of civil wars, imprisonments, and senseless murders, it was our prayer that our presence in any country, as a Christian Fellowship, would bring a peace that truly transcended human understanding.

Beyond the Democratic Republic of Congo, Wadikona went on to do phenomenal work for the Fellowship in the French-speaking countries, opening chapters in Equatorial Guinea, Congo-Brazzaville, and parts of Cameroon.

* * * * *

Jim Allenby, President of Proctor and Gamble, an American consumer goods corporation, served as the Vice President of the Fellowship, and stood side by side with founder Demos Shakarian. He had been a remarkable visionary and a Christian brother devoted to the work of the Fellowship. By 1991, Demos' declining health had become a cause for concern for the leadership, and we knew it was only a matter of time before he wouldn't have the energy to do the demanding work required of the President of the Fellowship.

Since 1951, Demos had availed himself to be voted on at the end of every three-year appointment to serving, and every time, the Fellowship unanimously selected him to serve as President. It was at a 1991 international convention in Florida that Allenby proposed that the Fellowship make Demos a *Life President*, arguing that it would be our way of honouring a man who carried a vision that God placed in his heart through the years.

At the next board meeting, we agreed to take the idea to a vote by the International Directors who represented Full Gospel chapters across the world. The proposal received a standing ovation from the International Directors, all of whom felt they owed a debt of gratitude to a shared vision that had brought us all together.

Two years later, we met at a board meeting in Anaheim, California where the Executive Board decided it was time for Demos to choose his successor. There was still work to be done across the world, and for the continuity of the Fellowship, it was best for the founder to begin the emotional process of handing over his work to anyone he chose to inherit it. Both of his sons had been actively involved in the Fellowship.

Stephen had spent years as an excellent administrator with an extraordinary sense of service, and it was the same for Demos' older son Richard who had also been by his father's side through the years and had served in the Fellowship faithfully. It was Demos' choice, and as a man who had been privileged to serve the cause of Christ through a network of businessmen from around the world, I would support anyone Demos chose, even if that person was not his own son.

I was with other leaders from the continents, Englishman John Jones and French Bruno Burton, both of whom served as International Presidents from Europe, Koo Entem from Singapore who represented Asia, and Benny Gray as the International President from Australia. Demos probably would have nominated several people, and allowed the Fellowship's directors to vote on who should be his successor, but every one of the directors understood the significance of the request, and we agreed it was most honouring to give the founder the chance to select the person he deemed would be best to carry on with his vision.

Demos chose his older son Richard to succeed him. Even before we left the meeting room and this news was to reach the Fellowship, the dissension and discord had set in. There were several people who preferred Demos' younger son Stephen to take over, while others supported the appointment of Richard. There were also others who believed that perhaps it was time for an outsider, someone other than the two sons, to lead the Fellowship. Even though I had heard of the grumblings and occasional suggestive comments, in one moment, there had been people nodding and smiling at Demos' decision, and the next minute lobbying to reverse that same decision.

As the International Secretary, both factions wanted me to support their position. I supported the founder's position, simply because we had asked him to select his successor, even when he wanted us to elect one. Even in that Anaheim conference room when he chose Richard, if anyone had a reason to oppose it, I imagined that would have been the ideal time to voice their concerns. My only recommendation was, rather than expend energy on who led, to not forget that no one person possesses all of the strengths and leadership traits that made the Fellowship the influential ministry it had become.

Demos was not perfect and did not possess every leadership ability, but as leaders, we had stood behind him with our talents and knowledge through the years, and I believed that we could do the same for Richard. I had absolutely no problem serving with Richard, and in fact, I welcomed him wholeheartedly. What drew me to the Fellowship in 1981 was the heart of men to build the kingdom of God, not personalities. I had not sacrificed thousands of dollars of my own money travelling around the world for the sake of notoriety or posturing for a business opportunity. I was not going to start now.

Rose Shakarian called. She was Demos' wife, and an incredible woman of faith who had stood by her husband for decades, working across America and in all the corners of the world. Now, members of the Executive Council were pressing her to influence Demos to change his mind. She spoke to me about the people who disagreed with her husband's choice, and the people who threatened plainly to break away from Full Gospel.

Regardless of who chose to walk away, the Fellowship had been the vision of a man who had been bold enough to follow God's calling on his life, and there was nothing anyone could say to persuade me to oppose him. More than a friend, he had been a brother in faith, and I couldn't help but marvel at the incredible doors God used him to open for hundreds of faith leaders and businessmen around the world. His absence was sure to leave a void, and the only consoling thought was that Almighty God in His own wisdom sets His plan in motion for its own time and its own season.

I remember a Brazilian entrepreneur in the Fellowship who was among the people lobbying for a complete change in direction so that he would be considered for the position of International President in Demos' absence. He invited me to Rio de Janeiro, Brazil, to see the manufacturing companies he had established and his business and political connections in the country. Even more, he had constructed a huge office complex and equipped it fully to serve as the international office in the event there was a splintering of the Fellowship, and he emerged the leader. It was a rather bizarre strategy, but that didn't change my position. A couple of the members on the Executive Council openly told me they had decided to walk away, but one thing I believed—I couldn't force other men to serve a vision in which they didn't genuinely believe.

I spoke with Demos. He knew which people disagreed with his choice and who was working behind the scenes to derail his vision. He acknowledged all of their opinions, but in the end, he had his reasons. *"Darko, I have given my word, and I will not change it. Richard is President of Full Gospel"*.

I headed to Ghana.

I had just landed at Kotoka International Airport when I received a telephone call from Richard, that his father Demos had gone to be with the Lord. He had died on that same Friday of heart failure in Downey Community Hospital, in California. The family, as part of Armenian culture, intended to perform any final rites as soon as they could arrange to. In his final days, Demos had requested that I serve as one of his pallbearers, and that required that I return to the United States quickly.

The days were difficult as I dealt with the grief and loss of a friend. It was even more overwhelming when Evangelist Oral Roberts, who had been friends with Demos for many years, handed me a pair of white gloves, with which I would be carrying my friend's body to the final resting place. We were soon to release 100 doves at his graveside, a touching image in a time of sadness even as we celebrated the life of a man who had finished his race. In the presence of hundreds of people gathered to bid farewell to Demos, Oral Roberts announced Demos' choice for Richard to lead the organization.

The same evening I met with the Executive Council and other international leaders before they headed back to their countries the next day. Without the founder of the Fellowship, the cracks widened, and if it was if there were some leaders who had been waiting on the perfect time to walk away. The American chapter turned this fracture into a legal battle, and ultimately many of the members left also. It was the same with the Fellowships in Europe and Asia.

The differing opinions on leadership had gradually ripped apart the unity beyond repair. We had become better individuals by learning, and serving, and growing together in faith. Our different skills and personalities from different cultures and countries made us colourful threads in a beautiful tapestry. We had a myriad of reasons to stand together in harmony, but it seemed what was binding us together had been Demos, not the vision he shared.

I continued as International Secretary, working with Richard, who devoted his life to the same passion as his father had done. We travelled extensively across Africa, to Russia, and many parts of Eastern Europe, and Australia. In 2009, Richard appointed a young Ghanaian brother Danny Mawuenyega to take over my work for the Fellowship.

The joy of serving, for me, will forever be a privilege. I had been honoured to carry the message of hope and grace to parts of the world that I never imagined I would reach. I was a poultry farmer who told God that I was willing, even if I was incapable, that He could use me for His own glory. What mattered to me had always been not where I served, but how I served. Through Full Gospel, I have been fortunate to reach the world and at every turn speak boldly in honour of the God who saved me and sent me to share his message. I have been blessed to share my faith, and hopefully encourage men and women to stand firm in theirs too.

For all the work I did as an entrepreneur, there was no amount of wealth or influence that rivalled the fact that God can indeed use men and women with fears and doubts and shortcomings just like me, and equip them to change the course of history. Serving others had become a living principle for me, just as the words of Peter encourage, *"Each of you should use whatever gift you have received to serve others, as faithful stewards of God's grace in its various forms. So that in all things God may be praised through Jesus Christ"*.

CHAPTER 22

OUTSIDERS

Boateng. GPC. Reluctant Politician.

Jerry Rawlings and his PNDC administration agreed to set up a 258-member National Consultative Assembly to engage different groups in the new constitution that was underway. The Provisional National Defense Council (PNDC) had been established after the military coup in 1981 as the supreme national government, and ten years later, their plan was to solicit feedback from all stakeholders in the country.

Ghana's path to multiparty democracy in 1992 meant eventually lifting the ban on political parties and the creation of a constituent assembly whose focus would be the drafting of a new constitution. The draft was to be submitted to a national referendum. Ghanaians of all political, social, and economic leanings looked forward to a new dawn in the country's history.

Kwaku Boateng reached out to me in 1990. I knew a little about him as a public servant in the late 1960s but this was the first time we met in person. He had served in President Nkrumah's Convention People's Party (CPP) administration as Minister for Interior and Local Government, Information Minister, and later Education Minister around 1964. He left Ghana after the 1966 coup d'état. He joined a British company, Cementation, whose work was similar to some of what Nkrumah had focused on during his tenure, building bridges and investing in infrastructure projects.

Kwaku returned to Ghana with political aspirations, and the decades away from Ghana had not stripped away that desire. He had done all he could to tuck it away, and reasoned that 1992 was a perfect re-entry into the political world, perhaps to reconnect with his CPP roots. He said he had friends and backers in Europe who were urging him to get involved in the politics in Ghana.

I didn't have any personal relationship with Kwaku. All I knew about him was that he was a lawyer and he spoke about his life grounded in faith and service to the Lord. I genuinely appreciated his shared sense of having godly leaders in authority. Where we struck a friendship was when Kwaku spoke about his active involvement in Kensington Temple, a charismatic church near London's Marble Arch in England. The church was one that I had visited several times when I was visiting England, and on finding out that Kwaku was a leader in the church, it was not difficult to imagine that his interest in the success of Ghana's politics would be driven by much more than a personal desire.

I was a leader in both the Full Gospel Business Men's Fellowship International and Assemblies of God church, and it was great to finally listen to a man who truly believed he could make a difference by participating in Ghana's politics. Kwaku desperately wanted to join the Fellowship, and the national leadership was happy to open a new chapter, the Accra City chapter at Novotel, where he acted as a leader to serve many of the people with whom he had worked through the years.

A few weeks later, with the PNDC seeking participation in the Consultative Assembly, Kwaku suggested that he had the time and was willing to represent the Ghana Pentecostal Council (GPC) at the Assembly, only if I could introduce him to the church's leaders. The Council was made up of The Apostolic Church of Ghana, Assemblies of God church, Church of God, and the Church of Pentecost, as well as several smaller charismatic movements. My relationship with the Council's elders had made me the perfect person who could vouch for Kwaku Boateng.

I mentioned him to Council Chairman Apostle Yeboah, the General Superintendent of the Assemblies of God church Reverend Asore, and other prominent figures in the Council. If Kwaku Boateng could help the church in any way to influence public policy, we needed to give him any support we could. Fortunately, the orthodox denominations had formed the Christian Council and were represented on the Assembly, so this would give another seat to a group that shared the same Godly principles as a foundation for governance. We needed a good lawyer and one who had a heart for Jesus at the Consultative Assembly, and they agreed to select Kwaku.

It was only a few weeks into the deliberations at the Consultative Assembly that Kwaku said he had met with some of his old CPP acquaintances who also had knowledge of what the PNDC administration was ultimately planning.

Apparently, Kwaku Boateng had made friends with political insiders who had assured him that Jerry Rawlings and his key advisors, who supposedly traced their political and governing ideologies to Nkrumah's CPP, were devising strategies to mount an opposition to the Progress Party, which was now the New Patriotic Party (NPP).

Once the ban on party politics was lifted, Kwaku planned to form a political party and contest the 1992 elections. He was adamant he didn't want to join either of the two main parties, or a coalition. I supported his stance, so that whether he won or lost, the platform upon which he had stood would remain. For Kwaku Boateng, having convinced himself that some of the influential political operatives would endorse his candidacy, he could afford to drift in any direction that supported his ambition.

I took Kwaku to every Fellowship meeting where he shared his vision for Ghana, but also his commitment to God's work. He needed our backing. His party would be the National Convention Party (NCP). I travelled with him to parts of the world where I had met godly men and women who were happy to financially support Kwaku Boateng's campaign.

Much of Kwaku's life was deeply woven into the entrenched character of Ghana's politics, and it was evident that he had kept a keen eye on developments in the country. He hadn't missed a pulse. He claimed men like John Tettegah, who had once headed Ghana's Trade Union Congress (TUC) during the Nkrumah years, and Kojo Tsikatah, who had been an influential politician and National Security Advisor, had reached out to him. The men supposedly assured him that they believed Jerry Rawlings and his military administration would hand over power to a civilian government, and have absolutely no interest in taking part in the 1992 elections. Rumours swirled on whether Rawlings would indeed step out of politics.

From a splintered CPP political slant, there were several parties that were to be formed, and one would be Kwaku's NCP. The tactic was for all the parties to campaign separately to earn the support of sections of the country where each was dominant. The plan would be such that when it was time to select a party head, the different parties would coalesce around one, and let Kwaku Boateng emerge as the presidential candidate. Somehow, Kwaku had convinced himself this was a much better path than to become president of Ghana.

Rawlings was still popular among the factions, but Kwaku was sure Rawlings was not interested in party politics and was ready to support the candidacy of a man with strong CPP roots. That was the turning point in my association with NCP, and my new friend Kwaku Boateng.

I had travelled across Ghana with Kwaku and assured everyone that I could find in the Fellowship, the Ghana Pentecostal Council, and the Assemblies of God church in particular, that Kwaku would be the best candidate to champion the values of the body of Christ, and committed Christians who truly sought the welfare of a nation. Now I couldn't be so sure.

Then the strangest thing happened.

The *New Nation* newspaper ran an advertisement on its front page: "Kwabena Darko for President". I had never thought of being President of Ghana, or even a political appointee. I was a chicken farmer who never lost sight of where God found me, and I was set on a mission that God had put into my heart. It seemed Ghana's transition to party politics had opened the floodgates to a host of viewpoints for governance, some unclear, others short-sighted, and some that could even set the country backwards.

Many people had seen me with Kwaku Boateng, and with our friendship headed in different directions, the political sponsors were not interested in finding out if I indeed announced an intent to compete in the upcoming elections. They must have had propaganda, to make the field murkier. I didn't know who was behind it, and certainly had no way of knowing the true intent. Some of the leading Fellowship members had decided to endorse Kwaku Boateng.

Then the advertisement "Kwabena Darko for President" ran again.

Hilla Limman, who had also decided to contest for the presidential elections, came to visit in Accra. He was a devout Christian and more than seeking my endorsement, he was considering selecting me as his running mate for the People's National Convention (PNC). I had first met Limann in 1981 when he was elected President in 1979 following the exclusion of Minister for Foreign Affairs Alhaji Imoru Egala by the then ruling Supreme Military Council (SMC). With some of his advisors, Limann came to my farms in Akropong Asante to outdoor his agricultural policy. Since then, much of what I knew about him was about the Rawlings coup d'état in 1981 that overthrew his short-lived government, and his desire to govern again. I declined his offer.

"Kwabena Darko for President".

Why not?

There were enough issues that I cared about, many of them about which I was even aggrieved. I had seen a country's reliance on state-owned companies unravel any promise it had, and seen first-hand how the collective mindset of a nation could crush every God-given opportunity we had to thrive. I had seen how fiscal policies that stifled private enterprises strangled economies, and how ordinary Ghanaians could rally around a vison that uplifts them and sets us all toward a future. Someone could stand up and avoid vulgar and vindictive attacks on other political opponents, and instead, choose to see the heart of everyone vying for the position as patriots seeking to make a difference. Our visions and subsequent policy agendas were markedly different, but perhaps not our love for the country.

Why not?

Why not Kwabena Darko for President?

If it was God's will for me to win an election, I would, and there would be nothing that any coalition or military could do to change it. If it was not God's will for my life, there was absolutely nothing I could say that would change the heart of the men and women to earn their vote. I might have had a great opportunity to sound an alarm on the need for righteous men and women to rise up and take leadership positions in their countries, because in the end, every action we took that day would affect generations to come behind us. In addition to the President who often became a prominent symbol of leadership, there were a host of leadership positions, all of whom influenced society in one way or another. Perhaps, one would hear the cry to stand for righteousness. *"When the righteous rule, the people will indeed rejoice".*

My wife Christiana couldn't help but think of Esther. She was a young Jewish woman living in exile in the world of the Persian diaspora. Eventually she becomes the wife of the Persian king Ahasuerus, and in place to persuade the king to retract an order for the annihilation of Jews throughout the empire. Unwilling, the young woman still found the courage that saved the Jewish people from destruction. If I could, but I didn't, and something awful happened to my people, it would affect all of us. Reluctant still, if I got involved in Ghana politics, I was stepping into a world without a sense of familiarity, safety, and certainty.

Unfortunately, much of what I stood for and tried to share didn't seem to resonate even with Christians. The tension and vitriol that filled partisan conversations forced well-meaning born-again Christians to become passive onlookers of governance. Politics for many had become a game that was to be won at all cost, not a quest to govern with a heart to serve. I was confident that my decision was much bigger than the moment. I had to step forward, but even more boldly, I had to be sure I would not compromise my faith and my integrity for votes and for political endorsement.

Several stalwarts in the former CPP, Komla Gbedemah and Kojo Botsio, and their colleagues called to support my candidacy. Unfortunately, every endorsement required a tradeoff and compromise, exactly what I had promised myself I would never succumb to. With my wife and children and a circle of believers, I had prayed for many days and nights about the decision to enter politics. I didn't have to give lofty and empty promises to trick Ghanaians just to satisfy my personal ambition. I didn't need to be president of my country, all I wanted was for God's will to be done. I was going with God alone, to speak His unvarnished truth.

Presidential and parliamentary elections were set for November and December 1992, and in spite of the endless string of challenges, shameful accusations, and bizarre suspicions, an independent interim National Electoral Commission was established in February of 1992.

I did not have a problem opening up to vulnerability to and even rejection from the people I would be stepping out to serve. Politics, for me, was unlike business or poultry farming where I needed to take calculated risks that benefited only me, or invest my own ambitions. Rather, I believed that unless a person truly committed themselves to serve his nation, their government would be a great disservice to the people.

My friend Sam Bamfo shared his opinion too. He was sure if only I could make the time to actively participate in party politics, there was certainly a need for new voices with new perspectives on leadership. He had recently retired from the military as Colonel, and never stopped advocating for civilian rule and a democratic system where the rule of law forced society to not descend into anarchy and chaos.

I remember he told of how he had confronted officers during his time in the military, only for a group to torture and leave him near death in the military barracks. He recalled the soldiers pushing burning cigarette into his ear lobe, as punishment for not towing the line. For man who had served his country for much of his adult life, he was haunted by a lawless society and prayed for a day when God-fearing leaders would emerge and challenge all Ghanaians to rise higher than the spite and hostility, and rather, fight for the future of our country.

*****

It was in 1991 that Kevin Callwood and the West African Network came to Ghana. The organization was designed by the United States Agency for International Development (USAID), an independent agency of the United States federal government focused on civilian foreign aid and development assistance, together with the Overseas Private Investment Corporation (OPIC), a government finance institution that mobilized private capital to assist with development initiatives. The West African Network had organized a trade mission to explore business opportunities in sub-Saharan Africa, and with Ghana on the verge of transitioning into a multiparty democracy, the organizers saw an avenue for bilateral investment with the private sector.

The reality in Ghana was such that in the absence of any major private enterprises, the group had only a handful of viable potential trade partners. Yet, it seemed there were enough economic indicators to lure investment if indeed the country shifted its policies to allow privatization to find a fair market to thrive. The companies that Ghana's first president Kwame Nkrumah built in the 1960s were barely functional, or operating at huge losses. The international organizations advised the government to consider divestitures of the state-owned corporations, in order for private businesses and entrepreneurs to join hands with the foreign investors.

At a meeting organized by the USAID at the Ghana Investment Centre in Accra, Callwood and his USAID counterpart Warren Weinstein hoped the discussions would mark the beginning of multisector negotiations, and that the private enterprises would be in a position to invest in the country shortly after the transition from military rule. Some of the people in at the event were private businessmen like John Kufuor who owned a brick factory in Akropong-Asante, and Texas-based businessman Chris Wilmot, and Emmanuel Botchway. In the same year, a real estate company, Regimanuel Gray Limited would be formed by a foreign investor with a local real estate entrepreneur Botchway to launch one of the many successful enterprises to be born out of the West African Network initiative. Other private businesses found opportunities to broaden their market.

I had been introduced to similar United States federal government agencies in 1972, so I was well aware of the opportunities they presented, even though the Americans weren't completely sure of the Ghanaian business landscape. I was appointed Chairman of the West African Network, and I hoped our work would lay the foundations for private enterprises, not only in agriculture, but also in industry, manufacturing, and other sectors. Even with changes in the country's constitution and political orientation on the horizon, there was still work to be done to realize any tangible results from the network.

From Accra, the group travelled to host a seminar in Dakar, Senegal, and extended the reach of private investments to other companies across the region. The discussions gave a real glimpse of what could be possible in Ghana, despite the internal economic challenges. My eyes were opened to what could be achieved if the leadership in the country was bold enough to embrace forward-thinking investment proposals that ultimately uplifted our people and the country.

It was some of the discussions in the West African Network that affirmed much of what I knew about the limitations of state-owned or controlled enterprises to attract any meaningful investment into the country.

What many of the foreign companies sought was a government that assured them of minimized risks while exploring new markets. They understood the challenges that were intrinsically connected to global markets, especially one like we had in Ghana with stagnating growth, but transitioning into an investment-driven economy.

Whether they were the financiers, investors, or contractors, unless there was a government that was willing to make tough decisions for our national interest, all of the optimism and bold ideas for accelerating economic growth would quickly fizzle into missed opportunities and empty dreams.

If I was to take a step toward presidency, I would be fighting attitudes on democracy and market capitalism that had become entrenched in Ghana's economic psyche, and had not been challenged. Governance would require providing a credible economic alternative, and one where the private sector generated jobs and fuels progress.

The network's vision was outstanding, with a clear objective for all West African countries where it set out to find business partners. Perhaps what was most fascinating about countries like the United States was in how the government promoted strategic initiatives around the world to allow its private sector to go out and build its businesses. The risk was borne by the private businesses, not the government, thus the government stood to gain for its tax base when the country was successful, yet with nothing to lose if the partnership fell apart.

From this point forward, the counsel to contest the 1992 presidential elections got louder. The life of a career politician had never been one that I found alluring, and there were the days that I reflected on how much business and farming brought me greater fulfilment, a peace that I didn't want to trade away. But there were millions of Ghanaians who didn't have the same peace and hope that I had. There were mothers and fathers whose faith in the future was dim, and every waking moment was only a step into a meaningless future. What if I could help change that?

Ghana needed to drive innovation and ingenuity. I had no interest in holding up privatization as a panacea for a supposedly sluggish bureaucracy and inherent inefficiency of government. Ghanaians needed leadership that would tout private enterprise as one with unparalleled capacity to generate prosperity, and boldly demonstrate the superiority of private ownership and the free market economy over its state-controlled counterpart.

With a hectic schedule of campaigns, conferences, and never-ending interactions with voters in local districts, I was not sure how I could accomplish every business endeavour I had undertaken through the years. Regardless of the outcome, a transition into politics was a service worth pursuing. My days were usually filled with the work of the Assemblies of God church and the Fellowship, but I had to be willing to devote time to party politics if this was indeed what God wanted for me in this season of my life. For many years, I had been so sure that nothing would convince me to be involved in party politics, until life took a series of unexpected turns.

And here I was.

CHAPTER 23

ON THE BRINK OF EVERYTHING

The Weight of Politics.

Now, with Kwaku Boateng having elected to join a different group that gave him the assurances he was looking for, I had a choice to make. My work in the Fellowship in Ghana and across Africa had created a platform whose reach I never could have imagined, and suddenly, there were several offers to join political clubs, especially as every club needed political or financial advantage.

Before the ban on political activities was lifted, the PNDC government allowed the formation of clubs and associations. The government had not passed any legislation against this, as long as they did not openly engage in political activities. There were groups like Our Heritage Club, Danquah–Busia Club, The Eagle Club, which quietly competed with Kwame Nkrumah Revolutionary Guards, and the Kwame Nkrumah Welfare Society was for membership, without openly declaring their intent.

Many of these had been formed to spread different political, social, and economic ideologies. The founders reasoned that the military government couldn't sustain its grip on the country for long, and this had become a back channel in preparation for a new republic. Most of the men who openly admitted that a 1992 transition into party politics was their opportunity seize needed my help to secure the backing of the Full Gospel, private businessmen, and Christians.

Convention People's Party (CPP) and Progress Party had been the two major political groups in the country, and even with the splintering that highlighted their differences, the fundamental ideologies remained. In the least, these clubs hoped they could provide some avenue to hold the government accountable on its policies. By 1991, this was a striking departure from a time when every known political critic of the government was branded a dissident or outright thief who was only out to loot the national coffers.

Two young men who were deeply involved in the activities of the Danquah-Busia Club visited me at my Akropong-Asante office and informed me of well-advanced plans to turn the club into a political party. For years, they had quietly laid the groundwork for party politics and perhaps used their contacts in the current government to pressure the PNDC military government to change directions. Other clubs had not carefully outlined all their options, but the Danquah-Busia Club had knowledge of timing, and were determined to find every one they could persuade to help them launch a resilient opposition. I chose not to accept membership.

On Saturday November 30, 1991, I was the featured speaker at the inaugural breakfast meeting of the Fellowship's Beach Chapter. The event was held at the Labadi Beach Hotel, and even though the Fellowship typically extended invitations to business and political leaders, this had become a place for presidential hopefuls to scout for potential partners and major donors. There were also several members of the National Consultative Assembly, the group that had been in charge of providing input to the new constitution.

At the podium, I spoke with the same excitement I had always done about my faith. Nothing about the men and women in the audience, or their intent, changed the truth about our God, and the mission for which we are called. For the people who had come only to find political sponsors, the Fellowship had never endorsed any politician, nor had we supported any party's campaign. Our organization's mission hadn't changed, even when it seemed that politics in Ghana was bracing itself for a bold new world.

After the meeting, I met Lieutenant General E. A. Erskine. He was a retired military officer who had gained popularity in the military ranks of the Acheampong administration, and also as Chief of Army Staff in the Ghana Army. He served as a commander of the United Nations Truce Supervision Organization (UNTSO) and the United Nations Interim Force in Lebanon (UNIFIL). Erskine had decided to contest the next presidential elections if indeed the PNDC give way in 1992, and he spoke of how he had been approached by some of the old Convention People's Party (CPP) loyalist to form a political party.

Since the CPP splintered after the 1966 coup that overthrew Kwame Nkrumah, pockets of CPP had tried to find their way into governance, but through new people who shared some of Nkrumah's vision, even if they didn't wholly accept the ideology. The CPP men were some of the same people who had approached me to also consider this. In Erskine's case, any presidential hopeful with a military background would be fighting an uphill battle having to convince the Ghanaian electorate that they would be any different from the PNDC military government that had ruled for ten years.

Some of the political strategists working behind the scenes had a different calculation. Their idea was for Erskine and me to join on the same party ticket. That afternoon in Labadi, we shared our thoughts briefly on what we assumed was the CPP strategy, but I didn't have an answer for Erskine or anyone. There was a lot to consider still.

It was in this climate that I was invited to the Overseas Private Investment Corporation (OPIC) conference on "Privatisation and Investment in Africa" in Dakar, Senegal. Much of the conversation by the investors and business leaders who had travelled to the event in Dakar centred on the economic problems facing African countries, despite their collective strength if we found ways to create markets for each other. Perhaps the harsh truth was that unless the country's leaders had the political desire to push toward true integration and cooperation in Africa, there was very little that the elaborate economic plans and policies could do for an individual country.

Year after year, African leaders had declared a commitment to economic integration and even made resolutions to accomplish them. It seemed the governments lacked the political courage to back such resolutions that were to provide long-term value for the countries even if they were a departure from the short-sighted gains the governments needed to win elections.

Some of the investors had formed the West Africa Network as a trade and investment group seeking to influence government's economic initiatives in a range of sectors. I served as Board Chairman for the organization in pursuit of significant foreign investments to the partner countries. Some of the businessmen in the network were lobbyists and venture capitalists seeking new markets, and with Ghana on the verge of transitioning into democracy, new opportunities were bound to emerge.

The investors, however, understood the reality of political ideologies, in that a government has the platform to open its country for investment or to close itself entirely. For the few who knew I was soon to decide on contesting the elections, I had become their ideal candidate who would champion meaningful private investments into Ghana.

In February 1992, I was invited to attend the annual National Prayer Breakfast in Washington D.C. The first time I had been to the event was in 1972, when Paris Reidhead and Al Whittaker arranged for me to join their Senator and Congressmen friends at the International Ballroom of the Washington Hilton Hotel. There, I sat patiently listening to American President Richard Nixon as he addressed an international audience, and with confidence in his nation to lead the world into its promise. I remembered vividly how he spoke about how leaders ought to give the very best they could of themselves *"to achieve goals that*

Chapter 23: On The Brink Of Everything

are bigger than all of us, bigger than differences between parties, faiths, and philosophies".

Twenty years later, I was attending the event from a completely different perspective. After it was first held in 1953 by President Dwight Eisenhower at the urging of the Reverend Billy Graham, the prayer breakfast had remained an important tradition for American leaders to gather and to pray. From what I knew, the breakfast event was a nonpartisan event organized by *the Fellowship*, a Christian network of economic and political leaders, the same people I had known since I had spent time with them in Arlington, Virginia and around some of the largest manufacturing companies across America.

For years, I had worked with my American friends, many through Opportunity International or the Fellowship to identify African leaders who would most benefit from such events. In 1992, I recommended the people who were seeking to contest the approaching presidential elections in Ghana. I travelled to Washington D.C. with J.A. Kuffuor, Kwaku Boateng, Roland Atta Kesson, all of whom held presidential aspirations, and Ato Dadzie who was serving with the PNDC.

The meetings with several of the world leaders, business executives, and leaders from the United Nations and other leading international agencies reiterated the urgency for Ghana to invest in its people and country to reap the enormous benefits that had lain dormant for so long. American President George H. Bush spoke of the four ideas that inspire his country's leadership: freedom, family, faith, and fellowship. That was what they wanted their country to stand for, a nation with a *"simple joy of praying to God"*. A nation can indeed turn its heart to God.

If I was to contest in a presidential election, sooner or later, I would wind up in one of the two traditional political camps. The parties may have broken apart and formed new ones, but they would essentially be espousing different variations of a central ideology. Then there would be political parties desperately seeking to recreate their identities and promise new ideals to Ghanaians, only to face a daunting reality: that the electorate themselves would accept one of the two political parties, not a third.

I was confident in what I stood for. I had chosen to part ways with Kwaku even though I had travelled the world to solicit financial support for his political ambitions, and introduced him at every Full Gospel event I could to give him a platform to share his vision. Nothing would persuade me to compromise what I believed in my heart, and how I expected a leader to fight for his country. The decision to serve my people was one that I was happy to leave in God's hands, and let His will be done. If I should end up with a political party, it would be one that accepted my stance on business, on society, and on faith.

S.K. Danso and a few others were the "elders" in one of the breakaway clubs that had their heritage tied to the Ghana's first president, Dr. Kwame Nkrumah. The name *Nkrumaist* subsequently defined their political philosophy. Even though I admired much of the work Dr. Nkrumah had done until his overthrow in 1966, I had never been in favour of any political agenda that leaned on socialist and communist ideas for building nations.

In Ghana, while the need to create jobs for our people remained the urgent priority, creating state-owned and state-run companies to compete with private businesses was never a useful development strategy.

The elders of the *Nkrumaist* group invited me to be one of the presidential aspirants of a political party which they would launch when the ban was lifted. The Kwame Nkrumah Welfare Society was later to become the National Independence Party (NIP). I was well received. The group leaders informed me that my name would be included on their official list, from which a candidate would be chosen by the group's Congress to be formed at a later date. I walked away with the assurance that the leaders were truly fighting for the welfare and future of ordinary Ghanaians, and that their break away from the other CPP groups wasn't motivated by their own short-sighted and selfish gain.

The gentlemen in the room were incredibly forthright and spoke candidly. They needed someone who would embody a departure from the *old ways of doing things in the Nkrumaist camp*. They spoke of how in the past, they had used "comrade" in referring to each other. Even though the word didn't have a negative connotation, because it had often been used by soldiers and also in socialist countries, the group had decided to refer to each other as "brothers" and "sisters", just as the Christians did. It was more than a change in vocabulary; it was about altering a mindset.

The ban on political activities was lifted on May 18, 1992.

I had my doubts still. Venturing into politics in Ghana didn't have to be a difficult decision for anyone, yet it was. Serving one's country didn't have to come with agony in thought. Unfortunately, ours had become a country that had once held its destiny in its grasp, only to let it slip away through our own desire to let apathy and distrust sow hate and insatiable greed. Not long ago, our national leaders and governing representatives were men and women of foresight and courage who stood together to declare independence and hope, and to be a shining light for all of Africa and the world to see.

Since 1957, we had found ways to overthrow leaders with one coup d'état after another, but short-sighted aspirations had taught men and women to skilfully siphon money that ought to have built roads, schools and hospitals in every village and town. With one government after another, we had cleverly mismanaged every asset and all the goodwill of Ghanaians, and left behind a revolving door of distrust and dread. My work with international financial institutions like International Financial Corporation (IFC), African Project Development Facility (APDF), World Bank, and the Commonwealth Development Corporation (CDC) had emphasized the need to attract foreign investment, while also being mindful of the cost of any debt to a country.

I didn't have to be a career statesman or a political insider to see the damage that had been done to our collective destiny. For a country whose forefathers had been able to stand on the world stage and speak boldly and in truth, now we struggled to tell our children what future lay ahead of them. We abandoned true patriotism long ago when leaders chose their own comfort over our collective gain and put every poor mother and child in harm's way, to save ourselves. We made a mockery of the songs we sang for *"God to bless our homeland Ghana"*, because we turned our hearts away from the Almighty God.

The world often frowned upon oppressive regimes that openly choked their people and killed their dreams, but missed the destructive traits in democratic systems where men and women led without integrity, and had no compass for what should be truth. The year 1992 could be a moment to change our country's course, it we chose to. The Ghanaian, like the people of most countries, had become adept at blaming institutions and people in authority, without pausing to wonder if indeed we too play our parts by not standing up or speaking up, and not encouraging the best in each other. It was time for a drastic shift if we wanted something different.

Politics affected us all. Incompetent leaders are a grim portrait of a society itself, and unless our voices as citizens are as loud as possible, and our actions the best we can do, however insignificant, the cycle of ineptitude will continue to ruin our nation. And also, every promise in our sons and daughters. For Ghana, our young nation still had a lot of painful memories to leave behind, and the transition from military rule to civilian rule will be a new opportunity to fix our missteps.

Politics could be honourable, if we wanted it to be. Politics will only be a *"dirty game"* as long as there were enough people willing to wallow in the mud. I rejected the notion that every politician was an incompetent fraud and dishonest in every way. Rather, any government is made up of men and women who are our brothers and sisters, and even when there are those who had chosen malice and violence to disguise their corrupt hearts, I knew many others who stood firm in honesty and who served their people with compassion and excellence.

Politics can also be an example of governance that seeks to truly lift everyone, and build systems that challenge the best in each other. A heart to serve will make itself accountable, and not give in to pride while its people suffered and many even died. Irrespective of the setbacks and frustrations, it will take an unrelenting attitude in a courageous leader to push ahead. I was a poultry farmer, business man, and industrialist, and most importantly, an evangelist. I knew who I was, and even in what could be an uphill battle, I was confident in my character, and trusted in my God in whom I have believed.

For its part, the PNDC government had successfully instilled a great deal of fear in men and women who were committed Christians and who sought to champion the values of the faith. I had seen young men who had once been devout Christians who had chosen to abandon their faith once they became involved with the military government. Ghanaians who were well informed of global affairs saw clear traits of Venezuela, Libya, and Cuba in every policy.

From 1981, the same fascist ideals that sought to create a regimented nation under a dictatorial authority had suppressed opposition groups and intimidated anyone or anything that sought to challenge the power. In Russia, I had known many missionaries and churches that lived through some of the horrors of such regimes, including the disdain for human rights, and fixation with national security. In some places, the missionaries were banned and had to flee their country.

The climate in Ghana bore a strange resemblance to some of these countries where the leadership preached the value of nationalism over that of any individual, and turned Christians in Ghana into spectators. Devout Christians with incredible leadership abilities convinced each other that politics was for unbelievers, not for them. But the leader that God wanted to step out of the shadows to lead his people would be one who stood firm on the Christian values of service, of selfless leadership, and of integrity.

If I contested the 1992 presidential elections in Ghana, I will compete not only with men and women with ambition to lead a nation, but also a mindset that a born-again Christian could not actively engage in partisan politics. Ghana had a large group of people who identified with the Christian faith, irrespective of their understanding of what it truly meant. Somehow they painted politics and politicians as people who enjoyed hurling insults and staining each other's reputation just to win a vote.

I believed that if anyone could stand in front of millions of people to lead the way, there will be no better person than one whose heart is set on God, and whose steps are truthfully guided by Christian values. I will have to be a leader who will inspire in truth, and serve every man and woman, every child and adult, irrespective of their wealth or fame.

Christian leadership will not be one that touts religious doctrines and affiliations with any church or a group. A Christian leader will not be another version of the millions of people who show up in churches across Ghana every Sunday, and yet, never car to let their lives demonstrate the values and character of Christ. Instead, a Christian leader will know they cannot succeed on their own, and that all that they are is because of God's abundant grace in their lives. It is this same grace that they will seek every opportunity to share with their brothers and sisters in every district across the country. *"When the righteous rule, the people will rejoice"*, was true centuries ago, and will be true forever.

For much of my adult life, I had learned the worth of perseverance from leading men and women in Town Fellowships, Scripture Union, church Councils, to large organizations like Darko Farms, Opportunity International, and Full Gospel Business Men's Fellowship International. Serving a nation will require an understanding that there will be a broad range of issues, diverse groups of people, and a near impossible task to satisfy the complex motivations that drove every individual. Yet, if I served with humility and integrity to bring God the glory, every decision would be one that sought the best interest of a society, not of the rich, the influential, or party loyalists.

Chapter 23: On The Brink Of Everything

In 1991, I travelled more than 50 times to different countries around the world for both business and ministry, and even with enormous opportunities ahead for me, contesting a presidential election meant that I was choosing to lift my hand and ask God for His will to be done in my life. In all of my work with local and international leaders, I truly believed Ghana had a golden opportunity to shift away from social and economic policies that had stifled our own development, and instead make a collective decision to move towards our God-given destiny.

If I was to serve my country, I had the model of Jesus washing His disciples' feet to guide my actions. It would be an incredible act of humility and service, one that showed authentic Christianity in a leader willing to be a servant to his people. I believed there was room for a leader who would genuinely refrain from the needless spite and violence that disgraced politics in Ghana, even if people had come to accept that as the norm. My journey had been guided by uncompromising faith and unwavering trust in Almighty God, and even on a national stage, I would stand firm to lead as best as I knew how. For meaningful change, a new breed of leaders had to rise to steer the affairs of Ghana, not because of what they stood to gain personally.

I was now a member of the National Independence Party (NIP).

I donated five million cedis to help defray some of the expenses for the official registration of the political party. There was also a string of expenses we expected to incur in the coming weeks, from printing posters to other campaign souvenirs. Then, I was invited to a Standing Committee meeting where I was introduced to members, and asked to join the team that was drawing the party's manifesto.

The party's Congress was still ahead. The party's constitution required its congress to elect presidential candidates, and it was only after I had been nominated and elected at congress that I could contest at the national level. I visited every region in Ghana and single-handedly provided funds for the opening of about half of the offices of the NIP throughout the country.

I travelled north to Brong Ahafo Region, and on several occasions to the capital Sunyani. My first visit as a presidential aspirant was to address a meeting of the regional executives. My message was simple, that Ghana needed a dedicated and selfless leader who truly understood the value of a private sector to uplift a nation. The problems that Ghanaian entrepreneurs and working professionals faced were largely engrained in the policies that touted socialist ideals even though they were not conducive to the welfare of our country. I took the time to speak with every party officer and supporter in towns like Atebubu and Dormaa Ahenkro.

In Dormaa Ahenkro, I addressed supporters who had gathered at Dormaa Ahenkro Community Centre, and continued in Berekum, Bechem, and Duayaw-Nkwanta. In another town, Wamfie, I donated 70,000 cedis to be used in opening a branch office. It was obvious that some of the local offices needed immediate help, and if I was in position to help, I didn't hesitate. It was while I was returning from Wamfie that I heard on the radio that Professor F. A. Botchway, one of the presidential aspirants, had withdrawn his candidature in my favour. If that was a sign of things to come, the march to the NIP congress wouldn't be as confrontational as some had predicted.

I knew I had to intensify my campaign in the Central Region because three of the presidential aspirants had roots in that part of the country, and it was very likely they would have several loyalty votes in their favour from people who valued the strength of their cultural bond, over any policies they sought to implement for Ghana. Both G. P. Hagan, and Dan Lartey, who was also serving as the Regional Chairman of the party, were seeking the same nomination. A lady who earned the nickname Obaatan Pa, as the only female aspirant in the party, was also on the ticket. I could only count on the worth of my character and the honesty of the platform upon which I campaigned.

Then I stumbled across a group of young men who called themselves the Darko Fun Club in Agona Swedru. They were a grassroots group determined to campaign in their area, and all they needed was a vehicle to help with their transportation. I had no hand in the affairs of their group and I did not attempt to direct them in anything. All I could was to strongly caution them to refrain from using the group to do anything that could tarnish my reputation. Apart from Agona Swedru, I had the chance to address the synod of the Presbyterian Church at Agona Nsaba, after which I spoke to some members of the party at Nsaba Township.

By far, the largest audience that I had in the Central Region was the delegates meeting at Mankesim. After the meeting I made sure to exchange greetings with every delegate and to listen to the concerns from their local constituencies. I wasn't sure what to expect from the Central Region, but all I could do was to do my best.

My pre-congress activities in the Eastern Region was unusually hectic. I was particularly bent on winning over the delegates in Koforidua, and surrounding towns. At a meeting with the delegates and party supporters at Legion Hall, my focus was to help each of them understand my economic platform, and hopefully, earn their vote as the presidential candidate.

The region was a large geographical area, but I left no stone unturned in my effort to win delegates. The strategy was to visit as many delegates and constituencies as possible from Kwahu Fodoa, Amma Dede, Danteng, Akwasiho, Nsawam, Anum-Apapam, Odumasi Krobo, Somanya, Atimpoku, Mpraeso, all the way to the Afram Plains. It would be difficult to convey complex social and economic ideas in the midst of cheering crowds, so reaching them individually was definitely an effective alternative.

My friend Colonel Sam Bamfo was incredibly helpful in introducing me to the electorate and delegates in the Kwahu area. He was a native of Mpraeso, and had spent many years developing professional relationships in Kwahu. He personally ensured that I visited almost every town in the region, and that none of the towns were too small to hear my message. Political campaigns meant reaching every possible voter.

Yet the campaign had its limitations. I could not visit the Akim Kotoku area of Eastern Region, towns like Oda, Kade, and Asamankese. It was the same with the Greater Accra Region, and because of the party headquarters in Accra, I assumed that I could deal with the representatives when they visited party headquarters. With the exception of Mamprobi, where I attended a meeting of the branch executives, I did not visit any other constituency.

Politics in Ghana had a rather fascinating side, where a constant stream of callers from almost every constituency in the country showed up to my office seeking help. Each constituency and every voter had a problem to be solved and somehow, they all believed I was the answer to their problems. For some, I had become the perfect person with the money to fix their personal problems. Then there were other disputes ranging from opening of constituency offices to solving personal conflicts between party members. Now, they were my headache.

Perhaps the most interesting groups of people who showed up at the party's offices were the artists, and songwriters of different genres, each wanting a job from me and the party. One after another, they brought along numerous souvenirs, songs, t-shirts, flags and a host other memorabilia, even though we hadn't asked anyone to do such a thing. Inadvertently, many of these people, in order to meet my preference, were unconsciously advertising me to the electorate and people in their network.

In Accra, the students at Ghana Fellowship of Evangelical Students (GHAFES) in Legon, invited me to speak on integrity. It was a good opportunity to introduce myself to the academic community and to win the confidence of the Christian students. Coincidentally, on the same campus, I attended the National Convention of Women's Aglow where my wife Christiana launched a new book, To God Be the Glory. She was serving as the West African International Outreach Director of Aglow, and gave me an opportunity to address the Christian women in attendance.

I also got the chance to address the closing ceremony of the Ghana National Convention of the Full Gospel Business Men's Fellowship International, where I used the opportunity to explain my involvement in politics to the members who felt that a Christian should only vote, and not be voted for, and also to encourage any fellow Christian brother who could help my cause outside the party hierarchy and campaign network.

I visited Tamale and Yendi in the Northern Region, where I met the regional executives and party delegates, canvassing for their support, before heading further north to Bolgatanga and Navrongo in the Upper East Region. The long distances between the major towns hampered my campaign activities in the northern parts of Ghana. Travelling in these areas, along some of the horrible roads, it was difficult to make it to the Upper West Region.

Time was not on my side, so I arranged for all the delegates from the southern parts of Volta Region to meet me at Sogakofe, and for the rest from the northern parts to meet me at Hohoe. I addressed the crowd and introduced myself and my political programme. At the end of both meetings, I was pretty convinced that I had made a good impression and that the delegates from Volta Region would cast their vote for me.

Before I attended the Regional Delegates meeting at Takoradi, I had already visited some towns in the region. Bibiani was the first town I visited in the Western Region, and the local office was opened without any fanfare. The executive members assured me of their support. Then I travelled through Sefwi Anwiaso, Donyina, Sefwi Bekwai, to Sefwi Wiawso. In all of these towns, I had fruitful discussions with old CPP officials who were now executive members of the NIP.

I travelled to Dwenasi, in the Western Region, where the Dwenasi chapter of the Full Gospel had invited me as main speaker to their breakfast meeting. It was another opportunity to share the word of God with the people of Dwenasi and to introduce myself to the electorate. In Takoradi, my trip coincided with the regional delegates' meeting with several of the presidential aspirants, and we had a rare opportunity to discuss some of the issues we had in common. In one town after another, campaigning for delegates for NIP congress had been a hectic ordeal.

Several people had formed their own alliances and even though I believed in my chances of winning the party's nomination, the reality on the ground would be a series of winding roads. The first group of people whose assertions I had to brush aside were those who claimed that I was not a true Nkrumaist and that I had only "hijacked" the party with my money. For them, the ideal scenario will be finding a way to force me to withdraw.

Oddly, every time they devised a strategy, a perfect stranger from among their own ranks would inform me of their plans. I had never cared to plant an informant within the party, but it was as if there were some who had reasoned that my candidacy would give them a fighting chance for the elections. My presence on the political scene had come as a surprise to some.

There was another group who had plans to drag the National Independence Party into political and electoral alliance with another political party. In their minds, I would be an obstacle because I had repeatedly spoken about how I had no plans of bending to doing politics as usual. Their strategy could not materialise if I was the flagbearer of the party and so they had to do all they could to remove me from consideration.

I wasn't naïve. Politicians weren't suddenly changing their tune because I was pleading with everyone to recognize why we had chosen to seek the country's highest office. There were some who only knew intimidation, and many others whose only tactic was launching verbal attacks, even with baseless allegations and demeaning remarks. Even before the party selected its presidential candidate, differing opinions had emerged, and each side was fighting to become the hallmark of the National Independence Party.

Out of nowhere, I received a message that the party's Congress was postponed. It was an internal tactic to delay the process long enough to

Chapter 23: On The Brink Of Everything

cast doubts in my mind. For some, I was still the outsider whose leadership wouldn't give them the leeway to do just anything they wanted. Twice, the dates changed.

Supposedly, some of the party elders were pushing for a merger with other Nkrumaist parties. Their real interest was to orchestrate an electoral alliance with a party which claimed to be pursuing the same policies that Dr. Kwame Nkrumah pursued. It took a third attempt, one where the party's Standing Committee had to forcefully intervene.

The party delegates arrived in Accra on September 11, 1992 for the NIP congress over the next two days. Some had travelled from different parts of the country, and the party arranged for accommodation in Akuafo Hall, at the University of Ghana. On one hand, all the delegates gathered in one place was a golden opportunity to canvass for support. I reasoned however that I had already endeared myself to the delegates through my repeated contact beforehand, by sending party posters and other items needed to run the party offices, all at my own expense.

Of all the presidential aspirants, I had been the only one who had travelled across the country to introduce myself to the delegates and party executives. A couple of the aspirants had visited some of the constituencies but there were others who had never taken the time to visit any constituency at all.

NIP Congress started at about 9 o'clock on Saturday September 12, 1992. The Congress elected Alhaji Imoro Ayarna the National Chairman, and elected three more people as National Vice Chairman. Other interim officers were confirmed in their appointments by Congress. The election process was supervised by the Interim National Electoral Commission (INEC), which opened with each aspirant given a few minutes to address the crowd. The speeches were intended to make a final impression on the delegates by outlining reasons why each of us deserved to be chosen as a presidential candidate. Needless to say, the speeches made no impact on anyone, because their minds were already made up.

I was the last to speak, with Christiana by my side. The cheers were deafening. I felt there was no need to read the prepared speech, and I used the time to thank the delegates for their support. By the time the INEC officials declared the results around midnight, I had won in a landslide victory, 963 votes out of a total 1082 votes.

A day after the congress, on Sunday, the NIP held a rally at Kwame Nkrumah Circle, in Accra, where I outlined my political platform. A week later, another rally was held in Kumasi, and another the following day, in Sunyani. Almost all leading members of the party attended all three rallies which were the preliminary stage of a strategy for our campaign.

The decision had been made and I had been given the mandate to lead the National Independence Party in the 1992 presidential elections. We were all working for the good of the party and Ghana as a whole. The other aspirants also assured me of their support and cooperation to ensure success at both the presidential and parliamentary elections. The weight of the party's hope was now my burden to carry.

CHAPTER 24

FOURTH REPUBLIC

Campaign. 1992 Elections.

On Thursday, July 30, 1992, I formally announced my candidacy as presidential aspirant of the NIP for the 1992 Presidential elections from an auditorium in Labadi Beach Hotel, Accra. This was the first time I declared my intent as a presidential hopeful to the general public. With Jerry Rawlings and his National Democratic Congress (NDC) having held on to power over a decade, through the PNDC military government, any opposition garnered a great deal of attention.

Africa and the rest of the world had taken a keen interest in Ghana's politics. Its success would demonstrate a new dawn in democratic institutions in Africa. A failure would be devastating for Ghana, and also paint a much broader picture of African countries as unable to shake off the grip of military leaders, and dangerously threaten the country with a wave of political and social instability.

National Independence Party (NIP) leaders, members of the diplomatic corps, as well as a host of local and foreign journalists were in attendance for the announcement. My wife Christiana's calming presence was particularly reassuring, and I could only imagine the sentiments rushing through the mind of my mother, Madam Yaa Serwaa, and my siblings who had travelled to Accra for the event. It was not more than a ten-minute statement, but that moment held years of struggle and pain, and hope too. They had been the ones who knew me best, and had seen my heart's commitment to integrity and service ever since I was a little boy in Asawaase and South Suntreso, in Kumasi.

In my mother's eyes, there was pride in seeing her son on a stage that seemed to have been an impossible climb from where I had started my life. There was also a reaffirming faith that God can indeed take anyone from anywhere and lift them up to places they couldn't have even imagined in their wildest dreams. My every moment in the political spotlight would tell a story of its own, and perhaps that in itself would be much more significant than any speech I would make.

Television lights and cameras flashed. In a concise speech, I outlined my reasons for contesting the presidency, and if I had the privilege to serve my country, what I wanted Ghana to be by the time I left office as the president of the fourth republic. I was well aware of the sacrifice I had chosen to make, and there was no insult, intimidation, or senseless threat that was to change my resolve. I had carefully decided to trust my journey into God's hands, and it was only His will that would be done.

The local newspapers took turns with my story on the front pages. The local radio and television outlets too. Many people whom I had never met wrote to congratulate me on my decision, and many more requested that I withdraw from politics entirely because there was no way I was a Christian, or could play clean politics. Some also imagined it was only a matter of time before the mudslinging began, and in the end, irrespective of which party won the elections, the decision to compete in presidential elections would have soiled my reputation.

What no one could know was the decision in my heart to prove that politics could and should be devoid of senseless violence, derisive insults, and antagonism. If we were all truly fighting for a chance to serve our people, and were not desperate for political power, we didn't have to bludgeon each other to death to do so. What had brought me to the national political arena wasn't to compromise my identity. It came from a choice to serve my country, and to offer a new direction.

Sure, I was a born-again Christian in a country that had prayed for God-fearing governance, and perhaps, my decision would challenge the Christian electorate in Ghana to rethink their passive attitude to governance, and be a prickly reminder that they could not afford to be bystanders in the political process and watch the country plunge into chaos.

As a presidential candidate, I wanted to reach all Ghanaians, irrespective of their political and religious beliefs. I wasn't campaigning for Christian votes. I was campaigning with Christian values like compassion and justice and hope. I was well aware of the millions of churchgoers, even in politics, who professed Christianity in one convenient moment, and turned to find any malicious and twisted opportunity to earn an advantage in the next.

All I could do was to share my party's vision plainly, without empty promises. In a few hours, I expected the opposition parties to begin their attacks on the NIP platform and my leadership abilities. The NDC had endorsed Jerry Rawlings as its flagbearer, the New Patriotic Party (NPP) had selected Albert Adu Boahen, the People's National Convention (PNC) had Hilla Limann as its candidate, and People's Heritage Party (PHP) having nominated Emmanuel Erskine.

Two days after the press conference, I left for London at the invitation of some of the old CPP members to introduce myself to supporters of the NIP in England. There were many of the party's supporters who had now taken residence in parts of Europe, most having left Ghana in the PNDC era. They were likely to join one of the Nkrumaist parties, and I wanted the opportunity to share my views on Ghana's economy and rally their support for the NIP to help rebuild the country.

I returned to Ghana quickly to continue the process of finalizing a campaign strategy across the country. For years, I had travelled around many of the towns and villages for business, but I was sure politics would offer a completely new perspective. In order to use the talents and organizational abilities of all the party members, we formed various committees on which they could serve. At any time during the campaign, a committee was required to present a situation report to appraise our performance.

On August 14, 1992 I headed to Kumasi, where I held a meeting with the Interim Regional Executives of the party at Adansiman Chambers. There were rumours that I had neglected the party hierarchy and was using the Christian community as my base. That wasn't true, and it was important that any misunderstanding between the regional executives and me be resolved quickly. In a few months, we would be challenging two major parties, the NDC and NPP, both of whom were desperate to discredit the NIP platform, so we couldn't allow internal divisions to fester. We all ended up at dinner at Roses Guest House.

After the NIP congress elected me as the party's flagbearer, I set out to introduce myself to the constituents, and the party establishment in the local districts. In areas where the supporters were opening the NIP regional offices, I had the chance to be introduced as the guest speaker for any occasions, and presented the party's platform to the smaller groups. The U.S.T. Youth Wing invited me as guest speaker at their inauguration, as another opportunity to unveil the NIP election strategy to a group of young men and women who had heard of my candidacy, but who had yet to form their own opinions. I was soon to head out on a long campaign trail in a hectic two-month period.

On September 21, I was invited as chairperson to commemorate the anniversary of what would have been Kwame Nkrumah's 83rd birthday. Besides the traditional leaders who wielded enormous power in their local communities, the party leaders are often in a constant jostle for recognition. Every politician who claimed to have some connection with the banned CPP, Kwame Nkrumah, or the Nkrumaist philosophy, attended the event as way of showing their allegiance to Nkrumah. Many were there to recruit political allies or identify worthy foes. For 1992 Presidential elections where every party was sure to scrounge for votes from every local district and constituency, any recognition at such events became a tacit endorsement.

Before the campaign across the country began, every regional branch was asked to draw an itinerary for the presidential candidate. The plan was to develop a workable approach, taking into consideration every logistic and cultural constraint. We were relying on the regional leaders because they knew their districts well, and could guide us to skilfully navigate their leanings. As much as it would have been ideal to visit every village and every town, time was very short. All itineraries were, therefore, scrutinised to ensure that they could be followed and that none of them would conflict with other events. Right at the start, we had a difficult time drawing a national plan because of the constraints time placed on us.

In 1992, political campaigning in all ten regions of the country began on September 25, with a tour of the Eastern Region, particularly the Akim Abuakwa, Kwahu, and Akuapem areas. Over five days, we commuted among the various towns in the region doing our best to listen and engage the voters in discussions that hopefully helped them to better understand what the NIP platform proposed.

The campaign team moved to the Western Region on October 1, starting with the regional capital, Sekondi-Takoradi. I wasn't particularly interested in screaming party slogans and meaningless catchphrases to the crowd if they didn't understand the message. Even though some had come to expect political rallies to be purely a popularity contest, the NIP was seeking to outline a specific economic and political agenda, and I hoped the people would hear and actually ponder. On our way to Sekondi-Takoradi, we made campaign stops in Beposo, Shama, and Kojokrom.

After spending the night of October 1 at the residence of the Western Regional Chairman of the party, the campaign team toured the Nzema areas including Axim, Half Assini, Anyinase, and Nkroful. Every district had its own pressing issues that drove them to the ballot box; my work was to give them a reason to trust my vision and provide an alternative to the parties that claimed to know how best to lead the country.

The following day, I was driven through Takoradi township in an open-top car greeting the crowds that had lined the sides of the road, after which I addressed a mini-rally. Later in the day, a regional rally was held in nearby Sekondi. We arranged for my presidential running mate, Professor Naa Afarley Sackeyfio, and most of the leading members of NIP to join us. It was our chance to present a united front and showcase the remarkable voice of Professor Sackeyfio on the campaign trail.

The campaign team left Sekondi-Takoradi on the morning of October 4 for Tarkwa where I attended a meeting of party members with Madam Sussane Halm, an old CPP activist in the town. I had been scheduled to address rallies later at Wassa Akropong, Wassa Amenfi, and Asankragwa. Travelling from one town to another took a physical toll from the constant grind of changing strategies, reworking rally speeches, and evaluating local contacts. The team planned to spend the night at Samreboi. I remember driving into a small petrol station where I had to beg the attendant for hours before he agreed to sell only a few gallons of petrol and diesel to us. This was not sufficient for the vehicles to travel the distance ahead.

We were campaigning in the months when Ghana's economy was near rock bottom, and essential commodities and petrol were in short supply. Travelling across the country had become an essentially difficult task, but there was no other way to meet voters unless we went to them. Often we had a large drum filled with petrol in one of the vans, to refuel in the event we ran out of petrol before we made our way to a station. By the time we arrived at Samreboi, we had exhausted every backup petrol, and were at the mercy of the petrol station attendants.

And there was an odd twist. We discovered that the Pyrex bowls containing food for the team had been stolen while the vehicles were being refuelled. Fortunately, the team learned that AT&P at Samreboi occasionally sold fuel to stranded motorists but coincidentally, the company had run out of petrol when we called at their office. They were able, however, to sell 25 gallons, just enough to take us to our next stop at Enchi. After a drive through the streets of Enchi, I visited the Omanhene of Aowin Traditional Area and later addressed a rally at the Enchi Central Lorry Park.

A near-disaster was averted at Enchi when a boy about ten years old who was among the crowd that enthusiastically welcomed us was nearly ran over by one of the NIP vehicles. He had been accidentally pushed down by an elderly man. Out of nowhere, an innocent boy was in a hospital for showing up to hear Kwabena Darko, and I could only hope I had made an enduring impression in his mind, for the sake of his future.

The boy was taken to Enchi Hospital where he was treated and fortunately was later discharged with minor bruises. I took this opportunity to visit him and other patients and to listen to some of the problems of the local hospital. As a gesture of my visit, I made a cash donation to the hospital for the upkeep of the facility. More than random gifts, many of the people in these areas needed significant help from the government to provide for the healthcare needs of the community. They couldn't afford to wait on politicians to show up in their communities once every four years with promises, only to forget everything they had said until it was time for another election, and return with another story. It was in places like these that I was running for president.

The team left Enchi later that afternoon and headed to Sefwi Bekwai, but because of poor road conditions, we reached Sefwi Bekwai around seven o'clock in the evening. There was an existing law against holding political activities after a certain time in the evenings, so I had only enough time to pay a short courtesy visit to the Omanhene before leaving for Sefwi Wiawso. The people of Sefwi Wiawso were expecting my arrival earlier in the day, and even though we didn't arrive until several hours later, surprisingly, the crowd had waited. It was promising to drive into a town where many seemed particularly excited to see a political newcomer speaking boldly and honestly for a change.

We had only a few hours get to the next scheduled campaign event, so I could not afford to spend the night at Wiawso. I had to leave for Bibiani that same night, and it was past midnight by the time the team reached Bibiani. The town was completely dark and quiet, and we thought it was best to continue to Kumasi.

The campaign had planned a tour of the Greater Accra Region to begin on October 11, but because another regional rally could not be held during the Eastern regional tour, we had to postpone it. Instead, we turned our attention to the rally in Koforidua that was to be held on the same Sunday afternoon. We managed to leave the next day together with some of the leading party members for a major campaign event in Accra. We drove through some of the main streets of Accra as an opportunity for me to introduce myself to the electorate.

NIP supporters with t-shirts and flags adorned with the bright red hen with baby chicks' symbol cheered me on, some of the young children running after the cars along the roadsides for as long as they could. The strategy had been such that the remaining campaign tours around Accra will be handled by the Greater Accra regional branch of the party, so we headed west to the Central Region.

The Central Region campaign started at Dunkwa-on-Offin, where I addressed a crowd at a rally after riding through the principal streets of the town. I paid a courtesy visit to the elders of the Denkyira Traditional Area who were hosting us on behalf of the Omanhene, the traditional chief, who was apparently traveling to Jukwa, the traditional capital of Denkyira Traditional Area. From Dunkwa, the campaign team travelled on a long stretch of poorly constructed roads to Twifo Praso. Every one of these trips, through any honest lens, should stir a sense of urgency and a deeper concern for many of the people who didn't have access to some of the most basic amenities we had in the large urban areas.

I had the opportunity to address people in towns and villages along that route. The team reached Praso at about 6 o'clock in the evening. The operators of the ferry at Twifo Praso were helpful in transporting the whole team to neighboring Praso. Owing to accommodation problems, some of us spent the night at the local Topp Guest House while the rest of the team lodged at another hotel a few miles away in Praso.

Before speaking to another crowd at Praso the next day, I had to address people in villages along the Twifo Hemang-Praso road. The rally was well attended, and I met many people who were optimistic about our chances, as long as enough people took the time to hear what I was saying. Unfortunately, at rallies, it felt the crowd had only come to cheer and applaud catchphrases. It was even more energetic if the candidate included a host of condescending comments and insults against the other candidates. Some didn't seem to care about much more.

I remember how a young man was arrested by the Praso police for removing NIP posters from a wall. I pleaded with the police to let him go with a warning, but they insisted that they wanted to prosecute that young man as a deterrent to other such people. In the middle of the country, I had seen how for every person who chose any opportunity to engage in lawlessness and dirty tactics, there were also law-abiding officers who were doing their best to curb any potentially violence. I had no alternative but to allow the law to take its course.

We left Praso and headed to Assin Fosu. I was driven through the main Fosu-Yamoransa trunk road before addressing a district rally. From Fosu the team travelled to Cape Coast but made stops in all the towns along that route. The campaign was forced to cancel a rally planned for Asebu because we reached the town much later than the six o'clock deadline. For many of the remote towns and villages without electricity, the narrow roads and entire town turned dark in the evenings, and many stayed home for their own security.

After a night's rest in Cape Coast, the team toured the interior parts of the Central Region including towns like Mankesim, Ajumako, Besease,

Enyan Denkyira, Nyakrom, Fanti Nyankomsi, and Assin Nyankomasi. A district rally scheduled for Agona Swedru could not take place, because the team arrived in the town late at night. The following day, we took another five-hour permit, starting at six o'clock in the morning to enable me to address some supporters and sympathizers of the party. The people of Swedru were disappointed I had not been able to address the district rally the previous day, but every chance I got, I tried to explain the NIP agenda, and especially my own commitment, to private sector growth as the architect for employment and development, and for that to serve as the economic catalyst for a new Ghana.

From Agona Swedru, the team left for Winneba. After a ride through the main streets of Winneba, I paid a visit to the Omanhene of Efutu Traditional Area before addressing a rally at the Winneba Central Lorry Park. The team then made stops in the coastal towns of Anomabu, Elmina, Komenda, and Saltpond. I got the chance, as a member of the Assemblies of God church, to visit the Southern Ghana Bible Institute, a school that trained local pastors for the church.

The group held a short service during which they joined together to pray for God's guidance for the presidential candidates and the upcoming elections. My running mate Professor Sackeyfio, who was also campaigning in that part of the region, attended the service too, and we had the chance to speak to the people about what we hoped to achieve. For the first time in Ghana, a woman was on a ticket for the nation's highest office, and that gave some of the people a reason to pause, and at the least, listen to our message.

A regional rally scheduled for Cape Coast had to be postponed because a police permit could not be granted for the rally. The explanation given was that this rally had coincided with that of another political party which had already secured a permit. The police could, therefore, not grant another permit for fear that their action might trigger confrontations between supporters of the two parties. The regional executive members managed to postpone the rally to a later date, October 18, 1992.

Chapter 24: Fourth Republic

The campaign team headed to the Volta Region through the Afram Plains. Campaigning in the area was particularly difficult because people there had received assurances that Jerry Rawlings, the presidential candidate of the NDC, had promised "opening of the Afram Plains". Persuading the electorate in Afram Plains with any other message was likely to fall on deaf ears. Even then, I was determined to break new ground and trust the Ghanaian voter's ability to sift through the noise, vain campaign promises, and focus on pragmatic economic reform.

My friend Sam Bamfo had been remarkably clever in making contacts in the area, and my visit was hugely successful. The Afram Plains area had been viewed by many as a Rawlings and NDC stronghold, one where no other politician dared to intrude. In fact, the people had chased away another presidential candidate just a few days before I arrived, so it was reassuring to be received with such warmth and spend a night at Donkorkrom without fear.

What worked to my advantage was that many of the voters in the area were farmers, and for many years, I had bought corn from many of them to feed my chicken. I never would have known that I would be running for president decades later, and now most knew I didn't have any malicious intent by campaigning in their towns. Politics, for me, was a fight for the honour to serve the people and my country. There was no reason to engage in any devious tactics just to gain an edge. I had also determined not to cede any ground to nasty verbal assaults on any candidate, because that wasn't worth my energy.

Another young man, Kenneth Aboah, had been a member of the Kumasi branch of Full Gospel when he was in medical school, before he was stationed in Donkorkrom. Now in 1992, many years later, he was excited to arrange for me to visit the main hospital where he worked and grant me an audience in the town. Perhaps, what had made the difference had been the fact that I had come to articulate a vision, a simple task that was rare in a heated political cycle.

For most of the electorate, they had spent much of their lives under military governments ever since the 1966 coup d'état that toppled

Nkrumah's government, and they had not known anything different since. At every rally, I had chosen to tell the crowd the truth, even when it was uncomfortable for them to accept. Everyone needed to understand that we were fighting for our future together. In our democracy, I wasn't asking for their vote in exchange for gifts or government contracts. Instead, I was challenging them to let their vote be their voices as we worked together, and embraced bold ideas that would move our country forward.

We headed to Adawso to join the ferry to Ekyi-Amanfrom. It was a twenty-minute trip on the Afram River, but due to the stops that we made on our way, we missed the ferry. In the absence of any other alternative, we had to wait. When the ferry returned from the other end of the river, we had to hire the entire vessel for our trip because our urgency and need to travel immediately was outside the company's scheduled times. The campaign team could not afford to wait any longer.

I chartered the ferry to take the team to Ekyi-Amanfrom at a full fee of 100,000 cedis for the 20-minute trip. We allowed all other passengers and vehicles to come on board at our expense. Suddenly, out of the inconvenience, we had a few people who were willing to listen to the NIP platform, at least for another 20 minutes until the ferry docked. On the other side of the river, we made stops in the towns along the Ekyi-Amanfrom main road just in time to address a scheduled rally, and spent time visiting the local hospital.

We left for Amankwakrom, where a smaller ferry was to take us to a village near Kpandu in the Volta Region. For some odd reason, the larger ferry that normally carried hundreds of people and cars across the river was not available. We had no option but to use a smaller dilapidated one. The trip was the most dangerous moment of my entire political campaign. I had no idea this had been orchestrated to derail our campaign, but there was perhaps nothing more frightening than to know the wickedness that people will accept in their hearts, just to win an election.

The ferry was unusually small in size, and could barely carry two vehicles. The other campaign vehicles had to return to Accra. Even worse, there was no dock in Amankwakrom to unload the vehicles, and the heavy rains that had flooded the entire area the night before made it even worse. We had to improvise to find a way to get the vehicles on the ferry, and hopefully be able disembark them at the destination dock.

Just as we had finished loading, the ferry got stuck in the mud. It was about another hour before we found our way through the sticky sludge, covered with sweat and dirt, and managed to float again. One operator sat in the front, and the other towards the back. The campaign team was exhausted and had all fallen asleep just as we set sail. My friend Sam Bamfo kept me company as we thought through the several rallies we had scheduled on the other side of the river.

Halfway through the trip, when we had just reached the deepest part of the river, about 400 feet, the ferry stooped. The operator said the engine had failed, and his apathetic demeanour was even more startling. The vessel apparently could no longer make the trip, and suddenly the silt and debris flowing downstream from the heavy rainfall was bearing down on us. We were stuck.

"What do you mean the engine won't work?" Sam Bamfo yelled at the operator.

"I don't know, sir".

"You don't know?" We both yelled at the same time.

The middle of the Volta River is the worst place to tell anyone that the operator doesn't know why a vessel's engine has suddenly stopped. The ferry shook over and over again. There was no sign of any rescue and the two operators seemed nonchalant, as if they could easily swim away and leave the rest of us there. I wasn't going to die.

Even though we were horrified, the team began to pray deafeningly, like our lives depended on it. There was nothing else that we could do. We were staring at a tragedy, and had no way of contacting anyone ashore about our predicament. It was then that we found that there were no lifesaving devices aboard and the crew operated the ferry without the aid of a compass. Supposedly, they had done this for many years, and knew where they were going, so we were supposed to trust our lives to perfect strangers. We prayed even harder and screamed loudly.

Suddenly the second operator, a young man who had tried to stay away from our heated confrontation with the first one, rushed forward.

"I will spark it, I will spark it".

He said he could restart the engine.

In one moment the men claimed the ferry was damaged, and in another, the operator mysteriously knew how to start the damaged engine. It took three hours to travel 26 miles on the Volta River, between Amankwakrom and Kpandu. At every turn we were clutching anyone or anything for support. For three hours, I was completely terrified. We finally arrived in the small villages near Kpandu, only to learn that it had all been a plot to drown my campaign team in the Volta River. The operators were part of the ploy, and had it not been the providence of our God, we would have perished and no one would have ever known what happened.

The Volta Regional executive of the party welcomed us and quickly arranged for me to address a group of NIP supporters in the village. From there, the team drove to Kpandu, taking the time to speak to any small pockets of villagers, on our way to pay a courtesy visit to the Chief of Kpandu.

I had chosen to preach the NIP platform rather than wasting time disparaging other candidates. When the opportunity had arisen, I had carefully outlined how I believed that the different political parties were all vying for the same work, with Ghana's interest at heart, hopefully. I disagreed with the other candidates' vision for the country, but that was no excuse for verbal assaults. Win or lose, history would remember the actions I took during this period, and I also had my own conscience to judge my actions.

Unfortunately, the Volta Regional executive had done a terrible job organizing events. Their itinerary was so haphazardly planned that it could not be followed, and as a result, we arrived at places where no one was expecting us. I remember on one occasion, when we reached a small village a few miles from Kpandu where a group of students had been hurriedly assembled and given NIP posters to parade as supporters of the party. It was a demoralizing spectacle.

Some of these hiccups were to be expected, as part of political campaigns. Others were inexcusable. I often told a story of how I had donated money to organizers in the Ho area to open a regional office for NIP in the region, only to arrive there two weeks before the presidential elections and find that the office was yet to be completed. Supposedly, the party executives had been locked in a stalemate over personal differences, and successfully sabotaged each other from doing any work for the party. Time was precious; we had to salvage what we could and live through the moments as best as we could.

We continued the tour of the region, spending a night at Jasikan after rallies in Jasikan and Kadjebi. The team visited the chief of Peki, and later, spent the night at Anum–Boso as guests of Dr. Vladimir Antwi Danso, who was a leading member of the NIP. The next morning, I addressed rallies at Anum-Boso, Atimpoku, and Akwamufie, before going to Tsito-Awudome and Anfoega to address another crowd at a rally. I also visited the paramount chief of Asogli Traditional Area of Ho. The regional rally could not be held in Ho, because the regional executives were refused a police permit. The police claimed it would coincide with a National Democratic Congress (NDC) rally in the town.

From Ho, we travelled to Kpetoe where I addressed another crowd. It was almost dark by the time we reached Dzodze around seven o'clock in the evening. I paid a courtesy visit to the chief of Dzodze, after which we finally left for Accra in the night.

Campaigning was a never-ending marathon with surprises lurking in every new moment. It took a huge physical toll too, and at times was even overwhelming, despite our having carefully evaluated all this beforehand, and prepared for the daily grind.

The tour of the Upper West Region began at Wa. We got there late at night. Early the next day, the team left for a campaign tour of the region, starting with Lawra, Nadowli, Jirapa, Nandom, Hamile, and Tiza. I addressed rallies in all these towns. A heavily attended regional rally was held at Wa, and I seized the chance to layout the NIP's vision. It didn't matter to me which campaign considered the area their stronghold, I was determined to tell our story and win their support.

In some of the Muslim communities, some of the people listened to find common ground on issues that affected their livelihood. A few others claimed that their communities would not vote for me because I was a devout Christian with a habit of gently converting every Muslim I came into contact with into Christianity. We often smiled about that comment, but it was good to be known as a man whose every step was to share the kingdom with anyone I met. Whether or not they voted for NIP would not make me change the message of the gospel in which I was grounded.

Men like Ahmed Adjei were happy to champion my campaign platform to the northern regions because he had a first-hand encounter of my willingness to assist entrepreneurs and visionaries irrespective of where they came from. I had been of assistance to his own vision when he needed the help. He was no different from the men in the Zongo areas where I travelled to buy rice bran for my poultry farm. I supported their businesses and didn't let my faith create a wedge between us as people. One thing I had always done was to respect every man and woman with whom I came into contact, so that even when I came across the people with whom I disagreed, we respectfully did so.

I visited the Chief of Tumu, after which I addressed a small rally in front of the Chief's palace. Both the National Chairman, Alhaji Imoro Ayarna, and the National Treasurer, Kofi Danso, were among the team that toured the Upper West Region. Alhaji Ayarna had been particularly instrumental in Ghana's politics even before the Nkrumah and independence, and had been a staunch member of the CPP. The crowds that showed up at the rallies in the northern part of Ghana were there because of the efforts of leaders like Alhaji Imoro Ayarna, who had faithfully represented their constituencies and earned their trust.

We reached Upper East Region through Tumu, and addressed large crowds in Fumbisi and Sandema. The reception in these two towns was incredible. For the first time, I had the chance to not only appreciate, but also understand the rich culture of the northern towns and villages and their genuine warmth and hospitality, even if our political views were different.

The reception at Fumbisi and Sandema paled in comparison to the reaction in Navrongo. After a "kingly" ride through the main streets of the town, I addressed a rally with a large and energetic crowd, complete with the traditional pageantry. There was a huge crowd when I visited the palace of the Navro-Pio, Dr. A. B. Adda, and it was difficult for the organizers to hold the supporters back calmly. They all wanted to meet the farmer turned politician. Ghanaians were desperate for a new direction, even though they weren't ready to shake off their old allegiances.

The entourage left that same night for Bolgatanga in advance of scheduled events in the region. The following morning, I attended a rally at Bawku before addressing another regional rally at Bolgatanga. Even though they were exhausted from being on the road, the National Chairman and the National Treasurer decided to stay with us on this trip despite the former feeling ill and weak. The NIP was determined to give the election our best effort, leaving nothing to chance, and having nothing to regret.

When we campaigned in the Upper West Region, we took advantage of the campaign in towns where we were granted an audience, even if we hadn't planned that ahead of time.

I addressed a hurriedly assembled crowd at Bamboi, and even though the people were not expecting us, they gave us a cordial reception. They were a very respectful crowd, open to hearing what the NIP offered and to give us a fair chance. The visit was a relief to our supporters in

Bamboi who never thought they would see their presidential candidate before the elections. This was because politicians often identified the areas where they rather let the surrogates reach, and focussed their attention on the large urban areas whom they imagined would decide the victory. When we reached at Bole, I visited the Bole chief and addressed a gathering in front of the NIP office in Bole. We arranged for a similar event at Sawla.

The campaign team arrived at Tamale at four o'clock before the break of dawn on October 20, for a formal tour of the Northern Region. The diversity in the country's landscape was striking. In one village after another, it was as though each was in a world of its own. It was especially humbling to see the mothers and fathers in some of the poorest areas in the country clinging onto their sons and daughters and hoping that they would have a much brighter future in Ghana than their own. They hoped for a better Ghana, and prayed their elected officials would not forget their plight once they were in office. Their unusual optimism gave me the energy to keep pushing along.

We travelled south to tour some of towns in the Brong Ahafo Region, and left Sunyani just before midnight. Before the team left Sunyani, the drivers had complained of weariness and preferred that we spend the night in the town and head on early the next morning. We thought that we were racing against time and far behind schedule, so we convinced them to try to make it through the night. The journey through the dark roads was to hopefully take advantage of the minimal traffic at night, even though we had no way of knowing what ditch or fallen tree would block the road ahead of us. Halfway to Kintampo, we didn't have much to worry about, and all the vehicles refuelled at the Kintampo Mobil Filling Station. The trouble began a few miles after Kintampo.

Everyone was asleep. The drivers too, apparently struggled to keep their eyes open, worn out by the long hours on the road. The vehicles swerved from one side of the road to another. Fortunately, at that time of the night, the Tamale road was virtually abandoned, so there were no oncoming vehicles that could cause head-on collisions. The drivers were so tired that at one of the toll bridges, one of them fell asleep behind the steering wheel even before he could find money to pay the toll fee. It was a miracle that all the vehicles arrived safely at Tamale.

Early the next morning, we left for Yendi, after making a stop at Sang. We held a rally at Yendi, and returned to Tamale to hold the regional rally. A planned trip to Chereponi had to be rescheduled because of the long distance and the bad nature of the road from Yendi, but the Tamale event had attracted a huge crowd. The campaign message was delivered in clarity to loud cheers and jubilant music. I was presented with a regal smock embroidered with the NIP party symbol by the northern regional branch of NIP. It was their way of expressing support, and faith in what we had set out to do.

Campaigning in the Brong Ahafo Region had to be done in two phases. We had previously visited towns like Tepa, Akwasiase, and Mabang, in Ashanti Region on our way to Acherensua, Hwidiem, Kenyasi No. 1, Kenyasi No. 2, Goaso, and Mim in the Brong Ahafo Region. The reception at Mim, though we arrived at night, had been particularly reassuring. The employees at Desmond Timbers and Mim Poultry Farm showed up in support, and rallied around every one of their neighbours. The team imagined that if we had arrived during the day time, it was reasonable to believe that the whole town would have been at the rally.

The second phase of the tour was undertaken when we were returning from Damongo and Yapei, the last two towns we visited in the Northern Region. We held a small rally in Nsawkaw and finally made it to Wenchi by nightfall. Developing a message that resonated with each group of voters was a constant battle because it was critical to explain complex economic and social policies in simple soundbites that made sense to the crowds. That was the critical challenge.

The following day, mini rallies were organized at Tanoso, Techiman, and Wenchi. We got to Seikwa around seven o'clock in the evening, just after Professor Adu Boahen of the New Patriotic Party (NPP) had left the town. Even though we could not hold a rally, we counted on our campaign volunteers in the local constituencies to persuade voters to support the NIP. After a short visit with the Chief of Seikwa, we left for Berekum in the night. I paid a courtesy visit to the Omanhene of Berekum Traditional Area, after which we left for Sunyani and continued south to Kumasi that same night.

Though Ashanti Region had been my home, it was the last place I toured. We had managed to intensify the grassroots campaign in an organized effort to reach voters. A large regional rally was held in Kumasi at Jackson's Park and a district rally also held in Bekwai, my hometown. On October 30, we traveled to Ejisu, Juaben, Effiduase, Asokore, Nsuta, Mampong, Kofiase, Anyinase, and Sekyeredumasi. By the time we arrived in Sekyeredumasi at night and I had to speak with the aid of very bright security lights. The following day, we held another district rally was held in Obuasi, after rallies at Odumasi, Konogo, Patriensa, and Agogo.

The Obuasi rally, held in front of Len Clay Stadium, was a complete success. The attendance was very encouraging, and either the NIP message was resonating across these constituencies, or the voters were fed up with the status quo and were clamoring for a new voice. The campaign hoped that this rally would have a significant impact on the votes in the Obuasi constituencies.

The campaign had strategically planned to arrive in Greater Accra in the final days leading to the elections, and push for a strong finish. We could count on our regional volunteers and party leaders to engage the local voters. The party held a district rally in Tema on Sunday, November 1. Before arriving at Tema, I was driven through the townships of Labadi, Teshie, and Nungua to meet the electorate, and seize the opportunity to explain the NIP manifesto. I remember addressing a rally at Ashiaman and another in the Tema district, in the Community 2 area. After the rally, I paid a courtesy call to the Chief of Old Tema township.

A grand regional rally was scheduled for November 2, 1992, a day before the presidential elections. Just as we were making final preparations for the rally, we learned that we could not hold the event because of instructions from the local police, or supposedly, someone from the government, that no political rally was to be held on that day.

We had spent an enormous amount of money and time on the road across Ghana, left our families behind to share the concerns of an electorate that was heading to the ballot box to vote for their hopes. If they chose to vote for the NIP, it was my job to ensure that we had not wasted their hope. Campaigning often forced me to pause and reflect on some of the challenges around the country and one that demanded an honest assessment of every unique challenge. The work will be to fix the backbone of society to address systemic issues. There were no easy answers, but around the country, it was easy to see the magnitude of the work ahead.

On the whole, the campaign tour had enlightened me on the problems facing Ghana, as it affected people on a very personal level. The tour across some of the remote villages and urban centres showed that while most Ghanaians were politically engaged, many were not prepared to sift through the political speeches to make any meaningful decisions. In fact, many were oblivious to the lasting repercussions of dangerous policies, especially one that was touted by the parties they supported.

What seemed to grab most people's attention were catchy phrases and slogans, and politicians who were happy to give in to their endless pleas for free party t-shirts and souvenirs. It was eye-opening to find that most Ghanaians didn't seem to have any time to listen to weighty matters that affected the economy and their individual lives.

Poor roads, poor sanitation, a lack of healthcare facilities, and a lack of basic amenities were all symptoms of a systemic failure. The issues were the kind that led the governments to react in order to remain popular, rather than taking the difficult approach of investing in infrastructure to help the people work to shape their own futures. If politicians were only interested in winning elections to satisfy their personal ambitions and selfish desires, the damage they caused to the families across the country was sad to fathom.

The 1992 presidential and parliamentary elections were to be a turning point in Ghana's political history. For all the work I had done, it was Ghanaians turn to choose what direction we wanted for our country. I had done all that I promised to the NIP on that Saturday afternoon when they elected me as their flagbearer. My focus had remained on listening to every concern and engaging in fruitful conversations that moves our country a step forward.

I spoke at a nationally televised broadcast at the Ghana Broadcasting Corporation (GBC) on the eve of the elections. Tired from a long campaign trail, I had learned a great deal more about my country than I could have in any other way. My friend Sam Bamfo had been right; there was always someone whose story was worth listening to, and someone who needed my example. Ghanaians would be going to the ballot box to vote for our own future.

Only a few decades earlier in 1957, we hoped our country would be like a city on a hill, shining for all to see. Now we had another chance to become the country our forefathers dreamed of, and stem the tide of political and economic upheavals and false starts. What we did with the opportunity would reveal the future we wanted for ourselves and for our children.

Regardless of the outcome, sharing my hope with Ghanaians in urban centres and rural villages, and perfect strangers who shared my optimism for the country, had been one of the greatest joys of my life. In both the presidential and parliamentary elections, the men and women we elected to lead us would be a reflection of the society we were, and perhaps embody the ideals we cherished. Now, it was Ghanaians' turn to decide, but most importantly, it would be for God's will to be done. I headed home to Kumasi.

CHAPTER 25

BEYOND SUNSET

Lessons after 1992 Elections

With the 1992 presidential elections behind me, there was nothing to regret. As the presidential candidate for the National Independence Party (NIP), we had done the best we could to win the confidence of Ghana's electorate for the high office of President of the fourth Republic of Ghana. We lost the election, one of only two outcomes. Like a flip of a coin, I was prepared for whatever result the voters handed to me, and my attitude would have been no different if we had won.

The NDC was declared the winner. The results of the presidential elections sparked discussions and tensions all over the country, especially in constituencies where some of the opposition parties had considered their voter strongholds and guaranteed themselves a win. The parties—NPP, PNC, NIP, and PHP—did not accept the results declared by the electoral commission. Our party's only recourse was to file a complaint, and for the Interim National Electoral Commission (INEC) to proceed with their independent investigations. In spite of protests from the four parties, the commission had determined it would not investigate any of the complaints.

On one hand, Ghanaians deserved closure. Many believed, and I did too, that the INEC should have at least acknowledged the complaints, and conducted a fair investigation into the matter, even if their findings were pre-determined, as a section of Ghanaians suspected. Allegations of electoral irregularities and fraud were not unusual in any democratic election, but for an African country that was seeking to set a precedent for a new chapter in our political history, any hint of conspiracy would be an indelible stain, and a sad model for free and fair elections.

Frankly, I had no reason to believe that any investigation or subsequent revelation of voter fraud would have affected the outcome, but some of the political parties were understandably livid that the results had been marred by alleged theft, and needless manipulations. Regardless of what the fact was, it was important for our young democracy to have the guts to confront their own shortcomings, even as they became the guiding light for future elections and strengthened our democratic institutions.

Observer Groups in the country declared the elections free and fair, and we had little choice but to accept their verdict. My party didn't. Many Ghanaians wondered how independent assessors of such a critical election could afford to briefly visit 500 polling stations out of 18,000 in the country and make broad conclusions about unique events happening in most of the stations. The reports of counting errors flooded in from the very start, and unless there was a system in place to rectify it, the outcome was inevitably tainted.

In one bizarre outcome, Emmanuel Erskine, who was presidential candidate for the PHP voted in a local constituency with his family and closest party aides. By the end of the night, the votes were tallied and Erskine had earned zero. The results implied that Erskine didn't even vote for himself. It was utterly embarrassing, just as it was hilarious to see a blatant display of election fraud, but Ghanaians being encouraged to ignore it for the sake of keeping the peace. There was one bizarre report after another, and unfortunately, we had found a way of making a mockery of our democracy. I wasn't surprised when the INEC officially wrote to the NIP about the mistakes that had occurred during the vote counting. Now it was too late.

Chapter 25: Beyond Sunset

Perhaps the brightest moment of the 1992 elections was that they ended without any of the suspected violence and unchecked tension that many feared could plunge the country into chaos as we had seen in different countries around the world. There had been blunders, incompetence at the polling stations, faulty voter machines, intentional vote tampering, and a host of other missed opportunities, no denying that, but perhaps the silver lining was that the country had been ushered into an era of civilian rule, and hopefully onto a path we would not stray from.

I was at home in Kumasi when the NPP presidential candidate Albert Adu Boahen called. He was furious. He requested that I join the rest of the presidential candidates who were planning a huge protest of the results at an impromptu demonstration. The organisers had chosen the grounds near the busy Kwame Nkrumah Circle in Accra for a rally the next day, and it would demonstrate solidarity against the NDC if all the candidates stood together.

Adu Boahen was convinced that it was a stolen verdict. I understood his rage, but I had chosen to move on. Every Ghanaian had a legal right to protest the outcome, but I was in no position to decide for the NIP on what they thought was best for the party. I politely declined Adu Boahen's offer.

Following the refusal of the four parties to accept the results of the presidential elections, each of the parties decided to boycott the parliamentary elections that were to be held on December 29, 1992. The NIP argued that there was no reason to compete with an organization determined it had to win at all costs, and there was nothing they would allow to derail that goal. The parties that contested the parliamentary elections, the National Democratic Congress (NDC), the National Convention Party (NCP), and Every Ghanaian Living Everywhere (EGLE) called themselves the alliance of progressives, but even among political allies, the malpractices surfaced. The thought was, if they could do it to one another, there was nothing they couldn't do to their opposition. But nothing justified a boycott, at least in my mind.

With the presidential elections over, the party chairmen and leaders took over. The parliamentary elections were eight weeks away, and rather than channelling any frustration into these important elections, the NIP boycotted. The other opposition parties walked away, too. This was the most disappointing part of the elections for me, and one that I could only hope would serve as a cautionary tale to our children and the future of democracy in Ghana.

Two parliamentary candidates with the NIP decided to contest the elections in their local constituencies, even though the party had boycotted across the country, and they won. This result was likely to be the case in many parts of the country, but Ghana will never know what our future could have been if a diverse parliament had been the fabric of the legislative branch in 1992.

In a sense, parliamentary elections were incredibly critical because in Ghana, they were the avenue to elect the men and women who would enact the laws of the land, and make policies that shaped our country. Parliamentarians assumed a remarkably important overseeing role to balance the government's actions. If opposition parties were effective, their presence in governance was probably just as critical as the ruling party. Boycotting parliamentary elections essentially gave a ruling party *carte blanche* to enact any policies it desired, rather than having a seat at the table to represent the local constituencies and districts. I hoped, at least in hindsight, some of these lessons would live in the minds of anyone who set out to serve.

My memory occasionally raced back to the evening I decided to run for president of Ghana. I hoped that regardless of which party won on election night, Ghana would win, too. Our democracy would be at stake, and our future would hang on the shoulders of men and women who would have sworn to voters to fight for their welfare. Now I was living in the moment I imagined, and as surreal as it felt, I only prayed that the hopes of the people I met in places like Yendi and Kadjebi, and in Fumbisi and Akwasiase would not disappear like vapor.

In 1992, I felt Ghana could easily plunge into a society that created a semblance of a multi-party system, while privately ensuring that the opposition was almost non-existent. In a democracy, even as imperfect as it could be, the opposition, if constructive, became an expedient check on governance, but if a progressive alliance were in no position to challenge the policies of the ruling party, what difference would they ever make.

It was only a matter of time before the government increased prices on anything it chose, and shut down any institution it deemed worthless. There were traces of the PNDC military government ideology that seemed to have morphed into the NDC agenda. I, like many, would move on with our lives and be back to the enterprises we had before the elections. What struck me was the millions of Ghanaians in towns like Anyinase and in Bamboi, in Fanti Nyankomsi and Sefwi Wiawso, who would have little or nothing to go back to. With their votes, they dreamed of a better Ghana, one in which a rising tide would lift all boats, and theirs, too.

* * * * *

My brush with death in 1969 had been a gift. After a near-tragic accident that left me wounded and in Okomfo Anokye hospital for more than six months, I cherished every breathing moment and chose not to give in to fear. There was nothing that demeaning remarks from politicians and total strangers could do to earn my attention. I had survived the dread of losing everything, and my very life, so competing for and losing presidential elections wasn't worth the gloom.

The fact that rumours swirled after an election and salacious falsehoods were peddled in the media wasn't lost on me. I had absolutely no control over what other people chose to say or believe. What mattered to me was that I hadn't lived my life under any pretence and had not left room for temptation and indignity.

Rumours that the NIP had been recruited by the PNDC military government to ensure that the CPP groups remained divided were baseless. Another headline claiming that my presidential campaign was sponsored by the PNDC was utterly false, but the newspapers didn't care to corroborate the story. I had spent millions of my own money travelling across the country, buying more than 30 Peugeot 404 vehicles to be used in the regional campaign offices, and even paid all the drivers across the country from my own pocket.

Just before the elections, there were rumours in Ashanti Region and parts of the Central Region that the NIP had merged with some of the political parties. First, they claimed there had been a merger of the NIP with the NPP, then another rumour started about a merger with the NDC. None of these were true, but the purpose had been to push misinformation and propaganda, and it worked. It sowed uncertainty.

After the elections, I received several congratulatory letters from friends and admirers, many of whom I did not know personally. I only hoped I had challenged them to stand on integrity, not only in politics, but also in life. Not everyone will lead a country, but all of us will have a chance to lead our homes, our communities, and our businesses. The need for empathy, integrity, and respect is no different in any of these walks of life. I could only hope, along the campaign trail, that I had treated people with respect, a quality that any child could use to guide his own future. Every time someone people who called to express their dissatisfaction with the election's outcome, I had to remind them that losing an election wasn't a reflection on a person's character or even a party's platform.

What mattered the most was that whoever won an election would build a government based on compassion for his brothers and sisters whose path may have been a bit more challenging than his own. The NDC government had work to do, and Ghanaians wished them well. The NPP had become the largest opposition party, and it had no choice but to learn from the 1992 elections and build on its platform. It was reasonable to imagine other parties would merge, and others would splinter. Yet, regardless of how political parties evolve, the duty to serve our country should remain the same.

I was fortunate to have built my companies in such a careful manner that I was able to step away for a year, and the company thrived even in my absence. Leaving behind the largest poultry farm in the country in the hands of a capable management team wasn't an accident. Years earlier, I had watched the film *The Unorganised Manager* as part of a management training program I had instituted in my company, Darko Farms. One of the central themes of the film was the art of delegation, - "taking your hands off but keeping your eyes on", and I had done so faithfully. Politics had taken me away for several months, but I didn't have to be in the board room for the people I had empowered to make tough decisions.

By the end of 1992, I was back at the helm of my company, having another privilege of continuing work with a great team that I had built. Darko Farms was set for expansion and new business opportunities, but whatever opportunity business affords us, it will be meaningless if we cannot reach back and inspire others. That is what I had been able to do for many years, and now I had met many more people who inspired me to do much more. I shared a great deal of the stories on the campaign trail with most of my employees, some of whom I had spent time with in their hometowns. I'd also visited with voters in their constituencies.

Across the country, there was a lot of work that needed to be done, and every Ghanaian could find a way to lend a hand. There were many places beyond Bawku and Bamboi where I saw young men and women eager to learn a vocation so they could contribute to the nation. Some needed mentoring, others needed the chance to start a trade, and most needed assurance. In Nsuta, Techiman, and coastal towns like Saltpond, some of the people wore their hopes on their faces as they spent long hours in their farms under the beating sun.

They were farmers, nurses, doctors, fishermen, and teachers. They believed the right leaders would pave the way for a brighter future for all. Perhaps my presence in their community had inspired some. As I shared my candid observations, I knew some of the employees would be able to impact people in their circles of influence, and I was happy to use my experience to encourage every one of them to also find ways to make a difference in any way they could.

Politics in Ghana was a fascinating experience. There were the men and women who made a living sowing discord among parties, just as there were those who were resigned to doing what they accepted to be the *dirty work*, even if it cost another person his or her life. It was the saddest manifestation of the stench in our humanity.

I had sat on a ferry with men with wicked hearts who were part of an elaborate scheme to drown me in the River Volta, just to ensure that I didn't campaign in their towns. I was of a firm belief that disagreements with political viewpoints shouldn't cause us to demonize and murder each other. Winning an election shouldn't consume our lives to the point of letting us miss the worth in each other, but throughout the campaign, television and radio debates easily turned into needless fights, juvenile name-calling, and vulgar exchanges.

I was sure they knew they could be more civil and decent, but perhaps it was much easier to wallow in filth in order to disgrace an opponent. Discussions on policy issues turned into shouting matches driven by pent-up anger and hate. That couldn't be our very best, and ultimately we had to choose what we wanted to become.

I remember when a young man rushed to my office to inform me that he had come across a supposedly scathing news article about me that was to be published in a local newspaper. He meant well, and he imagined I would do anything to save my reputation, so he suggested I pay the newspaper editor to prevent him from publishing the article. I smiled.

I had nothing in my life to hide, and I had no control over another person's opinion of me. As imperfect as I will always be, what mattered to me was pleasing my God, and doing the best I could for that purpose.

Chapter 25: Beyond Sunset

It was a teaching moment for the young man, and hopefully, one that he too would embrace. It was an attempt at blackmailing, but it fell apart. Living our lives honestly saves us from having to wonder which of our footsteps will bring us shame. The confidence I had was in the truth that I had chosen to guide my every step.

It had been a privilege for many people in places like Acherensua, Hwidiem, and Tanoso to welcome me into their communities and share their dreams like I was one of their own. If I didn't win an election, nothing stopped me from becoming an example, the best as I could be, to inspire their sons and daughters to also chase their dreams, whatever they might be.

With the election over, I was fortunate to gain incredible experience in 1992, and an understanding of the Ghanaian voter's psyche in a way I never would have otherwise. I often think back to my earlier campaigns in the Eastern Regions to become the NIP flagbearer. I overheard a group of party delegates in Nsawam make the most asinine of arguments about my education. It made sense to them that a presidential candidate be one with a string of academic degrees, irrespective of what they were.

Someone had told them I had never attended a university or any other school. In their minds, I wasn't a professor, a lawyer, or doctor, so it was difficult for them to imagine why I would be president. I was a farmer, and they couldn't fathom the idea that commercial farmers ended up in tertiary institutions just like many other professional careers. It was unfortunate that we had been conditioned to elect people who fit a certain stereotype, irrespective of the worth of their ideology.

The error in this reasoning wasn't theirs alone, and perhaps that was one of the many fruits of colonialism that we never moved past. Ghana inherited a British aristocracy mindset where the colonial masters chose to govern with men and women who had walked through the hallways of institutions like Oxford University and Cambridge University. Long after independence, Ghanaians never paused to wonder what value

Oxford University actually gives if the graduate is unable to serve his people with the knowledge acquired. As critical as education will remain in any society, it was dangerous to weigh a leader's ability by the type of institution he may have attended, and not by his character or commitment to the office.

All of our journeys are bound to be different. I have always believed there will be men and women who spend years in vocational schools, or learn in non-traditional ways, whose talent and passion will be the kind to change our country. But unless we confront the idiocy of some of the warped stereotypes, we will miss the opportunity to nurture people of character and substance to help build our nation.

As I listened as the man argue with the other regional delegates that they needed a presidential candidate *who looked the part, regardless of what he knew*, it was a bit disappointing to find that this was the mindset of a delegate. His comment was intended to discredit me, because I was not a neither a professor nor a doctor.

Then the young man next to me chuckled, and hinted that he was talking about me. I smiled too. If it was a matter of interacting with presidents, I had met many and sat with plenty. Serving Ghana was much more than vain appearances just to create an impression of sophistication. There were millions of people living in places like Enchi and Agogo who needed leaders with vision and courage to fight for their welfare, not just ones with a string of professional certifications to impress people.

In Nsawam, the young man had tried to demean me, but I was so confident in my own journey to appreciate the purpose for which God had called me. Three years in Ruppin College were the foundation of my career that I have been eternally grateful for. I was fortunate to have found my passion for poultry farming by the time I was 16, in a chance meeting with English missionary Reverend Sercombe, and set my heart on being a farmer. My dream was to be the best farmer I could be, never to be a professor, a doctor, or any other profession.

My stint in politics has been one of the most eventful parts of my life, with both sad realizations and happy moments. It enlightened me, and hopefully many of the people who worked with me on the campaign, on the problems facing Ghana, like the poor nature of the roads, the lack of communication systems, the vast natural resources that were not utilised and the abject poverty in which many Ghanaians lived.

There will be many more elections, and my prayer is for men and women with Christian values to seek to represent their people and lead, not only with competency but also compassion. Ghana was no different from other democracies where politics was unfortunately clouded by hate, deception, lies, and betrayal. For me, I was happy to have taken an unpopular stance in 1992, not just with empty words to win a vote. What I could never forget was that politics in Ghana had also shown me the tremendous power of kindness in the human heart, when a perfect stranger goes to great lengths to make a moment memorable. That is what gave me hope.

I had also made up my mind that my road in politics had come to an end. For any opportunity to share an experience, I will do all I can to build my country and help elected officials shape our future. It will not matter what party they belong to, what town they come from, or even the depth of the promises in their manifesto. What will matter is the candour in their hearts and their willingness to serve.

CHAPTER 26

TURNING POINTS

Devotion to Service, and Ghana.

In the mid-1980s Ghana's PNDC government invited me to join other private business owners and policymakers to serve on a national Think Tank on Privatization. We met several times in a month at the offices of the Ghana Investment Promotion Centre. To me, this was the military government's effort to better understand Ghana's unique economic crisis, and how private enterprises could help stem the dizzying rollercoaster.

It was a bit awkward that I had received the invitation despite the setbacks I'd had to endure immediately after the coup d'état, and the damage both government and military officers did to my business and to the agricultural sector as a whole. A few years later, God had relieved my every disappointment, and nothing I had faced had caused my heart to harbour any anger.

The fact is, a nation in turmoil affects everyone, and if I had an opportunity to help, irrespective of my disagreement with the policies enacted, the most important thing was to give any truthful advice I could, and for the leaders in power to make their own choices. It was a privilege to serve and uplift my country because our collective success was only possible with everyone pulling their weight and doing the best they could.

Ever since I started Darko Farms in 1967, with one government after another I had seen the effects of ill-conceived policies, and how they ultimately affected everyone. If I was a private entrepreneur in Ghana, it was in my interest to challenge the government to recruit the best minds to address our challenges. Interestingly, some of the same people who had done all they could to derail my work had years later become the same ones who needed my expertise and insight.

In Ghana, the British government and their European partners during the pre-independence years attracted private companies in Europe to invest in the colonies. The government itself was not an enterprise, but its focus was to create economic avenues in the colonial territories for private businesses who would in turn be subject to government taxes, so ultimately it was a win-win proposition for both sides.

I could safely assume that this was the strategy that attracted companies like the United Africa Company (UAC), Union Trading Company (UTC), and Lonrho to Ghana. Across Africa, the colonial government's model was no different, except perhaps in Francophone Africa where the French government constructed facilities in some of the colonies to ensure that the businesses ran the way they wanted. In Ghana, the private companies were the large conglomerates that hired Ghanaians as directors and managers, and trained them to run successful corporations.

What most Ghanaians didn't know was that the foreign investors were the private enterprises that pooled their resources for strategic investments in Ghana. The British government had used the private sectors to take the *commanding heights* of our economy and by bearing all the capital risks, the companies accumulated a disproportionate share of the wealth.

The evidence of their model's success was how the companies bought our cheap raw materials, took them to England to process and package, and returned to sell the final products to us. The rude awakening for the military government, the soldiers, and most Ghanaians was finding that the British government itself did not establish corporations in Ghana.

After our country achieved independence in 1957, President Kwame Nkrumah and his government set out to build the nation with strategic construction projects and state-owned corporations. Nkrumah, having lived in the United States during his university education, saw how private companies invested heavily in different sectors to allow free-market economy to become the bedrock of development. It is not difficult to imagine that he faced a different challenge in that era because there were only a handful of private entrepreneurs in the Gold Coast era.

In Ghana, without the large private enterprises as the engine, Nkrumah built companies, developed infrastructure, built schools, and trained Ghanaians. Perhaps the plan was to build an economic engine, but in a perfect world, the state-owned companies in the Nkrumah years would have best served as pilot projects, to set examples upon which the private entrepreneurs could build. It was a great start, but without the right mindset, it became our undoing.

I saw how creating industrial frameworks was critical to national development, but the citizens quickly saw that every state-owned and state-controlled business belonged to the government, not them. It was disheartening to often see Ghanaians professionals mismanage companies, political appointees condoned corruption, and employees looted state-owned facilities without any regard. Their justification was, "It is not my father's, and not my mother's". Indifference and laziness weren't causes for concern, because, in their minds, it didn't matter if the state-owned company survived. The apathy was stunning.

A thriving economy will be driven by market forces driving competition and innovation, not government price controls. These are some of the insights I was happy to share with anyone who cared to listen. Perhaps the best path forward was to incentivize the farmers, traders, fishermen and every professional and entrepreneur to work hard, and to fuel our growth. With the struggling economy, international organizations like the International Monetary Fund (IMF), USAID, and the World Bank could only make recommendations to the government, but they could not force any government to implement any measure.

Economic indicators in Ghana pointed to a downward spiral and soon, a disoriented PNDC government had to admit the failures of the economic initiatives they had embraced. The challenge wasn't insurmountable, but the leaders had to steer away from the socialist and fascist stance, and see Ghana's situation for what it was. Reality had forced them to confront the apathy and corruption rampant in state-owned institutions, but most importantly, they had to accept that the regulatory agencies were ill-suited to become enterprises on their own.

The Think Tank of Privatization could be a turning point. I wasn't alone in the opinion that when no one owned an enterprise, it was difficult to find someone to take care of it, and that attitude had haunted Ghana's economic progress. It seemed that attitude stifled even the most well-intentioned ideas. From my experience in business, I had seen how, if the employees actually had built their own companies with their hard-earned capital and sweat, they never stood idly to watch the companies fall apart. But for many, the companies were owned by the government, and it didn't matter if they succeeded or failed.

Sure, there is hardly a perfect economic system, but another recommendation to have come out of this privatization effort was the need to motivate the private sector and incentivize them to produce. If indeed the government could reap profits from private sector investment, then instead of nurturing the greed and corruption that turned most government agencies into looting machines, it had to guard its own actions against self-defeating and socialist-leaning policies. The military government would have to reign in its officers who harassed entrepreneurs because they were emboldened by the regime to do so. Ghana's government stood to benefit from a wider tax base, but most importantly, motivating the private sector would create job opportunities that would ultimately benefit the country as a whole.

I spent many months with the group, offering pragmatic insights to the PNDC government. Ghana had peculiar challenges, like how its business landscape was dominated by microbusinesses. Town Councils were given the responsibility of recording payments from market women and microbusinesses, many of whom were not registered in a national database. The revenue was intended to pay for construction, repairs and maintenance, but it easily became a loophole for corrupt officers to exploit. It was sickening, but the system was of our own making.

Over four years, I was with the group of private entrepreneurs, doing all we could to make several policy recommendations, including the registration of companies and the expansion of the Registrar General's department to include micro-businesses, irrespective of their size. If I had any knowledge or any resource that would benefit my country, it was a privilege to add my voice.

When I set up Darko Farms in 1967, my hope was to excel in private business and be able to support other businesses and institutions around the country. Setting up the Ghana Poultry Farmers' Association was an effort to help train farmers, and enhance individual ability to excel, just like some of the successful poultry farmers who had been mentors, and had given incredible support. My worldview had always been to become a resource to as many people as possible to help them be independent. From Akropong-Asante to Ejura and Techiman, I had been able to support many outgrowers to build successful enterprises and legacies.

Back in Israel, I had seen how the collective settlements, the *kibbutzim*, and the cooperative settlements, the *moshavim*, both found ingenious ways to inject life into the economy. From these arrangements, I had seen the value of companies and communities working together.

I was fortunate to create an outgrower network by investing in men and women interested in starting their own poultry businesses and other ventures in the agricultural sector. It was important to empower them to create sustainable businesses. In doing so, my company turned its focus to breeding baby chicks and producing feed. I worked with several outgrowers to secure low-interest bank loans and capital for construction and maintenance of facilities. The farmers stood to benefit, but that would also be a gain for the sector.

Year after year, any profit I earned had enabled me to expand my sphere of influence, with a focus on long term investment. I was able to extend my resources, share all my knowledge, and pass on every good thing I had acquired over 50 years in poultry farming. As a businessman, however, I had to manage my risk, and it was critical for every one of the farmers to also understand that a win-win outcome was only possible if they held up their end of the bargain. I was betting on a genuine belief that for every one of the outgrowers with the right attitude, if they succeeded, I succeeded. And our country would, too.

Sadly, I came across many individuals with tremendous potential who preferred to take unfair advantage of my generosity, and occasionally walked away with unpaid loans and mismanaged investments hanging over my head. I came across many who couldn't separate business decision-making from charity. In the end, there were farmers who ignored the arrangement and the fact that their diligence was critical to the relationship.

Despite the occasional flops, for many farmers and entrepreneurs whose companies I had been able to help establish across Ghana and beyond, I emphasized the need for them to guard their assets and invest in their families to also carry on the work. Building strong businesses was more than reaping quick benefits. It took patience and hard work, and the key to managing enterprises was no different from what it took a government to manage an economy. I was happy to have become a facilitator for many, and hopefully helped secure a much-needed lifeline.

*****

Since the 1992 presidential elections, I never felt the urge to contest another election, form a political party, or endure the gruelling days and nights on campaign trails. I was happy to share any business leadership insight or even political observations with any leader who found such thought of value. Ghana would rise if we embraced a leadership and governance driven by truth, dignity, and compassion. The value we placed on fruitful politics and political systems would affect our democratic ideals and our everyday lives.

Chapter 26: Turning Points

Without governance that was forward-thinking, selfless, and accountable, it was only a matter of time before our country descended into chaos, and the economy fell apart. A person's political party affiliation didn't matter. What was important was for their vision to lead, their mind to listen, and their heart to serve. There were years of wisdom gained from our own missteps to guide our years ahead. There was a lot everyone, including me, could do to actively support elected officials, irrespective of their perceived shortcomings, and to work together to uplift our country.

By February 2000, John Agyekum Kufuor and his New Patriotic Party (NPP) were preparing to contest a presidential election scheduled for November of that year. They were desperately seeking partnerships and strategic alliances that they could lean on to change the country's dim fortunes if they won the elections. The value of the currency and the economic instability that he would inherit, if elected as President, would be taxing. The country was broke.

Kufuor had seen the value of groups like the West African Network, on which I served as Board Chairman, and a chance to solicit mutually beneficial partnerships from foreign investors and donor agencies to revive the economy. In America, many of the people I had known for many years accepted the invitation to lend resources to Ghana's struggle to change the plight of Ghanaians steadily drifting into poverty. That is how our paths cross, again.

I was with Kufuor in Washington D.C. meeting with several business leaders, American senators, and congressional members who knew Ghana's story, and most of whom were well aware of our collective desperation to turn the economy around. Until he was elected president, this was only an opportunity to meet with other leaders to get a sense of what immediate plans its government would need to put in place to be able to secure any support from the first day of his administration. Kufuor won the presidential elections in 2000.

George W. Bush and the Republican Party won the American presidency in November of the same year. Some of the key business leaders were coordinating the upcoming inauguration in Washington, D.C., and mentioned they were happy to arrange for a delegation from Ghana to meet with several of their business colleagues during the inaugural events. By the time I received the phone call, a newly elected President Kufuor was working with the NPP Party Chairman Samuel Odoi-Sykes and other leading party members to select his cabinet.

Pat Robertson, whom I had known for many years through Full Gospel activities and the American National Prayer Breakfast network, was with the planning committee. He was arranging for us to meet with the Bush administration officials, and it was a huge opportunity for the Kufuor administration to gain an ally early for his government, to offer not only financial assistance, but a strategic direction to resuscitate the Ghanaian economy quickly.

President Kufuor's most urgent concern was building his government, so he nominated the party's Chairman to travel with me in his stead. The president also nominated Kofi Konadu-Apraku, a man he reasoned had an impressive grasp of international finance and global economic worldview, to join us. With the two men, we arrived in the United States in January 2001.

The events in Washington D.C. for the presidential inauguration allowed for very fruitful discussions with many decision-makers in charge of shaping their country's future. Some of the senators and members of Congress were the same people I had known through my work with Opportunity International and Full Gospel, and my network with the Fellowship, and they granted an audience to the NPP delegates.

I knew very well how several of the American business and political leaders had been genuine advocates of meaningful economic policies, especially in countries where despite a weak economic foundation, the leadership could be determined to seek strategic partnerships to reverse its dwindling fortunes. Ghana was broke, and we needed all the help we could find. Over the next five months, I travelled back and forth for frequent meetings in Washington D.C. and New York City. All I could do was to make an introduction, but soon it would be up to the administration's cabinet to make the decisions and broker the deals.

A few weeks after President Kufuor and the Ghanaian delegation returned from the United Nations General Assembly meeting in New York, I was back in the United States seeking meetings with private enterprises in several sectors which could significantly inject life into Ghana's economy.

In New York, Kofi Annan, who was then serving as the Secretary-General of the United Nations met me and President Kufuor. Kofi Annan was well aware of Kufuor's vision for Ghana, and some of the policies his government was putting in place to ensure efficient allocation of resources. If the NPP administration was willing to implement aggressive strategic investments, I was confident that Ghana had the potential to address the high inflation, a rapid exchange rate depreciation, and an untenable balance of payment deficits.

One of the pressing issues was how Ghana would address the mounting external debt and rising poverty, and that was what led the Kufour administration to seek debt relief through the Heavily Indebted Poor Countries (HIPCs) program. Fortunately, there was no harm that any incoherent economic policies had caused, that a sound and carefully orchestrated policy could not undo.

From the support of Millennium Challenge Corporation, Commonwealth, the United Nations, and other international institutions, I had the chance to continue working with elected officers, and introduce them to people and organizations who had become a part of my own network from serving across Africa and the world. Excellent business and governing minds across Africa were also willing to lend support, and they too understood Ghana's challenge. In 2001, Ghana had a chance to mobilize its private sector to actively invest in the country, but the government had to commit to a macroeconomic infrastructure that created a market and safeguarded investments.

Kevin Callwood had been instrumental in arranging meetings with senior business leaders, and from the multinational finance and insurance corporation American International Group, Inc. (AIG), Bank of America, to the New York Stock Exchange, we crisscrossed Washington D.C. and New York, one meeting after another. This was to be a turning point in Ghana's relations with the United States, a process that had taken a lot of years of working behind the scenes.

Dr. Bawuah-Edusei was Chairman of the NPP in North America, and his team helped coordinate Ghanaians across the United States to join President Kuffuor for a meeting at the White House with President George Bush. As a nation with a hobbling economy, it would be difficult to find countries that would do business with us. With America's backing, the Japanese government that had been reluctant to assist Ghana was willing to reconsider. It was the same with several other European countries.

One of the best outcomes became how a vast network of global decision-makers suddenly opened the doors for Ghana. We were on course to attract foreign investments from private enterprises and from other development institutions. In 2001, President Kufuor had to act decisively, if there ever was to be any real chance of implementing meaningful strategic initiatives.

It was on this trip that I got to know Paul Acquah, a Ghanaian economist with the International Monetary Fund (IMF) who had worked for many years in different parts of the world helping developing countries transform their economic fortunes in a systematic and transparent manner. I would later serve on the Bank of Ghana board with Paul as governor. Another important meeting was with the IMF Head, Horst Köhler, who was happy to share what he believed would be the building blocks to Ghana's economy, not just for debt relief, but for sustained growth.

Before heading back to Ghana, President Kufuor came along to visit Reverend Dr. W. Franklyn Richardson at the historic Grace Baptist Church in Mount Vernon, New York. A banquet with African-American leaders and entrepreneurs presented another chance for the president to share his administration's vision to this audience, and to welcome private partnerships from the United States into Ghana.

It was on another trip in May 2001 that I met with Susan Rice, who had served in American president Bill Clinton's administration as Assistant Secretary of State for African Affairs. She spoke candidly, not about politics, but about governance and the opportunity to make a lasting change on the continent. We also had lengthy discussions with Rosa Whitaker, the Assistant United States Trade Representative for Africa. They were two women whose insight added a great deal of value to the policies that the Kufuor administration would seek to pursue in Ghana. We met with James Wolfensohn, president of the World Bank, to discuss a host of issues desperately needed for major infrastructural development.

By 2008, the sacrifices had paid huge dividends for the country. It had taken an incredible amount of work, but it had all been worth it. If there was one thing that gave me joy and optimism, it was the National Prayer Breakfast. As Ghanaians, we had an opportunity to bring leaders together, without the partisan and ideological divisions, and letting God be the centre of governance.

This initiative had actually begun after the 1996 elections when a group of Christians, led by Minority Chief Whip S.K. Boafo, saw the urgent need to challenge elected leaders from all the political parties to join hands and pray. He founded the Parliamentary Christian Fellowship. I remember how the group had once requested to use the State Banquet Hall to host an event, and even though they had made arrangements with the State Protocol Officer, the officer changed his mind just a few hours before the prayer event.

Supposedly, the government insiders were not in support, and requested nine million cedis to use the facility, and that afternoon they reached out to me to help. A few years later, the Parliamentary Christian Fellowship became the vision and backbone to Ghana's National Prayer Breakfast, the first one held on September 10, 2004 with Nigerian President Olusegun Obasanjo as keynote speaker. That was two months after I had been part of a Christian group to organize a prayer and fellowship meeting for the African Union in Addis Ababa, Ethiopia.

From 2005, several groups joined in a determined effort to organize Prayer Breakfast meetings in different African cities starting with Abuja, Nigeria. We had the support of missionary networks including John Austin with the Christian Embassy, Ken Welborn from the Foreign Service Fellowship, and Dr Abraham Vema with the Abraham International Leadership Ministries who joined Dela Adadevoh to organize these ground-breaking Christian events. The objective was to bring together several heads of states across the African continent for fellowship and a chance to encourage them to take pragmatic steps to govern boldly with Christian values.

Egyptian President Hosni Mubarak, Malian President Amadou Toumani Touré, former Malian President Alpha Oumar Konaré, Ugandan President Yoweri Museveni, Nigerian President Olusegun Obasanjo, and Edem Kodjo, Secretary-General of the Organisation of African Unity, all travelled to Abuja for the event. We organized subsequent Africa Union Prayer Breakfast meetings in Khartoum, Sudan in 2006, another in Accra, Ghana the following year, and in Addis Ababa, Ethiopia afterwards.

With a vision much bigger than any one person's agenda, it was remarkable to see what we could accomplish by working together as a team. Other leaders, including Kenneth Kaunda, who was the former president of Zambia, Sudanese vice president Salva Kir Mayardt, Liberian President Ellen Johnson-Sirleaf, and Marc Ravalomanana, president of Madagascar, participated through the years.

We were united in a cause that would set our countries on a path to acknowledge the truth of God's word in leadership and society.

I was serving as the first chairman of the International Leadership Foundation (ILF), and the crux of my job had become working together with visionaries from across the African continent to create a platform that continued to bring leaders together to pray, and determine to lead

Chapter 26: Turning Points

their countries in the fear of the Lord, and with Godly wisdom. Pushing for a paradigm shift for effective governance demanded a collective effort and an unwavering commitment to teamwork.

In 2020, Ethiopian Prime Minister Abiy Ahmed made a profound observation in his remarks at the event in Addis Ababa, that "the solution to Africa's problems is Jesus Christ." More than just displaying empty religious attitudes, if we were willing to honestly embrace Christ's truth, and dedicate our lives to working our hardest, our continent was blessed with enormous opportunities and resources to rise beyond what had marred our progress for decades. It would be up to us to commit our nations truthfully to Christ's lordship, because *unless the Lord builds, we would only labour in vain.*

For governance that impacted lives, there was only so much we could do on our own. What will make the nation and continent stand was a people whose hearts were turned to Almighty God, standing together, working together, and praying together. It would take leadership that saw the work entrusted to them as a sacred mandate to govern in truth, with faith, and in excellence.

For governance that impacted lives, there was only so much we could do on our own, but what will make the nation stand was a people whose hearts were turned to Almighty God. It would take a leadership that saw the work entrusted to them as a sacred mandate to govern in truth, with faith, and in excellence.

I didn't have the chance to work with either President Atta Mills, except in the years when he had attended the Full Gospel meetings in Accra, or President John Mahama, both of whom were in the National Democratic Congress (NDC). For the latter, I vividly recall meeting him in the years when his father owned a rice milling company in the northern region, and I travelled to buy rice bran from the company. That was long before he was elected into office. It was during his years as vice president, when I was Chancellor of the Regent University that our paths crossed again.

From a distance however, I prayed for all the leaders, irrespective of political party, like I had done through the years, for their hearts to hear the cry of the millions of Ghanaians across the country who needed meaningful change in their communities. Regardless of which party won elections, leaders serving our country ought to fight for opportunities for their citizens to live their God-given destiny.

It was after my older sister Faustina's passing that my path crossed with Nana Akufo-Addo, long before my active involvement with Ghana's politics. At her funeral, we spoke at length about family, about friendship, and most importantly about our faith. During my work with the National Independent Party (NIP) in 1992, I knew about his involvement with the leading opposition party, New Patriotic Party (NPP). Together with Albert Adu Boahen, John Agyekum Kufuor, he had been one of the prominent leaders whose aspirations to lead the country seem to drive his every passion. It was evident then, that if he ever had the privilege of serving as president, he would set enormous expectations for himself and the country, and in turn create an enviable legacy.

When the NPP won the elections in 2000, President Kufuor appointed Akufo-Addo as Attorney General. I was volunteering my time to travel around the world, mostly to the United States, to reconnect with business leaders who would be in a position to assist Ghana to potential local investment, all at my own expense. With Akufo-Addo as the government's legal representative, I had to explain much of my work behind the scenes to him, and tell him about every discussion that I believed would be useful to their administration.

It was during President Kufuor's second term that Akufo-Addo was appointed Foreign Minister in charge of the country's foreign policy, and relations that any inroads I had built for the Kufuor administration became beneficial to him also. All I could do was to introduce him and any other government official to anyone whom I had been fortunate to know, in different countries, but all of whom saw Ghana's effort to regain its promise.

I was honoured to have had the rare opportunity to help presidents, ministers, business leaders, and a host of visionaries to impact our country. In all those years, I had never asked for any compensation or recognition, because all the work I had done was what I promised my God when I shared my passion with Evangelist Morris Cerullo after a crusade in 1966. My only prayer was to have a servant's heart to fulfil the destiny that God had called me to.

Perhaps what I always found humbling was how so much of my world had been connected to men like Al Whittaker and Paris Reidhead, two men I met in 1972, and who had an incredible network of Christian business and political leaders who had been instrumental to my own work, and to helping my country. I saw how God ordered my steps many years in advance, as if He knew what and who I would need some 30 years later. In fact, He did.

Truth is, none of us are ordinary, and nothing we have learned or endured in life is inconsequential. I have come to believe that patriotism ultimately is standing with the diversity and complexity that lives at the very core of a nation, and using our God-given abilities to contribute in any capacity we can.

Our voices and experience ought to stand for something, and ought to challenge not only the people we elect to lead, but also ourselves to help them lead. I also believe that serving our country ought not to be a blind acceptance of the status quo, or a conceited belief that our opinions are best. All of our seemingly ordinary moments have an incredible power to make an extraordinary impact in communities, many of which we may never know. I decided long ago to refrain from passing blame, or being fixated on people's shortcomings, and instead, challenge each of us to rise higher.

Ghana, like any other country, will have dishonest politicians and shrewd businessmen to take advantage of economic and political loopholes, but I am encouraged that we will also have disciplined elected officials and sound-minded politicians who will cherish our democratic ideals, our cultural institutions, human dignity, and compassion. We will have Ghanaians who will sacrifice to build our country, irrespective of what political parties they join, because the hope will be to build a better Ghana, toward a much greater destiny.

For governments, both military and civilian, whether it was my company donating poultry products to nongovernmental agencies or the ECOMOG peacekeeping missions in West Africa, or actively developing commercial projects across Ghana and Africa, what guided my work was a commitment I made to myself and my God long before I found any success as an entrepreneur.

Back in 1967, I had decided to pursue the life of an entrepreneur, a poultry farmer, and my hope was to be able to serve my church and my country in any way that would bring honour to the country, and to God. Some 30 years later, so many of the Christian men and women with whom I worked and travelled had become the prominent statesmen and business leaders from whom I could seek counsel on how best to assist any government.

My heart was meant to serve, and I had not chosen to side with any political party, but with any administration where men and women of integrity and compassion valued any insight I could share. My work and my prayer have always been to facilitate anything that is good, that is honourable, and that is of good report.

CHAPTER 27

A LEGACY OF FAITH

Serving. Giving. Standing in the Gap.

If there was one person whose presence and tireless service changed my life, it was my wife Christiana. I called her *Darling*. I had been blessed to build my life with a woman who was unashamed about her devotion to God's work ever since I first saw her in Scripture Union's Town Fellowship in Kumasi, and ignited a fire in my own heart. I remember how in 1967 when we were newlyweds and both committed to our faith, the ministry gave us indescribable joy, and our home was filled with prayer and praise with the joy of the Lord. As the years went by, her work in the Assemblies of God church increased and so did the unending desire to share the message of grace and hope.

By 1980, we had our children Sammy, Vernon, Joe, Maxine, Mercy, and Bernice who looked up to their mother's faith as one that was to guide their own. The long travels to remote towns and villages in Ghana to work with women in the Assemblies of God church fellowships seemed to strengthen her when most people would faint. I had seen how she had determined to make spreading the gospel the most important part of her life, and that began from our home, and to everyone with whom she crossed paths.

In 1984, Christiana travelled with me to a Full Gospel international conference in Anaheim, California. It was after a fellowship meeting, together with a couple of our friends from Ghana that we visited some of the Fellowship members who lived in the California area. In a casual conversation with an American brother, Dr. Drost, who was serving as International Director, we spoke about how impactful the women in our lives had been, supporting our ministry's work. We joked about how the women in Ghana had become active in meetings, and had taken over the Fellowship. I vividly remember all of us breaking into laughter, and my wife Christiana too in a bright smile, as if in appreciation of the recognition.

Apparently, that had been the case in America also. Dr. Drost shared a story about how the Fellowship's American chapters saw some of the member's wives being incredibly passionate for ministry and sometimes even more dedicated than the men who had invited them. This led a group of four women in Seattle to start the Full Gospel Business Women's Fellowship in 1967. Their hope was to minister to the spiritual needs of the Christian women in their communities, and just as the vision of the businessmen's fellowship did, to impact their world. The group eventually changed their name to Aglow International, but remained incredibly committed to a shared vision of fellowship as Christians without the denominational boundaries.

In California, Dr. Drost said he could arrange a meeting with another lady who was in charge of Aglow in the Santa Barbara area, and he did so the same day. By the time we left California, my wife Christiana was beaming as a new door of opportunity had been opened for her. We headed to Ghana with boxes filled with ministry resources and Christian literature to launch Aglow in Ghana.

I remember the afternoon when a few women who had been part of Archbishop Benson Idahosa's ministry visited Kumasi to invite Christiana to join a women's ministry that Idahosa was launching in Ghana. It would be called Quify, and its sole purpose was to uplift the name of Jesus in women, in every area of their lives. I saw Christiana welcome the vision, explaining passionately to me how she had met with the Aglow representative in the United States just a few weeks prior, and how God had laid it on her heart to carry the mantle in Ghana. The work was underway, and some of the women joined the new ministry.

Standing alongside Christiana, I saw a woman whose faith drove her to preach God's word with power and simplicity, and whose heart had no room for pretence. Her every encouraging word shaped my own commitment to serve in Full Gospel chapters across Ghana, and even in parts of Africa where the society didn't gladly invite Christians to share our message. She shared the pain and joys of the women with whom she fellowshipped, and did all she could to represent the heart of Jesus to her circle of influence.

I saw how Women's Aglow gave Christiana another outreach opportunity with insightful teaching resources to launch the ministry, from our living room in Kumasi. She returned to the United States, to Seattle where the ministry had begun, for a charter to continue the work in our part of the world. For the remainder of her life, a relentless pursuit of God's word and work filled her every waking moment. It affected my own leadership watching her sincere dedication to serving and leading women to the knowledge and freedom of Christ's salvation.

Over the next several decades, she coordinated Aglow as International Coordinator for Ghana, also as the International Coordinator for Africa, and later became the first African to serve on the organization's international board. Standing together with a team of dynamic Christian teachers like Collette Mbadinga in Gabon, and Esme Praah Siriboe in Ghana, I always saw the joy in her heart, an enduring legacy of an unwavering trust in God that strengthened the faith of the people who looked up to her, and many more she would never know.

In every African country where I travelled to launch Full Gospel Business Men's Fellowship International, she was there also, to launch a new chapter for Aglow. I remember in 2006 when Ellen Johnson Sirleaf was elected president of Liberia and the country desperately sought any help to uplift its people, not only economically, but also spiritually. Christiana was invited to the country to revive an Aglow that had fallen apart in the years of the country's civil war, and with the same passion as she had done in other African countries and in every city in Ghana where she reached out with the transforming power of Jesus Christ.

For every life she touched, it was as though she used her gift to build other men and women through their vulnerabilities, and heal painful emotional and spiritual wounds that had become gaping holes in their lives. God sought men and women who would be moved to act on behalf of others and stand in the gap for people on their own personal journeys. It was a conviction with godly compassion, and stepping out to share the same grace that we had the privilege of experiencing. God was calling us to bring hope and comfort, and even when circumstances were overwhelming, our work could become the interceding voice for our world, far beyond what we could comprehend.

It was in my wife Christiana that I saw the beauty of a faith that is stirred to expectancy, and a heart committed to serving with all glory and honour lifted unto Jesus' name. Together, what was to become our legacy were the seeds of faith that we planted in the hearts of our sons and daughters, and also, the communities and fellowships of which we had been a part. There was no greater gift we could give to any of them, or many of the people who we were fortunate to mentor, than the truth of God's abundant grace for people who sacrifice their time and wealth to serve with every spiritual gift and resource they were blessed with.

For every one whom God brought into our lives, we hoped they would find a testimony of integrity, for we had done all we could to be an illustration of living the truth of the gospel. Serving was much more than advancing an organization's reach or erecting impressive church buildings. The heart of Almighty God will be in our willingness to step away from our familiar comforts to reach our neighbours and strangers, meeting their needs, and pointing them to Christ's amazing grace.

Years ago, one man gave me a chance to serve in a great and fulfilling way. It was through John Agamah that I became involved with the Ghana Institute of Linguistics, Literacy and Bible Translation (GILLBT). The organization was a Christian mission that had taken on the incredibly important task of translating the Bible into local languages. From the early 1950s, John Agamah became "Uncle John" to many people and it was his devotion to Christian missionary work and evangelism that connected him to many institutions, and made him the leader of the Scripture Union in Ghana.

It was in England that he met the Wycliffe Bible Translators and learned about their interest in working in Ghana. He spoke of how there were more than 45 distinct languages in the northern parts of the country, and not surprisingly, those ended up being some of the communities where God's word could not reach the people because of a barrier created by language.

The importance of the work was easy to see. On mission trips and crusades, I remembered how we always had to find local translators to help spread the message to communities. There were many instances when the interpretation lost the meaning and context of a message. The Jewish Bible, what we know to be the Old Testament, was first written in Hebrew, and in a few places, Aramaic. Many of the books of the New Testament were first written in Greek, and other parts also in Aramaic. I had seen the impact of evangelism when we were able to share the gospel in a mother-tongue, for the listener to hear the message of grace and hope in their own dialect. That was what the GILLBT and its partners sought to do.

In my own travels around the world, from Germany, to France, and the Philippines, and across every African country, the need for translation was critical to help people understand the Word of God. I knew also that for any organization to undertake such a task in Ghana, it would be a huge individual sacrifice and investment.

Not many could afford to risk their own lives to live in remote villages for years in order to help document a language and create basic writing structures. Through Uncle John Agamah, I learned about how many of the translators, like Mary Steele, travelled to Ghana to live in remote northern villages for more than 50 years doing the work. I also met Grace Adjekum in 1981 who was heading to Chereponi, a small town in the northern region. She was to stay there for years helping to create alphabets and translate the Bible into the local dialect.

Often, the translators ended up in villages for many years to live with the indigenous communities, understand the language with its intricate idioms, and be immersed in the culture to be able to accurately complete the translation. This was work I was privileged to support, a chance to guide people to the same freedom and knowledge of Christ that I found many years ago.

A work of such magnitude required enormous financial support, and it was up to anyone who saw the urgency, and had the ability, to also help. I heard the calling and I was honoured to devote any resource and time to spread the knowledge of God's glory. From Tamale, in the Northern Region, where the GILLBT started its operations, there were many communities where the Word of God was to change lives, and shape destinies. There's no greater fulfilment than joining hands with men like Uncle John to build the kingdom of God in a way that transforms families, communities, and generations.

Through the years, the work required sponsoring local translators to spend time in Israel to learn Hebrew and gain a much deeper appreciation of every theological and historical context in the Old Testament, and then in Greece to study the native language, etymology and syntax in order to not miss any intricate detail of the writings in the New Testament. I served on GILLBT's board since the early 1970s. My desire was to extend God's kingdom, the same calling that led me to the Full Gospel Business Men's Fellowship International and other Christian organizations.

A young Paul Opoku-Mensah became Executive Director for GILLBT for many years, and in a heart-warming happenstance, he had followed his mother Grace Adjekum's footsteps to the same vision of spreading the needed gospel translations for the local communities to understand and appreciate the Word of God.

For me, the chance to share whatever I had to support the kingdom of God had been one that I always considered a privilege. Almighty God didn't need my money. I had made a personal commitment to give cheerfully in any way I believed would support mission work. I found how a simple act of generosity was a chance to trust my God even more, with my earthly resources, and every opportunity ended up helping me to step out on faith.

One after another, I was humbled by the men and women who found Christ through the outreach programs that I had been able to support. I didn't need any affirming or coaxing to trust my wealth in God's kingdom. It was a privilege to be part of something eternal. It was amazing to see how God was able to use one act of obedience to touch many lives and bless entire communities in ways that I couldn't even imagine.

In 1966, I vividly remember sharing my heart with American Evangelist Morris Cerullo when I was torn between the life of a preacher and that of an entrepreneur. I felt a burning desire to serve God's people and to preach the Gospel. It was a God-given conviction for my life's direction but I thought I couldn't do so in the towns and villages where I saw the preachers struggling to provide for their own families and their church. Maybe I didn't hear God right. Or maybe I heard His voice clearly, and He was not only asking me to preach and serve, but also to use my talents to build a business to support His work.

Maybe, for the preachers and missionaries, it would be up to men and women like me to obey God's calling on our lives to help their work. I had decided to take God at His word, with an unvarnished understanding of the fact that all money and every asset I could amass in this life could easily be lost or destroyed in a moment. Even my own life was not mine to boast of. This is the truth that loosened the grip on earthly possessions and gave me a personal reason to trust in God's provision for my life, and in turn, consider it a privilege to give sacrificially.

My conversation with Morris Cerullo took place the morning after a crusade in Kumasi where we invited the local pastors to join the missionaries on the stage. Their presence was most important to him because they were the ones who would be preaching the gospel in the rural villages and small towns, and who would shepherd the hundreds of men and women who gave their lives to Christ at the crusades.

The preachers had come from rural villages near Asante Bekwai, Konongo, and Mampong, and I watched each of them standing on the stage, next to the foreign missionaries, but seemingly lacking confidence. What struck me wasn't just their appearance, with the old oversized coats they wore, and the dirt-stained shirts they had tried hard to keep clean. They were struggling in the villages with little income, and tried their best to minister to their communities. It affected their psyches, and it was easy to see how their plight dampened their confidence. It broke my heart to think these men might never be able to go back to their villages to joyfully share the abundant grace of the Lord to their people.

My prayer, that morning, was to find ways to support as many of those preachers as long as I had breath and ability to do so. For every reward I received, and every profit my company earned, I found joy in working hand in hand with men and women in outreach and evangelism programs and supporting their needs. I had asked God to raise me to be a blessing in my enterprise, and my heart's desire was that I would in turn become a blessing to the body of Christ and my world.

If someday, I was to leave a legacy for my sons and daughters, I hoped it would be an urgent reminder to serve a God who had redeemed us, and qualified us, even when we were still unworthy, for Christ to die for us. My encouragement would be for them to serve Him unreservedly. In any work to support the kingdom, I had been particularly careful to guard my motives, strip my heart of any arrogance and not let my life be defined by what I earned.

Perhaps the most powerful realization for me was that all the help, healing, and caring for another person revealed my own brokenness and imperfection, and were a constant reminder of our need for a saviour. For many years, Christiana and I were able to travel across Ghana and

Africa, establishing churches and supporting mission work in cities and villages. Not everyone could afford to do so, and when we stepped aside to thank God for the work he had entrusted to us, we recognized that it was He who equipped us for every journey to be a blessing to another.

God is interested in our hearts, not our actions. I prayed for a heart to give cheerfully, never losing sight of a God who first loved me, and gave me much more than I could have ever asked for. Giving of my time and my wealth didn't have to earn me a front seat at any church or any ministry. I didn't need gratitude and misdirected recognition from preachers and pastors, and from mothers and fathers whom I had the chance to support. Our circumstances were different, and I was grateful that I could reach out to help another.

Over and again, I am reminded that it is God who gave me everything that I had, even the ability to share, and that was always humbling. In many places where I had the chance to speak of God's goodness, I taught and encouraged people to willingly seek to support and give freely in the humility God instills in their hearts. I had chosen to believe that God would truly *"rebuke the devourer for my sake"*, and because of that, there was nothing that hate or disease or even death could do to change my perspective on God's faithfulness. The Bible's illustration of the devourer is one of locusts and insects destroying a farm's harvests, its fruits and crops. But those who lean on Jesus will have a mighty army standing in position to protect them. It was up to me to stand in agreement with God's word, completely. Every promise in the scriptures was life to me, and that was enough to stand on.

I could never forget 1972, when a contagious Newcastle disease spread through Ghana like wildfire and killed thousands of birds in several poultry farms. There was nothing that any vaccine could do to stop it. It seemed overnight, poultry farms across the country were losing 1,000 birds, 6,000 birds, 10,000 birds, and even more in some places. On my Darko Farms property in Akropong-Asante, I had 50,000 birds on the farm, all at risk of serious infection, and death. It felt like a plague. It was overwhelming and I was unsure what was to happen next. Ghana Veterinary Services officers did all they could for the region, and some suggested that I slaughter the birds before the infection took hold and ravaged my entire farm.

In the gloomy days in 1972, I had two options, slaughter all 50,000 birds, or stand on the Word of God. I chose the latter. I knew the God I served, and the one I had trusted with everything I owned. I had chosen to believe that only He would deliver my company and save the birds, and there was nothing too difficult for Him to do. All I knew to do was to take God at His word and in those dark hours, let everyone else be a liar, and God alone be the truth.

In about a month, farmers across the country were struggling to survive the loss of thousands of birds suddenly killed by a deadly infection. When I had done all I could, by vaccinating every single one of the birds on my farm, and protecting every one of the feeding troughs and pens, I did the only thing I knew to do: I prayed. I asked Elder J.E. Acquaye and some of the elders in my local Assemblies of God church to join me in fasting and prayer. If God had promised that He would protect me, and protect a business that I had dedicated to supporting His kingdom, He would be faithful to His word. That is all I believed.

Eight birds died on my farm during the deadly Newcastle infections, not 50,000 like the experts predicted. Not even 10,000, like others imagined. For me, it was not a lucky break. An omnipresent God's generosity towards me was overwhelming, and there was absolutely nothing I could give to exceed His abundant grace in my life. I had chosen to serve, not because of religious duty or out of necessity but with gratitude for a God whose immeasurable goodness towards me never failed, and who extended an invitation to ordinary people like me to build His kingdom.

Whether or not I saw His hands in any moment, even in the hard places and troubling days, I trusted God to sustain me, and I found every comfort in His truth. No one compelled me to bring my tithe into God's house; I did it because I believed His word. Ever since I set out to become a poultry farmer in 1967, no one asked for Darko Farms company to bring its tithe to God's house. I did it because I knew what promise I had chosen to stand on. Whenever I had the chance to think back to every moment where I should have failed, or where deceitful people tried their hardest to harm my family, or when all human logic said my businesses ought to crash, the hands of Almighty God and His grace covered me.

For many years, I travelled across the world founding chapters for Full Gospel Business Men's Fellowship International, and my wife Christiana did the same for Aglow International. From Senegal and Sierra Leone to the Philippines and Japan, we travelled across the world for many years, willingly carrying every expense with joy to encourage men and women just like us to stand in their communities and nations.

Our encouragement was for committed Christians to determine to make a difference in their lifetime. I had decided to devote my time and everything I had to serve in the Assemblies of God church and other Christian fellowships. I gladly spent every penny and every minute without seeking any compensation or applause. Hopefully, my work would open doors for other men to find salvation through Jesus, just as Reverend Lonnie Fox and Reverend Gyan Fosu did for me, in 1962.

I first met my friend Charlie Duke, an American astronaut and Air Force pilot at a Full Gospel event in Houston, Texas. A few years later, he accepted my invitation to join us in Ghana for the first National Prayer Breakfast. We later travelled together to fellowships in Cairo and Alexandria, in Egypt, and also Larnaca, on the southern coast of Cyprus. Charlie's humility and devotion made an incredible impression on me, just as his powerful testimony did.

In April 1972, Charlie Duke was on the Apollo 16 spacecraft to the moon. In space, some 20,000 miles away, Charlie said the earth floated into view. He wasn't a born-again Christian when he walked on the moon, but one thing he never forgot was when he stretched his hand to find how it so easily covered the earth. At that moment, for Charlie, he couldn't help but believe that it was not difficult to imagine the whole earth to be in God's hands just as was written in the Bible.

At a meeting later that year, Charlie recalled, *"Isaiah 40:22 says God 'sits enthroned above the circle of the Earth.' Well, I saw that circle above the Earth. I didn't see God, but with these eyes of mine, I saw that circle"*. Charlie Duke spoke of how the scripture Job 26:7 came alive for him, *"God suspended the Earth upon nothing"*, and it changed the rest of his life.

I listened to him share his testimony over and again, and every time, it brought a reassurance to me, that indeed I had a Heavenly Father who knew everything, and owned everything, and was exactly who He said He was. What had given me strength to share my faith and reason to trust God with all that I am was because over and over I saw felt his covering over me, a God who was unchanging, and whose every word was life.

It was in Christiana that I found the power of intercession and standing in the gap for another. Our joy had become work that was lasting, and leaning wholeheartedly on God's unending grace. Through organizations like the Ghana Institute of Linguistics, Literacy and Bible Translation (GILLBT), we got the chance to share the good news with communities and remote parts of our world. I was merely an instrument, for God to use my energy, my talent, and every resource He had entrusted to me with praise and gratitude.

My hope is built on a God whose forgiveness, lovingkindness, and generosity towards us is beyond anything we could give to Him. My prayer and commitment is that everything we do will touch a life, and for God to be glorified.

CHAPTER 28

MIRACLE OF FAMILY

As for Me and my House.

I often searched for a memory of my father just sharing a smile with any one of his children, or of him holding my hand to guide my step. I saw how he chased his own dream, and even my mother's tears and his children's longing for his affection didn't bring him home. Long before he died, his absence left a void. My father Opanin Kofi Abebrese found happiness elsewhere, and both my grandmother and mother did the best they could to pick up the pieces. They raised our family in a Christian home the best they could, and gave us every reason to keep our focus on a God who cared for our every waking moment and had a perfect will for every one of us.

Nothing justified my father's absence; it was his choice. Sadly, I wasn't alone in a town where boys hardly knew their fathers and had to hope for another father to come along to teach them how to be men, hopefully, godly men. That was my lot in life, but the God who knew me before the foundations of the earth had a plan for my life, and it didn't change because of what I had to endure during my childhood. Then there was the Akan matrilineal society that traced kinship and lineage through mothers, and which gave some fathers an excuse to make their own children no more than an afterthought.

Our society at the time also inherited a culture that didn't seem to value the presence of women and treated them as inferior, their worth only in serving their husband's needs. Many mothers struggled to take care of their families, and even as a young boy, I saw the pain in my mother's eyes, of a woman now accustomed to loneliness. When a person's value is driven by their own ideas, societal norms, and a need for applause, it is easy to lose sight of a family longing for affection, and what it takes to uniquely prepare children for what God has called them to be.

Fortunately, the Lord found me, in 1962.

What I knew of love, marriage, fatherhood, and family was what I found in the Bible. Its teaching provided the principles that I was choosing to guide my life. I remember vividly that the first gift I gave to Christiana when we were married was a Bible. There was no gold, diamond, or silver that was worth anything close to God's word held in truth, and the assurance that we were to give. Our marriage was to be a foundation to alter the course of my family's future, and it was most important to have found a wife who had also chosen to walk in obedience to God's word. Our sons and daughters would see our fruits, which would guide their own lives.

As parents, we were imperfect, but our God would be *our everything*. We would have God's word to be our anchor, and that was the most important impression we could make on our children.

Years earlier, I had seen my father's priorities steer him away from his children, and now I was choosing to not take any moment for granted. There was nothing in my childhood that I would change, because it made me who I am, but my children and generations to come will know our story of salvation and grace.

Several years after we were married, Christiana and I had a rare argument. We can't even remember what it was about anymore. We were human, and just as fallible as any other person. I recall being irritated by something we disagreed on, and neither of us wanted to cede ground. I had a choice to make, but anger, even for a moment, clouded what I knew to be the truth in my heart. We argued, louder and louder. I was angry. Even though I cannot remember a word of what we said, I cannot forget what happened that afternoon.

Christiana's voice pierced my pride as she walked past me to climb the staircase in our home. I desperately wanted to be right. I was holding a small glass jar in my hand, and in the heated argument, I threw the jar near where she stood. I wasn't sure why I had done so, but watching the jar shatter into little pieces on that staircase was a stirring image of what I was doing to my marriage in that very instant, shattering it into little pieces.

Immediately, I felt the sharp rebuke of the Holy Spirit deep in my heart. It wasn't about anything she said, or even the frightened look on her face as I stood there numb. Tears began to roll down my face as I started to grasp the weight of what I had just done. I had been angry and allowed my anger to win. I had crushed my wife's heart. I remember kneeling down right there at the bottom of the staircase, in tears, and struggling to find the words to express my regret. I was asking for God's forgiveness because I had been given a charge of loving and protecting my wife at all costs, and for a moment, she was broken.

Nothing she had said, or any emotion I felt justified my actions, but all it took was a crack of anger to pull apart the home and the first mission field that God trusted into my care. We were fortunate to have God's word as our ever-present guide, and we quickly returned to it when we strayed from His best. I could only imagine how devastating it was for our young children to see, because someday, they too, would become mothers and fathers, and our prayers would be for them to guard the precious people that God put into their lives.

Just as my own father made his choices, I had my own to make. I had to guard the cracks in my life that the devil sought to exploit and unravel families. It was the little things and their ripple effects that took a person away from God's best, and I had to choose to stand firm every day. Guarding against pride and anger meant that I would do all I could to live by the principles embedded in God's Word to bring honor to His name.

The powerful lesson that lived with us for the rest of our lives was in our being mindful of our actions, both big and small, even inadvertently. Our judgments, choices, and actions would alter our children's. Everything we had told them would lose ground if the image we showed them with our lives was in conflict. What they saw us do would count more. As parents, we were modeling not only character, but also Jesus.

In Christiana, I was blessed with a virtuous woman who took every opportunity to provide comfort and affection as only a God-fearing wife could. What made all the difference in the world was her incredibly nurturing heart to elicit from both of us the best version of each other to achieve our family's goals. My life in ministry demanded that I share of myself and my time with perfect strangers around the world, and God brought Christiana into my life with unwavering trust. We knew very early on that it was both of our responsibility to pray ceaselessly and selflessly for our marriage, and stand on the very practical principles of God's word to strengthen its bond.

We cherished the marriage we had, and the harmony we found in each other. If we were determined to create a Christian home for ourselves and our children as God intended for us, we had to be particularly mindful to strip ourselves of anything that burdened our support for each other. We had chosen to love unconditionally with a Christ-centred relationship, and that meant we gave freely of ourselves without expecting anything in return.

I remember the afternoon I showed up with Christiana at Reverend Vernon Driggers' home in 1967 to introduce her. He saw my excitement and asked if we would delay our wedding plans for the routine church counselling program. I was sure that Christiana was my answered prayer. I told Reverend Driggers that we didn't need it. For many years, both of us had seen inspiring marriages that brought pride to families and glory to Almighty God. It was the kind we hoped that we too would create. We had also seen unions fall apart because of self-centred ambitions and decisions that were less than God's best. We were determined from the very start for our marriage to demonstrate perfect love and submission as God intended, and to reflect His image. Our foundation needed to reflect the perfect sacrificial love of Christ for the church and the church's submission to Christ.

With Christiana, we were anchored together through God, having sincerely chosen to put God first. We knew also that for any marriage to work, it would require a genuine commitment to nurturing the love we shared through many of life's ups and downs. We had made a scared commitment to spend a lifetime together, and we were incredibly fortunate to have the Word of God guiding our every step.

Nothing is better than being in love with your best friend, and the young woman I met in the Town Fellowship meeting many years ago in Kumasi turned out to be the best thing ever to happen to me. What remained our desire was to conduct our marriage according to the principles set forth by God, to magnify, and glorify Him. We both found our purpose in God, and were careful not to overwhelm each other to live up to our individual expectations. Christiana forgave, accepted, and modelled God to me.

The journey of lifelong love and devotion made a huge difference that we had both submitted ourselves to service from the very start. Country after country, we travelled together as much as we could for outreach and her work with women in Aglow, while I worked with the Full Gospel Business Men's Fellowship International. We did all we could to not miss appreciating the little things, because we were two unique individuals with differences, but who had made a choice to commit to each other. We were far from perfect and our light had to shine the brightest in our home.

What was to lead to marital joy for us was a commitment to sacrifice, devotion, and a love that only Almighty God can pull apart. The love that guided our lives was one that would be "patient, kind, not envious, not boastful, not arrogant, not rude, not insisting on its own way, not irritable or resentful, not rejoicing in wrongdoing, but instead rejoicing in the truth, bearing all things, believing all things, hoping all things, enduring all things." *1 Corinthians 13:4-7*

* * * * *

A few years ago I shared some of what I had observed as a father with a young man who was raising a family of his own. We spoke about a man's responsibility for his home and how successful marriages manage to keep God at the center. I had nothing profound to tell him, except that it took God's grace for anyone willing to lean on Him fully, and to follow His instruction completely. In my own marriage, I had come to learn how it was the simplest occasions that seemed to teach the greatest lessons. Our work was to find the God-inspired wisdom in ordinary moments and to teach its truth to our sons and daughters.

I told of how my wife and I did everything we could to spend time with our children, including sitting together to eat meals. My wife Christiana would prepare food and after we had prayed, we took turns serving. The children ate first, starting with the youngest. Christiana and I watched carefully while all the children scooped their food. Only then would we take our own.

It was a simple act, probably not too different from what millions of people did in their homes, but for us, there was a fascinating principle to share with our children. We chose to make sure the youngest among us got food, and that all our children had food before Christiana and I took anything to eat. We told them of taking care of each other, and of seeking the welfare of the least among us, even in our home. Sitting together and sharing a meal was an opportunity to develop our relationship, with our children having a chance to talk, and for us parents to instruct.

Raising our children had to be well thought out in every act and instruction. It is a parent's responsibility to teach a child "why", even in the mundane tasks. They saw why we trusted our God with our lives, and understood *why* it mattered that they gave their time and talent to serving. Years later, I remember some of my children reminiscing about waking up early Saturday morning to clean louvers and floors, pluck weeds from our front lawns, and paint the white wooden chairs on our compound. It was incredible to see the priceless memories we created and their worth in every minute of their lives.

In raising our sons and daughters, I believed that instructing our children didn't have to be a grand experience; it began with our presence, and our conscious choice to cultivate their confidence in us. It was my responsibility as a father to be interested in my children's welfare, not only their mere existence. I was a father who was choosing not to relegate my God-given responsibility as the head of my house to *"Train a child in the way he should go, and even when they are old they will not depart from it"*. It was a parent's duty to help their children walk into their God-given destiny.

Our faith gave us our worth in Almighty God to find our purpose. We were redeemed and set apart to be heirs of the kingdom. Our lives were to make a difference in our generation and lift the name of Jesus in everything we did. I was raising my family to know that it didn't matter that we had status or wealth, or fame. What mattered was our relationship with our heavenly father and doing our very best in every good area of life to glorify His name.

My family chose to pray together and serve the Lord. For many years, we woke up early to start our days with a morning devotion, and to encourage each other in God's word. We chose to sow seeds of faith in the hearts of our children, and our commitment was out of love and joy in our Christian way, not a sense of obligation or a ritual.

It was amazing some fifty years later to visit my grandchildren and see their young hearts immersed in the same early morning devotions that I had taught their fathers and mothers. They sat around a table, their young hearts taking turns to share the gospel of Jesus. In their hands were the same Scripture Union devotionals that had instructed my own life, and that of my young family many years earlier. Leading the hearts of generations to serve Almighty God was the most important legacy we could leave to our sons and daughters.

My son Jonathan spoke many years later of how he had learned to read from the small devotional booklets. With his siblings, they all took turns reading passages and scriptures, and when they were old enough to comprehend the values, we challenged them to share their views on what they had just read. Long before I knew what he would pursue in his own career, I saw a young boy who lived open-handedly, happy to share his days with anyone freely. Jonathan had become the same focused young man, now as an accountant, having returned to serve on the board of Darko Farms.

In all of my sons and daughters, their thoughts and understanding of the world through our lenses of faith were incredibly important to me, and I believed that it was the little seeds of faith that we planted in their hearts every day that would give each of them a foundation for the rest of their lives.

We prayed that they would have their own personal encounters with Almighty God, but in our own small way, Christiana and I did all we could turn their hearts to Him. As our children grew up, we shared our hope for each of them, that they too would build their families in a way that would honor our God. Some days we prayed for God to help them find husbands and wives, and when they did, to bring them home so they too would know who we were, and whom we had chosen to become.

My youngest daughters, Mercy and Bernice, didn't have to struggle for their father's attention. I had decided long ago that there was no meeting too important and no schedule too busy to push their needs aside. They were both particularly nurturing, seeking every avenue to create a sense of belonging for everyone. I wasn't sure what vocations they would pursue someday, but even then, it was refreshing to see the weight of their heart's compassion. Whether it was a career in medicine or in political science, they carried the same entrepreneurial worldview they saw early in their lives into their own careers. So much of what they would become was fashioned by the images we set before them many years earlier. I had to be in their lives to guide them.

We were raising sons and daughters, each with their own idiosyncrasies and talents. I remember how my son Vernon had a vivid imagination of the world even as a little boy. We watched as he fell in love with art, his work ending up at Oral Roberts University in the United States even when he had no idea of how the missionaries who took it had been captivated by every detail and color. For a parent, there was nothing more important than nurturing a child's gift and allowing him to grow into what God had called him to be.

Years later, Vernon had built a successful company that ended up facilitating all of Darko Farms' international transactions of materials and heavy equipment. What became his remarkable insight for growing businesses, negotiating contracts with international partners, and serving on international financing boards, had all begun with the broad view of the world, seeing the detail in the mundane. It was humbling to see my young son receive high recognition for his work—the President's E-Award for Excellence in Exports—from American President Barack Obama. He had chosen a path that nurtured his passion, pursued it with diligence, and gave himself permission to imagine.

Our biggest blessing had become our discernment at the instruction of the Lord. It was not enough to chastise them to listen to our instruction; it was even more important to help them understand why their actions would have lasting effects on their own lives and that of our family. Even when we missed the mark as parents, it was important to recognize our children as gifts that God gave to us to mold and shape, and to whom we should extend the same grace we would want if we missed a step.

I vividly recall when I had disciplined one of my sons for crawling under a hedge to a neighbour's house. The trepidation in the three-year-old's face every time he approached his father afterward broke my heart. What I thought was stern discipline had bruised his young heart, and I knew immediately how delicate parenting was if only we seek our children's best interest. All it took was a parent's single act and it could change the life of their child forever. We groomed each of our children towards their own passions and strengths and gave them the chance to see what they imagined. It was God who had deposited talents in each of them, and our duty was to guide them to their discovery.

On every trip that we could arrange, I traveled around the world with my wife and children. The moments mattered to me, and hopefully, there would be many experiences that they could also cherish. On the trips where I couldn't take them along, I purposefully returned home with a simple toy or a small gift. The object itself meant little; it was the intent that made it meaningful. It was years later, now that they were all grown, that some of them remembered the small chocolates from Holland and mini almonds that I used to save for them from my plane trips. Every gesture and kind word instilled confidence in their young hearts, and moulded their choices without my having to pressure them to conform.

Fortunately, Christiana stepped in to care for the children while I was travelling, and I didn't have to wonder if my time away from home would create empty moments. We were purposeful in our relationships because there was nothing more important than doing all we could to demonstrate godliness in every area of our lives.

The children saw the joy in their parents' eyes as we travelled across continents doing the work of the Lord, and we were blessed for open doors to give each of them a chance to widen their own horizons. In a summer 1996 convention of the Full Gospel Business Men's Fellowship International, a 15-year-old Bernice stood in front of thousands of people in a packed George R. Brown convention centre in Houston, leading them in worship. I prayed that all of my sons and daughters would find the joy in Christ, and never allow life's inevitable turbulence to strip away their trust in our God. It mattered to us.

Chapter 28: Miracle Of Family

When Christiana and I were first married in 1967, we sat down to plan every detail of our lives to be consistent with our faith. My wife was pursuing her nursing and midwifery careers, and even with a new station in life as newlyweds, we decided that our commitment to our church wouldn't change. Our lives were now together as one, and so were our focus and vision. Soon we would be blessed to have children, and we had to plan for their lives too. Our commitment to each other and to our God overruled any viewpoint that society or culture taught, because, in the end, the only sure foundation would be one built on Christ alone.

A year later in 1968, we completed the ownership and registration documents for Darko Farms company, with 40 percent ownership due to me, 30 percent for Christiana, and the remaining 30 percent belonging to my eldest son, Sammy. He was barely a month old, but he had become the representative of his brothers and sisters who would someday be born. We walked into the local Barclays Bank in Kumasi to open a joint account. That was all we needed.

It was in the ordinary choices in our lives that we affirmed our commitment to each other and what we knew was God's word. One truth we knew for sure was that everything we earned or lost was God's, and we were only stewards. Our assignment was to manage every resource, and to be able to be a blessing to our community and the body of Christ.

Each of my children was bound to pursue their own ambitions and I had decided not to force my children to become farmers like me. Still, I prayed for them to inherit my work. My prayer was to guide their minds and cultivate a passion for farming, especially in a rapidly changing world, because Darko Farms was our legacy to keep. God answered the prayer in a way I didn't expect.

Sammy was about eight months old when my wife was assigned to a midwifery residency program in Accra. She would be gone for a year, and we made arrangements with some of our relatives to assist when they could. At one time an elderly relative agreed to help. On more than one occasion my heart sank when I saw her flip little Sammy into the air playfully, and catching him right before he fell on the floor. She said it was common in her culture, and didn't see anything dangerous about it. I was petrified.

She had come to help, and she meant well. Over the next few days it was difficult to walk away from my son, and I wondered if we had made the right decision asking the lady for her assistance. I got home the next day to the smell of alcohol. She didn't deny it; instead, she explained how in her culture, it was understandable to give the little baby boys sips of alcohol to make them tough. I was stunned. There was nothing for me to understand.

I politely asked the lady to leave, and from that moment I made the decision to take care of my own son, irrespective of my busy schedule. I went to the UTC department store to buy a small bassinet. Sammy rode in the car with me to Darko Farms every morning, and the little boy ended up falling in love with being around the farm. God had a way of orchestrating our steps.

Years later, Sammy had graduated from university with an incredible understanding of animal science and commercial poultry farming. I still wanted to judge his practical experience from the start so I gave him a long pen filled with broilers to see how his knowledge translated into the field work. I recall Sammy quickly pushing for advancements in nutrition and breeding for Darko Farms to produce broilers ready for sale in a six-week period, instead of the ten-week period we had done for years. In every minute on the farm, a young Sammy was immersed in nutritional analysis and a host of experiments to find ways to save operational costs. It was then that we began properly measuring moisture levels in the feed in order to avoid insects and fungi that could infect our flock. Sammy's education had been incredibly vital to the future of Darko Farms, but it was his genuine love for poultry farming that made all the difference.

I had prayed for my oldest son to fall in love with my work, and be someone I could pass on my knowledge and legacy to. I hoped in turn he would pass them to his siblings and generations to come. God had a sense of humour. He answered my prayer, except that it wasn't how I had imagined.

In much the same way, my daughter Maxine became the *Iron Lady*, in charge of the processing plant at the facility in Akropong–Asante. Nurturing the managerial traits in her heart gave the confidence to lead in places where God's grace took her for a career. She set high standards for herself and the company's operations in a way that pushed employees to work their hardest and love the work they did.

At the company's office in Accra, it was Maxine whose skill made her the ideal person to manage operations in that part of the country, and help the company maintain our competitive advantage. Often it felt like Christiana had successfully transferred everything in her heart to her daughters, and Maxine embodied every one of her mother's traits. Fortunately, her husband agreed to travel to Accra to establish his own business alongside her, in order for Maxxine to help build our family's business, and we couldn't have been more grateful. A few years later, Christiana started Oasis Christian Academy, and fortunately we had Maxine to lean on to manage the institution. As parents, we had seized the opportunity to instil a sense of discipline in our children, so that in whatever area they ended up, their value would be in their commitment to effect change.

One after another, we were blessed to have all of our sons and daughters gladly choose to join hands to build a legacy, one that began in 1967. Ours was a reliance on God's word. All of their talents ended up serving the vision I had set for our family. When I chose to leave my stepfather's farm to start a new venture, my prayer was to build an organization whose success would support the kingdom of God, through missionaries, churches, and outreach. It is through my sons and daughters that the vision get to live much longer than I ever would.

I had determined that evening when I gave my life to Jesus in Abbey's Park in Kumasi that I wanted my life to stand on God's word completely. If I was to err, I would rather err on the side of grace and mercy. Nothing mattered more than giving my sons and daughters a glimpse of God through my eyes and my own journey. Through every one of them, I saw a version of answered prayers, and the worth of making a concerted effort to raise children in our faith from the very start.

There were also many young men and women around the world—from my church and my company, to a host of Christian organizations—whom I had the rare opportunity to mentor or encourage along the way. In the end, I hoped I had been a worthy example to challenge each and every one to reject the noise that drowns out our values and stand fierce against apathy and vanity.

My prayer is that they too will carry the message of hope to their families and for the generations to come to know when we must chose Christ to be our anchor, standing steadfast in the raging seas of life. I lived to see the fruits of our labour, and to see their offspring choosing to lean on the same God that carried us every step along the way. It was a joy for my eyes to see my sons and daughters do even better than I had, because they were committed to a kingdom's vision and a heart's desire not to depart from what we had taught them.

Christ will be the anchor for our souls, for our sons and daughters, and we will choose to not drift from His amazing grace. For our family, the meaning of a life well-lived will be in leaving a marker, one that is held together by grace. Our legacy will not be in material possessions, but in the urgency to lean on Almighty God's unfailing grace, together.

CHAPTER 29

THE MASTER STILL CALLS

Oasis. Challenges on a Great Commission.

Indeed, *"Many are the afflictions of the righteous, but the Lord delivers him out of them all"*. Making the choice to heed God's call to spread the good news to our neighbours and to the nations came along with winding roads filled with uncertainty, rejection, and sacrifice. Yet, I had chosen to walk ahead, my hope fixed on the promise that in the end, even though the darkest hours, it is God's providence that will prevail. If I was unmovable in my faith, even when I felt shaken and distraught, God's unfailing grace would order my steps in a way that I could never have imagined.

American evangelist Irvina Miller first arrived in Ghana in the early 1950s. Apparently, she had left her home in Shippensburg in Pennsylvania, and headed to Africa to evangelize. Her local church, which she had built with her husband in Shippensburg, was the Oasis of Love Church. She ended up in Prampram, a coastal town in Ghana, and it was here that her dynamic and prophetic ministry brought her in contact with local Pentecostal churches and prophetic ministries like Brother Lawson. In the area, Brother Lawson was popular for his spirit-based prophetic ministries, which the locals nicknamed *kyiri-bentoa*—which was much different from the predominant orthodox churches.

What attracted Irvina Miller to the Prampram area were the incredibly colourful festivals and the hospitality of the people with whom she felt compassion to share the gospel. Yet, she also felt threatened as her fiery preaching and deliverance ministry drew the attention of the traditional religious leaders and their elaborate rituals. Evangelist Miller headed west to Akim Abuakwa area at the invitation of several of the Presbyterian Church missionaries who were working with local communities in that part of the country. Nana Ofori Atta who was chief in the area welcomed her to continue her work in the local communities. Soon after, she would meet Reverend James McKeown in Asamankese whose evangelism with the Apostolic Church took him to parts of the Eastern and Ashanti Regions. It was Reverend McKeown who would bring Evangelist Miller to Kumasi, teaching God's word fiercely, with God using her ministry greatly for miracles and healing.

I was a young boy then, and didn't remember Evangelist Miller in those years. My mother, however, remembered every moment, and her powerful sermons. She recalled Evangelist Miller's commanding presence in the church as she invited many people to Jesus, and even though her small physical stature often required her to stand on a small table during her sermons, nothing dulled her passion for ministry and preaching the word of God. Evangelist Miller returned to Shippensburg, Pennsylvania in the mid-1950s. Our lives were to cross some 40 years later.

* * * * *

Ever since I turned over my life to Jesus Christ that Saturday evening in 1962 in Abbey's Park, Kumasi, nothing in life brought more purpose or joy than completely availing myself of the work of God. It was Reverend Gyan Fosu and Reverend Lonnie Fox who invited me to the Assemblies of God church the next day, and in the middle of the dusty field, it became my local church for the rest of my adult years.

From the very start, I had the joy of immersing myself into the Christ Ambassadors youth ministry of the church, the church's choir, and committing my every waking moment to evangelism and local outreach. I asked God to use my time and energy for His glory and I was choosing to dedicate my life to building the kingdom in any way that God led. It didn't matter if I had to buy vehicles, properties or land for the church. I gladly paid salaries of preachers and missionaries, met any need of the fellowship that I was capable of, and gave everything I owned to support the Assemblies of God church, because with every humbling act of generosity, I remembered the promise I had made to God in 1966. I had set out to become an entrepreneur whose heart would be to build God's kingdom, and that was the passion I shared with Evangelist Morris Cerullo. I was truly grateful to have seen God remain faithful to His word.

I remember vividly when Reverend Nicholas Opuni came from the village of Adusa to take over the leadership of the Lighthouse Assemblies of God church in Kumasi, and shared his vision to start churches in the surrounding areas. With other elders, we opened branches from Bantama, Santaase, Suame, Atonsu, Kwadaso, and Angonaga, all the way to Adiebeba. Often, we started the church in the classrooms of the local government elementary schools, teaching and serving the community until we eventually erected church buildings, one after another. We were not ordained ministers, and had not stepped foot in any seminary to study theology; rather, we were men and women with our hearts set on the Great Commission, and nothing was more important than leading other men and women to the knowledge of Jesus Christ.

The church in the Adiebeba suburb was the last location we set up in the area, before God opened huge doors of service to join hands with other witnesses to establish churches and ministries across Ghana and around the world. Christiana and I remained the overseers at the Adiebeba church, and we named it the *Glad Tidings Assemblies of God* church. As we had done with all the churches we founded, eventually, we had young preachers who had completed seminary school in Saltpond or elsewhere to take over.

Serving in the Assemblies of God church had taken me from Kumasi through almost every church in the country to the church's leadership in Springfield, Missouri, in the United States. Serving had become the most important thing in my life, and every moment and resource in my life would be devoted to building God's church. My heart was set on meeting the needs of anyone I could, and just as I had promised God in 1967, using my company's success as an opportunity to support every ministry that was proclaiming the name of Jesus to their world.

By 1981, the foreign missionaries were urging the church leaders in the United States to relocate the Assemblies of God Printing Press, which printed ministry resources and Sunday school materials from Ghana to Togo. I strongly opposed it. They feared that Jerry Rawlings' coup d'état would seize the printing press, just as the Nigerian military leader Emeka Ojukwu had seized the Assemblies of God church's printing press in eastern Nigeria during the country's civil war in 1967 to print Biafra's currency. I had sat with Reverend Phillip Hogan and the leaders in Missouri to discuss what I was convinced the church needed in Ghana, and tell them that I was willing to support it with any resource I could muster to make it work. The facility, Assemblies of God Literature Centre, A.G.L.C., continued to serve the entire West African region with Christian literature and training materials.

Over the years, my wife Christiana had also become the leader of the women's ministries across the nation, having devoted her life to the Assemblies of God church, working with women from all walks of life to find the same promise of Christ's salvation. Her work with women's Aglow ministry also granted her new opportunities to serve, and the more we opened our hearts for God to use us as instruments of His kingdom, the more He showed His amazing grace in our lives.

It was also in 1981, late one evening, when my lawyer Anthony Mmieh came to my house in Ahodwo's residential area, Kumasi. The PNDC military government had instituted a curfew in a society that had plunged into chaos and tension. I looked through my bedroom window, and saw him and another man, both of them looking nervous. They had to be desperate, having made their way through military checkpoints to find their way to my house.

Apparently, the man was a younger brother of B.M. Kuffuor, the same wealthy timber contractor who had sat next to me on a Ghana Airway flight to England, only to return to Ghana in a casket. He had never imagined that he would be returning to Ghana on a conveyor belt into a cargo compartment, but in what seemed like an instant, his family's life was turned upside down.

The young man had inherited his older brother's assets, never thinking he would also inherit unpaid taxes, which the military government deemed to be a crime. He probably had no way of knowing that inheriting from his brother would bring so much trouble, but now he was facing a firing squad from a ruthless military government that was supposedly rooting out all evil businessmen from the society. The young man had been paraded that afternoon along some of the main streets in the Kumasi area, along Prempeh II Street, shown to the entire community as one of the criminal businessmen to be executed in the abandoned racecourse in three days. If he was unable to pay the 10,000 cedis in taxes owed by his deceased brother's sawmill company, he would be killed too.

Christiana was perturbed, and we all knew what the soldiers were capable of. The man fell down begging for any help because they had tried every other avenue and didn't know anyone who could give him 10,000 cedis to save his life. Apparently he had gone to every one they thought would be able to help but even the ones who were financially able, were scared for their own lives. Christiana was gripped with fear, and she couldn't fathom why the soldiers would threaten the life of a man who probably had no way of knowing his brother's assets or business dealings. He didn't have the time to negotiate a reprieve from the soldiers.

My wife Christiana said *"Se nnipa bewu dea, nka sikka nwu"*, we would rather lose money than let a human being die. We agreed to help him. I wrote a check from our company's bank account and learned that the soldiers held the man in the military barracks only until they collected the money from the bank after a special clearance. Coincidentally, helping the young man brought me into the crosshairs with the military government. That was what everyone had been scared of. Supposedly private businessmen like me were the bane of society. They requested that I be vetted and face the same fate if they could prove that I had conducted shrewd business, or not paid taxes. Their attack on me failed.

Months later when the man returned to pay off the loan, the only way he could do so was to sell some of his brother's assets, and to pay the difference with whatever little money they could afford. It was an inheritance but they insisted that they had tried their hardest to find any amount money, and had no other option. They couldn't even find someone who would be willing to buy the properties. They begged for us to accept. We agreed.

After a few years, my wife and I decided that we would never use the land which had been another's inheritance for our personal use. Instead we would use the land to construct a church facility and a retreat centre, a facility that could help our Assemblies of God church use the property to expand the church's vision. My friend Professor Nii Adjere Wellington designed the facility for the church and the body of Christ. What I could never have imagined was that while I was working to find every avenue to build facilities with the land I had just acquired to support the church's vision, some of the leaders and elders in the church were plotting a different agenda.

Overnight, rumours turned to false reports on radio, and then the unthinkable happened. Some of the church leaders claimed I was building my own church, and sadly, there was nothing I could say to change their hearts. Our local Assemblies of God church in Adiebeba did not have a church facility and it was a blessing to move the local church into the new building. It was shocking and utterly disappointing that what I hoped would serve our collective vision didn't make any difference to the elders who were bent on pushing me out.

For some, even my decision as a Christian to contest the 1992 presidential elections was something they couldn't come to terms with, because they never imagined a committed Christian seeking elected office. For them, Christianity meant refraining from politics and governance, and instead spending time praying for God to raise righteous leaders from elsewhere. The disconnect in their thinking was baffling, but unfortunately, they were some of the people who were now leading the body of Christ.

The Church Council had met while I was travelling out of the country and decided that I had become too influential in the Assemblies of God church, and that my involvement in international outreach programs and ministries was overshadowing some of the leaders' own work. In one incident, Reverend Sumaila and some of his counterparts were against a young Kwasi Mensah's involvement. He was a committed young man who oversaw the child evangelism ministry and was incredibly dedicated to teaching children in the church. I disagreed with them, and even that minor disagreement had become one of the last pieces to unravel the relationship with the church's council.

The dishonest stories that I had opened a new church were more disappointing because there were elders and church leaders who knew my every intent. I remember one such person had been young Reverend Paul Dapaah whom I had encouraged for many years since he completed seminary, to use his talent and zeal to serve. He was the young man who had expressed interest in Christ for All Nations Bible School in Dallas, Texas, but he'd failed to gain admission on several occasions. Coincidentally the one of the founders, Mrs. Lyndsey who established the school with her late husband Gordon, was serving on the FGBFI board, and I met her at an event in Dallas. They were willing to accept Paul's application because I vouched for his dedication and passion to learn sign language to be able to minister to our communities after completing the seminary. I recommended him to lead the local church at New Tafo, through which he later became Treasurer for the Assemblies of God church council in the Ashanti Region.

Unfortunately it was Paul Dapaah who made the announcement of the local Ghana City Radio station that I had left the Assemblies of God church and started my own. That was not true, and the men who had carefully orchestrated that lie knew it. It was fascinating to see men and women who decried party politics and even disparaged politicians as being immoral and conniving manage to turn the church into a political spectacle.

I had done my best to nurture relationships with all the elders, and even when we disagreed, it was important that the interest of God's work take precedence over any personal desire. All I had done was to help the local church move into a new facility, and use the entire compound for other events and training activities to develop leaders and missionaries. The Assemblies of God church leaders said they were not interested in anything I had to offer, or any building I was erecting. I much more saddened than surprised by how we had lost our shared vision. I didn't get even the courtesy of a formal notification. I had to hear the announcement on radio.

I had no reason to fight the church, and in fact, I had seen how any fracture in any ministry can set people against each other and mute the church's impact in our society. I was focused on evangelism and outreach, and it didn't have to be in a building at any specific location to share the gospel. The burden on my heart was to equip leaders, and we decided to use the facility for a Bible School, to be called Oasis of Love.

Within two years, we had trained more than 350 ministers and given a great launchpad to young men and women whose heart's desire was to serve the kingdom. The facility grew. For people who were interested in heeding the Master's call to preach the gospel, our vision was for the centre not to charge fees. This had become another opportunity for God to honour His word and the commitment I gave in 1966 when I met American Evangelist Morris Cerullo. I had dedicated my life to becoming an entrepreneur whose only focus was to succeed in order to support the kingdom, and my heart was full of gratitude for yet another chance to do just that. The prayer sessions turned into fellowships and gradually we evolved into a church. We erected a huge signboard on the side of the Old Bekwai Road main road in Ahodwo, a suburb of Kumasi, with the words *Oasis of Love Center*.

What I never could have known was that Evangelist Miller, who had first come to Ghana in the 1950s from Pennsylvania, had just returned to Ghana some 40 years later. After her work in places like Cuba, Ecuador, and Vietnam, she told of how God had impressed upon her heart to return to Ghana. She arrived in Prampram, the same town she had first visited and where she had clashed with the traditional non-Christian religious leaders. This time, with her grandson, she wanted to build a vocational centre she called *Oasis of Love*, to serve young men and women in the area, just as she had done in places in South America. This time, Brother Lawson, with whom she had worked in the local communities, was frail with age and fallen ill. Evangelist Miller helped a local preacher in the Old Tafo area build a small church and named it "Oasis Church at Old Tafo," in Kumasi.

The word Oasis meant a great deal to her, the meaning and symbolism of bringing new life into challenging places. It was on her drive from Prampram in Accra to the Old Tafo that she saw a huge signboard on the side of the main road, with the words written in bold red letters, "Oasis of Love Centre".

The coincidence lit joy in her heart to find the organization that probably shared the same vision she had carried for decades around the world. Evangelist Miller was even more surprised to know that Madam Salormey, the woman who had hosted her in Prampram, knew Christiana and me. Apparently, the instant Evangelist Miller asked about the signboard, Madam Salormey spoke of our commitment to the body of Christ in Ghana and around Africa. It was she who arranged for Evangelist Miller to meet Mrs. Christiana Darko who was to be heading to Accra in a few days.

At nearly 85 years of age, she couldn't contain her excitement a few weeks later when she arrived at the facility in Kumasi to teach some of the students and share her own life's work. She ordained my wife and me, and we were all moving forward to work together, with a church that stood completely on the all-powerful word of Almighty God, and committed to equipping disciples for Christ.

For all the disappointments that had taken me from the Assemblies of God Church, I had gladly accepted the moments where God pushed me into new territory. I had not done any work because of any man, or for any accolade. If God was asking me to walk into in a new season, I was stepping out on faith to create an *oasis*—new life in a desert—for men and women whose desire was to serve Almighty God.

Heeding the Master's call meant the devil would fight back, but there would be no affliction or challenge that would overwhelm us, because the Lord had promised to deliver us from them all.

* * * * *

I sat in the back of the Nissan Patrol car on our way from Ouagadougou, Burkina Faso. My friend Reverend Frank Hatchful sat in the front seat, and Full Gospel President Joseph Kwao sat near the right window. We were returning from a Fellowship meeting where we had seen the amazing manifestation of God's presence on the Burkinabé people.

We had invited Burkinabé President Thomas Sankara, but only his wife Miriam was able to attend that morning. It was there in Ouagadougou that she accepted Jesus as her saviour, and like her, many of the people in the room found Jesus. Mamadou Karambiri, a young Christian gentleman, had also caught the Full Gospel vision and had committed to stand for the Lord and preach across the country. Karambiri had begun a prayer ministry in his home and it was refreshing to join him in the prayer meetings and encourage him as well.

The drive back to Kumasi was long, on a dusty and bumpy road, but I was too exhausted to care. I soon fell asleep, leaning my head against the window. Suddenly I was startled awake by the feeling of a heavy hand strangling my neck. I could hardly breathe. I tried to break free. I was panting, gasping for air, and struggling to scream the name of

Jesus. The men pulled the car to the side of the road and began praying forcefully.

I could hear their voices, even though I could hardly open my eyes. I woke up suddenly, shaken. I was terrified at the moment, but we were all alert to the challenge of the devil's opposition to ensure that we would give up on the Great Commission. If we chose to give in to fear and intimidation, the Devil would win. For every soul that the Holy Spirit was able to touch through our outreach, that was one soul that the devil lost. We were attacking the enemy's territory and he was hell-bent on doing anything he could to stop us.

As if I had broken free from whatever had gripped me, I was able to breathe again. Just as the word of God was true for every promise and assurance of His provision for our lives, the Word is also true that we wrestle against principalities and powers, spiritual wickedness in high places that will do everything it can to derail us from fulfilling the work set before us.

The work of ministry required a commitment to walk through the discomfort and the trepidation, and with our eyes fixed on Christ. The stakes for our salvation were too high to not step out of our comfort zones and be ambassadors of the gospel. For every attack, we chose to persevere so that the name of our Lord would be glorified.

In 1989, I returned home from the Lausanne Conference in the Philippines to a fellowship under attack. There was one moment after another when the circumstances looked grim and we prayed for *discernment to recognize the spiritual attacks in our lives*. I went to the Fellowship office in Accra only to learn that Dan Abebrese, one of the prominent leaders in the Accra chapter, had been involved in an accident on the Winneba Road. He died instantly. Another young brother in Christ who was travelling with Dan had both of his legs amputated and his life changed forever.

Then suddenly, we received news that another one of our members lost his young wife that very morning. She was healthy in one moment, and had never fallen ill, but had died suddenly. It was emotionally crushing, but even more, we felt a heavy attack on all of our lives. It was as though our work of passionately preaching the Word of God to men, and leading families to Christ's salvation had attracted the attention of Satan and every demonic force. The louder we preached, it was as if there was one tragedy after another to silence us. The leaders in the Fellowship had to stand firm and be vigilant.

We were fighting against spiritual wickedness, satanic instruments that we couldn't see with our naked eyes. We had chosen to serve God and take the message of grace and hope to communities and to nations. What I never would have known was the fierce spiritual opposition we would encounter, much more ferocious than any of us had faced in all of our Christian journey. We were not wrestling with flesh and blood, and the commitment to build the kingdom threatened our lives.

I went home to Kumasi, and all the leaders agreed to fast and pray. Our mission was too important to succumb to the pressures of demonic forces, and we were confident in the fact that the God we served was much more powerful than any satanic attack on our lives and those of our families. In moments when we were struck by fear, we had to encourage each other to stand firm.

In those unnerving moments, it was some of the incredibly powerful Bible stories of men like Paul, Stephen, and Jesus, which became our urgent reminders. Even though we felt the persecution and the journey had become one fraught with attacks on our lives, we had to remind ourselves that there was nothing that could happen to us that would surprise our Heavenly Father. God was watching over us, and we had to pray even more fervently.

A few months later, I was meditating on the Word of God sitting in my living room, and drifted into a moment of prayer. My hands were lifted as I prayed. Suddenly I felt a sharp object hit my left palm, like a gunshot. The pain was immediately excruciating and suddenly it was as if the devil had turned his attention to my life. I started praying loudly and my children rushed to the room and joined in prayer also. I could feel the sharp pain travelling forcefully along my arm, past my elbows.

I shook my hand over and again, and screamed the name of Jesus louder and louder. As I prayed, I felt the pain push away, only to press its way towards my chest, and I stopped praying momentarily. My wife and children rushed and joined in the prayer, holding my hand, calling for healing in a desperate time. Only then, I felt the pain disappear just as suddenly as it had hit me.

On another bizarre occasion, I fainted suddenly while I was at home with my family. A bright sunny afternoon immediately turned gloomy. I never had epilepsy or any medical condition that would cause me to faint for no apparent reason at all, but there I was on the cold floor. It was after a few minutes of my family praying frantically and interceding for my life that my eyes opened. I had been unconscious, and was now sweating and breathing harshly.

"What happened, what happened?" I remembered my wife Christiana's voice faintly.

"I don't know".

I was confused for a moment but it was as if I had suddenly fallen into a deep sleep and was dreaming.

"You were unconscious!"

Their faces were marred by trepidation and elation. I sat up slowly.

I hadn't been dreaming. My memory was clear. In what had felt like strange trance, I saw myself driving a green Mercedes Benz at full speed, and heading down a steep hill. My wife sat on my side, and my children in the back of the car, all holding tight to my arms and shoulders, pulling me back. I felt their hands pull, as they screamed and pulled even harder as if to yank me out of the speeding car. My eyes had opened just before the car crashed at the bottom of the hill. That was all I remembered.

For me, it was no coincidence that the Lord had snatched me out of the jaws of death. The bizarre encounters were not random imaginings.

My life was under attack, and I could not afford to take any part of it for granted. God's work was what I had chosen to spend my life doing, and even if that turned me into a target for Satan, there was nothing to fear because, through Christ, we already had the victory.

For every territory that we captured through salvation and where we ushered many men and women into a new life and a new spiritual quest, it stripped the devil of another soul it couldn't lure into the pits of hell. That was why the devil fought us the hardest.

I had decided to heed the Master's call to preach the good news to the nations of the world, and there was nothing that was to force me to turn back. No sickness and no demonic attack on my life and that of my family and fellowship would change my resolve to be an instrument for the kingdom. None of the *"fiery darts"* of the devil or his forces of darkness would dissuade us from our journey and our mission. Whatever work we were doing for Christ had gotten the devil's attention and he didn't want us to keep going. Nonetheless, we were determined to press ahead.

Stepping out in faith to become an ambassador for Christ had real consequences in the spiritual realm for the devil and his evil forces. Leading men away from promiscuity, adultery, dishonesty, and greed to the truth of Christ's salvation rattled the devil's cage. In countries across Africa where presidents and high ranking officials had allowed the devil and occult powers to reign over their people, we were lifting up the name of Jesus and breaking chains that had held people for many years.

God had called us for His purpose, and there was bound to be affliction along the way, but we were assured of a saviour who was more than able to deliver us from it all. The warfare with the devil was constant, and we, like any believer, were objects of focus for his attacks. In the years after, it was one attack after another, and one testimony of God's amazing rescue after another. There were some days when our faith wavered, but there was always God right there in the midst of the turbulence to help us see again.

Chapter 29: The Master Still Calls

Years ago we were in Togo, along the eastern Benin border when we learned that there was a failed coup d'état on President Eyadema's government and the officials had suddenly decided to shut its borders. In a tense environment, the government's suspicion lay with everyone who wasn't part of their inner circle. I was travelling with Christiana and my brother Joseph Kwao. We were foreigners in Togo, and in the eyes of the military, we could easily be operatives under the disguise of a missionary group.

The young military officers, the *gendarme*, pointed their guns angrily at us and instructed us to step out of the car. They threatened to shoot anyone who disobeyed their orders. Nothing we told them about why we were in Togo satisfied them, and the fact that we were crossing into Benin for a Full Gospel outreach program didn't make any difference to them. Their eyes were red with anger, the loaded guns strapped to their shoulders. The guns swung back and forth callously.

My wife began praying, in a deep and passion-filled petition to God. Some of the soldiers mumbled to each other and there was nothing we would say to them to assure them that we were not conspirators in any coup d'état. We called some of the government officials who were members of the Fellowship in Togo, Yagne Nim and Kofi Essaw. They authorized the border guards to release us, and we continued into Benin, with hundreds of people stuck on either side of the border.

Every choice to preach the good news, and open a new chapter for the ministry in different countries brought along one hurdle after another. Some people threatened our lives and most sought to scare us into walking away. The journey to challenge men and women to rise and become what God had created each of them to be, came with a struggle of our own and we could only pray for the grace to press on. We had chosen to take on the cross, and had come to believe that the assignment was too important to let the devil win.

The work of the Lord was taking us to remote towns and villages, breaking barriers and chains that had held many people captive. We were preaching Christ's salvation and amazing grace to people and places where the Word of God had never found an audience. The devil launched his assault on our lives and our ministry, but we served a God who indeed promised our triumph. The devil did all he could to make us lose sight of the truth that he was soundly defeated at the cross. Our confidence was in the fact that despite the persecution, all we had to do was to stand on the word of Almighty God. We were not fighting spiritual battles with our own strength, but through Jesus Christ, in whom we found the strength to *stand against the wiles of the devil*.

The Master is still calling men and women to lead their communities and their nations to His kingdom. When we stand and choose to pursue the heart of God, Satan will do anything he can to attack our health, our families, our careers, and every good area of our lives. He will slander and smear. He will turn hearts against us, and tempt us to give up. We are covered by the blood of Jesus and anything sent to fight us will miss its mark because our God will be our shield and ever present help.

In Ghana, I saw how God used a young man like Ahmed Adjei to impact his community and the world in remarkable ways. He was raised in a Muslim family, but he decided in his adult years to turn his heart to Jesus. He joined the Assemblies of God Church and that was how our paths crossed. Later, he founded the Converted Muslims' Church which he renamed Father Abraham's Church as a vessel to share his testimony about God's grace and His love for many people in the Muslim communities.

For years, despite the harassment that his choice had brought upon him and his family, Ahmed became an evangelical missionary working with organizations around the world sharing Christian principles for living. In some traditional Muslim regions, conversion from Islam was guilty of apostasy and regarded as a capital offense. For people like Ahmed, choosing to become Christians meant risking their lives, being ostracized by their families, or even facing death.

Chapter 29: The Master Still Calls

Taking a courageous step to be sent by the Master to the nations brought them face to face with men and women with other belief systems, some of whom vowed to never allow Christianity to take root in their communities. Witnessing to Muslims, for Ahmed, had to be through the leading of the Holy Spirit. It was Him who had called us, and it was His love that would draw men and women to Him. All we have to do is heed the call, and be ready to take the first step.

The Great Commission had become my life's purpose. My mission was winning souls for Christ. But the devil fought back. Over and again my personal life had been under spiritual assault, but I had committed my life to a God who was stronger than any devil who sought to crush our work. None of the threats on my life had shaken me enough to make me give up on the message of eternal life through Jesus Christ.

In the 1970s and 1980s, every trip on the small aircrafts and all the long drives through deserted alleyways across the African continent were risks I had chosen to take. Every news report of plane crashes and road accidents in remote parts of the continent reminded us of God's provision for my life, and even though the journeys had been treacherous and the tasks seemed daunting, I had decided in my heart to go anywhere the Holy Spirit led, will full confidence that He would be faithful to keep my life in perfect peace.

With brothers and sisters in Christ, we had faced border guards who threatened our lives if we didn't pay bribes, and devious people who orchestrated our arrests, all of which were a stirring reminder of the cost we had chosen to bear for His name's sake. We had accepted the call to preach the message of Christ and despite the afflictions in our lives, our hope rested on a God who had promised to deliver us.

As I travelled the world, I shared the message of the gospel of Jesus Christ, that the Master is still calling men and women to build His kingdom and preach His good news. The joy of serving the Lord took me outside my comfort zone, but there was nowhere I was to go that would take me out of the protective care of my God.

I had decided to let my life and work be a testament to the kingdom. Men and women walked into Darko Farms as accountants, scientists, farmers, and farmhands, and left as preachers and missionaries. I was unashamed of sharing my faith wherever the Lord took me, and even though the devil was determined to fight me the hardest, my confidence in my God was sure. We are equipped with the sword of the Spirit, sharper than any double-edged sword and with every power to demolish strongholds and attacks of the devil.

From Ghana to the ends of the world, there is much more work to be done. God is looking for willing hearts ready to take a bold step of faith. Even when our world seems to be spinning out of control, our confidence ought to remain in God's promises that He will protect us from every adversary and turn every turmoil into a testimony for His glory.

The Master is calling, still.

CHAPTER 30

WHAT LEADERS HOPE FOR

Governance: Bold Visions for Generations

It was in a Hilton Hotel auditorium in Washington D.C. in 2019 that I listened as Ghana's President Nana Akufo-Addo shared his heart in a way I had never seen from another president. With about five thousand political and business leaders from around the world converged at America's National Prayer Breakfast event, it was as if President Akufo-Addo was reliving his entire political journey in an instant, and was humbled by the rare opportunity to serve.

He was standing in front of a captivated crowd, and every word he spoke carried an unembellished sincerity of heart and immense gratitude to have earned the trust of his nation and His God to lead his people. I watched as the room erupted to a standing ovation, like a resounding endorsement of a message of hope that his world so desperately needed. What I knew of him painted a portrait of worthy governance. It was like seeing the pieces a puzzle come together wonderfully.

Back in April 2011, Nana Akufo-Addo had reached out to me through a mutual friend, S.K. Boafo. Much of what I knew about his political life had been from a distance, but privately, our stories were woven together by my older sister Faustina's relationship with Akufo-Addo's family many years prior. I met with him in Nhyiaso, at the home of Asantehene Nana Osei Tutu while he was visiting with several of his NPP leaders. Akufo-Addo asked for my help, the same assistance he had seen me give to President Kufuor for several years, all the while without any fanfare or credit seeking. My heart longed for any opportunity to help my country, not party politics. I was happy to help, reaching out to my network of business people and institutions to support his vision for Ghana.

From my ministry work and relationships with American missionaries Paris Readhead and Al Whittaker back in 1972, and from serving with both Opportunity International and the Full Gospel Business Men's Fellowship International, much of my work had become supporting impactful initiatives that uplifted communities and became catalysts for sustainable change. My prayer had been for God to use my every resource to build His kingdom, and to help leaders who sought God's righteousness to lead their people. In a few weeks I would be travelling to the United States to meet with Douglas Coe and my friends at the Fellowship, who would be instrumental in planning the National Prayer Breakfast in 2012. I arranged for Akufo-Addo and a couple of his closest aides to be in Washington D.C. for the event.

After a disappointing presidential election campaign in the same year, the whole world looked on, as if to judge whether Akufo-Addo's ideology on governance and unapologetic pronouncements on upholding the rule of law at all costs would be any different. A majority of Ghanaians seemed to share his outrage and disapproval of the election outcome, and unfortunately, this had every potential to sow chaos in a young democracy. Akufo-Addo was willing to fight for the truth to stand. A long string of election malpractices had stripped him of victory, yet he knew the weight of every one of his actions to ensure peace in our country. It had to be infuriating.

Soon after, rather than let the seeds of doubt gain a footing in his mind, he knew it was God who opens doors and closes others. Only His will is done in His perfect time. It was remarkable to find how

Akufo-Addo had travelled to Israel, stood at the Wailing Wall and the Hebrew Ha-Kotel Ha-Ma'aravi in the Old City of Jerusalem, and lifted a prayer to Almighty God. The urgency to impact his country drove his relentless pursuit, if it was God's will.

As I watched his stride and countenance, I felt he had been prepared for the stage for much of his life. He hoped for a new direction for a country, one that appealed to the best in all of us. There was nothing we could not do together if we leaned on Almighty God. Contesting the next presidential elections would be about a man driven to his wit's end to accept that indeed *the battle had to be the Lord's*. In 2016, Nana Akufo-Addo and his New Patriotic Party (NPP) won the presidential elections in Ghana. Akufo-Addo was devoting himself to serving with Christian values at the core of his governance.

Back in 1992, when I contested the presidential elections, I didn't have any particular interest in elected office, but every one of my encounters with people across the country had been worth it. Since the elections, I had never once entertained seeking any elected office. Instead, my commitment had become to support any leader or public servant whose heart was truly guided by the principles that guided my life, and the same ones that I had always fought for. As a presidential candidate, I spoke loudly about a government's role in privatization and the urgency for all Ghanaians to reorient our ideals to embrace the God-given potential in each of us to add our talents and voices to our nation's success.

I had lived through the different governments and military rulers since our country's independence, and seen first-hand the incredible impact of national leadership on the plight of a people and the future of generations. Ghanaians had seen Dr. Kwame Nkrumah, Major-General J.A. Ankrah, Brigadier General Akwasi Afrifa, and lived through the years of Edward Akufo-Addo as Prime Minister. Then we lived through Lieutenant-General Kwasi Akuffo, Dr. Abrefa Busia, and Colonel Kutu Acheampong before Hilla Limann, and Flight Lieutenant Rawlings.

In all of them, I had seen the aftershocks of revolutions, coup d'états, and short-lived civilian governments.

With some of these leaders, I had seen enormous potential dissipate overnight. Rather than seeing them working together to seek the best in each other, it had been disheartening to watch greed and resentment reign while the nation plunged into corruption and the people suffered. If we were a people willing to let God's truth lead our nation, *humble ourselves and turn from our wicked ways*, God had promised *that He will heal our land*.

The years after 1992 turned the country on a path to meaningful democracy with glimpses of a forward-thinking agenda and bold ideas. As a nation, we'd had our share of false starts, broken promises, and short-sighted policies for selfish gain. Yet, Ghanaians had survived the years. It was my own journey that affirmed my belief that indeed when the righteous ruled, with God's truth, the people rejoiced. What was even truer was, *unless the Lord builds, we laboured in vain*.

Building a nation would take much more than one man; it would mean setting the direction where a nation could take one man. If President Nana Akufo-Addo was willing to seek the face of God in everything he did, he would be challenging Ghanaians to take pride in every ability that God had given us to innovate and be industrious. Our actions were to shape our own future. As a leader, President Akufo-Addo would be serving a heterogeneous group of people with diverse beliefs and expectations, yet, if he had a chance to walk in truth, he could create a lasting legacy of hope.

For many years I had the privilege of selecting leaders from African nations to participate in the America's National Prayer Breakfast events. It became a great avenue for leaders to see their counterparts from different parts of the world committed to the work of God and using their positions of influence to create meaningful change. This time, it would be a rare chance to share Ghana's vision with many of the business and political leaders who would be honoured to help.

As a country, Ghana stood at the cusp of opportunity and destiny, but it would take God's grace for the country to see its hopeful years become its shining moment. President Akufo-Addo called on all Ghanaians to support a call to build a cathedral to God's glory. As a people, the significance of a cathedral would be much more than embarking on an overt display of faith. Rather, it was to be an incredible symbol of a nation turning its heart and submitting its future to Almighty God.

More than building a cathedral with sand and stone, putting faith at the center of nation building was a virtue that the country had always inspired to, even proudly weaving that inkling into our national anthem and hymns. As a leader, President Akufo-Addo had to be humbly aware that this wasn't something he could do in his own might. One truth that wasn't lost on President Akufo-Addo was how God's grace had spared the country from some of the horrific civil wars, terrible famine, and awful chaos that gripped many African nations through the years. An inter-denominational cathedral would be a daunting task, but it would take bold ideas and paradigm shifts to move Ghana towards its collective destiny. It would be an opportunity for a sacred marker to be a public monument with significance beyond the shores of Ghana and Africa to the world.

For such a dream to see the light of day, only God could raise men and women who would stand and work without any need for recognition, but only to lift the name of Almighty God on the African continent. And that was all God was asking of people like me. In any small way that I could, I had decided long ago to support any leaders who shared the same core values and vision I wholeheartedly believed in. I didn't care about a political party affiliation, tribe, or belief. What mattered were the principles upon which a person stood and the humility with which they embraced the task of leading a nation. For Akufo-Addo, his policies reflected much of what I had championed more than thirty years earlier. These were pillars upon which my own life and faith were anchored.

Even from a distance, it was refreshing to see the fundamental belief of putting God at the center of nation building, flanked by progressive economic and industrial policies, and inclusive society and private enterprise as a path to development. This was forward thinking, and it struck me as the kind of policies that had every chance to be transformative. I admired the audacity of Akufo-Addo's vision, but even more, his confidence in God's guiding hand in his service to Ghana. Our people had to take responsibility for our future, because there was no miracle waiting in the wings to drop into our laps.

A Christian leader had to be committed to lead with humility and with the resilience to embrace a governance that lifted its people rather than serving corrupt and selfish gain. For Ghana to rise to our collective potential, every man and woman would have to step out from a narrow outlook on life, and break free from the warped sense of entitlement that had hampered our competence. It would start with a leader willing to sacrifice his popularity to do what was right for his people, and nothing had given me more joy than to see a president embody the same values that I had championed nearly 30 years ago. I am grateful to have lived to see it.

What I knew was that it would take good governance that embraced transparency and accountability, and sought the interest of every person, especially the least fortunate among us. Transforming our nation with good governance would be about prudent policies that would challenge all of us to bring our strengths and shortcomings to build a nation together. It would bring hope and fuel opportunity. Yet, despite the most noble of intentions, much of what derails great ideas and even leads to the downfall of many leaders are the *handlers*.

From party leaders to Chiefs of Staff and personal secretaries, Ambassadors to cabinet appointees, they were often the men and women who sabotaged any vision that didn't feed their personal agendas. I had seen their unfortunate influence at work over and again, and it rarely helped any leader to execute their vision. I saw the same phenomenon in my own business and even ministry, and unless the leader was cautious of the men and women who surrounded them, it was only in hindsight that they saw the damage done by the same people they had trusted. For Ghana, irrespective of what missteps we had lived through for decades, we could still rise to become the shining city on a hill, the same one that our forefathers dreamed of many years ago.

So much of Ghana's future would hinge on an investment in its private sectors who would become the engine of its economy. It would be the private enterprises setting out to seek opportunities around the country that offered competitive advantages and leveraged available natural resources, solicited private investment, and harnessed local expertise. President Akufo-Addo's government, like most forward-thinking institutions, had a chance to invest their efforts in building critical infrastructure, conducting research, and enforcing its regulatory authority. What had the potential of turning the tide in our country's economy was an environment that didn't strangle individual initiative but challenged citizens to contribute their ideas and expertise.

I saw President Akufo-Addo's administration set an agenda to encourage the construction of factories and commercial manufacturing facilities in every district across the country. It was One District One Factory (1D1F). Beyond the fact that it was incredibly foundational to our country's success, it was a policy that I believed, if managed well, could have a significant long-term impact on the economy. From what I had lived through since the Nkrumah years, it was to be a change in our national psyche to incentivize innovation and challenge a new generation of Ghanaians to live in a world where we sought to create value in a variety of industries in our own backyards.

It was a bold idea, much different from the privatization of government assets and services. Policies of this nature allowed private entrepreneurs and enterprises to engage in a wide range of provision of goods and services that met local needs and targeted a wider market beyond our borders. The underlying philosophy was that competition and innovation in a free market economy incentivized performance and ultimately promoted efficiencies in meeting the demands of customers.

Employment opportunities, wider tax base opportunities and economic growth were the intended result. As an entrepreneur, I had seen corporations across America, Europe, and other parts of the world benefit from strategic government incentives to remain viable operations, because, in the end, the governments understood the enterprise's pivotal role in its economy. In Ghana, the hope would be to shift the country's reliance on imports to one that exploited raw materials in different parts of the country and turned them into processed goods and marketable products.

Yet, in a society like ours, it was not farfetched to find a prevailing thought that it was the government's duty to establish factories in districts across the country, and the government's duty to hire every citizen into a government job. Those were sentiments I saw first-hand back in 1992 when I contested the presidential elections, and it was as startling and unsettling at it is in recent years. Decades of reliance on parastatals had shifted much of our expectation into what we expected any government to do. I hoped most Ghanaians, irrespective of personal differences, would rally behind a chance to build an economic engine that our children and future generations could benefit from. Governments can only create an environment and infrastructure for enterprises to thrive; it cannot set out to build a business. Over the last 60 years, I have seen government enterprises fall apart when they had every support needed to succeed, and private enterprises thrive even in the face of incredible odds.

In 2020, Darko Farms received financial support through the Ghana EXIM Bank to inject capital into existing enterprises with the potential to increase productivity. Even though much of our business structure has evolved since I first set out in 1967, it was a welcome opportunity to expand aspects of our enterprise to continue contributing to the local economy and the country as a whole.

Like Darko Farms, the government was offering the same financial support to nearly two dozen poultry companies across the country. Ghana continues to import large quantities of poultry products, just as it does basic foodstuffs like wheat and rice, to meet growing demand. More than 30 years ago, Tyson Foods ventured into Ghana, only for our efforts to fall apart because of policies that probably didn't value the enormous opportunities that private enterprises brought to society. The missed opportunities hopefully had become cautionary tales for governments to be wary of trade and investment policies that stifle local enterprises.

With a hatchery, breeder, feed, and chicken processing factories and a network of about 200 outgrowers, my focus remained strategic expansion that created jobs and returns on the investment. For Ghana, progressive agricultural policies and targeted government interventions had every opportunity to continue driving growth initiative that fostered sustained productivity and economic prosperity.

In my own journey, I had been fortunate to lead men and women in both industry and ministry, and I had seen how leadership takes the same honesty and intention to make a lasting impact in the lives of the people we get the privilege to serve. The young woman who showed up at Darko Farms on a hot afternoon with a tray on her head to buy eggs was not worth any less than the celebrated astronaut who walked on the moon. Whether it was in helping President Akufo-Addo honour a pledge to Almighty God, or taking the time to assist the young child in a refugee camp who needed a meal, I didn't deserve any of the credit. God did.

* * * * *

Over and again, I have found how God always has an amazing way of using every gift and open door He had given to us to affect the world around us. Often it may look like a coincidence, but I know enough about my God to recognize how He alone orders our steps perfectly if only we are willing to follow His voice. It was in 1993 that Larry Reed, Jonathan Wilson, David Freeman, and Kwame Opoku showed up in my office. I was travelling to China that evening and I asked that they give me any brochures they had on what they wanted to discuss.

I remember fondly how I read about their Opportunity International organization on the long flight, and saw how it had the same goal I did with my own initiative, the Kwabena Darko Foundation. We joined hands to work together, starting with sending Kwame Opoku to learn all he could about Zamboku, Opportunity International's program in Zimbabwe.

We began the work in my office in Kumasi, and I recall how all the office equipment and desks we needed, like the ones I had used for my presidential campaign the previous year, had been left intact, as if God knew what I would need. J.E. Acquaye, who had retired as accountant from my farms, agreed to come on board as the Executive Director, helping to build every organizational structure and outline the foundation for the program. A couple of years later, Ken Appenteng, who was originally treasurer for Sinapi Aba Trust and had a successful career with Merchant Bank, agreed to take over as Executive Director to help build the foundation. What became Sinapi Aba Trust micro lending organization was an Opportunity International program. It was one that, even though I had emerged as a promoter in Ghana, just as in Zambia, Uganda, Malawi, Jamaica and across Latin America, was a non-profit organization and no one person owned it.

After a few months, I remember when Larry Reed prepared a business plan and advised that I go to the USAID office in Washington D.C. to seek assistance, and I found that the same Warren Weinstein with whom I had worked on the West Africa Network initiative in 1991 was the head of the USAID program for Africa. His guidance to comply with every requirement assisted us in securing a $1.5 million grant that was to be the backbone of our lending operations in Ghana.

For several years, I had spent time travelling around places like the Philippines, Indonesia, England, Germany, France and Australia, working with community organizations and local business leaders to create avenues to uplift people from poverty, and be the hands and feet of Jesus as we reached out to people of diverse backgrounds. Larry Reed, by now, had become Executive Director of Opportunity International Worldwide. The Implementing Partners and Supporting Partners created the Network Design Council, on which I represented Africa for two years. Jim Duncan was appointed the head of the council. After a series of conferences and meetings with the Implementing Partners in their respective countries, the Council submitted its report. One of the outcomes was the establishment of a Network Board to take over the Council's work and oversee all of the activities of the organization, Opportunity International.

Opportunity International's conference brought about 400 people to the Founders' Inn, in Virginia Beach, Virginia. I was still chairman of both Opportunity International Africa and Sinapi Aba Trust, and I arranged for the board members to also travel to the Virginia conference, because as an Implementing Partner of the program, I believed it was important for them to see the magnitude of the work around the world.

The Founders' Inn on the campus of Regent University was owned by my friend Pat Robertson, a former Southern Baptist minister and media pioneer who had made significant contributions to Christian programs and organizations. It was in a private meeting that Pat graciously donated $1 million to support Opportunity International's work in the Philippines.

In the eyes of several of the Supporting Partners whose work was raising funds for the organization, I was the ideal choice for the role because of my business experience, and involvement with other initiatives that took me to the frontlines of our outreach programs. The Americans, Germans and several of the Asian delegation shared the same opinion, and for an organization with such diversity, I had emerged as the neutral choice to be chairman of the Network Board for Opportunity International.

Back in Ghana, Opportunity International had secured the license to operate a savings and loans venture, and the hope was for this new chapter to widen our lending outreach. There were men and women across rural Ghana who found that our program gave their family an opportunity they never had, and for the first time in their lives, they were able to sustain their families and open a new window of hope for themselves. Opportunity International Savings and Loans (OISL) would be a banking institution, and its business would be properly scrutinized by the Bank of Ghana. I was elected to serve as Board Chairman for OISL at the same time when I was chairman of Opportunity International's Network Board.

In addition to the funding we received from Opportunity International's head office in Chicago for this new venture, Sinapi Aba Trust used three of the local branches in Accra, Techiman and Kumasi to acquire shares in Opportunity International Savings and Loans. FMO, a Dutch organization became the third shareholder. Ken Appenteng led a group of accountants and banking professionals to successfully grow the savings and loans enterprise, the first of its kind for Opportunity International programs in Africa.

David Freeman, whom I had first met with Larry Reed and Jonathan Wilson, was appointed Board Chairman of Sinapi Aba Trust in my stead, after I'd served for ten years. Sinapi Aba Trust remained a micro lending institution, but with Opportunity International's work stretching across the globe, the organization found itself in a season where it was difficult raising funds to continue its work. I spoke to Opportunity International to agree on an interest-free loan of $2 million to Sinapi Aba Trust, one that would be recorded appropriately in its accounting records, as the value of the shares Sinapi Aba Trust held in Opportunity International Savings and Loans.

Shortly thereafter, the remaining 14 chapters of Sinapi Aba Trust realized they couldn't secure funds to support its work. The Sinapi Aba Trust board members told me they needed help. The recommendation was for Opportunity International USA to give Sinapi Aba Trust the $2 million interest-free loan. This was to help sustain Sinapi Aba Trust as a lifeline to operate a successful organization, and hopefully continue their work of assisting local entrepreneurs in small towns and villages across Ghana.

At a point, Opportunity International USA decided it wanted to sell Opportunity International Savings and Loans venture in Ghana. Their plan was to shift away from the banking business completely and focus on micro lending. I opposed the proposed sale, especially since there was an existing regulations from the Bank of Ghana that prevented it. It wasn't long before I retired from the board of Opportunity International Savings and Loans after serving for 10 years.

For Sinapi Aba Trust's $2 million, I told Opportunity International USA to review the assets of the three Sinapi Aba Trust branches that had been taken at the start of the savings and loans enterprise, so that their value would be used to defray the amount. Sinapi Aba Trust officially wrote to Opportunity International USA who agreed to close the deal. Later, Sinapi Aba Trust decided to start Sinapi Aba Savings and Loans. I did not have any part in that new venture.

Since we'd embarked on the journey in 1993, what guided the organization's attention was an urgent need to serve communities that were typically stuck on the fringes of enterprise and commerce. The cycle of poverty and destitution continued in their children. Sinapi Aba was like a *mustard seed* blooming into its full potential, just as men and women in small towns and villages who had to fight through impossible situations and overcome their limitations to fulfil their destiny.

Through all the years, my aim as a leader had been to support as many families as we could, and reassure them that it didn't matter what little opportunity they'd had. Every one of us had an ability to transform that opportunity into something powerful. I had not set out to make any profit from any of the ventures, because for me, it had been a mission more than a business enterprise. I had done all I could to put the right people in place to build a good foundation that would live long after my work was done.

In the end, I have no way of knowing what future Sinapi Aba will have and what hope it will represent for many in Ghana. One thing I know for sure: any entity not belonging to one individual eventually needed to carve its identity, and someday, it might be up to a Board to decide its fate. Even then, nothing would take away from the joy in the faces of the people who found tremendous hope in our work.

For more than 30 years, I had been a promoter of all that Sinapi Aba represented—*the mustard seed*—and perhaps my life's story will forever be intertwined with the opportunity to change lives. If there is only one family whose future had been transformed by an investment in their own effort, the journey will have been worth it. My only gratitude is that my work will not have been in vain.

I had decided long ago to seek the welfare of everyone whom God brought into my path irrespective of their station in life. Only He can raise us into places we never imagined we would be. In the same way, the bank manager who belittled my vision to become a poultry farmer in 1966 had no more impact on who I was to become than the insolent soldiers who stormed my farms in 1981 to crush my business. What life taught me was that if I was to walk in sincerity, as a leader with my heart set on serving a bold vision, the God who ordered my every step would honour every one of them.

In 2018, I accepted an honorary doctorate degree at Gordon College, a private Christian college in Wenham, Massachusetts. Later I received another doctorate degree at Babson College's business school in Wellesley, Massachusetts. I was being honoured for decades of work in Christian leadership and service around the world, and on both occasions what struck me was the rare chance to challenge a new generation of Christian men and women to remain steadfast in their own pursuit of excellence. They too would be leaders in their communities and nations, and my prayer was that they would allow Christ's lordship over their lives to guide their every step.

Just as I did with my own company, Darko Farms, leadership is about setting out with a vision and taking an audacious stand to make it thrive. I remember vividly Israeli Prime Minister David Ben-Gurion's counsel back in 1959, to motivate men and women to give their best in every endeavour. That is how successful leaders seek people committed to their visions and encourage them to build incredibly successful organizations.

When I first set out as a chicken farmer, I had a single focus tucked in my heart, to succeed as a businessman to support the kingdom of God. That was the faith I shared with Evangelist Morris Cerullo in 1966 when I was torn between becoming a preacher and an entrepreneur. That deep-seated persuasion of serving the kingdom is what guided my every step. It is only by God's grace that I can truly say I lived every moment in pursuit of that calling.

CHAPTER 31

THE PROMISE OF TOMORROW

Education: A Priceless Investment

What became the Christian Service College in Ghana started with Christian men and women in the Scripture Union joining hands for a bold dream of an interdenominational bible-based tertiary institution. More than a seminary, in our hearts we imagined an institution that was driven by Christian ethos and with instructional models that addressed the tangible needs of our community. In the early 1960s Trinity Theological Seminary had been founded in Accra as an orthodox seminary, and in every facet of society, we prayed for many more institutions that would be steeped in Christian values and seek to impart those to its students.

WAC Mission, a Christian non-profit headquartered in England had done missionary work in Ghana, including building local churches in parts of the country, especially in the north. Later the organization sent an Australian missionary, Greg Francis, to continue its work in the country. He settled in Kumasi and it was through the Scripture Union meetings that I met Greg.

Around 1969, to widen his outreach efforts, Greg and his organization saw an opportunity to start a radio ministry to reach more people in the country. This endeavour required recording the sermons in Twi and other local languages in advance and then finding a radio station that could broadcast. At the time, Ghana Broadcasting Corporation (GBC) was the only government broadcast network in the country but there was no one Christian program on their platform. Greg Francis travelled to Monrovia, the Liberian capital, to meet with an American non-profit organization, Eternal Love Winning Africa (ELWA), who founded its Christian radio station in 1953. ELWA agreed to broadcast the sermons through shortwave radio in Ghana.

Together with my colleagues Godfred Bamfo who had become the Scripture Union Travelling Secretary for Ashanti Region, Brong Ahafo Region and Northern Region; Kwadwo Kyere, Martin Asamoah-Manu, Kwabena Agyei, and Brobbey, we took turns recording the Twi sermons for the radio outreach program. Encouraged by the success of the pilot project, Greg believed it was the perfect time to establish a full-fledged radio ministry, and he arranged for us to use part of his home for the project. We often recorded late into the evening.

Working hand in hand with other Christian brothers and sisters, the WAC mission purchased land in Kumasi to build a mission residence, but also a facility that will accommodate the broadcast program. At the Scripture Union, we had continued to pray for our vision of a Bible school. Greg Francis showed interest in our vision, and he spoke to his team in England in case they would be interested in helping with such a project. Shortly after, we arranged to meet with prominent statesman William Ofori-Atta, to discuss much of the help we needed to make the vision a reality. He was also a member of the Scripture Union, and an elderly committed Presbyterian whom we believed could be one of the elders we could reach out to. Our prayers were answered and our years of hard work found their reward. What began as an idea for a Christian institution found its roots from an unlikely start.

In 1974, the Scripture Union and WAC Mission together started the Christian Service College near the Santaase area of Kumasi. Jesus Christ was to be the focal point of everything the institution did and for that, we would stand boldly on the Word of God. Isaac Ababio was selected to be the principal of the institution. Not much later, Ransford Sinavor and his wife returned from training in the United States to oversee the school with the help of several other missionaries who continued to be instrumental in the effort. Through Paris Reidhead, another American Christian businessman, Dan Swanson, stepped in with financial support to pay the lecturers. Later, it would be through his help that the school, together with the WAC Mission, would successfully raise finds to expand its facilities and widen our reach to people across Ghana.

What Christian Service College reminded all of us was that God was faithful to bring any dream to pass when it served a purpose much bigger than our individual aspirations. It also was a powerful reminder that we had every ability to create institutions and programs devoid of mediocrity even if we didn't have all the resources in the world. The men and women whose prayers and hard work carved the vision of the college were willing to sacrifice their time and resources. We believed it was a worthy investment, and Almighty God honoured it.

Adu Boffuor returned from his studies abroad to work as a lecturer at Christian Service College, and to have young men like him commit to the kingdom mission and become ambassadors of the college. My work as a Christian businessman had been to support institutions like these, so it was in these years that my paths crossed with Adu Boffuor. After a while, he arranged to return to the University of Edinburg, in Scotland, to pursue a doctorate degree. It was in Scotland that he met another Ghanaian student, Emmanuel Kwabena Larbi, who was also pursuing his doctorate. I saw the impact of Christian Service College, and prayed for other such institutions across the country.

From the time Professor Emmanuel Larbi left Scotland and returned to Ghana to oversee a newly established university, Central University, he had embraced his work shaping minds to influence every aspect of society. Professor Larbi was a member of the Church of Pentecost and set out to write a book, *Pentecostalism: The Eddies of Ghanaian Christianity*. That was when we first met.

A few years later Professor Larbi was stepping out on faith to start a new university that embodied every vision of excellence that had nurtured his every step, and one that latched on to a faith in almighty God to excel. He believed God had called him into a different direction, and reached out to me to support his vision. What God had put in his heart was Regent University College of Science and Technology.

What Professor Larbi envisioned was a Christ-centred institution committed to training men and women to be change agents to influence different sectors of society with their skill and faith. The hallmark would an overarching philosophy to serve the needs of the Ghanaian marketplace and equip men and women to step into positions to create value. For Ghana to make strides towards a promising future, institutions like Regent University would have to choose a practical vision to engage every student intellectually. What was at stake was our nations' future, and for that reason, I believed that no institution could afford to compromise on any investment we believed would be instrumental to a student's success.

From the moment Professor Larbi first shared his vision, Regent University College of Science and Technology was not only seeking to offer a quality education, but would be shaped by thoughtful leadership to create an excellent model for education that suited the society in which we lived. I was honoured to share in a bold idea to impact generations, and that started with giving the students every practical arsenal they needed for their future. The success of the institution would not be driven by a desperate need for recognition, but shaped by intellectual probity and a deep respect for diligence and merit. I served as Chancellor of the university for ten years, and then as Chancellor Emeritus.

* * * * *

When I returned from Israel in 1961, the enormous value of applied education had left indelible imprints on my mind. I had spent years in an environment where they invested a great deal of resources into huge farms for students to experience in a way that they never could forget. It was a love for scientific research that brought them a unique understanding of poultry. Animal breeders went to great lengths to understand the genetic characteristics in animals, develop new breeds or conduct extensive research to ensure the offspring would have the desired traits.

More than once, I couldn't help but wonder what it would take for societies like ours in Ghana to become dissatisfied with information that they couldn't use in practical application. My encounter with several of the students in our universities and technical schools were young men and women spending years amassing information without any sense of how to translate it to affect our economy. As children we'd teased each other about the *chew-pour-pass-forget* syndrome, but it was hardly a joke.

From institutions like Ruppin College in Israel, Cornell University and Kansas State University, to Texas A&M University in the United States, huge investments were poured into research and the construction of farm facilities to equip students with emerging technologies and new scientific research. The investment was careful and planned. For Ghana, in every area of education, if we were to someday compete with a steadily evolving world of technology and knowledge, we would have to shift our priorities and make our learning purposeful.

It was during my years as Chairman of the Ghana Animal Science Association that I saw much of the problem first-hand. In the agricultural departments, basic facilities like chicken houses and hatcheries were non-existent, and there was nothing like academic journals or research materials for students to get a sense of what technologies or practices were developed outside their community.

It was painful to accept that reality because I had learned all too well that any education without practical experience is almost worthless. More than once, I erected pens on my farms for the university students' research work, and handed down every insight I had gained in the vocation. I could do my best helping to raise funds to buy essential equipment because of its importance, especially in a tertiary institution where we were relying on the knowledge of the students to impact our nation.

If we wanted young men and women to walk out of our university halls to contribute their expertise and knowledge to our country's future, it would be our responsibility to make that a priority. Unfortunately, in some of the tertiary institutions that I got a chance to visit, we were spending the years churning out scientists and researchers with little value to give, and putting our own futures at a disadvantage.

In countries like Israel, tucked in the middle of a desert, they have little choice but to live with a sense of urgency and force themselves to innovate. It was in the company of young men and women whose societies were counting on their practical knowledge to sustain their existence that I saw the worth of education that was oriented to build a nation.

The value of education is immeasurable, much more significant that handing out diplomas and trusting that our sons and daughters will find their place in the world. Exposing students to a wealth of information and practical knowledge is especially crucial in a world that is increasingly transitioning into a global society. If the men and women who walked through the hallways of the local universities are to compete with the rest of the world, it will be incredibly important to acknowledge the role of education in shaping our future.

In Darko Farms, I recruited university graduates for work, but I had to retrain every one of them. What was painfully evident, at least from seemingly dedicated animal science graduates, was that the lack of technology and resources had hampered their professional development. To enable them to work in my hatcheries and feed mills, I sent them to training in technical schools and hands-on training with companies in Israel, England and Holland. I had to invest in every one of them, because sure, they could read and write, but they hadn't seen any of what they'd read about.

I made up my mind to learn the world around me. I was fortunate to have had mentors who pushed me to step outside my comfort zone and never stop learning. It had been the best education I could have ever received, and it was all free. Every person and place carried knowledge and wisdom, and I tried my hardest to not miss the fleeting opportunities that life gives us to glean all we can from people and circumstances. It started with granting ourselves the permission to observe, and the discernment to find valuable nuggets in the mundane.

I remember when I first joined the World Poultry Science Association in the 1980s. The organization held the International Production and Processing Expo conferences in Atlanta, Georgia, every year and invited a host of industry leaders to display emerging technologies in agriculture and animal science. The displays featured producers and processors of broilers, eggs, and breeding stock, to integrators, pharmaceutical companies, ingredient suppliers and equipment manufacturers.

Year after year, a host of remarkably informative seminars on anatomy, physiology, reproduction, genetics and nutrient management gave me incredible insight into what I could apply in my farms back home. Every single year, every one of those events became avenues to see a world outside my own, and to quickly apply everything I saw and heard to my business.

In a sense, the most powerful part of my education had been the opportunity to apply all my knowledge in a real sense that reinforced the information or gave me the basis to sift its practicality. Even then, it was only by God's grace that I was able to value learning and invest in myself through the years. I did not have anyone to nudge me to study or apply myself in elementary school. I recall how I didn't have enough money for secondary school, and even when I applied for a scholarship that was earmarked for children from less fortunate backgrounds, I was probably too poor to qualify. Something urged me to keep fighting for my education. I managed to enrol with a correspondence course because that was all I could afford, and I didn't want life to leave me behind.

When I had the chance, in a room full of hopeful young men and women seeking scholarship for an agricultural program in Israel, it was what I had learned on my own, sitting by hencoops in the middle of the night in my stepfather's home that made me stand out in the crowd.

For Ghana, and for future generations, there is perhaps nothing more pivotal to their future than investing in the present, because of the enormous potential it holds to transform our own lives and that of our world. It is my prayer that God grant us the wisdom to do the best we can with whatever opportunities come our way. Someday our nation and world will count on us to contribute whatever we can, and I hope we can all rise to the occasion. And future generations too.

CHAPTER 32

BY HIS GRACE

Adom Ara Kwa

If there was one thing that shaped the rest of my life, it was that the Lord found me early. On one Saturday evening in 1962, in the dusty fields of Abbey's Park, I reached the turning point in my young life. Reverend Lonnie Fox and Reverend Gyan Fosu had seen me shiver and sweat and cry and scream on the ground. By the time my eyes were opened, the hundreds of people who had gathered in the park were gone. I was covered in dirt, but I had taken the most important step of accepting Jesus as my personal saviour. I had been baptized in the Holy Ghost, and suddenly spoken in a spiritual language, the same as I had heard my grandmother speak in prayer. My life was never to be the same.

I joined the Assemblies of God church and poured my life into outreach and evangelism. Months later, I joined the Lighthouse Assemblies of God church choir in Kumasi. All I wanted my life to represent was a man whose every desire was to heed the Heavenly call, every day and every night. When I heard His call, I was not disobedient. I ran to Jesus. Only He was able to keep me safe in His arms.

It was at a Sunday service that one of the most amazing moments in all of my life happened. After the service's closing prayer, the preachers stepped down from the pulpit and lined up in a procession at the centre. The choir would typically follow the preachers, as we sang a hymn, to the front door, and descend through the staircase of the sides to the basement.

While the choir sang Charles Wesley's hymn "And Can It be that I Should Gain?" I was in tears and I felt moved by the lyrics. I raised my hands, and lifted my head. The hymn book in my hand fell on the floor as I felt an unusual feeling of helplessness and went down on my knees. I was weeping still, as in a gaze, looking past the pillars above. In the next instant, I was down on the cement floor. The choir continued to sing, walking ahead, and some of the young preachers quickly rush to surround me. Tears flowing from my eyes, I was in worship still. I could almost see what looked like the heavens open, as if with bright lights piercing through the roof of the church building.

And can it be that I should gain,
An interest in the Saviour's blood?
Died he for me, who caused His pain?
For me, who Him to death pursued?
Amazing love, how can it be that Thou, my God, should die for me?

The words of the song were weighty. Each word jumped at me. In that morning, I saw how it is truly the gospel that stirs a searching soul, and reveals God's amazing truth to anyone who seeks Him. That Christ had died a painful death on the cross for my sins was incredible to me, and the image of his blood on Calvary seemed as fresh as if it had just happened. Just to fathom Jesus loving an ordinary me, so much as to hang on a wooden cross in exchange for my sins was incredible. I saw Him. It was personal.

Whatever you do, work at it with all your heart, as working for the Lord, not for human masters, since you know that you will receive an inheritance from the Lord as a reward.

Colossians 3:23-24

For the rest of my life, I was a child of Almighty God and for nearly 80 years, I had seen His grace carry me every step of the way. I found that God hears our heart's cry, and all He asks is our willingness to be vessels for His glory. I asked God to bless the work of my hands so that I would in turn be a blessing to my people and the church, and He had been faithful at every turn. When I shared my passion with Evangelist Morris Cerullo in Kumasi In 1966, I didn't know how much God could transform my humble vision to reach a world around me.

When all I had was chicken and eggs, that was all God needed from me to serve in refugee camps, mission homes, military barracks, prisons, and school campuses. God knew there would be days when incarcerated people and soldiers at the frontlines of peacekeeping missions would need every bit of what I could help with, and He would need me to serve them. God knew when famine and starvation would grip a nation, and when the corn stored in silos on my farms would be just what people needed.

I took a leap of faith to set up a business without any guarantee of success. But I handed it over to Almighty God because if I was to succeed, it would build His kingdom as far as He took me. The same joy that kept a teenage boy fascinated by day-old-chicks in a tiny hencoop in my stepfather's garage, was what gave me the enthusiasm to devote every energy to the vocation. Darko Farms became a "Paradise in the Bush" as one journalist wrote in the *Poultry World Journal*, but it was a paradise to reach men and women with the power of the Living God.

God needed my willing heart, irrespective of who I was and what I thought my limitations were. From Indonesia and the Philippines to Senegal, Liberia, and Sierra Leone, all God needed of me was a willingness to go. To Equatorial Guinea and Tanzania to South Africa and Malawi, even in the face of danger, God was looking for people who felt the freedom in Christ's salvation and were willing to share His message. It was only by God's grace that my life had been different, and that was what drove me.

Almighty God plants each of us for our season, and His grace ushers us into greatness for us to blossom in our generation. Far beyond my personal ambition, I am humbled by what the grace of God has revealed to me for decades, in places I never dreamed of, and by the opportunity to share His message with people whom I would have never imagined meeting. All I needed was a heart of obedience for the privilege to be of service to Almighty God. Nothing has given me more comfort than knowing how God has anointed each of us to walk into our destiny and impact our world, for such a time as this.

The steps of the righteous man are ordered by the Lord.
Psalms 37:23

Nothing in the hands of God is a coincidence. It is He who orders our every step, and sets futures in motion long before we are able to see His guiding hand. Serving in ministry didn't make me immune to duplicity and disappointment, but God orchestrated new doors of opportunities. When my work was done at the Assemblies of God church, I had a choice, either to dwell on the untrue reports that some of the elders shared about me, or accept the pain of the moment and look ahead.

I couldn't allow myself to feel lost in my faith because of closed doors, and because men and women had turned the church into politics to serve their personal ambitions. It was unfortunate but God who already knows the heart of every man, knows how to turn moments around. What I believed was that it was God closing the door in its season.

It took a signboard beside the main road in the Ahodwo suburb of Kumasi for Evangelist Irvina Miller to come into my life. I never would have known that back in the 1950s she had set out with a vision for an *oasis*—a place of restoration and newness. Our paths didn't cross in the 1950s when she was travelling through Kumasi with Reverend James McKeown, but 40 years later, the vision we shared together brought transformation and healing to many. God set our lives in motion long before we met. My work had become to raise men and women to carry on with the Great Commission in Ghana and around the world. Nothing had been a coincidence.

It was through Uncle John Agama that I will get to know about Wycliffe Bible Translators and their work in Ghana. With people like Mary Steele, who spent decades of her life in rural villages in Ghana's northern regions, they sacrificed their time and effort in such an impactful way. It was through him also that I got to meet Mary Agyekum, a young Christian lady whose work in Sandema, Northern Region Uncle John stressed I should support.

Many years later, Grace's son Paul had risen to become a *Nehemiah* in his generation. I had no way of knowing how much my own work with Ghana Institute of Linguistics, Literacy and Bible Translation (GILLBT) would come full circle to become the pillars of a faith that would lift the banner of Christ high for all to see. But God knew.

For our struggle is not against flesh and blood, but against the rulers, against the authorities, against the powers of this dark world and against the spiritual forces of evil in the heavenly realms.

Ephesians 6:12

I was once a boy who dreaded darkness and night because of large scary hands and a shadowy figure that haunted me. It was more than a premonition; it felt real. Throughout my teenage years, I was living every day and night coping with the horrors of demonic attacks. I lived much of my childhood and adolescence in fear of these ghastly moments.

More than once, in the middle of the night, these same episodes woke me while I slept with the brothers. I would carry my mat to sleep in the middle of a nearby street. My poor mother had to rush to find me lying there. My grandmother prayed night after night. If God had any purpose for my life, the devil was eager to rip it apart to prevent it from becoming a reality. In spite of the horror, I thought I had little choice but to suffer the torment. Then grace stepped in.

For the rest of my life, the devil attacked my life and my family's. Prayer had become my only weapon and I knew there was nothing that could stand against the power of God. The devil seemed to fight the hardest when God lifted me higher. My Christian way didn't have the luxury of resorting to empty talk and perfunctory religious rituals. I had determined to not just go through the motions or to be a casual church-goer or religious bystander, but rather, I poured my every moment into a relationship with Almighty God.

For me, the faith that I professed wasn't passive. I wasn't waiting on God to rain miracles. From road accidents with petrol tankers to trancelike moments when I saw my car speeding to the bottoms of hills, my choice to serve Almighty God made me a target for the devil.

We chose to stand firm in our faith, knowing the power we had because of Christ who had saved us. Indeed, "For the weapons of our warfare are not carnal but mighty in God for pulling down strongholds, casting down arguments and every high thing that exalts itself against the knowledge of God, bringing every thought into captivity to the obedience of Christ, and being ready to punish all disobedience when your obedience is fulfilled." *2 Corinthians 10:4-6.*

No matter what happened to me or against me, I was sure of this, that I wasn't defenceless. When high-ranking political officials and soldiers threatened my life and spewed anger to crush my business, I could still afford to keep my joy, because I knew whose I was, and what every one of those encounters were. They weren't happenstance. But I believed that with God on my side, I was far more powerful than any adversary that rose against me.

My driver heading to the airport in 1981 had a road accident in Nsawam, so that I wouldn't end up in the Full Gospel Business Men's Fellowship International meeting for many lives to be changed in one evening. In another strange occurrence, I tumbled down a steep staircase in London's Heathrow Airport, and was rushed by ambulance to a local hospital. I couldn't be on the flight to Indonesia for Opportunity

International's outreach event. For what had been nearly 80 years, the devil's flurry of attacks persisted, but I had a God whose provision for my life promised that nothing designed against me would succeed. And God was faithful in every step along the way.

> *"And I will rebuke the devourer for your sakes, and he shall not destroy the fruits of your ground; neither shall your vine cast her fruit before the time in the field", says the Lord of hosts.*
>
> Malachi 3:11

I was in Kentucky, in the United States, in 1972 when a tornado swept through the quiet neighbourhood where my friend Maury Cable lived. In one instant it seemed like the cloudy skies were filled with rain, only in the next, we looked outside the windows to see the spinning clouds heading our way. In the air, anything the winds could pick up floated high in the sky; benches, animals, and trees. It was frightening.

We hurried to Maury's basement for shelter. About an hour later, the tornado had passed. We walked outside the house, only to find the tornado had swept away the houses on both sides of his home. An entire neighbourhood was destroyed in an instant, and my heart sank for the people who were suddenly staring at the ruins left behind. Their memories and livelihoods were swept away. They had no choice but to salvage what they could, and I could only imagine the long road ahead for them. Even in the devastation I couldn't help but see the gratitude in the eyes of Maury and his family. The devastation was overwhelming, but they had a reason to be grateful for life. Regardless of what their communities lost, the only thing that gave them comfort was a God who restores, and who made everything beautiful in its own time.

In the same year, I returned to Ghana only to live through unimaginable devastation on my farm as the infectious Newcastle disease spread through Ghana. One day after another, farmers across the country lost several hundreds and thousands of birds. It all happened suddenly and

Ghana Veterinary Services officers scrambled to find answers. There were 50,000 birds on my Darko Farms site in Akropong-Asante, all at the risk of death. I have often recounted when I was left with two options—slaughter all 50,000 birds, or stand on the Word of God. I chose to let God's word be true.

By the time the Newcastle infection ran its deadly course in poultry farms across the country, I had lost a total of eight birds. The experts predicted I would lose at least 10,000 of the animals if not all. Unfortunately, many farms in the region and across the country had suffered devastating losses. Every forecast was grim and every fact suggested a worse outcome. There was no escaping life's trials, but I chose to believe in God's report, one that said that he would rebuke every devourer for my sake. I believed it, and I stood on that word, and Jehovah-Jireh gave me testimony even in a dark hour.

> *Many are the afflictions of the righteous, but the Lord delivers him out of them all.*
>
> Psalm 34:19

Many years ago I read the Psalm, "I have been young, and now am old; yet have I not seen the righteous forsaken, nor his seed begging bread." I have lived to see the truth in that promise. I remember how I chose to let the Word of God guide my every action, my outlook on business, governance, and even personal relationships. What brought me comfort was being able to ask myself what the Word of God said about every step I took. I had seen how the Bible is perfect for its direction for our lives, only if we made the choice to follow.

When Tyson Foods arrived in Ghana for an international partnership with Darko Farms, it was a chance to open new markets for Ghana's Agriculture sector and help revive an industry to international standards. I had spent ten years developing a business relationship with the American multinational company who was set to invest more than

$50 million, but the PNDC military government crushed the opportunity. That was after another high ranking military official reached out to my Chinese partners to derail a timber project that was close to its construction in Takoradi. It was one devious interference after another, but the God I served brought more rewarding opportunities my way.

In 1992, in the middle of River Volta, wicked men had plotted my death on a ferry. The engine of the small ferry suddenly shutting down was part of an elaborate scheme to let me drown. But God's watchful eye covered me and it was His peace that kept me through it all.

Like the Bible story of Daniel whose righteousness and commitment to prayer led him into a den with hungry lions ready to devour him, but who was resolute that even if his God didn't come to his rescue, he wasn't going to turn away from the truth he knew. A king who didn't serve Daniel's God saw the faithfulness of a man who was willing to die for what he believed to be the truth. Daniel was sure that the God he served was capable of shutting the mouths of hungry lions and that there was nothing impossible for Him to do.

I didn't have to be perfect for God's grace to be sufficient for me. I served a God who knew my heart's desire to please Him in everything I did. Time and again in my own life, my confidence was stirred by a God who delivered me from one accident and danger after another. I had put my trust in Almighty God, because only He was able to save my life from any shame and from death. Break to start a new line from military soldiers to angry gendarmes and pestilence, God's hedge of protection around my life made provision for me when all I had was a faith to believe. All I needed was faith the size of a mustard seed, and I came to believe that for those who lean on Almighty God, it all ends well because He is our redeemer, and He lives.

> *And we know that all things work together for good to them that love God, to them who are the called according to his purpose.*
>
> Romans 8:28

God's grace had kept me, and even when the devil tried his hardest, His grace turned every misfortune and setback into my testimony. When national leaders turned their hearts toward hindering my work and livelihood, they closed one door after another, but God opened much bigger doors that He had in store for me. What those men and women meant for evil, God turned around to set me on higher ground and made something beautiful arise from the ashes of the damage they did.

I had to let the truth be my anchor and walk with integrity at all costs. My yes had to be a yes, irrespective of the circumstances. I had chosen to not only profess the faith, but to walk in the Word of God, and nothing that happened to me came as a surprise to Him. I knew this, that I had been bought with a price, and for my life to glorify Almighty God. There were people whom I had never met, yet something about what I represented irked them. I had earned enemies who plotted my downfall but God used their traps to thrust me further into my purpose.

I often recalled the Bible story of a young Joseph, whose brothers sold him into slavery to get rid of him because of a dream God had revealed to him. If it were up to his brothers, they could have left him to die in a pit. As a servant, his diligence earned him the trust of Potiphar, one of Pharaoh's officials, the captain of the guard.

What left a profound mark in my own life was the words that guided Joseph's life. At a point when Potiphar's wife forced Joseph to resist her tempting advances, Joseph responded that he could not only do such a heinous act against his master, but most importantly he could never do that in the sight of his God. It was his God that he couldn't afford to grieve.

But God had anointed him, and nothing the devil did to derail his purpose would succeed. It was after he had been falsely accused by Potiphar's wife and unjustly thrown into prison, and a Pharaoh's cupbearer with whom he had been in jail forgot to recommend his release, that he would learn first-hand that it was God who did his masterful work in His own time. Until then, His grace was sufficient to keep Joseph in perfect peace.

What was truly incredible was learning how the misfortune didn't stop him serving his God. He worked diligently in what had become another rough patch in his life. That profoundly inspired my own journey especially when I had to suffer many unfair attacks from people who disliked me or what I stood for, and betrayals from people I knew or trusted.

It wasn't until Pharaoh himself had a dream that he desperately needed answers for, one that confounded his astrologers and soothsayers, that the cupbearer remembered a man who interpreted his dream while he was in jail, Joseph. He had forgotten all about him for two long years. In his due season, Joseph rose from a Hebrew slave and prisoner to becoming Prime Minister in all of Egypt, a foreign land. God's promise for Joseph came to pass because of his commitment to the truth.

Many years after his brothers had sold him into slavery, with the whole region in famine, they came to Egypt to buy grain. Joseph recognized them. For the next few days he would use the opportunity to test their character and see whether they would leave their young brother Benjamin behind as they had done with him. Joseph was overwhelmed with emotion as he revealed himself to his brothers having forgiven them completely, even for such a heinous offense. In his words, "I am your brother Joseph, whom you sold into Egypt, but now do not be sad, and let it not trouble you that you sold me here, for it was to preserve life that God sent me before you."

When the men were getting rid of Joseph, God, who had ordered his steps, was taking him into the future He had ordained for his life. It had not happened the way Joseph imagined, but God had proven Himself faithful to keep His every word, and it didn't matter how long it took or what challenges he faced along the way. He knew the God who had promised to watch over him was true. *"The preaching of the cross is foolishness to those who perish; but unto us who are saved, it is the power of God."* (1 Corinthians 1:18).

Like Joseph, if we are to lean wholly on our God, no matter what consequences we have to endure, God will lift us up just as He has promised, and that is a reassuring reminder to every committed Christian who seeks to please God irrespective of adversity. In the end, nothing can stand in the way of every promise that God has in store for those who love Him and commit their every step to Him.

> *For I know the plans I have for you," declares the Lord, "plans to prosper you and not to harm you, plans to give you hope and a future.*
> Jeremiah 29:11

Ministry took me to presidents and kings across Africa and the world. I shared with them what I had come to find was true about my God. The God who knew me before the foundations of this earth had a purpose for my life. I am grateful that God's grace found me early, and that fellowships like the Scripture Union, Town Fellowship and Assemblies of God church nurtured my faith. I made a decision to follow His every word, and there was nothing that was to sway me to turn back.

A stranger, Paris Reidhead, had to meet a Ghanaian student in America who barely knew my name to share my story enough to intrigue him. He had to travel to a country he had never been, and meet a man he had never met to strike up a friendship that was to open doors that only God could open.

I was a chicken farmer who walked in the path God ordained for my life. I was a teenager who fell in love with a vocation and it was precisely what God needed for me to spread the gospel. There is not a legacy and gift much more powerful than having given men and women the incredible gift of Christ's salvation, and the eternal freedom from the bondage that kept us from God's best. My background and starting point was irrelevant to Almighty God; all he needed was a willing heart.

And I said yes.

I didn't go into politics as a presidential candidate in 1991 to earn prominence and wealth. I stepped out to inspire a governance driven by God-fearing people, and saw the heart of men and women from Yendi and Bawku to Hohoe and Donkorkrom. All over the country, people searched for a glimmer of hope, but it was only when the righteous ruled that the people truly rejoiced. I championed Christian values in governance even when the Christian electorate didn't seem to understand why I had chosen to take that step of faith. It was a call, and only God knew why.

For the rest of my life, I hoped to lead men and women to find their own encounter with Jesus, and for salvation to have a transforming impact on their lives. There had to be a reason for which I had been saved, and it certainly wasn't to seek applause in church buildings or to jostle for recognition in pulpits and church councils. I can only look back and thank Almighty God for His grace that opened countless doors for me to serve in the body of Christ and in many communities around the world.

God knew the plans He had for my life, and only He knew how to bring them to pass. Perhaps, if the Apostolic Church never splintered in the last 1950s, the elders wouldn't have forced Reverend James McKeown to return to England. Perhaps if he hadn't gone to England, Reverend C. B. Sercombe would never have arrived in Kumasi.

I often can't help but wonder, what if the Catering Guest House where the church had arranged for Reverend Sercombe to stay had a room available, and the elders didn't have to bring the missionary to the church on Sunday to ask for any volunteer to be his host. If my grandmother hadn't been in the church that Sunday morning, she wouldn't have recommended Reverend Sercombe to stay in my stepfather F. K. Gyamfi's home. And perhaps, if Reverend Sercombe had not lived in my stepfather's home, I would never have seen *Poultry Keeping in Modern Days*, the small booklet that took my life into my God-given destiny.

In all of this, God gave me a partner with whom I would take every step, and without my wife Christiana, I cannot imagine fulfilling the work God had in store for me. Organizations like Full Gospel Business Men's Fellowship International, Women's Aglow, Opportunity International, Sinapi Aba Trust, and Edify were only vessels for Almighty God to use us to reach people from around the world. From presidents and kings to widows and orphans, we travelled the world together and served together.

I had not taken any one of these journeys for granted because there was nothing that I had done on my own. I have been able to do everything I set out to do because of Christ in whose grace I find courage.

Adom som bo, na y'anya yi / Unmerited grace is that we have found
Yesu awu ama y'anya nkwa / In Christ's death, we have life
Adom som bo, na ye nsa aka / Unmerited grace is what we have been given.

I am what I am, only by His grace.

AFTERWORD

Nothing about Kwabena Darko's long overdue memoir is ordinary. It is the work of an important and interesting man, both as an entrepreneur and a leader whose every measure of success and fulfilment is only one rooted in faith. Streaks of active political life are passing moments, more like a subplot, yet many in his native Ghana remember him as a man who, perhaps in a different political climate, might be president.

Courage to Lead is carefully pulled together like an intricate puzzle that shines a light on a splendid life of a visionary who managed to be a towering figure in agro-business across Africa, and one who had a seat at some of the defining moments in Ghana's political turning points. It is an eye-opening account distinguished by a level of introspection that makes him incredibly engaging, but in a very real way.

Sitting next to Kwabena Darko for many months, and working through pages that have been several years in the making has been truly humbling. He is calm, yet full of life and laughter. He is patient, quick to acknowledge that mistakes are part of being human. He is incredibly detailed, combing through every word and page with careful intent. I was fortunate to have worked with him on this literary project, a chance to learn much about history as to learn from it.

He is a man whose every word reaches a depth of emotional honesty, and any reader easily sees why. His wife's role is central, as a partner and most importantly as an intercessor. He recalls fondly everywhere they travelled together and many challenges they overcame as a couple, and is the first to admit her incredible influence.

The book intentionally drifts and strings together one-off vignettes and other longer, coiling stories that paint the powerful protection of God's grace in Kwabena Darko's life. The colourful memoir traces his work with the Assemblies of God church, Full Gospel Business Men's

Fellowship International, Opportunity International, Edify, Sinapi Aba, Luke Society, and several others into which he poured himself to serve his community. What stands out will remain the impact of his faith at the centre of it all.

Even more powerful was his careful intent to not use his book for a malicious purpose or for settling scores. Without losing the storyline, he insisted on not shining any needless light on the identities of the perpetrators of the hurt against him. The book wasn't about any of them, and in fact every hurdle turned out to be a stepping stone God used to raise him up. He only tells his side of the story without any pent-up anger or repugnance. I remember his words so clearly, that "My life is much bigger than any person or petty vendetta." And there was Romans 3:28 to drill that point home: "And we know that all things work together for good to them that love God, to them who have been called according to His purpose". They do indeed.

Regarding politics and his contesting the presidential election in 1992, he remembers this fondly, especially the people he met in many of the small towns and villages. Most people who claim to be Christians in Ghana, and perhaps in other parts of the world too, live with the vague assumption that politics is a dirty playing field not meant for "good people", but end up wrestling with the nagging realization that if "all the good people" stood aside, governance would be left in the hands of "bad people". Men like Kwabena Darko saw governance through a lens of service and obligation to others, and not as self-seeking undertaking. His belief was driven by what he deemed to be Christian values, not empty spirituality and commercial evangelism.

Darko Farms became a household name in Ghana, and soon across the African continent. At several peaks, the company saw years of annual revenue of nearly $100 million, and was supplying poultry products to hundreds of major clients across Africa. Yet, it is hard to miss how Darko talks less about his company's earnings since it first opened in 1967, and rather, recounts every moment he was privileged to lead someone to Christ. As an entrepreneur, he quickly discovered an open secret to lasting success: God's word, simply and entirely.

It is what guided his every step, and also where he found the courage to make bold decisions. It is what makes him different, and also what keeps him grounded. Thus, when Kwabena Darko makes reference to any scripture, it is far from an exercise of rote memorization. Instead, it is a humble reliance on every word, just as it is written.

For a man who never saw himself as a missionary, at least in the traditional sense, his whole life was immersed in a mission field, one whose only passion is demonstrating the managing grace of Christ to anyone he met. I remember working through one of the chapters with him, one word after another, only for the conversation to shift into an in-depth Bible study about the significance of water baptism and the baptism of the Holy Spirit. I listened carefully as he used the characters and stories of Paul, Ananias, Stephen and Cornelius to weave together a powerful Christian doctrine and its practical application in contemporary society. Kwabena Darko is a man who decided to seek the Lord with all of his heart, and more than once, he reiterated a guiding principle for his own life: having known the truth, to choose to walk in it, completely.

In working on *Courage to Lead*, what I found important and impressive was how Kwabena Darko has a natural sense of influencing other people, and it is evident in the conversational tone of the book which makes even some of the most difficult moments easy for a reader to absorb, without losing the ability to bring a genuineness and immediacy to the story. Such an audacious journey through business, politics, and life, with faith at the heart of it all. The work is a profoundly honest memoir, glowing with wisdom and gracious candour, and most importantly, uplifting. It certainly did that for me.

E. Obeng-Amoako Edmonds

ENDNOTES

- Diploma in Poultry Science, 1960
- Farms Manager, Central Egg Farm, Kumasi, 1960-1969
- Deacon (Elder), Assemblies of God Church, 1965-1996
- Chairman & CEO, Darko Farms & Co. Ltd., 1967-Present
- President, Ghana Animal Science Association, 1979-1983
- Interim President, Ghana National Council on Poultry, 1979-1984
- President, Ghana National Council on Poultry, 1984-1987
- Chairman, Board of Directors Assemblies of God Literature Center Ltd, Ghana, 1986-1997
- Chairman, Board of Directors Assemblies of God Bookshops, 1989-1995
- Member, Ghana Government "Think Tank" on Privatization, 1989-1991
- International Vice-President, Full Gospel Business Men Fellowship International (FGBMFI) Africa, 1990-1995
- Presidential Candidate, Ghana National Election, 1992
- Member, Nominating Committee of the African Prize for Leadership, 1994-Present
- First Board Chairman, Sinapi Aba Trust, 1994-2004
- International Secretary, FGBMFI, Costa Mesa, USA, 1993
- Vice-President, African Business Roundtable under the African Development Bank, 1995-1996
- Board Member, Empretec Ghana Foundation, 1995-2002
- Chairman, Africa Regional Board, Opportunity International, 1996-2000
- General Overseer, The Oasis of Love International Church, 1996-Present
- Board Chairman, Opportunity International Network, 1997-2000
- Board Member, Oasis International Training Center, 2000-Present
- Board Member, Opportunity International, 2000 - 2010
- External Board Member, The Bank of Ghana, 2001-2008
- First Founding Chancellor of Regent University 2008 – 2018
- Executive Board Member of Regent University 2008 – Present
- Chancellor Emeritus of Regent University – Present
- Chairman, Executive Board, Ghana Institute Of Linguistics, Literacy and Bible Translation, Kumasi Chapter (GILLBT) 2014 – Present

- National Board Member, Ghana Institute of Linguistics, Literacy and Bible Translation (GILLBT) 2018 – Present
- Member of Edify International Board – Present

* * * * *

- Grand Medal "Order of the Volta" The Highest National Award in Ghana for his Contributions to Agriculture Business In Ghana, 1978
- Honorary Certificate for Selfless Devotion to Charity by Christian Voluntary Society, 1978
- Award by Ghana Animal Science Association for Outstanding Contribution to the Association, 1982
- Best Farmer Award, Royal Agriculture Show, London, 1984
- Honorary Member, Ghana Science Association, 1985
- National Best Poultry Farmer, 1986
- Meritorious Award for Contribution to Charity by the Ghana National Trust Fund, 1990
- Certificate of Honor for Voluntary Service and Contribution to Charity by the Ghana Department of Social Welfare and Community Development, 1990
- Certificate of Honor From The First General Superintendent of Assemblies of God, Ghana, 1990
- Certificate of Honor for Outstanding Contribution to the Ghana Feed Millers Association, 1992
- Junior Achievement of Ghana Business Hall of Fame, 1992
- Ordained as The Minister of The Gospel by Bishop Elvina E. Miller, 2000
- Honorary Doctorate of Science Degree by Kwame Nkrumah University of Science and Technology KNUST, 2002
- Honorary Doctorate of Divinity by Global Missions and London Bible College, 2002
- Obasanjo Institute Award, a Distinguished African Farmers with Global Influence, 2009
- First Lewis Institute Social Innovator Award from Babson Entrepreneur College of USA, 2013.
- Honorary Doctorate, Gordon College, 2018

INDEX

A

Abebrese 3, 355, 379
Asawaase 4, 10, 186, 187, 294
Asamankese 8, 288, 370
Anyinam 21, 56
Avenin 22, 23, 24, 25, 52,
Agricultural Development Bank
    (ADB) 79, 80, 81
Akropong Farms xxiii, 86, 74
Akoko Photo 25
Ajamal Figueroa 63
Akomadan Afantwo 63
Animal Husbandry Farm 54
African Business Roundtable 131,
    132, 425
Alfred Nyamekye XXII, 119
Anta Babacar Ngom 129
Advanced Learning Training Seminar
    (ALTS) 130
African National Congress (ANC)
    131
Assemblies of God Literature Center,
    L.L.C. 425
All Africa Convention 254
Amprollium 159
Al Whittaker 143, 145 ,164, 175,
    278, 341, 388
Apino Soap 191
Archbishop of Australia Fund 173
Armed Forces Revolutionary Council
    (AFRC) 192
Aglow 287, 344, 345, 353, 372
African Project Development Facility
    (APDF) 281
Adiebeba 371

B

Bill Bright 115
Brenhya Distributive Agency 140
Builders' Brigade 20, 54
Bantama Local Authority (LA) 12
Black Star Line Shipping 53
Book it Dead 53, 54, 140
Buduburam 161
Benji Montemayor 185
B. M. Kuffuor 109, 110, 111, 373
Brother Lawson 369,377

C

Cocoa Marketing Board 19, 96, 101,
    136
Convention People's Party (CPP)
    263, 276, 277
Central Egg Farm 21, 51, 56, 58, 73,
    80, 83, 235, 425
Converted Muslims' Church 384
Central Intelligence Agency (CIA)
    240
Chicken Unlimited 246
Colonel Sanders 147, 148
Coccidiosis 158
Clopidol 159
Christian Life Center (CLC) 163, 173
Commonwealth Development
    Corporation (CDC) 281
Charlie Duke 353, 354
Christ Ambassadors 71,370
Campus Crusade for Christ 115
Corporate Council for Africa 129,
    132
C.K. Annan 52

Col. Ignatius Kutu Acheampong 95, 99, 101, 149
Chief Uwadie 119

D
Dr. Kwame Nkrumah 20, 21, 35, 280, 291, 389
Dr. Babacar Ndiaye XXII, 131
David Ben-Gurion 36, 46, 401
Deganya 37
D. L. Moody 56, 57
Dela Adadevor 118
D.W. Amoah 118, 120, 123
Demos Shakarian 120, 123, 125, 133, 248, 249, 253, 257
Downey Community Hospital 260
David Freeman XXII,164,3 96, 398
David Bussau XXII,164
Dr. Peter Boelens XXII, 178, 181
Danquah–Busia Club 275

E
Edify XXIV, 177, 183, 185, 186, 187, 424, 426
E.O. Gyenin 87
Étienne Tshisekedi 131, 256
Edufinance 184, 185
Ellen Johnson Sirleaf 345
Emeka Ojukwu 372
Ejura 99, 144, 331
ECOWAS Ceasefire Monitoring Group (ECOMOG) 161
Evangelist Irvina Miller 369

F
Father Abraham's Church 384
Full Gospel Business Men's Fellowship XVII,XXII,XXIV,118-123, 125, 126, 128, 129, 130, 131, 132, 133, 174, 182, 247, 248, 250, 251, 253, 254, 255, 264, 284, 289, 345, 348, 353, 359, 364, 388, 416, 424

F. K. Gyamfi XXIV, 9, 10, 17, 21, 93, 423
Fourah Bay College 128
Food Distribution Corporation 99
Five Year Plan 99

G
Grand Medal Order of the Volta XVII
Ghana Farmer's Council 21
Ghana Agricultural Poultry Farms 24
Ghana Veterinary Services 87, 352, 418
Givatos Settlement 38
Gabardine 53
Great Commission 118, 120, 128, 249, 254, 369, 371, 379, 385, 415
Gaddaffi 245
Grenoble 247, 248, 250, 252
Gracien Desouza XXII, 251
Ghana Pentecostal Council (GPC) 264, 266
Ghana Broadcasting Corporation (GBC) 314, 404
Ghana Fellowship of Evangelical Students (GHAFES) 288
Ghana Institute of Linguistics, Literacy and Bible Translation (GILLBT) 346, 354, 415, 427
Glad Tidings 371
Golda Meir 22

H
Hilla Liman 98, 243, 295, 389
Haggai International 173, 174
Hilden Charitable Fund 173

I
International Production and Processing Expo 154, 194, 409
Institute for International Development Incorporated (IIDI) 145, 175

Interim National Electoral Commission (INEC) 269, 291, 315
International Finance Corporation (IFC) 100, 190
International Leadership Foundation (ILF) 118, 338
International Monetary Fund (IMF) 329, 336
International Tobacco Ghana Limited (ITG) 192

J
Jack Delaney XXII, 145, 147, 148
Jamesway 147
Jonathan Wilson 163, 164, 167, 396, 398
John Ndebugri 192
John W. Tyson 195
John Njaw 256
John Agamah 346, 347
Jerusalem 36, 117, 238, 389
John Austin 115, 118, 338
Joseph Kwaku Kwaw 119
Jerry Kibarabara 130

K
kyawkyaw 3
kente 3
kaji kaji 3
kayayei 171
Kejetia Market 29
Kyebi 2, 5
Kuduo 4
Kayembe Wadikonda 130, 256
Kofi Amponsah Effah XXII, 122
Kojo Akowuah 74
Kwame Amponsah 29, 90, 232
Kibbutz 37, 38, 39
Keta School Boys 86
Katanga Hall 106, 109
Kwesi Andam 106

Kwame Nkrumah University of Science and Technology (KNUST) 105, 115
Kofi Abrefa Busia 98
Koo Entem 258
Kamina Tolbert 159, 160
Kentucky Fried Chicken (KFC) XVIII, 148, 175
kafo didi 149
Kwame Opoku 163, 167, 396
Kwabena Darko Foundation 165, 166, 396
kashire 166
Kumasi Asafo Jamboree 232
Kwakugan Apaloo 247, 248, 249, 250, 252
Kevin Callwood XXII, 270, 335,
Kofi Essaw XXII, 251, 383
Kwame Nkrumah Revolutionary Guards 275
Kwame Nkrumah Welfare Society 275, 280

L
Larry Reed 164, 166, 167, 396, 397, 398
Luke Society 178, 179, 181, 182, 183, 187
Lausanne II 179
Lonrho 328

M
Manhyia Palace 3, 253
Muus Agency 140
Mobutu Sese Seko 131, 256
Modupe Tilapiers XXII, 126, 129,
Moshe Dayan 45
Moshav 37, 45, 135, 331
Morris Cerullo 61, 62, 65, 67, 69, 231, 341, 349, 371, 376, 401, 413
Meat Marketing Board 99
Mac Obiri-Mainoo 122
Martin Asamoah–Manu XXII
Millennium Challenge Corporation 335

N

National Independence Party (NIP) XVII
Nii Adjere Wellington 122, 374
National Redemption Council (NRC) 99
Nelson Mandela 131, 132
National Convention Party (NCP) 265, 317
New Patriotic Party (NPP) 295, 312, 333, 340, 389
National Prayer Breakfast 175, 278, 334, 337, 353, 387, 388, 390
Navro-Pio 308
National Democratic Congress (NDC) 293, 307, 317, 339
Nkrumaist 280, 281, 290, 291, 295, 296
National Consultative Assembly 263, 276

O

Omar Bongo 131, 254
Okomfo Anokye Hospital 105, 107, 108, 319
Operation Feed Yourself 99
Opanin Kofi Poku 3
Opportunity International 163, 164, 165, 166, 167, 168, 172, 173, 174, 175, 183, 184, 185, 279, 284, 334, 388, 396, 397, 398, 399, 424
Obaapanin Yaa Serwaa 4
Overseas Private Investment Corporation (OPIC) 270, 277
Our Heritage Club 275
Oral Roberts 363
Opportunity International Savings and Loans (OISL) 175, 185, 398, 399
Opportunity Knocks 175
Official Development Assistance (ODA) 173
Oasis of Love Center 377

P

Pan-Africanist Congress (PAC) 131
Paris Reidhead 136, 141, 144, 175, 278, 341, 405, 422
Patience Bar 3
Paul Aidoo 89, 105
People's Defense Council (PDC) 103
People's Heritage Party (PHP) 295
People's National Convention (PNC) 267, 295
Pomadze Poultry Enterprise 97
Poultry Keeping in Modern Days 11, 14, 23, 74, 423
President Frederick Chiluba 255
President Gnassingbé Eyadema 251
President Thomas Sankara 378
Professor Kuperstein 41
Professor Yudith Klein 43
Provisional National Defense Council (PNDC) 101, 263

R

Rapid Results College 19, 24
rayon 53
Regent University College of Science and Technology XVII, 406
Reinhard Bonnke 249, 252, 253
Richard Morris 160, 165
River Birim 1, 2, 5,
Robin Hood 7, 12, 13, 14
Rose Kogombe 254
Ruppin College (24, 35, 40, 41, 48, 52, 80, 324, 407)
Reverend Arthur Hokett 239
Reverend Gyan Fosu 30, 65, 231, 234, 253, 370, 411
Reverend James McKeown 7, 370, 414, 423
Reverend Lonnie Fox (xxii, 30, 231, 233, 353, 370, 411)
Reverend Phillip Hogan 239, 244, 372

Reverend Sercombe 9, 10, 11, 12, 14, 15, 16, 17, 20, 23, 50, 72, 238, 423
Reverend Vernon Driggers 92, 109, 235, 358
Reverend Zimmerman 239

S
Sam Bamfo 269, 287, 303, 305, 314
Samuel Doe 156, 158, 159, 160
Scripture Union 61, 89, 91, 105, 106, 115, 119, 179, 182, 284, 343, 347, 361, 403, 404, 422
Senya Breku 86
Simpa 4
Sinapi Aba Trust XVII, 169, 170, 172, 173, 174, 175, 396, 397, 398, 399, 424
South African Communist Party (SACP) 131
South Suntreso Clinic 92
Southern Ghana Bible School 71
State Fishing Corporation 99
Stibokir Settlement 38, 40
Stonely Poultry Show 118
Sudan Interior Mission 142
Supreme Military Council (SMC) 267

T
Tata Brewery Limited 192
Teacher Nsiah 12, 13
Tel HaShomer Hospital 45
Tetrachromatic 51
Thomas Hope 126
Think Tank on Privatization 327, 425
The Fellowship 90, 120, 122, 123, 125, 130, 131, 132, 143, 145, 150, 160, 165, 175, 247, 248, 249, 250, 251, 253, 254, 255, 256, 257, 258, 259, 260, 261, 264, 266, 273, 275, 276, 277, 279, 334, 344, 371, 379, 380, 383, 388

Trade Union Congress (TUC) 266
Tyson Foods 155, 194, 195, 196, 197, 198, 199, 395, 418

U
Union Trading Company (UTC) 328
United African Company (UAC) 4
United Gold Coast Convention (UGCC) 20
United States Agency for International Development (USAID) 172, 270
Unorganised Manager 321

V
Victor Jocktane 254

W
West African Cocoa Research Institute (WACRI) 138
West African Network 270, 271, 333
William Tolbert 157
World Bank 148, 150, 175, 190, 281, 329, 337
World Poultry Science Association 154, 194, 409
Wycliffe Bible Translators 347, 415

Y
Yentua 100, 149

Z
Zamboku Micro Lending Institution 164

www.ingramcontent.com/pod-product-compliance
Lightning Source LLC
Chambersburg PA
CBHW031053080526
44587CB00011B/671